Birnbaum's

Walt Disney World

Expert Advice from the Inside Source

Wendy Lefkon EDITORIAL DIRECTOR

Jill Safro EDITOR

Elliot Kreloff DESIGN DIRECTOR

Rob Eberhardt DESIGNER

Jody Revenson CONTRIBUTING EDITOR

Alexandra Mayes Birnbaum CONSULTING EDITOR

Stephen Birnbaum FOUNDING EDITOR

DISNEP EDITIONS

Table of

Getting Ready to Go

Here is all the practical information you need to organize a Walt Disney World visit, down to the smallest detail: when to go; how to get there; how to save money and work within a budget; plus sample schedules; and hints for parents, travelers with disabilities, singles, and older visitors.

Transportation & Accommodations

Two big questions about Walt Disney World are where to stay and how to get around. Accommodations range from concierge suites to modest campsites, with thousands of rooms and villas in between. Our guide describes every Disney resort, with details presented in a handy chart. And we explain the World's vast transportation system, to boot.

Magic Kingdom

The enchantment of Walt Disney World is most apparent in the wealth of attractions and amusements that fill this, the most famous entertainment zone of all. Our land-by-land guide describes all there is to see and do, where to shop, and how to avoid the crowds, plus plenty of other insider tips.

Epcot

A gleaming silver geosphere introduces Walt Disney World's wonderland of discovery—an ambitious exploration of the world of the future as well as the present. Future World and World Showcase offer every visitor the opportunity to be a global and cerebral voyager, without setting foot outside Florida. Here's how to make the most of this uniquely fascinating destination.

Disney-MGM Studios

Now's your chance to be part of Hollywood's golden years. Everything from the magic of animation to the excitement of daring stunts and special effects is waiting to be enjoyed. There are also opportunities to go behind the scenes, create sound effects, and even experience a thrill ride or two. We've developed strategies for seeing this Tinseltown, ensuring the most fun and the least time standing around.

Disney's Animal Kingdom

This latest addition to Walt Disney World's theme park lineup celebrates the circle of life and all the wonders of the animal world. Amid nature's soothing majesty, you'll experience a stirring African safari, dodge dastardly dinosaurs, and ride raging rapids. Our detailed coverage guarantees a fun-filled trip to a place where humans are humbly reminded of their tenuous position in the food chain.

Contents

Everything Else in the World

Beyond the theme park boundaries lie countless acres full of just the sorts of wonders for which Disney is famous: state-of-the-art water parks, and a night-time entertainment, shopping, and dining district among them. So if you want to ride down watery slides, dance the night away, shop at elegant boutiques, pamper yourself at a spa, or even learn a few tricks of the trade by slipping behind the scenes, this chapter will help you find your way.

Sports

Walt Disney World has more tennis courts and golf greens than most posh resorts, plus plenty of places for boating, biking, horseback riding, swimming, and fishing. Here's how to combine these options with the rest of the fun at Walt Disney World.

Good Meals, Great Times

Restaurants around Disney World property run the gamut from simple snack shops to bastions of haute cuisine. Choices are nearly endless, so we've organized them into an area-by-area directory that lets you know where each restaurant is located and what specialties it offers, and a roundup of the dining spots we consider Birnbaum's Bests. We also tell you about the dinner shows, the best family fare, where to dine with Disney characters, and where to enjoy an after-dinner drink.

WHAT'S NEW?

To spotlight attractions making their Walt Disney World debut, some listings are marked with the special stamp shown here. Look for it throughout the book. Here are few highlights:

- **Saratoga Springs Resort & Spa** (page 74)
- **Mickey's PhilharMagic** (page 101)
- **Mission: SPACE** (page 129)
- **Reflections of China** (page 145)
- **Carriage Rides** (page 196)
- **Princess Storybook Breakfast** (page 220)
- **The Spirit of Aloha** (page 248)

For Steve, who merely made all this possible

Other 2004 Birnbaum's Official Disney Guides

A Word from the Editor

For some of us, our first Walt Disney World experience dates back to 1971, the year this new "Disneyland in Florida" made its debut. At that time, the Magic Kingdom was the only theme park, and it could be explored easily in a few days. Early visitors will remember, too, that many of the attractions were still under construction. Nonetheless, for those who came, it was love at first sight, and we've returned again and again.

Never before has there been so much incentive to visit (and revisit) the memory-making capital of the world. We are both privileged and proud to provide readers with our extensively researched, insider look at some of the most cherished attractions on Earth.

Editor Jill Safro consults with Mickey and Minnie, the ultimate Disney insiders.

When Steve Birnbaum launched this guide back in 1981, he made it clear what was expected of anyone who worked on it. The book would be meticulously revised each year, leaving no attraction untested, no snack or meal untasted, no hotel untried. First-hand experiences like these, accumulated over the years, make this book the most authoritative guide to the World. Our expertise, however, was not achieved by being escorted through back doors of attractions (although we would have thoroughly enjoyed that). Instead, we've waited in lines with everyone else, always hoping to have a Disney experience like that of any other guest. Happily, logistical pickles are few and far between, leaving us with ample time to investigate all the nooks and crannies of Walt's vast World.

After more than 30 fun-filled years, the World and the number of visitors have expanded—and so has our knowledge of the most popular vacation destination on the planet. On some occasions we've encountered sweltering weather and swelling crowds, times when even the happiest of families or best of friends turn into archenemies for a day. At times the lines seemed endless and, in a triumph of bad planning, we managed to take in just a few attractions before dinnertime. Had we known then what we know now, we could have spared ourselves some trying experiences. In one typical case, a staffer waited more than an hour to take a backstage tour at the Studios. Standing in line with a notebook, she was asked by another guest if there was a quiz at the end. When she explained what she was doing, he expressed surprise to learn that she was waiting with the rest of the masses. How better, she replied, to help people like you?

Take Our Advice

We've done our best to keep you from making any mistakes. We realize that even the most meticulous vacation planner needs *detailed, accurate, and objective information* to prepare a successful itinerary. To achieve that goal, we encourage the submission of factual insight and information from Disney staffers—but the decision to use or lose such information is entirely up to the discretion of the editor.

To that end, we have also packaged handy bits of advice in the form of sample itineraries and "hot tips" throughout the book. This advice comes directly from the copious notes we've taken during our hundreds of trips to Walt Disney World. We've also used our "Birnbaum's Best" stamp of approval wherever we deemed it appropriate, highlighting our favorite attractions and restaurants—the crowd pleasers we believe stand head, shoulders, and ears above the rest.

You, the reader, benefit from the combination of our many years of experience that, together with our access to current insider information from the Disney staff makes this guide unique. We like to think it's indispensable, but we'll let you be the judge of that a few hundred pages from now.

Credit Where Credit Is Due

Both in the parks and behind the scenes, Walt Disney World personnel have been a critical source of factual data. I hope I'm not omitting any names in thanking Chris Howd (Entertainment), Craig Dezern, Rick Sylvain (Media Relations); Alain Boniec, Gene Duncan, Mark Drennen, Janice Hilliard (Photography); Tim Lewis (Disney Publishing); and Bo Boyd, Charlie Ridgway, Karen Haynes, Linda Warren, Ken Potrock, Darlene Papalini, Laura Simpson, and Jeff Titelius. Special thanks to Dave Herbst, who has done so much to ensure the factual accuracy of the Birnbaum Guides.

Kudos to Michelle Magenheim, for her outstanding fact-checking effort, and to Diane Hodges, Monica Mayper, and Robert Rohr, copy editors extraordinaire. Thanks, also, to Duryan Bhagat, Janet Castiglione, and Sue Cole, for their editorial support and production panache.

Hats off to those for whom doing Walt Disney World research is truly a labor of love (as in no financial compensation whatsoever). The class of 2004 includes Irene Safro, Roy Safro, Joy Safro, Amy Safro, Margaret Verdon, Linda Verdon, Trace Schielzo, Heather Pommerencke, Joan Nickel-Sohn, Judith Lagano, Donna Sabino, and Suzy Goytizolo.

Of course, no list of acknowledgments would be complete without mentioning our founding editor, Steve Birnbaum, whose spirit, wisdom, and humor still infuse these pages, as well as Alexandra Mayes Birnbaum, who continues to be a guiding light—to say nothing of a careful reader of every word.

The Last Word

Finally, it's important to remember that every worthwhile travel guide is a living enterprise; the book you hold in your hands is our best effort at explaining how to enjoy Walt Disney World at this moment, but its text is in no way etched in stone. Disney is constantly changing and growing, and in each annual edition, we refine and expand our material to serve your needs even better. For this year's edition, though, this must be the final word.

Have a great visit!

Don't Forget to Write

No contribution is of greater value to us in preparing the next edition of this book than your comments on what we have written and on your own experiences at Walt Disney World. Please share your insights with us by writing to:

Jill Safro, Editor
Birnbaum's Walt Disney World 2004
Disney Editions
114 Fifth Avenue, 12th Floor
New York, NY 10011

Getting Ready to Go

The key to a fabulous vacation at Walt Disney World is advance planning. This remarkably varied complex is too vast and diverse to allow a spontaneous visit to be undertaken with much success—especially when you consider the rapid rate at which the World has expanded. That does not mean that even the most casual visitors can't have some significant fun, but they are bound to have regrets about things they missed because of time pressures or a simple lack of information. The purpose of this guide is to eliminate potential frustration, while getting the most bang for your vacation buck.

What follows, then, is meant to provide a sensible scheme for planning a satisfying visit to Walt Disney World, one that will offer the most fun and the least amount of disappointment. But how do you know which of the countless activities will be the most enjoyable for you and your family? Do your homework. The best strategy is to make sure you have a clear idea of all that is available long *before* you arrive in the Orlando area.

When to Go

When talk finally turns to the best time to make a trip to Walt Disney World, Christmas and Easter are often mentioned, as well as the traditional summer vacation period—especially if there are children in the family. But there is also good reason to avoid these periods, namely the tremendous crowds they attract. And when Disney World is crowded, it can be very crowded, indeed. On the busiest days, visitors may wait as much as two hours to experience the more popular attractions when waiting in lines. That's at least twice as long as during less busy times of the year. What's more, Fastpass assignments (see page 19) have a tendency to be maxed out early.

Considering seasonal hours, weather, and the crowd patterns described in the charts that follow, optimal times to visit Walt Disney World are usually mid-January through early February, late April through late May, and September through December (except Thanksgiving and Christmas weeks).

Note that during some of the less crowded times of the year—particularly during the winter—some attractions are closed for renovations. In addition, water parks are often closed for refurbishment during cooler months. Call 407-824-4321 or check *www.disneyworld.com* for a current schedule, updated each season.

December is an especially festive time of year the world over, and Walt Disney World is no exception. All of the theme parks are decorated to the nines for the holiday season. The Magic Kingdom, Epcot, and the Disney-MGM Studios feature nightly tree-lighting ceremonies. Many other special events are held during this period, including Mickey's Very Merry Christmas Party in the Magic Kingdom

(a separate admission ticket is required). The party brings a dusting of snow to Main Street from about 7 P.M. to midnight for several days during the first three weeks of December. It also features holiday shows around the park, including Mickey's Very Merry Christmas Parade, plus a special finale of Fantasy in the Sky fireworks. Select performances from Mickey's Very Merry Christmas Party are also staged in the park during regular hours throughout the holiday season. Note that this event is extremely popular and usually sells out long ahead of time. Plan to purchase tickets in advance by calling 407-W-DISNEY (934-7639).

Epcot celebrates the season with Holidays Around the World, including the nightly Candlelight Processional, complete with 450-voice choir, 50-piece orchestra, and a reading of the story of Christmas by a celebrity narrator. Dinner packages are available for some World Showcase restaurants. (We recommend the dinner package: It guarantees seating for dinner as well as preferred seating at the Candlelight Processional. Without a package, you should arrive at least one hour before showtime or risk being shut out of your preferred performance.) In years past, the Disney-MGM Studios has featured a display of about five million lights depicting holiday scenes. At press time, the fate of this event was uncertain. For updated information regarding the status of the Osborne Family Spectacle of Lights, visit *www.disneyworld.com*.

There are holiday decorations at each WDW hotel, too, including a Victorian Christmas at the Grand Floridian, a seaside party at the Yacht and Beach Club, and a Cajun holiday at Port Orleans Riverside.

For reservations, call a travel agent or 407-W-DISNEY (934-7639) or the Walt Disney Travel Company at 497-828-8101. Special-event tickets are available separately. Call 407-934-7630 or visit *www.disneyworld.com* for information.

Hot Tip!

The period between the end of Thanksgiving and the week before Christmas is one of the least crowded and most festive times of the year. It's a wonderful time to visit.

Crowd Patterns

Day-to-Day Trends

In general, the weekends tend to be among the most crowded days at Walt Disney World theme parks—most notably during the summer months and other peak periods. Monday is also a notoriously busy day, especially at the Magic Kingdom. Morning through early afternoon is a bustling time for the theme parks and their respective "E-ticket" attractions. Days that are kicked off with an "Extra Magic Hour" tend to be more crowded at their respective theme parks. When the weather's steamy, the water parks tend to reach capacity soon after the gates open—so be sure to get an early start if you're headed to Blizzard Beach or Typhoon Lagoon.

When the time comes to plot an itinerary, it's helpful to know about crowd patterns beyond the four theme parks as well. As a rule, Downtown Disney and Disney's water parks host their largest throngs on weekends. Of course, in these circles, a bigger crowd could possibly mean a better time. Golfers should note that weekend tee times are typically in the highest demand, while Monday and Tuesday tee times are the easiest to come by.

Seasonal Shifts

The chart below indicates the density of crowds in the theme parks throughout the year. Though it's tough to generalize about a property as vast and ever changing as Walt Disney World—special events and package deals can swell park attendance during a period typically marked by smaller crowds—the chart highlights historic trends.

"Least Crowded" means that there will be lines, but most attractions can be visited without much waiting.

"Average Attendance" refers to times when there are lots of people around, but lines are manageable.

"Most Crowded" reflects times when lines at popular attractions can mean a wait of as much as two hours. As a rule, when school is out, the crowds are in at Walt Disney World.

Least Crowded

- 2nd week of January through 1st week of February

- Week after Labor Day until Thanksgiving

- Week after Thanksgiving through week before Christmas

Average Attendance

- 1st week of January

- 2nd week of February until Presidents' week

- End of February through 2nd week of March

- Last week of April through May

- Thanksgiving week

Most Crowded

- Presidents' week

- 3rd week of March through 3rd week of April

- June through Labor Day

- Christmas through New Year's Day

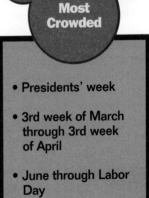

Holidays and Special Events

Special affairs are staged throughout the year, not only to mark holidays but also to celebrate other interests. *The dates and details below are subject to change without notice*; call 407-824-4321 to confirm, or check out *www.disneyworld.com* for up-to-the-minute information about specific events.

JANUARY

Walt Disney World Marathon (January 9–11): Some 15,000 entrants run through several theme parks, Disney's Wide World of Sports complex, and many other areas of the World during this 26.2-mile race. Live bands, hot-air balloons, and Disney characters are on hand to inspire runners. There's also a 5K run for children. Special packages are available. Call 407-939-7810 for additional information.

MARCH

Saint Patrick's Day (March 17): Everyone is Irish on Saint Patrick's Day—especially at Pleasure *Ire*land. Epcot's United Kingdom pavilion marks the day with Irish dining and dancing, plus special appearances by a leprechaun or two. Don't forget to wear green while you celebrate the Emerald Isle.

APRIL

Easter (April 11): of Disney World theme parks stay open late during the two weeks straddling the Easter holiday. Keep in mind that this is an extremely busy time to visit.

Epcot International Flower and Garden Festival (late April through early June): Epcot is blooming with elaborate gardens (including more than 30 million fragrant blossoms) and topiary displays, behind-the-scenes tours, gardening workshops, and guest speakers. Learn from the experts how to create a beautiful garden of your own.

MAY – JUNE

Star Wars Weekends (May–June): Disney-MGM Studios salutes Star Wars with celebrities and characters from the movies, plus autographs and photo opportunities, trivia contests, and more.

JULY

Fourth of July Celebration: Double-size fireworks over the Magic Kingdom, Epcot, and the Disney-MGM Studios make for a very colorful night. Pleasure Island kicks off the Independence Day festivities with fireworks on the evening of the Fourth (following a lineup of special entertainment). This is a very busy time to visit Disney World.

SEPTEMBER

Night of Joy: Two nights of celebration highlight contemporary Christian music. For dates and to purchase tickets, call 407-827-7200 or TicketMaster. Note that this very popular event attracts a bit of a rowdy crowd (of mostly teens and groups of young adults).

OCTOBER

Funai Golf Classic (October): Top PGA Tour players compete alongside amateurs in this big tourney, played on the Palm and Magnolia courses. Special packages are available. For more information, call 407-824-2250.

Epcot International Food and Wine Festival (October–November): World Showcase celebrates the flavors of a variety of countries (even those not usually represented around the lagoon) through tastings ($1 to $4.50 per sample), demos from top chefs, and wine and cooking seminars. It's a very satisfying way in which to wander World Showcase.

Halloween (late October): The festivities vary from year to year. Past celebrations have included spooky window displays and performances by storytellers at World Showcase.

Fort Wilderness Resort and Campground generally hosts a pumpkin-carving contest and a children's costume contest, followed by a screening of a scary movie.

Downtown Disney has hosted kids' costume contests. Grown-ups have competed in costume contests at Pleasure Island.

The Magic Kingdom will certainly play host to its usual Halloween spectacular: **Mickey's Not-So-Scary Halloween Party.** The special-ticket activities include a Halloween costume parade, dancing, appearances by Disney villains, trick-or-treating, and fireworks. This is an extremely popular Magic Kingdom event. Purchase your tickets as far in advance as possible. And don't forget to wear a costume!

As a special spooky bonus, **Mickey's Not-So-Scary Halloween Parade** makes its way through the Kingdom during the Halloween party. For more information about the specific dates on which the not-so-scary party and/or parade will take place, call 407-824-4321.

NOVEMBER

ABC Super Soap Weekend: A celebration of ABC daytime dramas is held at the Disney-MGM Studios each year. Guests can meet soap stars; collect autographs; compete in trivia contests; and see sets, props, and costumes. For more information, call 407-397-6808.

Festival of the Masters (November): This three-day fine-arts show draws more than 150 of the world's top artists to the Downtown Disney area.

DECEMBER

Disney's Magical Holidays: Decorations and festivities abound in Walt Disney World's parks and resorts. The Magic Kingdom hosts **Mickey's Very Merry Christmas Party** on several nights during the first three weeks of December, complete with snow flurries on Main Street and hot cocoa. Entertainment for the special-ticket party includes **Mickey's Very Merry Christmas Parade** and a holiday edition of the fireworks; select performances are staged during regular hours throughout the holiday season.

Epcot's **Holidays Around the World** (November–December) features "The Lights of Winter" and a Candlelight Processional, including a choral concert. The event is free, but seating is limited and it is extremely popular. Arrive at least an hour before showtime, or book a dinner package (which combines dinner at a World Showcase eatery with guaranteed seating at the Processional). For information, call 407-824-4321.

The Osborne Family Spectacle of Lights (November–January), which brightened the Disney-MGM Studios with about five million lights on annual basis, was in limbo at press time. It may be moved elsewhere in the Studios for 2004, to another venue altogether, or not presented at all. For updates on the status of this popular holiday event, call 407-934-7639.

New Year's Eve Celebration (December 31): There are extra-large fireworks displays over the Magic Kingdom, Epcot, and the Disney-MGM Studios. (The Magic Kingdom and Epcot are open until 2 A.M., and the Studios stays open until 1 A.M.) Pleasure Island hosts a grand special-ticket bash. Many of the resorts, as well as the nightspots at Downtown Disney West Side, also welcome the new year Disney-style.

www.disneyworld.com

So you've made the big decision to go to Disney World. What are you going to do now? Go to *www.disneyworld.com*! In addition to finding current theme park hours, special-event information, Fastpass updates, color photos, and the lowdown on what's new, you can reserve a room at a Walt Disney World resort, purchase a vacation package, order Disney theme park admission tickets, and a whole lot more.

Keeping WDW Hours

Since operating hours fluctuate quite a bit, we strongly advise calling 407-824-4321 or visiting *www.disneyworld.com* for the most current schedules available. The automated system is updated every three months or so.

THEME PARKS: Theme park hours vary seasonally. In May, September, October, parts of November and December, and all of January, the Magic Kingdom is usually open from 9 A.M. to 6 P.M.; Epcot is open from 10 A.M. to 9 P.M. World Showcase opens at 11 A.M. and Future World closes at 7 P.M.; the Disney-MGM Studios is open from 9 A.M. until about dusk; and Animal Kingdom is open from 9 A.M. until about 5 P.M. The parks take turns offering an "Extra Magic Hour" throughout the week. That is, on any given day, one of the parks may allow Walt Disney Resort guests to enter an hour early. For information and Extra Magic Hour schedule, call 407-824-4321 or inquire at your resort's front desk when you check in.

The Magic Kingdom usually keeps later hours through summer and other busy periods, including Christmas and Easter. The parks may be open until 1 A.M. on New Year's Eve. The Disney-MGM Studios often stays open until 10 or 11 P.M. in the summer, too.

DOWNTOWN DISNEY MARKETPLACE: Shops are usually open from 9:30 A.M. until 11 P.M. daily. Restaurant hours vary.

DOWNTOWN DISNEY PLEASURE ISLAND: Clubs are open from about 7 P.M. to 2 A.M. nightly; shops generally close at about 1 A.M.; and the restaurants, from about 11:30 A.M. to 11 P.M. Admission must be purchased after 7 P.M.

DOWNTOWN DISNEY WEST SIDE: At the AMC Theatres cineplex, movies begin at about 1 P.M. Restaurants are generally open from about 11:30 A.M. to midnight. Shops are generally open from 11 A.M. to 11 P.M.

WATER PARKS: Although hours vary, the water parks are generally open from about 10 A.M. to 5 P.M., with extended hours in effect during summer months.

WDW Weather

	TEMPERATURE AVERAGE		RAINFALL Average
	High	Low	(inches)
January	71	49	2.3
February	73	50	3.0
March	78	55	3.2
April	83	59	1.8
May	88	66	3.6
June	91	72	7.3
July	92	73	7.2
August	92	73	6.8
September	90	72	6.0
October	85	65	2.4
November	79	58	2.3
December	73	51	2.2

How to Get There

By Car

While most visitors to the Orlando area fly in, some prefer to drive. If you opt for a road trip, pack lots of music and figure on logging no more than 350 to 400 miles a day—a reasonable distance that won't wear you down so much that you can't enjoy your trip.

Contact state tourist boards to inquire about the availability of free maps; for a Florida map and guide, call 888-735-2872, or pay a visit *www.flausa.com*. Other map sources are the *Rand McNally Road Atlas* and the *AAA North American Road Atlas*; both are sold in bookstores. Driving directions from most cities are also available on the Internet. One site to try is *www.mapquest.com*.

Reputable automobile clubs offer help with breakdowns; towing; insurance that covers personal injury, accidents, arrest, bail bond, and lawyers' fees for defense of contested traffic cases; and travel-planning services, including free maps and route mapping. Services vary from one club to the next, and membership fees range widely, from $42 to $90 a year. (For information, refer to page 14.)

Did You Know?
It's perfectly legal to make a right turn at a red light on roads throughout the state of Florida.

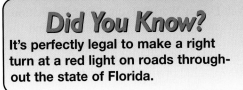

From the Airport

By car: During rush hour, take the airport's South Exit to the Central Florida Greeneway (Route 417) to Route 536, which leads to Walt Disney World. The tolls run about $2.

For the shortest route to WDW, take the North Exit to Route 528 (Beeline Expressway), going west toward Tampa. Pick up I-4 west, and follow it to a WDW exit. The trip takes about half an hour, and tolls are $1.25. This route is heavily trafficked.

By shuttle: At Orlando International Airport, Mears Motor Shuttle offers vans 24 hours a day. It serves Disney resorts, Hotel Plaza Blvd. properties, and other hotels. Shuttles make multiple stops; a trip can take an hour or more. On the return trip, Mears requires guests be picked up at least 3 hours prior to flight times. Reservations must be made 24 hours ahead. Bell services can call a cab for the return trip.

The shuttle cost to most hotels is $16 one way, $28 round-trip per adult; $12 one way, $20 round-trip per child age 4 through 11; free for children under 4. Fares to International Drive properties are $2 to $4 lower. Call 407-423-5566 for information, or visit *www.mearstransportation.com*.

Cabs cost between $35 and $50 each way, depending on the destination. A taxi can accommodate up to 9 people and the trip is direct, so it's a good alternative to the shuttle. There's a taxi stand by baggage claim. Bell services can call for a cab at any WDW resort.

By car service: Florida Towncar offers direct service to Disney World resorts for a round-trip rate of $85–$95 (for up to five passengers). Call 407-277-5466 or 800-525-7246 or visit *www.floridatowncar.com*. Reservations should be made at least a week ahead.

Towncar service is also available from A Selective Limousine, Inc. Selective's drivers take guests directly to their resort. Round-trip rates to WDW area resorts start at about $80 for up to four passengers. Reservations are required and cancellations must be made at least 24 hours in advance. To make reservations, call 800-730-0211 or 407-854-7503.

Gratuities are not included in any of the transfer rates. It is customary to tip for good service.

By Air

When it comes to airfares, there is a trick to unearthing the most economical ones: Shop around. Call a travel agent, browse the Internet, and keep these tips in mind:

- Watch your local newspapers for ads announcing short-term promotional fares. When a deal presents itself, grab it.

- The more flexible you can be in your dates and duration of stay, the more money you're likely to save.

- Take advantage of advance-purchase fares (lower rates that apply if a ticket is bought at least two to three weeks prior to the scheduled departure).

- Keep in mind that the lowest airfares usually carry a penalty if you have to revise your flight schedule, and that certain discounted tickets are nonrefundable.

- When you call to make a reservation, ask about any fare restrictions, including an obligatory Saturday night stay-over.

- Fly when most people don't: For vacation destinations, that usually means leaving the ground midweek.

- If a fare comes down after you've purchased a ticket, you can request a refund from the airline.

- Check out airline websites. They may e-mail information to you about discounted fares. Some sites even offer a discount for purchasing tickets online.

- If you live in the New York metropolitan area, seriously consider flying JetBlue. Their prices are unbeatable and the service is second to none; visit *www.jetblue.com.*

By Train

Amtrak serves the Orlando area twice daily from New York City, with various stops made along the way. The trip takes approximately 22 hours and costs from about $130 to $350 round-trip, coach. (Book as early as possible for lower fares; discounts are often available, so be sure to ask.) If you're staying at Walt

Resources for Road Trippers

There are a variety of reputable national automobile clubs to choose from. Among the leading clubs:

- **Allstate Motor Club**
  1500 W. Shore Drive
  Arlington Heights, IL 60004
  800-214-5132

- **American Automobile Association (AAA)**
  1000 AAA Drive
  Heathrow, FL 32746
  800-564-6222

- **Ford Auto Club**
  Box 224688
  Dallas, TX 75222
  800-348-5220

- **Gulf Motor Club**
  929 N. Plum Grove Road
  Schaumburg, IL 60173
  800-633-3224

- **Montgomery Ward Auto Club**
  200 N. Martingale Road
  Schaumburg, IL 60173
  800-621-5151

- **Motor Club of America**
  3200 W. Wilshire
  Oklahoma City, OK 73116
  800-227-6459

Travelers may also check with their state tourist boards about the availability of free maps. Other excellent sources for maps are the *AAA North American Road Atlas* and the *Rand McNally Road Atlas*; they are sold in many bookstores.

Disney World, plan to take a cab or shuttle to the area hotels. The cost varies, depending on the destination. Rental cars are also available by shuttle.

For reservations and information on this and other routes, call 800-USA-RAIL (872-7245), visit the Amtrak website at *www.amtrak.com,* or contact a travel agent.

By Bus

Greyhound provides frequent direct service to Orlando and Kissimmee (the latter is closer to Walt Disney World). From either destination, you can take a taxi to your hotel, but first check if your hotel offers shuttle service.

For more information, contact Greyhound at 800-231-2222 or visit *www.greyhound.com.*

Planning Ahead
Logistics

Organizing a trip properly takes time, but most travelers find the increased enjoyment well worth the effort. The fact is, planning can become a pleasant sort of "armchair" exercise, and kids will enjoy their visit to Disney all the more if they, too, are involved in the process.

To assist in that effort, we immodestly recommend *Birnbaum's Walt Disney World For Kids, By Kids*, a colorful look at the World from a young person's perspective, written for readers ages 7 through 14. For adults traveling *sans* children, *Birnbaum's Walt Disney World Without Kids* is the definitive source.

Information Sources

For information about Walt Disney World, call 407-824-4321. Lots of current specifics, such as park hours, ticket prices, refurbishment schedules, and directions are available through an automated system 24 hours a day. To speak with a representative, call weekdays 7 A.M. to 7 P.M. or weekends 7 A.M. to 8 P.M. For information by mail, write to Walt Disney World, Box 10000, Lake Buena Vista, FL 32830-1000.

Internet users can tap into updates about happenings in the World, get information on trip planning, reserve a room, order tickets, and get theme park hours and special-events listings by entering *www.disneyworld.com*. Disney Cruise Line vacation packages may be booked at *www.disneycruise.com*.

For information and discounts on area attractions, restaurants, and hotels, contact the Official Visitor Information Center, 8723 International Dr., Suite 101, Orlando, FL 32819; 407-363-5872 or 800-551-0181. Another good resource for Orlando-area happenings is *www.orlando.com*.

For details about other Central Florida attractions, contact Visit Florida, Box 1100, Tallahassee, FL 32302; 888-735-2872 (to request a free visitors guide and map) or 850-488-5607; *www.flausa.com*.

Disney Information Center: This full-service visitors center, located at the intersection of I-75 and S.R. 200 in Ocala, Florida, about 90 miles north of Orlando, can help WDW-bound vacationers plan their time, book (or confirm) hotel reservations, purchase park tickets, and even make priority seating arrangements. For departing guests who didn't buy enough Mouse ears, it also stocks character merchandise.

On-site Resources: Those staying at Walt Disney World resorts should consider their hotel's Guest Services desk the primary resource. Resort guests also receive WDW information via their room's television. Fort Wilderness campers are advised to stop at the Pioneer Hall Information and Ticket Window, call extension 2788, or touch 11 on a phone near any restroom.

What to Pack

While there is hardly a dress code at Walt Disney World, casual clothing is the rule, with few exceptions. Most notably, jackets are required for men at Victoria & Albert's restaurant in the Grand Floridian resort. More generally, T-shirts and shorts are perfectly acceptable during the day. For evening, slacks, jeans, or Bermuda shorts are appropriate. Bathing suits are a must, along with the appropriate attire for any sport you want to pursue.

Lightweight sweaters are necessary even in summer—to wear indoors when the air-conditioning gets chilly. From November through March, warmer clothing is a must for evening. Pack for weather extremes so you'll be comfy should it become unseasonably warm or cool. Always bring plenty of sunscreen, and don't forget the bug spray. If possible, pack lightweight rain gear and a compact umbrella. The most important item of all? Comfortable walking shoes.

Guests at the resorts on Hotel Plaza Boulevard may access a tourist-information TV program of their own. Some other area hotels also show a version of the orientation, usually aiming to provide an overview of all Central Florida attractions.

For Day Visitors: All day visitors—that is, those staying off Disney property—receive a useful handout at the Auto Plazas (if you don't, just ask). When purchasing one-day admission to a given theme park, guests receive a complimentary guidemap and entertainment times guide for that park. Ticket holders may receive all four park guides upon request. Extra guidemaps are available at City Hall (in the Magic Kingdom) and at Guest Relations (in Epcot, the Disney-MGM Studios, and Animal Kingdom), as well as in many shops and restaurants throughout the park.

Package Pointers

The sheer number and diversity of packages offering vacations in Central Florida are enough to bewilder even the savviest traveler. Still, such plans are worth exploring. Most offer the convenience of a vacation that's completely organized in advance, and one that will generally cost less than the sum of the same transportation, accommodations, and admission elements purchased separately. In addition, since most package providers purchase blocks of Disney resort rooms, they are an excellent source for securing a room on Walt Disney World property when the hotel of your choice is booked.

American Airlines Vacations (800-321-2121), US Airways Vacations (800-455-0123), Southwest Vacations (800-243-8372), *www.expedia.com, www.travelocity.com*, and the Walt Disney Travel Company (407-934-7639 or *www.disneytravel.com*) offer packages that feature WDW on-site hotels, as well as choice off-property accommodations. Many packages include the added attraction of low-cost air transportation. The American Automobile Association (800-222-4357) offers AAA Vacations and other travel packages, which include certain perks and discounts. For other possibilities, consider Go Go Worldwide vacations (*www.gogotour.com*), check the

travel section of your local newspaper, or consult a travel agent.

Walt Disney Travel Company vacation plans start with a value-packed base package that includes room and theme park admission. Base packages may be augmented with a selection of add-ons that feature keepsakes, meals, and recreation, as well as other WDW experiences. These vacation plans are available year-round; others, are offered seasonally. Packages may be designed around a specific type of vacation: i.e., a golf getaway, honeymoon, or family reunion. They may include extra elements such as unlimited tee times or a carriage ride. Still others are tied to an annual event, such as the Walt Disney World marathon (see "Holidays and Special Events" on page 10 of this chapter). Finally, Disney's Sand and Castle package combines a Disney World vacation with a stay at Disney's Vero Beach Resort, or other Florida beach resorts. (See page 71 in the *Transportation & Accommodations* chapter for more information about these options.) Air transportation, rental car, or airport transfers can be added to packages.

Hot Tip!

When selecting a Walt Disney World package, pay close attention to the type of WDW pass or ticket that's included—and make sure it's the one that best suits your needs.

The value of a package depends on your specific needs. Before considering options, use this book to help determine which of the myriad accommodations, activities, and attractions at Walt Disney World most appeal to you. There's real value in some package elements, such as airport transfers and meal discounts. Several packages also include meals with the Disney characters, tennis lessons, golf greens fees, tennis court fees, boat rentals, and the like.

Never choose a package that includes elements you don't want or won't have time to enjoy. While extras such as welcoming cocktails may sound appealing, their cash value is negligible. Also beware of any packages that tout as selling points certain services that are available to every Walt Disney World guest.

All About Theme Park Tickets

When it comes to selecting the perfect type of admission ticket, it pays to do some homework. Study all the options, evaluate your priorities, and make no hasty decisions. The following information was correct at press time and is meant to help you make a wise choice. Keep in mind that *Disney ticket structures and prices are likely to change in 2004*, so call 407-824-4321 for up-to-the-minute information.

Ticket Options

One-Day Ticket: One-day tickets are valid for admission to one park only—the Magic Kingdom, Epcot, the Disney-MGM Studios, or Disney's Animal Kingdom. (The one-day ticket does not allow for park-hopping.)

> ## Hot Tip!
> At the end of your visit, make a note of the number of unused days on a multi-day ticket. Write it on the ticket itself.

Park Hopper Ticket: This ticket can be used at all Walt Disney World theme parks on the same day. It includes use of Disney transportation. The ticket is available for four or five days that need not be used consecutively. Unused days never expire.

Park Hopper Plus Ticket: Available for five, six, or seven days, this is one of the more comprehensive options. It can be used at all theme parks on the same day. It also comes with a number of "plus" options to choose from: admission to Blizzard Beach, Typhoon Lagoon, Disney's Wide World of Sports complex (on event days), or Pleasure Island. Five-Day Park

> ## E-Ride Nights
> Imagine having the Magic Kingdom practically to yourself for an entire evening. It can happen if you're a WDW resort guest with a multi-day pass and about $13 to spare (about $11 for kids). The E-Ride pass lets you stay in the Magic Kingdom after it closes to enjoy the park's best attractions time and time again. It's available on select nights throughout the year, so ask about it when you check in.

> ## Did You Know?
> The phrase "E-ticket ride" is American slang for "the ultimate in thrills." It comes from the early days of Disney parks, back when tickets were used for each attraction. E-tickets were reserved for the most exciting rides of all.

Hopper Plus Tickets include two plus options, Six-Day Park Hopper Plus Tickets include three, and Seven-Day Park Hopper Plus Tickets include four. Days and plus options need not be used consecutively and never expire. It includes use of Walt Disney World transportation.

Ultimate Park Hopper Ticket: WDW resort guests can buy a multi-day ticket geared to the length of their visit. It offers unlimited admission to the theme parks, water parks, Disney's Wide World of Sports complex, Pleasure Island, and DisneyQuest for the length of a guest's stay. *This ticket expires on the evening of check-out.*

Theme Park Annual Pass: This pass offers admission to the four theme parks for a year. It can be used in more than one park on the same day (also known as park-hopping), and includes use of Disney transportation, as well as free parking at the theme parks. Annual passes can be purchased at the entrance to any of the theme parks (they can be renewed there or by mail). A photo ID must be presented for purchase by adults and may be required for future use of the pass. Passes are non-transferable.

Annual pass-bearers (including those who have the Premium Annual Pass described on page 18) qualify for many Walt Disney World discounts and benefits, such as reduced rates at select Disney resorts at certain times of year. A special newsletter called the Mickey Monitor keeps pass-holders up to date regarding discount offers. The pass expires one year after it is purchased. A discounted renewal rate applies if the pass is renewed within one month of expiration. (The expired pass must be presented in order to receive the discounted renewal rate.) A pass may be renewed by mail or at the entrance to any theme park.

Premium Annual Pass: This pass has everything the Theme Park Annual Pass has to offer and more—namely, admission to the water parks, Disney's Wide World of Sports complex, DisneyQuest, and Pleasure Island for a year. Premium Annual Pass-holders are eligible for the same discounts and benefits as Theme Park Annual Pass-holders; Premium Annual Passes can be purchased at the entrance to any of the four theme parks (they can be renewed there or by mail). A photo ID must be presented for purchase by adults and may be required for future use. Premium Annual Passes are non-transferable. These passes expire one year after the date of purchase.

Deciding Factors

Choosing the Right Ticket: Before you make your decision, it helps to map out your vacation. Only have a few days? Pick which parks you'd like to visit and get day tickets. Each is valid for admission to one park only, while most multi-day tickets can be used at all parks on the same day. Will you have lots of time to explore the rest of the World? Consider the Park Hopper Plus Ticket. If you plan to focus on theme parks, skip the plus option and get a Four- or Five-Day Park Hopper Ticket.

Disney resort guests can get an Ultimate Park Hopper Ticket, good practically everywhere for the entire trip. The downside? Unused days on the Ultimate Park Hopper Ticket expire the day of check-out.

The Park Hopper Plus has some limitations, but unused days and "plus" options never expire. Before you purchase the Ultimate Park Hopper Ticket, create a day-by-day itinerary to determine if you'll have time (and energy) to make use of all it has to offer.

If you are planning a longer visit, or two trips in a year, we highly recommend an annual pass. In addition to unlimited admission to the parks, you'll get discounts on everything from dinner shows to room rates.

Note: Only one person per party need possess an annual pass to net a discount on a resort rate. This option is great for travelers with flexible vacation schedules, as the discounts do vary and are often announced just weeks before they go into effect.

Tickets with Unused Days: Remaining days on any multi-day tickets—with the exception of those on the Ultimate Park Hopper Ticket—may be used during a future visit to Walt Disney World. They never expire.

Admission Prices

ONE-DAY TICKET

Adult	$55.38
Child*	$44.73

PARK HOPPER TICKET

Four Days

Adult	$221.52
Child*	$177.86

Five Days

Adult	$254.54
Child*	$204.48

PARK HOPPER PLUS TICKET

Five Days

Adult	$286.50
Child*	$230.04

Six Days

Adult	$318.45
Child*	$255.62

Seven Days

Adult	$350.40
Child*	$281.18

ULTIMATE PARK HOPPER TICKET

Length of Stay	Adult	Child*
2 days	$179.99	$144.84
3 days	$241.76	$193.83
4 days	$289.68	$232.17
5 days	$323.76	$259.86
6 days	$356.78	$285.42
7 days	$392.99	$315.24
8 days	$424.94	$340.80
9 days	$456.89	$366.36
10 days	$484.58	$387.66

THEME PARK ANNUAL PASS

Adult	$392.99
Child*	$334.41

Renewals

Adult	$350.39
Child*	$298.20

PREMIUM ANNUAL PASS

Adult	$520.81
Child*	$467.56

Renewals

Adult	$443.05
Child*	$397.27

Prices are subject to change. They include sales tax, were correct at press time, and are the prices charged at the gate. Some tickets are cheaper if purchased in advance.

*3 through 9 years of age; children under 3 free

Save Time In Line!

For those of us who'd prefer not to waste time standing in line for theme park attractions, Disney's Fastpass is nothing short of a miracle. Basically, the system allows guests to forego the task of waiting in an actual line for a number of theme park attractions. How? Simply by walking up to the Fastpass booth (located near the entrance of participating attractions) and slipping their park ticket into the Fastpass machine. In return, guests get a slip of paper with a time period printed on it (in addition to the safe return of their park ticket). That time—for example 4:05 P.M. to 5:05 P.M.—represents the window in which guests are invited to return to the attraction and practically walk right in—without standing in a long line!

Once you use your Fastpass to enter an attraction (or the time on it has passed), you can get a new Fastpass time for another attraction. It may be possible to get another Fastpass within 45 minutes or sooner (depending on availability). To find out, read the fine print on your current Fastpass ticket. For example, if one pass was issued at 2 P.M. you can get a Fastpass for another attraction at 4 P.M. (possibly sooner). Sound confusing? It won't be once you've tried it.

Disney's Fastpass service is free and available to everyone bearing a valid theme park ticket. It should be available during peak times of the day and all peak seasons. Fastpass assignments are limited and tend to go quickly on busy days. Always start the day with your "must-see" attraction. We've placed the Fastpass logo (FP) beside the listing for all of the attractions that were participating at press time. However, since more attractions are scheduled for inclusion, check a park map for a complete listing of Fastpass attractions.

Note that all Walt Disney World attractions offer the option of standing in a traditional line. If you enjoy the standing-in-line experience, by all means, go for it. Otherwise, take our advice: Fastpass is the way to go!

Purchasing Tickets

Admission tickets are sold at park entrances, WDW resorts, the resorts on Hotel Plaza Boulevard, Orlando International Airport, the Transportation and Ticket Center (TTC), and Downtown Disney Guest Relations. Cash, traveler's checks, personal checks (with ID), American Express, Visa, MasterCard, Discover, Diner's Club, JCB Card, and the Disney Visa card are accepted. Not all tickets are available at each location, so be sure to check. Call 407-824-4321 to confirm.

We recommend buying tickets in advance from a travel agent, or in one of these ways:

Tickets by Phone: Multi-day tickets can be purchased by phone; call 407-824-4321. There is a $3 handling fee. Allow two to three weeks for delivery.

Tickets Online: Multi-day tickets can be bought through *www.disneyworld.com*. There is a $3 handling fee. Allow at least three weeks for delivery.

Tickets at the Disney Store: Select multi-day theme park tickets are available for purchase at any local Disney Store.

Tickets by Mail (multi-day tickets only): Allow at least three to four weeks for processing, and include a return address. Send a check or money order (for the exact amount plus $3 for handling), payable to Walt Disney World Company, to: Walt Disney World, Box 10140, Lake Buena Vista, FL 32830-0030. Attention: Ticket Mail Order.

Hot Tip!

Prior to your visit, call 407-824-4321 or visit *www.disneyworld.com* for current ticket information. You may be able to save time and money by buying tickets before you arrive at Walt Disney World!

Money-Saving Tips

While there's no denying that a Walt Disney World vacation can be an exceptionally expensive undertaking, it is possible to keep costs down. When budgeting for your trip, keep in mind that WDW prices are comparable to those in a large city. Here are a few tips to help you conserve cash.

Lodging

- When it comes to saving money on accommodations, timing is truly the key. While off-season dates tend to vary, depending on the hotel, value season for most Walt Disney World resorts generally means January through mid-February, late August through late September, and early November through late December.

- Consider how much time you will actually spend at your hotel, and don't pay for a place with perks you won't have time to enjoy. Hotels often allow kids to stay free in parents' rooms, but the cutoff age does vary. Budget chains are economical but usually offer few frills.

- When considering the cost-effectiveness of off-property lodging, factor in the time, money, and inconvenience of commuting to and from attractions.

- Realize, too, that the advantages of staying on-property (tops among them, the "Extra Magic Hour" perk and access to Walt Disney World's transportation system) also apply to those staying in the least expensive rooms in Disney's hotels. The most important addresses for budget-watching Disney fans, the All-Star and Pop Century resorts, offer the lowest rates on Disney property. Rooms at Caribbean Beach, Port Orleans French Quarter and Riverside, and Coronado Springs are slightly higher priced. Also, note that the only difference between the least and most expensive

guestrooms in a hotel is often the view. Consider how often you'll be looking out that window.

Food

- Visit costlier establishments at lunchtime (if you so desire) rather than at dinner; entrées often cost a bit less at the midday meal.

- Sometimes certain Epcot eateries have early-bird dinner deals; it pays to ask.

- Carry sandwich fixings and have lunches alfresco when possible (keeping in mind that outside food is not welcome inside Disney theme parks).

- Look for lodging with kitchen facilities: The savings on food, especially at breakfast time, may be more than the extra accommodations expense.

- Refrigerators are available for about $10 a day at many Disney resorts.

- A souvenir mug can be purchased at most resorts, good for refills during your stay at the resort. (Note that similar mugs are sold in the theme parks, but do not come with free refills.)

- The Trail's End Buffet at Fort Wilderness has an inexpensive, yet satisfying, all-you-can-eat country breakfast buffet.

- Pack kid-friendly snacks, such as fruit, cereal, or even a lollipop. (Snack stands are plentiful, but not always handy or cost-efficient.)

- Don't plan on eating three big table-service meals a day. It gets expensive—and filling!

> ## Hot Tip!
> Staying hydrated can get costly. Refill water bottles as often as possible—rather than buy new ones.

Satisfying Substitutes

Fewer frills rarely means less fun at Walt Disney World. Here are money-saving alternatives to two of Disney's higher-priced treats.

If you'd rather not spring for admission to Downtown Disney Pleasure Island ($21), consider taking a trip to Disney's BoardWalk resort. Among other diversions, you'll find Jellyrolls (a sing-along piano bar with a cover of $10 or less), Atlantic Dance (a nightclub with no cover charge), and ESPN Club (a cover-free sports bar). A short walk will take you to the Swan hotel, home to the karaoke-friendly Kimono's Lounge.

If the Grand Floridian ($339–$755 a night) doesn't quite fit into your budget, consider staying in a Mansion room at Port Orleans Riverside ($133–$194 a night). Southern society replaces Victorian splendor, and, though the guestrooms aren't quite as spacious, the understated elegance and air of sophistication make for a most satisfying stay.

Discounts

- Theme Park Annual and Premium Annual Pass-holders receive so many discounts on meals, dinner shows, tours, room rates, and more that it may be worth purchasing an annual pass for longer visits or if you plan to take more than one trip within a year. Although the pass entitles the bearer to a slew of discounts, the potential for reduced room rates is the most valuable of them all.

- The lineup of Walt Disney resorts that offer Annual Pass-holder rates varies from month to month (with occasional periods devoid of any special offers), and discounted rooms aren't always available for booking more than a month or so in advance (although we've been able to get reservations as far as a season ahead). It's best to be flexible with your travel dates. Call 407-560-PASS (560-7277) for additional details.

- Discounts on Disney World resort rates and theme park tickets are available to Florida residents, and other seasonal promotions occur. Call 407-824-4321 for specifics.

- Several off-property hotels offer discounts to seniors and AAA or AARP members as well. Some AAA branches offer members ten percent off some park passes, as well as discounts on rooms and select packages with the AAA Disney Magic Moments Savings Program. Contact your local branch for additional information.

- Web-based *travelocity.com* offers a variety of Disney vacation packages. Vacation Outlet also offers some packages at a reduced rate. Visit *www.vacationoutlet.com* or call 800-690-2210 for details.

- To receive a free copy of the Orlando Magicard (included in a complimentary packet of Orlando information), call 800-643-9492. Cardholders receive many discounts at Orlando-area hotels, restaurants, attractions, and shops, as well as on rental cars. Similar coupon offers can be found at the airport.

- Disney's Visa cardholders earn reward dollars when they use the card. These dollars can be redeemed at Walt Disney World, the Disney Cruise Line, and Disneyland.

- It's possible to save a few bucks by purchasing some Park Hopper tickets in advance (as in before you arrive at Walt Disney World). For example, a 4-day hopper will cost $199 on Walt Disney World property but just $192 if ordered and paid for ahead of time. Multi-day tickets can be purchased at *www.disneyworld.com*, by calling 407-934-7639. Keep in mind that this policy may change at any time.

- When you call to make your resort reservation (401-939-7639), ask if any discounts apply. Hey, you've got nothing to lose.

Hot Tip!

It may be cheaper to spread out over two rooms in a "value" or "moderate" resort than to cram everyone into one room at "deluxe" Disney digs.

Making a Budget

A stay at Disney's kingdom need not cost a king's ransom (though it easily can). In fact, with a well-planned budget, money at Disney World can stretch relatively far.

Vacation expenses tend to fall into five major categories: (1) transportation (which may include any combination of costs for airfare, airport transfers, train tickets, car rental, gas, parking, and taxi service); (2) lodging; (3) theme park tickets; (4) meals; and (5) miscellaneous (recreational activities, souvenirs, postcards, film, toiletries, and home expenses such as pet boarding, etc.).

When planning your budget, first consider what level of service suits your needs. Some people prefer to spend fewer days at Disney but stay at a deluxe hotel or dine at pricier restaurants, while others would rather make their money cover a longer vacation that includes a value-priced resort and less expensive meals. The choice is up to you. Once you've established your spending priorities, determine your price limit. Then make sure you don't exceed it when approximating your expenses—without a ballpark figure to work around, it's easy to get carried away.

Sample Budget

The following is an example of a low- to moderately priced budget designed for a family of four (two adults and two kids planning to stay at WDW for five nights and six days). Totals include tax.

GETTING READY TO GO

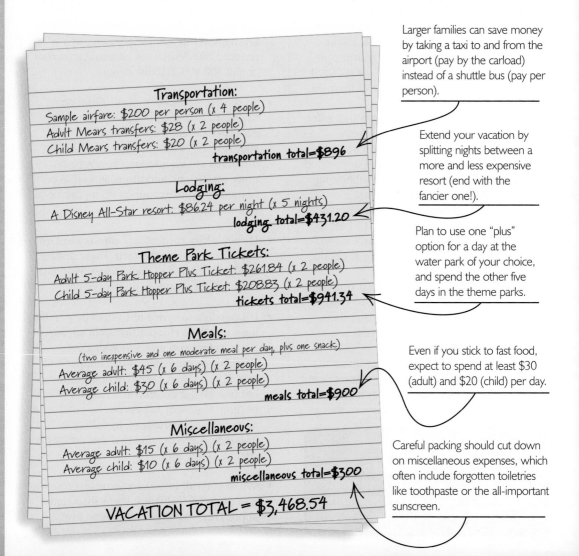

Transportation:
Sample airfare: $200 per person (x 4 people)
Adult Mears transfers: $28 (x 2 people)
Child Mears transfers: $20 (x 2 people)
transportation total=$896

Lodging:
A Disney All-Star resort: $86.24 per night (x 5 nights)
lodging total=$431.20

Theme Park Tickets:
Adult 5-day Park Hopper Plus Ticket: $261.84 (x 2 people)
Child 5-day Park Hopper Plus Ticket: $208.83 (x 2 people)
tickets total=$941.34

Meals:
(two inexpensive and one moderate meal per day, plus one snack)
Average adult: $45 (x 6 days) (x 2 people)
Average child: $30 (x 6 days) (x 2 people)
meals total=$900

Miscellaneous:
Average adult: $15 (x 6 days) (x 2 people)
Average child: $10 (x 6 days) (x 2 people)
miscellaneous total=$300

VACATION TOTAL = $3,468.54

Larger families can save money by taking a taxi to and from the airport (pay by the carload) instead of a shuttle bus (pay per person).

Extend your vacation by splitting nights between a more and less expensive resort (end with the fancier one!).

Plan to use one "plus" option for a day at the water park of your choice, and spend the other five days in the theme parks.

Even if you stick to fast food, expect to spend at least $30 (adult) and $20 (child) per day.

Careful packing should cut down on miscellaneous expenses, which often include forgotten toiletries like toothpaste or the all-important sunscreen.

Planning Your Itinerary A Time Line

First Things First

- Make hotel and transportation arrangements as far ahead as possible. Note that many Disney hotels fill up more than six months in advance. Call 407-W-DISNEY (934-7639) to book a room at a Disney hotel; your confirmation should arrive within two weeks. Log it and other pertinent information in your Birnbaum Trip Planner at the end of this book. (Don't forget to take the Trip Planner with you!)
- Create a day-by-day schedule, deciding which area of WDW to visit on each day of your vacation. This will help when it's time to make restaurant and recreation reservations.
- Dinner-show reservations may be secured up to two years in advance. Consult page 248 for details, and call 407-WDW-DINE (939-3463) for reservations.

6 Months

- Unless you purchased a package that includes theme park admission, it's time to order tickets. Refer to pages 17–19 for details, and call 407-824-4321; passes should arrive within four weeks. Keep in mind that you may save money by purchasing tickets in advance.

4 Months

- Choose dining spots from those listed in the *Good Meals, Great Times* chapter. Call 407-WDW-DINE to make priority seating arrangements. Add restaurant names, dining times, and priority-seating numbers to your daily schedule.

3 Months

- Find out park hours for your stay, and add them to your day-by-day schedule. Closing times will be particularly helpful when making evening plans. Call 407-824-4321, or consult Walt Disney World's website (*www.disneyworld.com*).
- If you have purchased a golf package or will be staying at a WDW resort or a resort on Hotel Plaza Boulevard, you may book a tee time on one of WDW's golf courses now (see pages 204–205 for details on the courses). Golf lessons may also be reserved at this time. Call 407-WDW-GOLF (939-4653) for reservations. Those not staying on WDW property may make reservations one month ahead.
- Fishing excursions (see pages 208–209) may be booked by calling 407-WDW-PLAY (939-7529).
- Tennis lessons and courts may be reserved by calling 407-WDW-PLAY. Turn to page 206 for more information.
- Parasailing and waterskiing excursions (for details, see pages 207–208) may be booked by calling 407-WDW-PLAY.
- If you'd like to add a behind-the-scenes tour to your vacation, now is the time to make a reservation. See pages 200–201 for details, and call 407-WDW-TOUR (939-8687).
- Some attractions may be closed for refurbishment during your visit. A new refurbishment schedule is released each season. Call 407-824-4321.

1 Month

- Trail-ride reservations may be made up to 30 days in advance. Call 407-WDW-PLAY.

2 Weeks

- Airline tickets and travel-package vouchers should have arrived in the mail by now. Contact your travel agent or the travel company if they have not.

1 Week

- Reconfirm all reservations and priority-seating arrangements. Finalize your day-by-day schedule, including all confirmation numbers. Make one copy for your suitcase and one to carry with you in the parks.

Step-By-Step Sample Schedules

Many visitors have a deep desire to cover each and every inch of Walt Disney World in the span of a few short days. While we hesitate to discourage these most ambitious of travelers, we feel the need to enlighten them: Walt Disney World is a staggeringly large place. In fact, it's as big as San Francisco, and jam-packed with about as many diversions as you'd expect from a city that size. You could spend two full weeks on Disney property and still not have time to do it all. The theme parks alone require every bit of four days just to see the major attractions.

What's the best strategy for organizing a Walt Disney World visit? Make a list of the parks, attractions, and activities you *most* want to see and use it to create an itinerary. Don't forget to allow time for swimming, boating, or relaxing in a hammock. This is, after all, a vacation.

Assuming you've narrowed your "must-do" list to the barely manageable, we recommend a stay of at least four to five days. This allows for a visit to each of the theme parks and some time to enjoy many of the recreational activities at your resort. Longer stays can include water parks, Downtown Disney, a dinner show, and more. When planning your days (which you should do before leaving home), be sure to take into account theme park hours and seasonal temperatures in Central Florida.

The following sample schedules assume that you eat breakfast at your resort (unless otherwise stated) and arrive up to 30 minutes before the official opening time. These schedules, though tirelessly tested and proven successful by Birnbaum's editors, are not written in stone. Use them as a guide, tailoring the itineraries to suit your family's individual tastes.

Note that we have not included specific instructions with regard to Fastpass in our sample itineraries. It's not because we don't love the service. In fact, we highly recommend using Fastpass, even if working it into a daily schedule is still an inexact science. As more and more attractions are added to the program, it gets easier to breeze through the turnstiles in a highly organized manner. By all means, take advantage of the Fastpass opportunity every chance you get—not only will it make you feel like a VIP, but it will free up time in your schedule to do things you otherwise might not have gotten to.

Magic Kingdom One-Day Schedule

- Begin the day with a brisk stroll down Main Street, U.S.A. Cut through Adventureland on your way to Splash Mountain and Big Thunder Mountain Railroad. Backtrack to Pirates of the Caribbean, Jungle Cruise, The Magic Carpets of Aladdin, or The Enchanted Tiki Room—Under New Management.

- Access Frontierland via the path near the Tiki Room. Consider lunching at Pecos Bill Cafe or Columbia Harbour House.

- If time allows, squeeze in The Haunted Mansion before the afternoon parade. Watch the parade and move on to Fantasyland. (But visit The Haunted Mansion first.)

- See as much of Fantasyland as possible, including Mickey's PhilharMagic, It's a Small World, Peter Pan's Flight, and The Many Adventures of Winnie the Pooh.

- Cool off at Ariel's Grotto. If the wait to see the Little Mermaid is daunting, consider visiting other Disney characters at the Fantasyland Character Festival or in Mickey's Toontown Fair.

- Explore Mickey's Toontown Fair. Take daring kids on The Barnstormer. As a calmer alternative, hop on the railroad. Afterward, tour the country homes of Mickey and Minnie Mouse. Mickey greets guests in the Judge's Tent.

- If the evening parade is scheduled to run twice, explore Tomorrowland during the earlier showing. See Space Mountain, Buzz Lightyear's Space Ranger Spin, Alien Encounter, and the Speedway.

- View the fireworks from Main Street or the bridge to Tomorrowland.

- Watch the nighttime parade from Main Street, U.S.A.

- If there's time, revisit your favorite attraction (guests are admitted until closing time).

IF YOU HAVE YOUNG CHILDREN

Head directly to Fantasyland (walk right through the castle) and ride Dumbo, Peter Pan, Cinderella's Carrousel, Mickey's PhilharMagic, and Winnie the Pooh. Take fans to meet Ariel in her grotto.

Go to Toontown Fair to meet Mickey in the Judge's Tent. Explore Toontown and stop at the teacups on the way to the Fantasyland Character Festival.

Check showtimes for Cinderella's Surprise Celebration before riding the carousel and It's a Small World.

Line up for the afternoon parade about 30 minutes early. Or skip the parade, finish up Fantasyland, and take a magic carpet ride in Adventureland.

LINE BUSTERS

Even when the park is packed, there are some attractions with shorter or faster-moving lines. Among them are: Tomorrowland Transit Authority, Walt Disney World Railroad, The Enchanted Tiki Room—Under New Management, Pirates of the Caribbean, Country Bear Jamboree, It's a Small World, and Tom Sawyer Island.

Magic Kingdom Musts

Short on time? Here's a list of the attractions that put the magic in the Magic Kingdom:

Splash Mountain • **Big Thunder Mountain Railroad**
Pirates of the Caribbean • **The Haunted Mansion**
Peter Pan's Flight • **It's a Small World**
Buzz Lightyear's Space Ranger Spin • **Space Mountain**
The Many Adventures of Winnie the Pooh

Epcot One-Day Schedule

- Start the day by making a beeline for Future World's Mission: SPACE and Test Track. (If the Test Track line is long, consider jumping on the "single riders" line. It moves much faster.) Follow it up with Wonders of Life, Universe of Energy, and The Living Seas pavilions. (Keep in mind that World Showcase doesn't open until about 11 A.M.)

IF YOU HAVE YOUNG CHILDREN

Begin the day at the Wonders of Life pavilion, making sure to explore the Fitness Fairgrounds. Make your way over to The Living Seas before popping in at The Land. Be sure to hit ImageWorks in the Imagination! pavilion (but skip Honey, I Shrunk the Audience—it scares little ones silly).

At World Showcase, head to Mexico's boat ride and, for braver tots, Norway's Maelstrom. Visit the Kidcot Funstop at each country.

LINE BUSTERS

Tired of long lines? Go to: The Living Seas, *The Circle of Life* movie in The Land, Universe of Energy, or The American Adventure. The Spaceship Earth line thins in the afternoon.

- Stop for lunch at The Land's Sunshine Season Food Fair or Garden Grill, or the Coral Reef restaurant in nearby The Living Seas.

- After exploring The Land, be sure to see Honey, I Shrunk the Audience in the Imagination! pavilion (though it may frighten small children). Save time to enjoy ImageWorks, a high-tech playground.

- If you're in the mood for some serious pin-trading (or shopping), stop by Pin Central in Innoventions Plaza. (Note that pin-trading can take place just about anywhere at any time. All Disney employees who are wearing pins are willing to trade.)

- Visit Spaceship Earth before heading to Innoventions. Be sure to explore the interactive area known as Global Neighborhood, located at the exit of the attraction.

- Make your way to World Showcase by early evening and start your circular tour of the world at Canada. Proceed counter-clockwise around the lagoon. Don't miss the *Impressions de France* movie in the France pavilion, the show in the American Adventure pavilion, and the Maelstrom attraction in Norway.

- After dinner, scope out a spot to watch IllumiNations: Reflections of Earth. (We enjoy the area near Japan, but there are excellent viewing locations all around the World Showcase lagoon.)

Epcot Essentials

There is a lot to see and do at Disney's discovery park. Don't leave without investigating these outstanding attractions:

Universe of Energy • **Honey, I Shrunk the Audience**
Living with the Land • **Test Track**
Cranium Command • **IllumiNations: Reflections of Earth**
The American Adventure show • **Impressions de France**
Mission: SPACE

Timing Tip: If you have priority seating arrangements for dinner at World Showcase, give yourself 30 to 40 minutes to get there from the front gate. Taking a *FriendShip* water taxi can shave a few minutes off your trip (although it isn't much faster than brisk walking).

Disney-MGM Studios One-Day Schedule

- Some attractions open later in the morning: Consult a park times guide for exact times. Also, many shows here run on a schedule, so check for times throughout the day. Note that this park is not the easiest to navigate. You'll need a map to get your bearings in the region beyond the Chinese Theater.

- Daredevils should begin the day with Rock 'n' Roller Coaster, followed by some eye-opening drops at The Twilight Zone Tower of Terror.

- If Beauty and the Beast is playing soon, grab a seat. Otherwise, plan to come back later and go to The Magic of Disney Animation, Voyage of The Little Mermaid, Walt Disney: One Man's Dream, and Who Wants to Be a Millionaire—Play It!

- Pause for lunch at the ABC Commissary, 50's Prime Time Cafe, Sci-Fi Dine-In Theater, or Hollywood & Vine.

- Line up 20 to 30 minutes early to watch the Disney Stars and Motor Cars parade. (Note that if you skip the parade, it is an excellent time to see The Magic of Disney Animation, Who Wants to Be a Millionaire—Play It!, or The Great Movie Ride.)

- Be sure to see (and hear) Sounds Dangerous starring Drew Carey, followed by the Disney-MGM Studios Backlot Tour, Star Tours, Jim Henson's Muppet*Vision 3-D, and the Indiana Jones Epic Stunt Spectacular.

- Be sure to take tots to the Honey, I Shrunk the Kids Movie Set Adventure. (It's an elaborately themed playground.)

- If you missed Beauty and the Beast—Live on Stage, go now and, if you haven't hit it yet, The Great Movie Ride.

- Keep an eye on the clock: You want to get a spot for Fantasmic! *at least 60 minutes* before showtime. Note that if you choose to skip Fantasmic!, plan to exit the park before the last performance breaks. If you do stay for the show, know that you can meander through select shops while the throngs file through the turnstiles at the exit.

IF YOU HAVE YOUNG CHILDREN

Begin with the Voyage of The Little Mermaid attraction followed by a visit to Jim Henson's Muppet*Vision 3-D.

Have lunch at Toy Story Pizza Planet, then watch the parade. Romp in the Honey, I Shrunk the Kids Movie Set Adventure, catch a show at Playhouse Disney, and see Beauty and the Beast—Live on Stage. Skip Fantasmic!— it tends to terrify tots.

Be sure to catch up with Disney characters on Mickey Avenue and New York Street.

LINE BUSTERS

When lines abound at the Disney-MGM Studios, we suggest the following: Indiana Jones Epic Stunt Spectacular (the theater accommodates 2,000 guests at a time), Honey, I Shrunk the Kids Movie Set Adventure, Disney-MGM Studios Backlot Tour (the line moves relatively quickly, and you get plenty of bang for your waiting buck), American Film Institute Showcase, and Toy Story Pizza Planet (as an arcade, it's not an attraction per se, but still a pleasant diversion).

Studios Standouts

If you're short on time, be sure to catch as many of the following four-star attractions at the Disney-MGM Studios as possible:

The Twilight Zone Tower of Terror
Rock 'n' Roller Coaster starring Aerosmith
Beauty and the Beast—Live on Stage • The Magic of Disney Animation
Jim Henson's Muppet*Vision 3-D • Star Tours
Fantasmic! • Who Wants to Be a Millionaire—Play It!

Disney's Animal Kingdom One-Day Schedule

- Many shows here run on a schedule, so check for times throughout the day. Make a point of seeing Festival of the Lion King—it appeals to all ages.

- As you enter the park, pass through the Oasis and head toward DinoLand U.S.A. Ride Dinosaur before eating breakfast with Donald Duck at Restaurantosaurus (priority seating is highly recommended). Explore DinoLand before catching a performance of Tarzan Rocks!

GETTING READY TO GO

IF YOU HAVE YOUNG CHILDREN

We recommend lingering a bit in the Oasis on your way into the park. Then make a sharp left and head straight to Camp Minnie-Mickey. Visit with some Disney characters, and watch Festival of the Lion King. (Warn sensitive youngsters that the music may be a bit loud.)

Stop by The Tree of Life to notice all of the animal carvings in its trunk. (Note that the show inside the tree, It's Tough to be a Bug!, is very intense and may frighten young children.)

Eat lunch at Pizzafari or head to DinoLand U.S.A.'s Restaurantosaurus. Explore DinoLand, making sure to see The Boneyard playground and Chester and Hester's Dino-Rama!

In Asia, go to the Maharajah Jungle Trek. Consider riding Africa's bumpy Kilimanjaro Safaris. See the Pangani Forest Exploration Trail. Then take the train to Rafiki's Planet Watch.

LINE BUSTERS

When herds of guests mob Disney's Animal Kingdom attractions, there are a few places to escape the stampede: the Oasis, Pangani Forest Exploration Trail, Maharajah Jungle Trek, Discovery Island Trails, The Boneyard playground, and Rafiki's Planet Watch. (You'll need to take the Wildlife Express train to Rafiki's Planet Watch.)

- In Asia, ride Kali River Rapids, then visit the tigers at the Maharajah Jungle Trek, and, if it's playing soon, see Flights of Wonder at the Caravan Stage.

- Check a park times guide for the Festival of the Lion King schedule. Plan to arrive in Camp Minnie-Mickey at least 45 minutes before it starts (it's a wildly popular show). If possible, mingle with Disney characters before seeing Festival of the Lion King.

- Stop at Tusker House for lunch. Then jump aboard the Wildlife Express train to Rafiki's Planet Watch. Don't miss the Song of the Rainforest and Affection Section (the latter, a small, outdoor petting farm, allows for up-close encounters with little critters).

- After experiencing Africa's Kilimanjaro Safaris, take a relaxing hike on the peaceful, animal-laden Pangani Forest Exploration Trail.

- Wander the Discovery Island Trails that surround The Tree of Life, taking time to search for the many animals carved into the tree and its roots.

- Finish off the day with a screening of It's Tough to be a Bug!

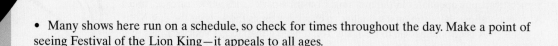

Animal Kingdom Aces

An abbreviated visit to Disney's Animal Kingdom is enough to make anybody growl. The following attractions should help soothe the savage beast, er, guest:

Dinosaur • Kali River Rapids

Kilimanjaro Safaris • It's Tough to be a Bug!

Festival of the Lion King • Pangani Forest Exploration Trail

Maharajah Jungle Trek

Hot Tip!
Many attractions are in the steamy outdoors. Bring a refillable water bottle when you visit.

Half-Day Schedules
Magic Kingdom

Morning at the Magic Kingdom

- Where to begin—Tomorrowland or Frontierland? It's a big decision. Know that the area you postpone may have long lines by the time you get there. We'd start with Tomorrowland.
- Move rapidly from one attraction to the next—first to Space Mountain, then to Buzz Lightyear's Space Ranger Spin.
- Cut across Main Street and head for Pirates of the Caribbean, Splash Mountain, and Big Thunder Mountain Railroad.
- Visit The Haunted Mansion and, if there's time before the parade, the Country Bear Jamboree.
- Watch the afternoon parade in Frontierland. Or skip the parade and see Fantasyland's Peter Pan's Flight, Winnie the Pooh, It's a Small World, and Mickey's PhilharMagic.

> **HALF DAY WITH YOUNG CHILDREN**
> Start at Mickey's Toontown Fair. (You can get there easily by boarding the Walt Disney World Railroad at Main Street Station.) Meet Mickey Mouse inside the Judge's Tent. After fully exploring Mickey's Toontown Fair, move on to Fantasyland. Soar on a magic carpet in Adventureland before calling it a day.

The Magic Kingdom After Lunch

- Start in Adventureland. Ride the Jungle Cruise and Pirates of the Caribbean.
- Head to Frontierland. Do Splash Mountain and Big Thunder Mountain Railroad. Then see the Country Bear Jamboree or stop by Goofy's Country Dancin' Jamboree. Hop on the Walt Disney World Railroad to Mickey's Toontown Fair.
- Explore Toontown. If the wait to meet Mickey Mouse is more than 30 minutes, consider coming back in the late evening.
- Take a spin at the Mad Tea Party, and see the highlights of Fantasyland, including It's a Small World, Peter Pan, Mickey's PhilharMagic, and Winnie the Pooh.
- Pop in at The Haunted Mansion before dinner.
- Now it's time for Tomorrowland. (If you have the energy and the nighttime parade is running twice, plan to stay in Tomorrowland during the early run. See the parade later.) Go to Alien Encounter, Buzz Lightyear's Space Ranger Spin, and Space Mountain.
- Watch the nighttime parade.
- Shop on Main Street, U.S.A. while the exiting throngs file out.

Epcot

Morning at Epcot

- Head right to Mission: SPACE and Test Track. Then move to Honey, I Shrunk the Audience (inside the Imagination! pavilion) and The Land.
- See Universe of Energy and the Wonders of Life before moving on to World Showcase—it opens at 11 A.M. (Note that Wonders of Life may be closed for refurbishment during your visit.) When hunger calls, stop for a light lunch. See the countries that interest you most, making sure to see the show inside the American Adventure and the boat ride in Norway.
- Finish up by seeing Future World's Spaceship Earth.

> **HALF DAY WITH YOUNG CHILDREN**
> Begin with a visit to Imagination!, taking time to fully explore the ImageWorks interactive play zone. After making the trip to The Living Seas, move on to the Wonders of Life, making sure to enjoy some hands-on fun at the Fitness Fairgrounds, and catch Cranium Command.

(Continued on page 30)

(Continued from page 29)

Epcot After Lunch

- If you don't have priority seating arrangements and would like to have dinner at a World Showcase restaurant, stop by Guest Relations to make them. If not, consider dining at the nearby BoardWalk resort (it's a short stroll or boat ride away).
  - See as much of Future World as possible before going to World Showcase for dinner.
  - Spend the evening touring World Showcase. Keep an eye on the clock so you can secure a good spot around the Lagoon to watch the evening's presentation of IllumiNations.
- Avoid the crush of exiting crowds by browsing in Mouse Gear in Future World.

Disney-MGM Studios

Morning at the Disney-MGM Studios

- Kick-start the day with Rock 'n' Roller Coaster, followed by a trip to The Twilight Zone Tower of Terror. From there, move to Jim Henson's Muppet*Vision 3-D and Star Tours.
- Before lining up for the parade, see The Magic of Disney Animation, Beauty and the Beast—Live on Stage, Who Wants to Be a Millionaire—Play It!, and The Great Movie Ride.

The Disney-MGM Studios After Lunch

- Begin with Tower of Terror, Rock 'n' Roller Coaster, Beauty and the Beast—Live on Stage, and The Magic of Disney Animation.

HALF DAY WITH YOUNG CHILDREN
Start with Voyage of The Little Mermaid, followed by Playhouse Disney—Live on Stage, the Honey, I Shrunk the Audience Movie Set Adventure, Jim Henson's Muppet*Vision 3-D, and Beauty and the Beast—Live on Stage. Skip Fantasmic!—it is just too intense for most tykes.

- See Voyage of The Little Mermaid, Who Wants to Be a Millionaire—Play It!, Star Tours, Jim Henson's Muppet*Vision 3-D, The Great Movie Ride, and Disney-MGM Studios Backlot Tour.
- If there's time, see Walt Disney: One Man's Dream, Sounds Dangerous, and Indiana Jones before securing a spot for Fantasmic!

Disney's Animal Kingdom

Morning at Disney's Animal Kingdom

HALF DAY WITH YOUNG CHILDREN
Scope out animal life in The Oasis before heading to Camp Minnie-Mickey. Meet Disney characters and see The Festival of the Lion King before visiting DinoLand U.S.A. Explore The Boneyard and ride TriceraTop Spin. If time allows, take the train to Rafiki's Planet Watch where kids can bond with live animals (mostly goats) in the Affection Section.

- Go directly to Dinosaur in DinoLand U.S.A. Then head to Asia for Kali River Rapids and the Maharajah Jungle Trek.
- Experience the Kilimanjaro Safaris and the Pangani Forest Exploration Trail in Africa.
- Check a times guide for the next Festival of the Lion King show. Arrive at least 45 minutes ahead of time. (It's a very popular show.)
- Finish up with It's Tough to be a Bug!

Disney's Animal Kingdom After Lunch

- Check a times guide for the Festival of the Lion King schedule. Arrive 45 minutes early. Then visit Disney characters in Camp Minnie-Mickey.
- If there is entertainment or a parade scheduled, stick around Discovery Island to enjoy it. Otherwise, head to the Kilimanjaro Safaris ride. Do the Pangani Forest Exploration Trail, and take the train to Rafiki's Planet Watch.
- In Asia, ride Kali River Rapids and experience the Maharajah Jungle Trek.
- Wander the Discovery Island Trails and see It's Tough to be a Bug!
- Before dinner, dodge dinos on Dinosaur and catch a performance of Tarzan Rocks!

GETTING READY TO GO

Making the Most of Longer Visits

Longer stays allow the chance to sample some of the World's myriad offerings. Spend another day in the one park you most enjoyed. Lounge by the pool, play tennis or golf, or bike. Go shopping at Downtown Disney. Cool off at one of Disney's innovative water parks. Have lunch at a WDW resort, and try a special dinner at Victoria & Albert's, in the Grand Floridian, or at California Grill, in the Contemporary. Check out the clubs at Pleasure Island or Downtown Disney West Side, or spend the evening at the BoardWalk. Take golf or tennis lessons. Go fishing, water-skiing, or horseback riding. Visit a spa. Participate in a behind-the-scenes program. Play a round of miniature golf. See a game at Disney's Wide World of Sports complex. For even more ideas, see our *Sports*; *Everything Else in the World*; and *Good Meals, Great Times* chapters.

How to Save a Rainy Day

Florida rain showers come and go with such regularity that you could set your watch by them, especially during summer months. They're usually brief, though torrential. Of course, there are times when gray clouds linger longer. Here are some ways to make the most of a soggy day:

- Head for DisneyQuest, a huge interactive play zone at Downtown Disney West Side. It'll keep the whole family entertained (and dry) for hours.

- See a movie on one of AMC Theatres' 24 screens at Downtown Disney.

- Consider taking in an indoor event at Disney's Wide World of Sports complex. For information, call 407-363-6600.

- Don your rain gear and go to Epcot. The pavilions in Future World house a bounty of sheltered diversions. (Ponchos are sold throughout Walt Disney World for about $6 each.)

Customized Travel Tips
Traveling with Children

Tell youngsters that a Walt Disney World vacation is in the works and the response is apt to be overwhelming. Our guide *Birnbaum's Walt Disney World For Kids, By Kids*, written for children ages 7 through 14, can be a useful resource for getting them involved in the planning from the outset. Filled with information about the World from a kid's perspective, it can be used as a reference before and during the trip, and as a souvenir afterward.

Walt Disney World ranks among the easier spots on earth for families with children. Keep in mind, however, that kids under 7 must be accompanied by an adult to enter the theme parks; kids under 10 must be accompanied at the water parks. With most teens, however, it is enough to establish a meeting place and time inside the Magic Kingdom, Epcot, Disney-MGM Studios, or Animal Kingdom.

Child Care: In-room child care service can be summoned to all Disney-owned resorts. The service is available 24 hours a day, seven days a week. For pricing information and to make a reservation with a company called Kids Night Out, call 407-827-5444, or inquire at your resort's guest services desk. Another outside company, All About Kids, offers this service as well. To reach them, call 407-812-9300.

The Polynesian, Grand Floridian, Contemporary, Animal Kingdom Lodge, Wilderness Lodge, Yacht and Beach Club, BoardWalk, and Dolphin resorts each have an on-site children's activity center. These centers accept (potty-trained) kids ages 4 through 12. For details and availability, phone 407-939-3463 for all but the Dolphin. For information on "Camp Dolphin," call 407-934-4000.

Baby Care Centers: Located in all four theme parks, these centers are for parents with young kids. There are rooms with rocking chairs and couches for nursing mothers, and cheery feeding rooms. Centers have facilities for changing infants, preparing formula, and warming bottles. Diapers, bottles, formula, pacifiers, and baby food are among the supplies for sale. There are changing areas in most women's and in some men's restrooms, as well.

Lost Children: Disney employees know what to do if a child starts to call for his or her parents. If your child wanders off, stop in at the Baby Care Center or City Hall in the Magic Kingdom; at Guest Relations or the Baby Care Center in Epcot; at Guest Relations at the Disney-MGM Studios; or at Guest Relations in Animal Kingdom. A computerized system allows for a detailed description of the child and his or her status, help reunite families quickly. There are no paging systems, but in emergencies an all-points bulletin can be put out among Disney employees. The Guest Relations staff of each park can also help.

It helps to prepare your child for the possibility of an accidental separation. Direct him or her to contact an employee (anybody wearing a name tag) and ask for help.

Refrigerators: For parents of young children, an in-room fridge is not a mere luxury, it's a necessity. Disney's "home away from home" accommodations generally come equipped with a small refrigerator. However, it is possible to rent one for a standard hotel room. The rate is about $10 per day. Request one when you make your reservation, and be sure to confirm that request shortly before you arrive.

Parental Perk

Families with small children should know about the "rider switch" policy at the theme parks. At attractions with age or height restrictions, a parent who waits with a young child while the other parent rides the attraction can go right on when the first parent comes off. Be sure to ask the attendant.

Baby Food: It's possible to purchase jars of baby food at most Disney resorts. However, the selection isn't huge. For a wider variety of foodstuffs to choose from, consider Gooding's grocery store. It's located at the Crossroads shopping center, near Hotel Plaza Boulevard. For directions, inquire at your resort's front desk, or ask a parking attendant. Gooding's, as well as nearby convenience stores, are also within a reasonable cabbing distance.

Be sure to hire an authorized cab for your trip (one with regulated rates). Your resort staff can make the arrangements and give you an estimate of the cost. Publix supermarket is another good choice. It tends to be less expensive than other options, but it's a bit further away. If you've got a car, this is the way to go.

If you have a milk (or other food-supply) emergency after hours, know that the following resorts have 24-hour snack bars: Grand Floridian, Polynesian, Contemporary, Dolphin, and Wyndham Palace.

Cribs: Most WDW resort rooms come with a small, playpen-like crib. Be sure to request one when you make your reservation and to confirm that request before you arrive. They're free. If you'd like something a little sturdier, consider renting a crib from Children's Rentals (407-522-0233) or All About Kids (407-812-9300).

Diapers: Each Disney resort has at least one shop in which to pick up diapers. If you're brand loyal, pack your own. Be sure to throw a few waterproof diapers into your bag each morning. You never know when you'll run into an interactive fountain on Disney property. They're necessary for pool use, too.

Resort Fun: All Walt Disney World resorts have at least one room stuffed with video games. Most of the hotels have little playgrounds as well as small, toddler-friendly wading pools.

Strollers: Available for rent for $7 (plus a $1 refundable deposit) at stroller and wheelchair rental shops at each of the theme parks. (Strollers are not available for rent at the water parks.) Double strollers cost $13 plus a $1 deposit. Present the receipt when returning the stroller to get a Disney Dollar back.

Keep in mind that strollers are not permitted inside the attractions (they can be parked near each attraction entrance). If a stroller disappears while you're in an attraction, a replacement may be obtained. Ask a park worker for the nearest replacement location.

Guests have to pay only once a day for a stroller. If you rent one in the morning and plan to spend the afternoon at another park, just present your receipt for a stroller there.

You may also choose to bring your own stroller into the parks, or rent one at your hotel by calling Children's Rentals (407-522-0223) or All About Kids (407-812-9300).

Tips for Teens

When it comes to teens at Disney World, *The Little Mermaid*'s Ariel has plenty of company. Of course, be they of the fish or human variety, teenage guests have special needs all their own. Here are some tips, courtesy of Amy Newcomer, Birnbaum's WDW teen expert:

- Bring a Walkman. It's perfect for the trip to Walt Disney World and for sitting poolside at your resort. But you don't have to pack every CD you own. Just take a few of your favorites.

- Have some of your own money on hand. If it's your hard-earned cash, you won't spend it as fast as you would Mom and Dad's!

- Pack a hat. Why? It's much easier to throw a hat on than taking time to do your hair.

- There are lots of great restaurants for teens: Rainforest Cafe has a lot of action going on. Planet Hollywood does, too. It's fun to look at all the movie memorabilia. One of the best restaurants is 50's Prime Time Cafe at the Disney-MGM Studios. It's great to see your parent get yelled at by the "Mom" and "Dad" waiters! It's also fun to sit in a car and eat at Sci-Fi Dine-In Theater.

- Try to get along with your brothers and sisters—even if it isn't always easy. Don't bug them to do the things you want to do all the time. Offer to do things they want to do, too.

- One of the coolest things for teens to do is an "E-Ride Night" at the Magic Kingdom. It lets you stay in the theme park after hours and ride all the best rides with basically no wait! Another good thing to do at night is go shopping, especially at Downtown Disney.

- *Attention parents!* Try to include your teens in planning your trip. If they get a say during planning, they will be much happier when they arrive at Walt Disney World. Also, don't make them get up every morning at 6 A.M. Try to give them a day or two to wake up late and lounge around the pool or a water park.

Traveling Without Children

Walt Disney World has become a popular destination for adults without children, appealing to singles, young couples, and empty nesters alike. Disney has responded to the demand with an entertainment complex and dining for grown-ups without kids in tow.

- Consider perusing *Birnbaum's Walt Disney World Without Kids*, our adult-oriented companion guide to this book.

- Crowds can be extremely heavy during traditional school break times. Schedule your visits for off-peak seasons.

Older Travelers

Walt Disney World can sometimes be overwhelming for older travelers. The theme parks can be disorienting because of the crisscrossing pathways. And the heat, particularly in summer, can be hard to take. But with the proper planning and precautions, it's just as delightful for older visitors as for kids.

- Try to eat early or late to avoid the mealtime crowds. In the Magic Kingdom, select restaurants such as Cinderella's Royal Table, in Cinderella Castle. Or take the monorail to the peaceful Polynesian, Contemporary, or Grand Floridian resorts, where pleasant dining options abound (check ahead to find out which restaurants serve lunch). In Epcot, the Coral Reef restaurant and Le Cellier Steakhouse are pleasant spots. At the Disney-MGM Studios, the Hollywood Brown Derby offers a relaxing sit-down meal.

- The Florida sun tends to be brutal year-round. Always wear sunscreen!

- Don't underestimate distances at Epcot or Animal Kingdom; you may need to walk more than three miles in a day. If that's daunting, consider renting a wheelchair. (Epcot's *FriendShip* boats on the lagoon can also ease the burden on weary feet.)

- Pace yourself. It's smart to head back to your hotel for a swim or a nap in the afternoon and then return to the parks later on.

The hotels connected by monorail are particularly convenient for this.

- Many Orlando-area hotels and attractions offer discounts to seniors and AARP members. Contact the Official Visitor Information Center (407-363-5872) for details.

Young Singles

While it's not exactly a happening singles scene, Walt Disney World is a lot of fun to visit with friends.

- Downtown Disney's clubs and restaurants can prove to be fertile meeting places. The BoardWalk is another lively destination. Sports fans find the ESPN Club most inviting.

- The lounges at WDW hotels are relaxed and welcoming. The same atmosphere prevails at the Tune-In Lounge in the 50's Prime Time Cafe at the Disney-MGM Studios, and at the Rose & Crown Pub (in the United Kingdom pavilion) and the Matsu No Ma lounge (Japan) in Epcot.

Solo Travelers

Those who travel alone for the freedom and fun of it can have as memorable a time here as they would anywhere else.

- Solo travelers with extra time should consider taking a behind-the-scenes tour.

- Many of the finer restaurants now have counters to sit at—perfect for lone diners.

- Need a tennis partner? Be sure to check out the player matching program at Disney's Racquet Club (407-824-3578).

- Other recreational opportunities for unencumbered travelers include parasailing and water-skiing (at the Contemporary), horseback riding (at Fort Wilderness), taking a spin around the track in a racecar (at the Richard Petty Driving Experience), and watching a pro baseball game (at Wide World of Sports). Call 407-WDW-PLAY (939-7529) for information.

Tips for International Travelers

Visitors from outside the U.S. need not feel like strangers in a strange land when they arrive at Walt Disney World—even if they speak a language other than English. Information is readily available in many different languages. These tips may also be helpful:

- International Welcome Centers are open in the theme parks during regular hours.

- Free park maps can be found in different languages at the entrance to all parks, as well as at Guest Relations.

- Several Disney resorts offer services for their international guests. Ask about them when you inquire about reservations.

- When making priority seating arrangements through 407-WDW-DINE (939-3463), ask to speak with a foreign language host.

- Most WDW restaurants offer menus in various languages. Some have picture menus.

- Foreign currency exchange is available at Guest Relations in each of the theme parks. Traveler's checks may be purchased at the SunTrust bank by Downtown Disney.

- Most Disney resort room keys can act as a charge card. Purchases made at WDW will be billed to a credit card that is presented at check-in (reducing the amount of currency that has to be exchanged).

- Many Disney employees are fluent in more than one language. Flags on their name tags symbolize which languages they speak.

- Guided tours of theme parks are offered in several languages. Ask at Guest Relations or the International Welcome Center for details.

- A tape-recorded walking tour is available for the Magic Kingdom and Epcot in a selection of languages. The device may be rented for a small fee (with a $100 refundable deposit) at the park's International Welcome Center.

- Guests traveling long distances and through time zones should conserve energy. It might be wise to relax by the pool on the day of arrival, instead of trying to fit in a full day at a theme park—it's never beneficial to start a vacation exhausted!

- Phone cards good for international calls can be purchased at several Disney World shops. Look for a yellow star on the theme park map to locate one of the stores.

Telephone Dos and Don'ts

It's a common practice for hotels to assess a surcharge for phone calls, and Disney is no exception. To avoid whopping bills, charge calls to a phone card, and keep these tips in mind:

- A direct-dialed long distance call will set you back the cost of the call at the AT&T operator-assisted day rate *plus a 55 percent surcharge*. (A recent one-minute call from a Disney resort to a New York City number cost $6.77.) The price-rate applies to both domestic and international long distance. Applicable taxes are included. Rates are subject to change.

- Prepaid phone cards are available for purchase in most WDW resort lobbies.

- Guests making credit card, prepaid phone card, or any type of operator-assisted call from a resort room phone will be charged a 75-cent fee per call.

- It costs 75 cents to call an 800 number from a WDW resort room.

- Calls made between most WDW resorts are toll calls.

- Directory assistance phone calls cost $1.40 each.

- There is no charge to call from room to room within a resort.

- If saving money is key, make calls from pay phones whenever possible.

- All Disney–owned-and–operated resorts support mobile computing through a data-port connection on the guestroom telephone, with applicable charges.

Travelers with Disabilities

Disney tends to get high marks from travelers with disabilities because of attention paid to special needs. Here is an overview:

GETTING AROUND: Special parking is available for guests at the theme parks; ask for directions at the Auto Plazas upon entering. From the Transportation and Ticket Center (TTC), the Magic Kingdom is accessible by ferry or by monorail. All monorail stations are accessible to wheelchairs.

Wheelchairs: Wheelchairs can be rented in all theme parks; they cost $7 per day, with a $1 refundable deposit. In the Magic Kingdom, they are available at the Stroller and Wheelchair Rental, at Epcot's rental area inside the main turnstiles on the left, and at the International Gateway entrance. Oscar's Super Service rents wheelchairs at Disney-MGM Studios. At Animal Kingdom, wheelchairs are available at Garden Gate Gifts.

Walt Disney World resort guests may request a complimentary wheelchair at the front desk. Supplies are limited. It helps to request one when you make your reservation.

Electric Convenience Vehicles (ECVs) are available for rent in every park. They cost $30 plus a $10 refundable deposit, per park per day. They usually sell out early.

Equipment rented at a park cannot leave that park. If you'd like to hold onto yours for your whole trip, consider calling a company called ScootAround. They rent standard and electric wheelchairs, as well as scooters. Pick up and delivery is available at all hotels in the Walt Disney World area. Call 888-441-7575 for information.

There are designated areas for guests in wheelchairs to view the fireworks at Epcot and to view the parades in each of the theme parks. Check a park guidemap for locations.

Accessibility: It's easy to get around the theme parks by wheelchair. Most attractions are accessible to guests who can be lifted from chairs with assistance from a member of their party, and many can accommodate guests who must remain in wheelchairs. Consult the *Guidebook for Guests with Disabilities* (for a free copy, write to Walt Disney World Guest Communications, Box 1000, Lake Buena Vista, FL 32830) for details about wheelchair access, or check with the ride host or hostess. At the water parks, special life jackets are available for travelers with disabilities.

All Walt Disney World hotels have accommodations for guests with disabilities, including roll-in showers. For assistance in selecting the hotel that best fits your requirements, ask for the Special Reservations Department when you call Central Reservations (Voice: 407-934-7639; TTY: 407-939-7670).

RESOURCES: Visual Disabilities: Guests can get a tape recorder and a cassette that describes each park, as well as a Braille guidebook. Each requires a $25 refundable deposit.

Hearing Disabilities: Pay phones with Text Typewriters (TTYs) are available throughout Disney World. For more information, call 407-824-4321 (voice), or 407-827-5141 (TTY). Sign language is available for some shows. Call at least two weeks ahead for arrangements.

Listening devices that amplify attraction sound tracks are available at City Hall in the Magic Kingdom and at Guest Relations in Epcot, Animal Kingdom, and the Disney-MGM Studios. A $25 refundable deposit is required. Sites with assistive listening systems are listed on park guidemaps.

Ask about the availability of reflective and handheld captioning devices. The former project show dialogue onto panels in front of a guest; the latter provide captioning on personal devices at certain attractions. Scripts are available for some shows and attractions.

Note: *Service animals are permitted in all Disney parks.*

Booking the Trip: The following organizations specialize in assisting physically disabled travelers:

• The Society for Accessible Travel and Hospitality (347 Fifth Ave., Suite 610, New York, NY 10016; 212-447-7284; *www.sath.org*)

• Accessible Journeys (Ridley Park, PA; *www.accessiblejourneys.com*; 610-521-0339 or 800-846-4537)

• Flying Wheels Travel (Owatonna, MN; 507-451-5005; *www.flyingwheelstravel.com*)

Vehicles: Wheelchair Getaways (800-242-4990 or 407-292-7614) and Rainbow Wheels of Florida (800-910-8267) both rent wheelchair accessible vans and offer pick-up and delivery options for most hotels in the area.

WDW Weddings & Honeymoons

Believe it or not, Walt Disney World is the most popular honeymoon destination in the United States. Why the appeal? The resorts offer some romantic stretches of white-sand beaches for evening strolls, fine restaurants for candlelight dinners, and a host of activities to rival almost any European or Hawaiian destination. Add to that the fantasy of the Magic Kingdom, the wonder of Epcot, the glamour of the Disney-MGM Studios, and the majesty of Animal Kingdom, plus Downtown Disney and BoardWalk nightlife, water parks, and the Disney Cruise Line, and it's not hard to see why Walt Disney World is number one with newlyweds.

After years of fending for themselves, folks looking to honeymoon here now have help at hand. A variety of packages cater specifically to newly married couples. For information, call toll-free: 877-566-0969.

The folks at Walt Disney World have also received oodles of requests from couples who wanted to actually get married at one of the theme parks. Today, happy couples can tie the knot in evening ceremonies at some parks during seasons when they close early. (The area in front of Cinderella Castle in the Magic Kingdom is one of Walt Disney World's wedding hot spots, as are several Epcot sites.) Morning ceremonies are offered at Epcot's World Showcase.

The Yacht and Beach Club, BoardWalk, Polynesian, and Wilderness Lodge resorts also host their share of weddings. The Wedding Pavilion, on the grounds of the Grand Floridian Resort and Spa, offers a Victorian-style indoor setting with a prime view of Cinderella Castle and the Seven Seas Lagoon. A combination of stained glass, sage green and soft pink florals, and benches with heart-shaped cutouts (seating around 250 guests) creates the romantic ambience. Couples can fill their wedding albums with photos taken at Picture Point, under a trellis of climbing white roses, with the faraway castle prominently in the background. Private ceremonies may also be performed at this scenic spot.

Weddings range from elegant affairs, without a hint of Disneyana, to ceremonies in which the bride arrives in Cinderella's coach and Mickey and Minnie are among the guests at the reception.

At Franck's Bridal Studio, Walt Disney World specialists work with couples to customize each wedding. Unique merchandise is available for purchase. Among the services offered are cakes, photography, hairstyling, flower arranging, and musical entertainment. Specialists can help secure accommodations, rehearsal dinners, bachelor parties, and more.

For information about planning a Walt Disney World wedding, call 407-828-3400 or visit *www.disneyweddings.com*; for honeymoon packages, call 877-566-0969 or visit *www.disneyhoneymoons.com*.

MAGICAL MILESTONES

Even frequent visitors have trouble keeping up with all the changes at Walt Disney World. The time line below will help you determine which major attractions have opened since your last visit.

1971–1982

1971
Magic Kingdom

1973
Pirates of the Caribbean, Tom Sawyer Island

1974
Star Jets (now Astro Orbiter)

1983–1990

1983
Journey into Imagination pavilion (now Imagination!)

1984
Morocco pavilion

1986
The Living Seas

1991–1996

1991
Jim Henson's Muppet* Vision 3-D, Beauty and the Beast—Live on Stage, Spectro   Magic

1992
Splash Mountain, The Voyage of The Little Mermaid

1993
New production of The Hall of Presidents

1997–2002

1997
Downtown Disney West Side, Disney's Wide World of Sports Complex

1998
Disney's Animal Kingdom, Buzz Lightyear's Space Ranger Spin, Enchanted Tiki Room—Under New Management, Fantasmic!, DisneyQuest, Disney Cruise Line

1999
Sounds Dangerous starring Drew Carey, Kali River Rapids, Maharajah Jungle Trek, Test Track, Rock 'n' Roller Coaster, The Many Adventures of Winnie the Pooh, Cirque du Soleil

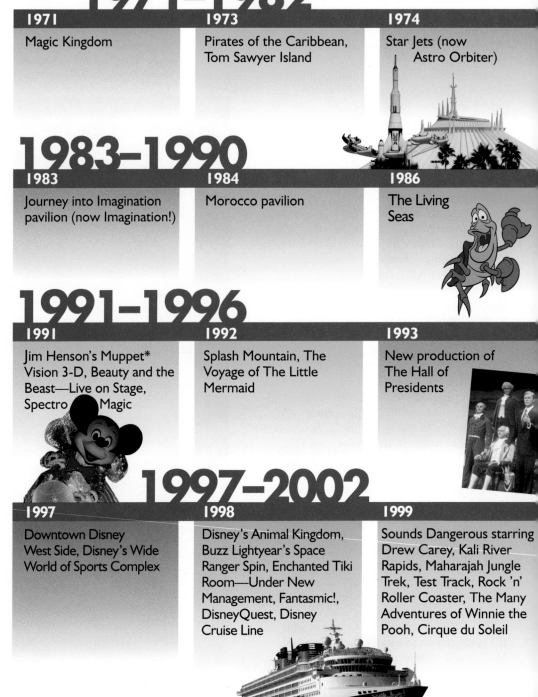

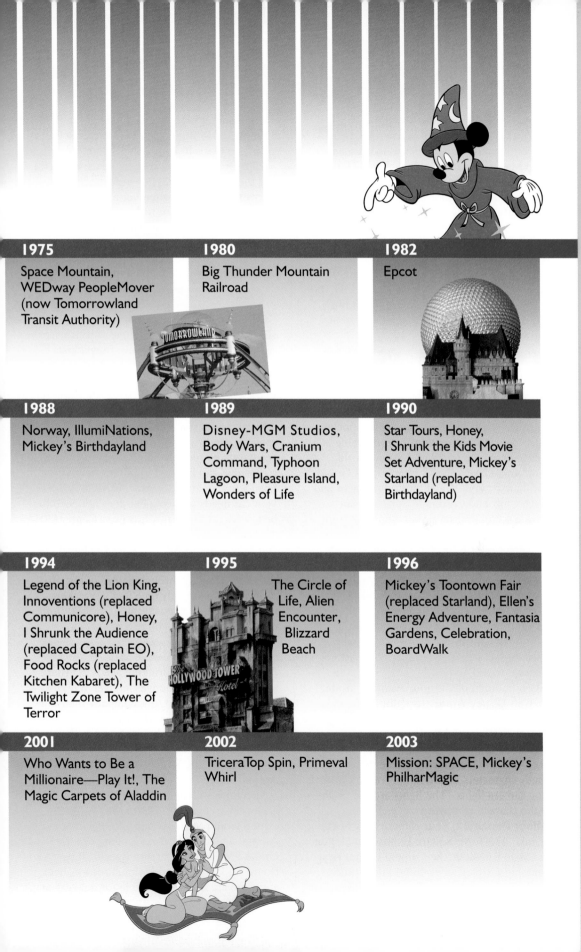

1975

Space Mountain, WEDway PeopleMover (now Tomorrowland Transit Authority)

1980

Big Thunder Mountain Railroad

1982

Epcot

1988

Norway, IllumiNations, Mickey's Birthdayland

1989

Disney-MGM Studios, Body Wars, Cranium Command, Typhoon Lagoon, Pleasure Island, Wonders of Life

1990

Star Tours, Honey, I Shrunk the Kids Movie Set Adventure, Mickey's Starland (replaced Birthdayland)

1994

Legend of the Lion King, Innoventions (replaced Communicore), Honey, I Shrunk the Audience (replaced Captain EO), Food Rocks (replaced Kitchen Kabaret), The Twilight Zone Tower of Terror

1995

The Circle of Life, Alien Encounter, Blizzard Beach

1996

Mickey's Toontown Fair (replaced Starland), Ellen's Energy Adventure, Fantasia Gardens, Celebration, BoardWalk

2001

Who Wants to Be a Millionaire—Play It!, The Magic Carpets of Aladdin

2002

TriceraTop Spin, Primeval Whirl

2003

Mission: SPACE, Mickey's PhilharMagic

Fingertip Reference Guide

BARBERS AND SALONS

One of the most amusing places to get a haircut is the Magic Kingdom's old-fashioned Harmony Barber Shop. It's located beside the Car Barn in the Town Square section of Main Street.

Haircuts, coloring, manicures, and other services are available at the following resorts: the salon in the Contemporary (407-824-3411), the Periwig Salon at the Yacht and Beach Club (407-934-3260), Ivy Trellis at the Grand Floridian (407-824-3000, ext. 2581), the Niki Bryan shop at the Swan and Dolphin (407-934-4250), and the Casa de Belleza at Coronado Springs (407-939-3965).

BUSINESS SERVICES

Disney provides a range of services for those who simply must mix business with pleasure. Photocopiers, fax machines (also found at Guest Relations in the theme parks), pocket pagers, and FedEx materials are available at Guest Services at any Walt Disney World resort. In addition, the Contemporary, Grand Floridian, Animal Kingdom Lodge, Yacht and Beach Club, and Coronado Springs resorts provide secretarial services, computers, printers, and Internet access for a fee. A videoconferencing center is located near Downtown Disney. For information, call 407-827-2000.

CAMERA NEEDS

Photo spots around the theme parks can help you capture the best shots. To photograph fireworks, your camera must have a manually adjustable shutter speed and aperture (it helps to have a tripod, too).

Flash photography is not permitted inside any Walt Disney World attraction. Film and disposable cameras are available at many shops throughout the World. The best selection can be found at the camera shops in each park. Also, when capturing moments with Disney characters on videotape, refrain from using camera lights. (The lights are too bright for the characters' sensitive eyes.)

Minor Repairs: If your camera isn't working, take it to Town Square Exposition Hall in the Magic Kingdom; the Camera Center near Spaceship Earth, Cameras and Film at the Imagination! pavilion, or World Traveler at International Gateway in Epcot; The Darkroom on Hollywood Boulevard in the Disney-MGM Studios; or Garden Gate Gifts near The Oasis in Animal Kingdom.

Film Processing: Processing is available at the theme parks, all WDW resorts, and Downtown Disney wherever a Photo Express sign is displayed. Film is developed on site.

If you're traveling by plane, be sure to pack your film in your carry-on bag. (Airlines can't guarantee that equipment used to screen checked bags won't damage film.)

CAR CARE

Several Exxon gas stations with convenience stores are on the property, some of which are open 24 hours a day. One is on Buena Vista Drive across from Pleasure Island; another is on Floridian Way near the Magic Kingdom Auto Plaza. The third, near the BoardWalk resort on Buena Vista Drive, also has a car wash.

Breakdowns sometimes occur, but they don't spell disaster. All WDW roads are patrolled constantly by security vehicles equipped with radios that can be used to call for help. If you need a tow, contact security (407-824-0976). If your car needs servicing but does not need to be towed, call the AAA Car Care Center (407-824-0976). Located in the Magic Kingdom Auto Plaza, the AAA Car Care Center offers full mechanical services and free towing on property, Monday through Saturday. For off-property car care, rely on Riker's Wreckers (407-855-7776) for towing; 407-238-9800 (for repairs), or AAA (if you're a member).

DRINKING LAWS

In Florida, the legal drinking age is 21. There are many bars and lounges all over WDW; minors are permitted to accompany their parents but are prohibited from sitting or standing at the bar. No alcohol is served in the Magic Kingdom, but alcoholic beverages are sold in Epcot, the Disney-MGM Studios, Animal Kingdom, and Downtown Disney.

Alcohol is sold in at least one shop at most Disney World resorts. Liquor may be purchased from room service at the Polynesian, Animal Kingdom Lodge, Contemporary, Grand Floridian, Yacht and Beach Club, BoardWalk, Swan, and Dolphin resorts; beer and wine are usually available for delivery at other resorts.

LOCKERS

Attended lockers can be found in the following theme park locations: underneath Main Street Railroad Station in the Magic Kingdom, beside Spaceship Earth in Epcot, next to Oscar's Super Service inside the main entrance at the Disney-MGM Studios, and just inside the entrance and to the left at Animal Kingdom. Lockers are also available at the Transportation and Ticket Center (TTC).

Items too big to fit can be checked with the locker attendant at the Magic Kingdom, at Package Pickup in Epcot, and at Guest Relations at the Disney-MGM Studios and Animal Kingdom. Cost is about $5 per day (plus a $2 deposit) for unlimited use. Items may not be stored overnight. Lockers are cleaned out after the park closes.

Note: Be sure to save your rental receipt; it can be used again that day to secure a locker in any of the four theme parks.

LOST & FOUND

The extensive indexing system maintained by Walt Disney World's Lost and Found department is impressive, especially when a prized possession turns up missing, whether it's false teeth or a camera. (Both have been lost in the past; the dentures were never claimed.)

If you lose (or find) something, report it at any one of these Lost and Found locations: the Transportation and Ticket Center (TTC), City Hall in the Magic Kingdom, the Guest Relations lobby in Innoventions East at Epcot, Oscar's Super Service just inside the Disney-MGM Studios, Guest Relations near the Animal Kingdom entrance, or Guest Services at any WDW resort. At Fort Wilderness, dial 7-2726 from a comfort station telephone; from outside the campground, phone 407-824-2726; and from Downtown Disney, phone 407-828-3058.

Items lost in a theme park may be claimed on the day of the loss at the park's Lost and Found, and thereafter at the Transportation and Ticket Center (TTC) Lost and Found station. To report lost items after your visit, call 407-824-4245. Hats, strollers, sunglasses, and WDW merchandise are kept for one month; everything else is kept three months.

MAIL

Postage stamps can be purchased at all WDW resorts; at City Hall in the Magic Kingdom; at shops near the lockers in Epcot, the Studios, and Animal Kingdom; and at Guest Services in the Downtown Disney Marketplace.

The old-fashioned mailboxes in the theme parks are not official U.S. post boxes, but letters (with postage) can be mailed from them. Postmarks read "Lake Buena Vista," not "Walt Disney World."

A post office at the Shoppes at Lake Buena Vista shopping center (opposite Summerfield Suites) is open from 9 A.M. to 4 P.M. weekdays and 9 A.M. to 12 P.M. on Saturday.

Mail may be addressed to guests care of their hotel. The address for all WDW resorts is Walt Disney World, Box 10000, Lake Buena Vista, FL 32830.

MEDICAL MATTERS

Travelers with chronic health problems should carry copies of all prescriptions and get names of local doctors from hometown physicians. However, Walt Disney World is equipped to deal with many types of medical emergencies. In the Magic Kingdom, next to the Crystal Palace, there is a First Aid Center staffed by a registered nurse; there is another such facility at Epcot in the Odyssey Center complex. At the Disney-MGM Studios, the First Aid Center is inside the Guest Relations building at the main entrance, accessible from both inside and outside the park. The Animal Kingdom First Aid Center is located on Discovery Island near the back side of Creature Comforts.

Walt Disney World resort guests and those staying at other area hotels have access to services providing nonemergency medical care. Centra Care Walk-In Medical Care, owned and operated by Florida Hospital, has two locations near Walt Disney World. Both are adjacent to pharmacies, and one has X-ray facilities. For information, call 407-238-2000.

One of the facilities, at 12500 South Apopka-Vineland Road, is open 8 A.M. to midnight weekdays, 8 A.M. to 8 P.M. weekends. The other, at 7848 W. Irlo Bronson Highway in Kissimmee (407-397-7032), is open 8 A.M. to 8 P.M. Call 407-239-6463 to be connected to a Centra Care facility.

Courtesy transportation is available from most area hotels to Centra Care clinics, and there is a no-tipping policy. Waits in walk-in clinics can be lengthy, but Centra Care drivers call ahead to learn which has the shorter wait. For patients who prefer to have the doctor come to them, Centra Care offers 24-hour, in-room visits (407-238-2000), as does Doctors On Call Service. A 24-hour house-call only medical service, Doctors On Call can be reached at 407-399-DOCS (399-3627).

The most common maladies reported by Walt Disney World guests? Sunburn (Don't forget to wear your sunscreen!), blisters, colds, fevers, earaches, and injuries from falls. For emergencies, dial 911, or call nearby Sandlake Hospital (407-351-8550) or Celebration Health (407-303-4000).

For Diabetics: All Walt Disney World resorts can provide refrigeration services for insulin. All villa accommodations have their own refrigerators, and small refrigerators are available for rent at other resorts for about $10 a night.

Prescriptions: For a referral to a pharmacy or to find out how to have medications delivered to your resort, contact Centra Care (407-239-7777).

MONEY

Cash, traveler's checks, personal checks, American Express, MasterCard, Visa, Discover Card, Diner's Club, JCB Card, and Disney's Visa card are accepted as payment for most charges at Disney. Checks must bear your name and address, be drawn on a U.S. bank, and be accompanied by proper ID—a valid driver's license and a major credit card. Note that some snack stands only accept cash.

A Disney resort guest perk: Leave a credit card imprint at check-in and the hotel IDs may be used to cover purchases in shops, lounge and restaurant charges, and recreational fees incurred inside Walt Disney World. A bill will be sent home for all charges made past check-out time.

ATMs: Automated Teller Machines are scattered throughout Walt Disney World. Theme park locations include the Magic Kingdom

(under the train station on Main Street, U.S.A., in Adventureland near The Enchanted Tiki Room, and in the Tomorrowland arcade), Epcot (near the main entrance, on the pathway between Future World and World Showcase, and in Germany), the Disney-MGM Studios (at the entrance, and inside Toy Story Pizza Planet), and Animal Kingdom (at the entrance), plus the Transportation and Ticket Center (TTC). Most Disney resorts have ATMs in the lobby; the Fort Wilderness ATM is outside Pioneer Hall. Three can be found in Downtown Disney: near the Rock N Roll Beach Club at Pleasure Island, next to Guest Services in the Marketplace, and by the West Side's Forty Thirst Street. Most bank cards and credit cards are accepted; the fees range from $2 to $2.50.

Banking: SunTrust, located across from Downtown Disney Marketplace, offers a variety of services. Guests can get cash advances on MasterCard, Discover, and Visa credit cards; receive incoming wire transfers (for a $50 fee); and cash, replace, or purchase American Express traveler's checks. This branch is open from 9 A.M. to 4 P.M. weekdays, until 6 P.M. Thursdays (407-828-6114 or 800-786-8787). The drive-thru is open until 6 P.M. Monday through Friday.

Disney Dollars: Money bearing the image of Mickey, Goofy, or Minnie is available for purchase at City Hall (Magic Kingdom) and Guest Relations (Epcot, the Disney-MGM Studios, and Animal Kingdom) in $1, $5, and $10 denominations. (The exchange rate is always a buck for a buck.) Disney Dollars are accepted as cash throughout the World.

Traveler's Checks: Even the most careful of vacationers occasionally loses a wallet. Traveler's checks can take the sting out of that loss. Look for promotions by banks at home in the months preceding a vacation to see if one of the major brands—American Express, MasterCard, Visa, Citibank, and Bank of America—is available free. Stash the receipt bearing the check numbers in a place separate from the checks themselves, along with a piece of identification such as a duplicate driver's license or a spare credit card to speed the refund process should your checks get lost.

To purchase, cash, or replace American Express traveler's checks, go to the SunTrust bank across from the Downtown Disney Marketplace. (If you do not have a record of the check numbers, first contact the place where you purchased the travelers checks. Then, an American Express referral number is required; call 800-221-7282.)

AAA members can visit the AAA Travel Center in the Magic Kingdom for traveler's check assistance.

Foreign Currency Exchange: Up to $50 per person in foreign currency may be exchanged daily at Guest Relations in the theme parks, and up to $500 at the Guest Services desk at WDW resorts. Foreign currency exchange is also available at the SunTrust bank across from Downtown Disney and in the Gooding's grocery at the Crossroads shopping center near Hotel Plaza Blvd.

PETS

No pets (other than service dogs) are allowed in the theme parks or the Walt Disney World resorts, except at certain campsites at Fort Wilderness (request a pet site for $3 extra per day). Travelers who bring pets along can lodge them in one of the five air-conditioned Pet Care Kennels: near the Transportation and Ticket Center (TTC), left of Epcot Entrance Plaza, at the Disney-MGM Studios entrance, at the Disney's Animal Kingdom entrance, and at the Fort Wilderness campground entrance. (The last one is next to a field where owners can take their pets out for a run.)

During busy seasons, it is best to arrive before the 9 A.M. rush. Kennels close one hour after the closest theme park closes. In case of emergency, a vet will be called on your pet's behalf.

Owners must put more unusual animals into the kennels' cages. Rabbits, birds, turtles, hamsters, nonpoisonous snakes, and other animals unsuited (because of their size) to cat- and dog-size cages must have their own escape-proof carriers.

Guests may board pets overnight in any of the kennels on property. While there are no staffers on duty overnight, it just takes a phone call to gain access to your pet after hours (guests receive the number when they check their pet in). Cost is $11, including Friskies dry food (Walt Disney World resort guests pay $9 per night to leave pets

overnight); a day stay is $6, with one feeding. Guests who board pets overnight are required to walk their pets throughout the a day, as animals are not otherwise let out of their cages. We recommend owners make at least three visits per day. Pets will be fed special food, if provided. For information, call 407-824-6568. Reservations are not accepted.

Be sure to bring along your pet's certificate of vaccinations, since Florida law requires proof of immunization for animals involved in biting incidents. It's always a good idea to pack your pet's favorite blanket, pillow, or toy, too. Never leave a pet in your car. It is extremely dangerous for the animal and is against the law.

Outside Walt Disney World: A few hotels in the Orlando area, including the Quality Inn Plaza (for $5.55 a day), let pets stay with guests. Call the Orlando/Orange County Convention & Visitors Bureau (407-363-5871 or 800-551-0181; the latter is a recording).

POCKET PAGERS

Two types of devices are available to signal a phone call or message. They can be rented at nearly all WDW hotels; ask at the front desk.

RELIGIOUS SERVICES

Note that religious services are no longer offered on Disney property, though one need not venture far to find them.

Protestant: Sundays at 10:30 A.M. at River of Life Presbyterian, 8323 W. Sand Lake Rd. Call 407-351-4333. Also, Sundays at 11 A.M. at Lake Buena Vista Baptist Church, 11551 County Rd. 535. Call 407-239-6030.

Muslim: Prayer takes place five times a day at Jama Masjid, 11543 Ruby Lake Rd. Call 407-238-2700 for more information.

Catholic: The closest Catholic church is Mary, Queen of the Universe Shrine, 2½ miles north of Lake Buena Vista, at 8300 Vineland Ave. This church seats 2,000 people and has beautiful gardens, fountains, and a large gift shop, which is open daily. Call 407-239-6600 for mass times.

Jewish: Reform services are held at the Congregation of Liberal Judaism (928 Malone Dr., Orlando; 407-645-0444), near Winter Park about 20 miles from Walt Disney World. Conservative services are held at Temple Ohalei Rivka, also known as the Southwest Orlando Jewish Congregation (11200 S. Apopka-Vineland Rd.; 407-239-5444), less than two miles from Downtown Disney.

SHOPPING FOR NECESSITIES

Almost any everyday item can be purchased right on the property. At least one shop in every Disney resort stocks a small selection of toiletries. In addition, over-the-counter health aids, plus many other useful items, can be purchased at the Emporium on Main Street in the Magic Kingdom; they're kept behind the counter, so ask for what you want.

Aspirin and sunscreen are also available at Island Supply in Adventureland and Mickey's Star Traders in Tomorrowland. In Epcot, sundries are sold in at least one shop in each World Showcase pavilion and at all Future World stores. At the Disney-MGM Studios, stop by the Crossroads of the World and Movieland Memorabilia shops. At Animal Kingdom, you can pick up bare necessities at Island Mercantile.

Local supermarkets include Winn-Dixie and Gooding's (which are close to Hotel Plaza Boulevard), and Publix (a bit farther afield, but still worth considering).

SMOKING

A strict Walt Disney World smoking regulation took effect in 2000. It prohibits smoking in the four theme parks, with the exception of specifically designated areas.

Smoking is also prohibited at all Disney-owned-and-operated restaurants, with the exception of some outdoor seating areas. However, most clubs (except the Adventurers Club and Comedy Warehouse at Pleasure Island), as well as many resort lounges, allow smoking in some spots. The same goes for water parks, miniature golf courses, and Disney's Wide World of Sports Complex. Tobacco products are not sold in the theme parks. Guests may purchase tobacco products at WDW resorts and Downtown Disney.

All Disney resorts have rooms for smokers and nonsmokers alike. Be sure to request the room type of your choice as you check in.

Lost Adults

Occasionally, traveling companions get separated in the crush of the crowds, or someone may fail to show up at a meeting spot. When this happens, it's good to know that messages can be left for fellow travelers at Guest Relations in any of the four theme parks.

TELEPHONE CALLS

It takes more than the traditional seven digits to make a local call in this neck of the woods. Every time a local call is placed in Central Florida, callers must dial the area code and the seven-digit number. The rule applies to calls made within the same area code as well as for those that connect with other area codes. For local calls, it is not necessary to dial a 1 before the ten-digit number.

Local calls made from pay phones cost 35 cents each. Rates charged by local resorts tend to vary quite a bit (for local and long-distance calls alike). Be sure to ask about rates and fees before you make any calls beyond your resort. See page 35 for more telephone tips.

Hot Tip!

It's fine to stash a cell phone in a backpack, but don't forget to turn it off (or at least switch it to vibrate mode). That way you'll ensure that the magic—for you and those around you—will be uninterrupted.

If you plan to connect to the Internet via personal computer, don't forget to bring a list of local access numbers. And know that even if the area code is 407, it doesn't guarantee that the number is a local one.

TIPPING

Tips are no less valued at Disney resorts than at any other hotel—$1 per bag is appropriate for lugging luggage; $1 to $2 per night for housekeeping services. Gratuities of 15 to 20 percent (excluding tax) are customary at full-service restaurants. (If service is exceptional or otherwise, adjust the tip accordingly.) Gratuity is included in the room-service bill at WDW resorts and some off-property hotels. Check before you tip twice. Note that a 10 percent gratuity is included at the Pepper Market food court in Disney's Coronado Springs resort (despite the self-serve setup).

Give cab drivers a 15 percent tip for good service. Baggage handlers at the train station and airport expect about $1 per bag.

WEATHER

Call Walt Disney World Weather Information (407-824-4104), or check the Weather Channel website (*www.weather.com*).

Transportation & Accommodations

The popularity of Walt Disney World has made the region around Orlando one of the world's major tourism and commercial centers, and transportation facilities, from a state-of-the-art airport to an efficient network of highways, bring visitors to the area by the millions.

There's no doubt that getting to and around the Walt Disney World region can be very confusing. The only more perplexing dilemma may be choosing the best accommodations for your family from among the huge assortment of hotels and motels.

The accommodations operated by Walt Disney World itself range from futuristic high-rise towers to cabins buried deep in piney woods. In between are resorts that evoke striking images of Africa, the South Pacific, historic Florida, the Pacific Northwest, the Caribbean, New England, early Atlantic City, New Orleans, the Southwest, Mexico, and the sports, movie, and music worlds, plus a sprawling, beautifully maintained campground. And that list doesn't include the many villas or the studios and homes with one, two, and three bedrooms that can be purchased through a special vacation-ownership system. What follows should help travelers sort out all the lodging options on Walt Disney World property, as well as shed light on the broad range of possibilities that exist outside the WDW gates.

Getting Oriented

Orlando, the Central Florida city of more than one million residents, is the municipality with which Walt Disney World is most closely associated. Walt Disney World, however, is in a far smaller community called Lake Buena Vista, 15 miles from Orlando's business center. A number of hotels and restaurants are located in Lake Buena Vista, though there are many more in Orlando.

ORLANDO-AREA HIGHWAYS: The most important Orlando traffic artery is I-4, which runs diagonally through the area from southwest up to northeast, cutting through the southern half of Walt Disney World. It then angles on toward Orlando and Winter Park, ending near Daytona Beach at I-95, which runs north and south along the coast.

All the city's other important highways intersect I-4, and each has a name as well as a number. From south to north, they include U.S. 192 (aka Irlo Bronson Memorial Highway), which takes an east-west course that crosses the WDW entrance road and leads into downtown Kissimmee on the east; S.R. 528 (aka the Beeline Expressway), which shoots eastward from I-4; S.R. 435 (aka Kirkman Road), which runs north and south and intersects International Drive, where many motels catering to WDW visitors are located; U.S. 17-92-441 (aka the Orange Blossom Trail), which runs north and south, paralleling Kirkman Road on the east; and S.R. 50 (aka Colonial Drive), which runs east and west.

WALT DISNEY WORLD EXITS: The 47-square-mile tract that is Walt Disney World is roughly rectangular. I-4 runs through its southern half from southwest to northeast. The major Disney destinations are most efficiently reached by taking the I-4 exits suggested in the paragraphs that follow; off the highway, clear signage makes it easy for

visitors to get anywhere in the World. This road is congested more often than not. Keep in mind that construction work and special events will often require rerouting of traffic patterns, so it's best to follow signs as directed:

- **Exit 64A**, marked "192/Magic Kingdom," leads to the Magic Kingdom, Disney-MGM Studios, Disney's Animal Kingdom, Blizzard Beach, Fort Wilderness, Palm and Magnolia golf courses, Disney's Wide World of Sports complex, and Pop Century, Disney's Animal Kingdom Lodge, All-Star Music, Sports, and Movies, Coronado Springs, Contemporary, Polynesian, Grand Floridian, and Wilderness Lodge resorts.
- **Exit 65**, leads to Disney's Wide World of Sports complex, Disney's Animal Kingdom and Animal Kingdom Lodge. It is also a good alternate route to the Disney-MGM Studios.
- **Exit 67A**, marked "Epcot/Downtown Disney," leads to Epcot, Typhoon Lagoon, Downtown Disney, Lake Buena Vista golf course, Disney's Saratoga Springs Resort & Spa, Bonnet Creek Golf Club, the BoardWalk, Caribbean Beach, Swan, Dolphin, Yacht and Beach Club, Port Orleans, and Old Key West resorts.
- **Exit 68**, marked "S.R. 535/Lake Buena Vista," is the route taken to the resorts on Hotel Plaza Boulevard and the Crossroads of Lake Buena Vista shopping center.

TRANSPORTATION & ACCOMMODATIONS

WDW Transportation

Walt Disney World transportation is extensive, with boats, buses, and the monorail all doing their part to shuttle guests around. Visitors staying at WDW hotels should receive a detailed brochure about transportation options at check-in. (If you don't, just ask.) For transportation information, call 407-824-4321.

One of the system's hubs is called the Transportation and Ticket Center (TTC), located near the Magic Kingdom. Monorail, bus, and ferry service connect the TTC to points throughout the World. Day visitors must park here before taking a monorail or ferry to the Magic Kingdom. (Most Disney resort guests can bypass the TTC via direct buses.)

The monorail runs along a circular route near the Magic Kingdom, stopping at the TTC, Polynesian, Grand Floridian, Magic Kingdom, and Contemporary. A separate extension of the monorail system connects the TTC to Epcot. Bus service is the cornerstone of the WDW transportation system. It is efficient, if occasionally confusing. With a few exceptions, buses arrive every 15 to 20 minutes, from one hour before park opening until about an hour after closing; bus stops are clearly marked. Travel times vary, depending on the route.

Although Disney resort guests are provided with complimentary transportation to all sites on-property, that transportation is not always direct. *Build in extra time for travel*, especially if you have made priority seating arrangements at a restaurant. Also, know that traveling

Should You Rent a Car?

If you plan to spend all of your time on WDW turf, you can spare yourself the expense. Shuttle service from the airport to all area hotels is available around the clock, and taxis are in good supply. Within the World, an exhaustive (sometimes exhausting) network of transportation brings guests from point to point. Most area hotels offer their own bus service to and from Disney theme parks (inquire in advance about schedules and costs, if any).

However, for those planning to visit Orlando-area restaurants and any attractions outside Walt Disney World, a rental car is a must. Also, certain routes are more convenient by car. It is easiest to rent from one of the companies at the airport: National (800-227-7368), Avis (800-331-1212), Budget (800-527-0700), or Dollar (800-800-4000). Other rental agencies provide shuttles from the airport, so it may be worth the extra time if you get a good deal. For day trips, consider Alamo at the Magic Kingdom Auto Plaza (407-824-3470) or one of the rental agencies that have desks at the resorts on Hotel Plaza Boulevard, or simply inquire about car rental at the front desk of your resort.

between resorts can be time-consuming and usually requires at least one transfer.

From several Walt Disney World locales, water launches usher guests to the Magic Kingdom, Epcot, the Disney-MGM Studios, Downtown Disney, or between resorts. Boats generally depart every 20 to 30 minutes.

TRANSPORTATION ID REQUIREMENTS:

Guests who wish to use the Disney transportation system may be asked for proof of riding privileges. Accepted IDs afford different degrees of access. WDW resort ID cards, Park Hopper Tickets, Park Hopper Plus Tickets, Ultimate Park Hopper Tickets, and Annual Passes let guests use all Disney buses, monorails, and boats. Valid one-day theme park tickets permit guests to use monorails and the ferries running between the TTC and the Magic Kingdom, but do not allow use of buses.

TAXI SERVICE: Cabs are available for $2.50 for the first mile, $1.50 per extra mile (though it may vary, depending on the number of passengers). Stick with authorized cab services. Many independent cab services charge outrageous rates. Disney employees can direct you to authorized taxis. If you plan to travel between resorts that aren't joined by water taxi or monorail, and time is of the essence, take a taxi.

THE MONORAIL: The Disney World monorail system is an efficient (and to many, downright exciting) way to travel. There are two main loops, which converge at the Transportation and Ticket Center (TTC) stop. One loop connects the Contemporary, Polynesian, and Grand Floridian resorts with the Magic Kingdom and the TTC. The other loop links Epcot with the TTC, making the monorail a park hopper's dream come true. Note that guests staying in the aforementioned resorts have a private track on the Magic Kingdom loop, making for a hastier exit at closing time. All Disney resort guests are entitled to unlimited use of the monorail (with a valid resort ID), as are day visitors with a valid transportation ID. Monorails run from 7 A.M. until about two hours after park closing.

Did You Know?

The Walt Disney World monorail system—a 14.7-mile highway in the sky—has carried more than a billion passengers since 1971.

Timing Tip: It takes about three to four minutes to get from stop to stop on the Magic Kingdom monorail loop, making for a grand circle total of about 15 to 20 minutes (depending on the size of the crowds waiting to board).

Transportation Tips

• If you are staying at a Disney resort, request a complimentary Walt Disney World transportation guidemap at check-in.

• Most buses are equipped with wheelchair lifts. Such buses have a blue emblem on the windshield and rear door.

• When using the WDW transportation system to travel between your resort and a theme park or from one park to another, allow an extra 30 minutes to get to your destination.

• The interval between the arrivals of most Disney buses is about 20 minutes.

• Be forewarned: It takes a long time to travel by bus from resort to resort. Plan on a trip of up to 90 minutes.

• Monorails usually run until two hours after the latest theme park closing time (one hour after Magic Kingdom E-Ride Nights).

• Note that there is no direct transportation between Disney's BoardWalk and most other resorts. You must first travel to Downtown Disney and transfer to the appropriate bus.

• Never attempt to vacate a theme park just as a park closes. Instead, plan to linger a bit in a shopping area, or grab a seat and watch the crowds crawl toward their respective buses, boats, cars, and monorails.

• It is not uncommon, especially at park opening and closing times, for guests to be asked to stand on the bus or monorail.

• Keep in mind that the most obvious mode of transportation may not be the quickest. For example, it is much faster to walk to the Magic Kingdom from the Contemporary resort than it is to take the monorail or boat.

• It's possible to rent a car from any Disney resort. For details, inquire at Guest Relations, or contact the front desk.

• WDW resort guests who arrive with a car receive a complimentary parking permit upon check-in. The permit, good for the length of your stay, allows you to park most places on property for free.

Accommodations

With hundreds of resorts in the Orlando area to choose from, it's definitely a challenge to select a hotel. Our advice is to approach the matter in stages and make no hasty decisions.

Weigh the Options: First decide whether to stay on or off Disney property. We recommend staying at a Disney resort because the conveniences and perks offered to resort guests are appealing (see page 50). That said, there are two major factors that tend to lure guests off property: budget and schedule.

Travelers on a tight budget will find some off-property options that are quite reasonable. Remember, however, that Disney offers rooms as low as $77 per night, so choose off-property accommodations only if the difference in price is substantial.

Guests who will spend only part of their trip exploring Disney may also prefer an off-property hotel—one that's closer to the other attractions on their itinerary.

There's one final aspect to consider—the Disney atmosphere. Every Disney resort offers whimsical diversions and a never-ending supply of festive ambience. From shower soaps bearing the tri-circle imprint of Mickey's head to wake-up calls by the Mouse himself, every detail sings of Disney.

Deciding Factors: Once the on- or off-property decision has been made, it's time to look at hotels. The big differences among accommodations, at both Disney-owned and independent resorts, are in the size of the rooms and bathrooms, attention to decor, level of service, dining options, recreational facilities, landscaping, location, and, of course, cost.

Consider how much time you plan to spend in the room, whether you'll need to return to the hotel during the day, and if you'll have time to use the facilities (golf courses, tennis courts, etc.) and room amenities that are included in the price. Parties with five or more members have an additional concern: how best to accommodate their group. It may be less expensive to reserve adjoining, value-priced rooms instead of one luxury room or villa.

Ask the Right Questions: Once a hotel that meets all basic criteria is selected, it's best to do one last round of research, so there will be no surprises at check-in.

For example, ask about any possible hidden costs, like shuttle service to and from Walt Disney World (which can be more than $20 per person, round-trip) or taxes that may not be included in the quoted price. Though most off-property hotels offer transportation to WDW, the frequency and number of buses vary significantly. Find out the exact schedule and the stops made.

Some hotels advertise a misleading proximity to Disney. Remember that Walt Disney World is 47 square miles, so while a hotel may be only a short distance from the border, the actual commute to the theme parks may be considerable. Get specifics.

Finally, check the age at which kids staying in the same room with adults will be billed as extra adults. (At Disney resorts, the age is 17.)

Reserve a Room: Found the perfect hotel? Now book it before someone else does, and don't forget to ask about any special discounts or seasonal promotions.

A Room with a View

There's a lot to be said for throwing back the curtains and gazing at a breathtaking view, provided you have the time to appreciate it and that your view is within your price range. The following is a breakdown of different "views" you may select from at the various WDW resorts. It will help you determine the best view for your budget.

Although the categories vary, depending on the resort type, the "standard view" is always the lowest rate available.

Value Resorts

Standard View = Parking lot, pool, garden, and everything else

Moderate Resorts

Standard View = Parking lot or landscaping

Water View = Pool, marina, lake, river

Deluxe Resorts

Standard View = Parking lot

Garden View = Landscaping

Water View = Pool, lake, or other water

Lagoon View = Seven Seas Lagoon

Savanna View = Animal pastures (at Animal Kingdom Lodge)

Walt Disney World Resorts

Walt Disney World hotels fall into two categories: Disney-owned and non-Disney-owned resorts. Of all the WDW properties, the Swan and Dolphin, and the resorts on Hotel Plaza Boulevard do not belong to Disney. Expect services and benefits in the non-Disney resorts to be slightly modified (see pages 67 and 83).

On-Property Perks: Disney resorts offer guaranteed admission (with ticket) to the theme parks—even when they're filled to capacity and closed to the general public; use of the WDW transportation system; the "Extra Magic Hour" allows, entry into a select park on select days; the convenience of charging most purchases to your hotel bill; access to a Guest Services staff, plus in-lobby showings of Disney's animated films, and wake-up calls from the Mouse.

Room Amenities: All Disney rooms have alarm clocks; toiletries; safes; voice mail; TVs with local and national channels, including the Disney Channel and ESPN, as well as WDW event information. There are hair dryers, irons, and coffeemakers in many rooms. These extras are always available upon request. Laundry facilities, dry cleaning, and room service are provided in most resorts (for a fee).

Resort Primer

Payment Methods: Hotel bills and room deposits may be paid by credit card, traveler's check, cashier's check, money order, cash, or personal check. Checks must bear the guest's name and address, be drawn on a U.S. bank, and be accompanied by proper ID (a valid driver's license or government-issued passport will do).

Room Deposit Requirements: When booked through Central Reservations, a deposit equal to one night's lodging (or campsite rental) is required *within 14 days* of the time that a reservation is made. Reservations are automatically canceled if deposits are not received by the 14-day deadline. (Reservations booked less than 30 days prior to arrival will receive special instructions for deposits.) Reservations booked through the Walt Disney World Travel Company are subject to a more substantial cancellation fee. Be sure to ask about the cancellation policy when you reserve your room.

When booking by phone, guests may pay the deposit by giving a major credit card number. Those who wish to use another payment method may do so by mailing or faxing it with the payment stub that comes with the reservation confirmation.

Cancellation Policy: Deposits will be fully refunded if the reservation is canceled at least five days before the scheduled arrival.

Additional Charges: When more than two adults (age 17 and up) occupy a standard room, the added per-day fee for each extra adult is $2 at Fort Wilderness campsites; $5 at Fort Wilderness Cabins; $10 at the Pop Century and All-Star resorts; $15 at Caribbean Beach, Port Orleans French Quarter and Riverside, and Coronado Springs; and $25 at all other WDW resorts. Note that in some resorts, an additional bed may be required to sleep an extra adult. If so, the cost is $15.

Check-in and Check-out: The early check-out time (11 A.M. at all WDW lodgings) and the late check-in times (1 P.M. at the campsites, 3 P.M. in most hotels, 4 P.M. at BoardWalk, Wilderness Lodge, and Beach Club, plus All-Star resorts, and Old Key West) often come as a surprise. Guests who arrive before check-in time can preregister, store luggage at Guest Services (without fee), and head to the parks or relax by the pool.

Hot Tip!

On select days, WDW resort guests are allowed to enter a theme park one hour before the general public. It's known as the "Extra Magic Hour."

WDW ID Cards: Issued on guests' arrival at Disney resorts, the cards (which double as room keys) entitle guests to use of WDW transportation (through the last day of your stay) and charge privileges (provided you leave a credit-card imprint with the hotel) to cover purchases in shops and restaurants, as well as recreational fees incurred in the World.

Note: Charges incurred on a hotel ID after check-out will be reflected in a revised bill, which will be sent by Disney. Swan and Dolphin guests may use their IDs to charge meals inside the two hotels only. Other restrictions may apply. Read the cards when checking in.

DELUXE

Name & Location	Setting/ Theme	Favored By	Romantic Hideaways	Kids Adore	Dining Tip	Resort Category & Amenities
Animal Kingdom Lodge Animal Kingdom area (page 77)	African wildlife preserve	Animal lovers—nearly every room affords a view of wandering wildlife Art aficionados—authentic African artwork abounds	Private balconies by moonlight Sunset lounge overlooking the savanna	The kopje, a rocky outcropping from which to spy on critters Story time beside the lobby fireplace Rustic bunk beds (on request)	Sample the exotic eats and atmosphere of Boma while savoring the sights of the savanna	Full-service restaurants, fast food spots, room service
BoardWalk* Epcot area (page 69)	Turn-of-the-century Atlantic City	Night owls—the entertainment options are numerous and right in the backyard Epcot-lovers, who will appreciate the short commute Disney Vacation Club members	Moonlight strolls along the boardwalk A special fireworks cruise	The Keister Coaster, a 200-foot water slide at the main pool The face-painting booth on the boardwalk at night	Snack on saltwater taffy, cotton candy, or old-fashioned sticky buns while strolling along the boards	Bellhop luggage service Valet parking Swimming pools
Contemporary Magic Kingdom area (page 56)	Retro-futuristic	Families—the monorail whisks through it and the Magic Kingdom is a short walk away Professionals, who can take advantage of the hotel's many business services	The rooftop lookout (available only to California Grill patrons) helps make up for the resort's otherwise less-than-romantic atmosphere and decor.	One of the best Disney resort arcades The party held every 45 minutes at Chef Mickey's fabulously fun character meals	Request a seating during the fireworks. The view is good from some tables and from the outdoor viewing area (standing room only). ♣	Beach access‡ On-site recreation, such as boat rentals‡ On-site kids' activities
Grand Floridian Magic Kingdom area (page 59)	Victorian seaside resort	Honeymooners—who will love spending much of their vacation basking in the resort's unebbing romantic atmosphere Magic Kingdom and monorail fans	Manicured rose gardens Honeymoon suites The Grand Lobby for a cocktail while an orchestra performs on the balcony	Child-size robes can be sent to the guestrooms The complimentary activities, like face painting and storytelling	Have a spot of traditional afternoon tea, accompanied by a scone, at the Garden View Lounge ♣	Most rooms sleep five guests Monorail, bus, or boat transport to all parks
Polynesian Magic Kingdom area (page 57)	South Pacific	Romantics—the white-sand beaches and lush, tropical setting may make you swoon Vacationers looking for a hotel with a real resort feel Magic Kingdom and monorail fans	Hammocks or beach coves for two Sunset Pointe	The weekend torch-lighting ceremony in the Great Ceremonial Hall The slide- and waterfall-endowed pool	The Polynesian Luau is favored by many for its knock-out entertainment and revamped menu. ♣	($199–$755) ‡Except Disney's Animal Kingdom Lodge

♣ This resort hosts character meals.   * Beach Club, BoardWalk, Wilderness Lodge, and Fort Wilderness also have Home Away from Home accommodations.

Name & Location	Setting/Theme	Favored By	Romantic Hideaways	Kids Adore	Dining Tip	Resort Category & Amenities
DELUXE						
Swan & Dolphin Epcot area (page 67)	Maritime whimsy	Conventioneers—the services are excellent; Guests who want many of the Disney perks but not necessarily the Disney hotel; Serious swimmers—the only WDW resort lap pool is here	The Lobby Court cigar bar at the Dolphin; The small beach tucked behind the main pool at the Swan	The swan-shaped pedal boats; The giant swan and dolphin statues perched atop their respective resorts	Save room for Dolphin Fountain's Banana Fo-Fana Split or a seven-scoop doozy called the Dolphin Splash	Full-service restaurants, fast food spots, room service; Bellhop luggage service; Valet parking; Swimming pools; Beach access‡; On-site recreation, such as boat rentals‡; On-site kids' activities; Most rooms sleep five guests; Monorail, bus, or boat transport to all parks ($199–$755) ‡Except Disney's Animal Kingdom Lodge
Wilderness Lodge* Magic Kingdom area (page 61)	America's grandest national parks	Sweethearts—love is always in the air at this resort; Winter visitors—the warm, cozy atmosphere is even more inviting when the many fireplaces are roaring; Disney Vacation Club members	Steamy, bubbling "hot springs" whirlpools; The cozy alcoves hidden on each floor of the main building	Totem poles, an erupting geyser, and countless Hidden Mickeys—there's even a free tour to help guests find them	Sample the tomato salad (when it's in season), an Artist Point signature dish; Savor morning coffee from a fireside rocking chair	
Yacht & Beach Club* Epcot area (page 65)	Martha's Vineyard and Nantucket Island	Ambitious guests—those who plan to see and do everything Disney has to offer will like the central location; Everyone—deluxe atmosphere and amenities appeal to all; Disney Vacation Club members	The Yacht Club's peaceful gazebo; Secluded whirlpools; The beach—perfect for twilight strolls	Stormalong Bay—the sand-bottomed, three-acre pool, with water jets, a series of water slides, and a shipwreck to play on	Cape May Café's bountiful nighttime clambake has many a surf-and-turf fan lining up for more	
HOME AWAY FROM HOME						
Disney's Old Key West Downtown Disney area (page 75)	Key West	Guests looking for a homey, village atmosphere; Disney Vacation Club members	Private whirlpool tubs—they come with all resort rooms except the studios	The weekly Tiny Tot Tea Parties and Un-Birthday Parties with snacks, games, and treats, held at Community Hall	Good's Food To Go can box up any item from Olivia's (the table service restaurant next door)	Kitchens, restaurants, pizza delivery; Luggage service; Swimming pools; On-site recreation, such as boat rentals; Front-door parking; Rooms sleep 4–12 guests; Bus or boat transport to all parks ($289–$1,695)
Disney's Saratoga Springs Resort & Spa Downtown Disney area (page 74)	Historic Saratoga Springs, NY	Peace seekers—the atmosphere is meant to soothe; Disney Vacation Club members	Pretty gardens and meandering pathways	The kids-only waterspray area near the pool	Downtown Disney's tempting array of eateries is a mere stone's throw away	

Resort	Theme	Good for	Don't miss	Pool / recreation	Insider tip	Amenities
Caribbean Beach Epcot area (page 64)	Tropical islands	Families—while all Disney resorts have kid appeal, the colorful design, themed pool, and beach setting make this hotel ideal for families with kids of any age	Aruba beach—the hotel's longest, most secluded strip of sand	The fortress pool and Parrot Cay Island / The coconut postcards sold at the Calypso shop (real coconuts!)	Try a food court kids meal—it's served in a sand bucket with a shovel (and keep an ear out for the talking trash cans!).	**MODERATE** — Restaurant, food court, limited room service; Bellman luggage service; Swimming pools with slides; On-site recreation, such as bikes and boat rentals; Rooms sleep four guests; Bus transport to all parks ($133–$194)
Coronado Springs Animal Kingdom area (page 78)	Mexico and Southwest USA	Conventioneers—which means more business services (and a health club), higher food prices, and slightly less family entertainment than at the other moderate resorts	The waterfront in the peaceful Casitas area / The gazebo-style boat-rental dock at twilight	The Dig Site—which encompasses the resort's playground and main pool with its Mayan temple water slide	Carryout items at the Pepper Market food court are spared the 10 percent gratuity charge	
Port Orleans Riverside and French Quarter Downtown Disney area (pages 72–73)	Antebellum South and New Orleans French Quarter, respectively	Lovebirds on a budget—the Riverside decor is like many of Disney's deluxe hotels, as is the romance factor, but the price is considerably less. The French Quarter provides a peaceful, urban alternative	Any room in Magnolia Bend's stately mansions / The peaceful gardens scattered about the Riverside quarters.	The pool, fishing hole, and playground at the Riverside's Ol' Man Island / The French Quarter's Doubloon Lagoon—a sea-serpent-themed family pool	Sample the fresh beignets from the food court. You'll think you're in Jackson Square!	
All-Star Movies, Music & Sports Animal Kingdom area (page 76)	Comic book	Penny-savers of all ages—these three resorts offer fun theming and bold decor, plus all the Disney perks, at a notably lower price than at other Disney resorts	All-Star Music's Jazz and Broadway areas (note that Music tends to attract more couples without kids than the other two themes)	Awe-inspiring, super-size icons—the movie and sports themes score the highest points / Extra-large arcades	Pick up a pizza at the pick-up window in the food court and have a pizza party.	**VALUE** — Food court, pizza delivery; Hourly luggage service; Swimming pools; Bus transport to all parks ($77–$121)
Pop Century Animal Kingdom area (page 79)	American pop culture	Budget watchers and nostalgia buffs—this sprawling resort celebrates pop history with bright colors and big icons / Young athletes and their families—Disney's Wide World of Sports is located nearby	Sipping specialty cocktails poolside	The state-of-the-art arcade / Wildly oversize cell phones, yo-yos, bowling pins, and more / The interactive water fountain near the playground	The refillable mug, good for use at the resort throughout your stay, definitely scores points as far as bargains go.	
Fort Wilderness Resort and Campground* Magic Kingdom area (page 63)	Rustic woods	Motor-home mavens—Disney's hook-ups are considered top-notch / Families—who appreciate the kitchen and extra space of the cabins, which fit six	The Fort Wilderness beach at night—perfect for viewing the Electrical Water Pageant on Bay Lake	Pony rides, hayrides, a blacksmith's shop, and a petting farm	Join the nightly campfire circle and roast marshmallows with Chip and Dale.	**CAMPGROUND** — Recipient of perfect ratings from Trailer Life and Woodall's magazine; Bus transport to all parks ($35–$299)

❤ This resort hosts character meals.   * Beach Club, BoardWalk, Wilderness Lodge, and Fort Wilderness also have Home Away from Home accommodations.

Rates at WDW Properties

	Value	Regular	Peak*
DELUXE‡			
Animal Kingdom Lodge			
Rooms (sleep 4 to 5)	$199–$340	$239–$385	$289–$445
Rooms–Concierge (5)	$425	$480	$545
BoardWalk Inn			
Rooms (5)	$289–$360	$329–$405	$394–$470
Rooms–Concierge (5 to 6)	$425–$505	$480–$555	$550–$610
Contemporary			
Rooms–Garden Buildings (5)	$239–$280	$264–$315	$309–$365
Rooms–Tower (5)	$335–$395	$370–$435	$435–$505
Rooms–Concierge (4)	$480	$540	$610
Grand Floridian Resort & Spa			
Rooms (5)	$339–$415	$384–$475	$444–$560
Rooms–Concierge (5)	$450–$595	$520–$670	$600–$755
Polynesian			
Rooms (5)	$299–$385	$344–$430	$404–$505
Rooms–Concierge (5)	$390–$470	$440–$525	$515–$605
Swan & Dolphin (Rates were accurate at press time, but are likely to change. Call 800-227-1500 for current prices.)			
Rooms (5)	$337–$375	not applicable	$360–$445
Rooms–Club Level (5)	$455	not applicable	$519
Suites (5 to 10)	Call 800-227-1500 for prices		
Wilderness Lodge			
Rooms (4)	$199–$250	$239–$290	$289–$340
Rooms–Concierge (4)	$350	$385	$435
Yacht & Beach Club			
Rooms (5)	$289–$345	$329–$395	$394–$455
Rooms–Concierge** (5)	$425–$470	$480–$530	$550–$595
**Yacht Club only ‡For information about suites, call 407-934-7639.			
HOME AWAY FROM HOME			
Disney's Beach Club Villas			
Studios (4)	$289	$329	$394
1-BR Villas (4)	$390	$435	$505
2-BR Villas (8)	$545	$705	$890
Disney's BoardWalk Villas			
Studios (5)	$289	$329	$394
1-BR Villas (4)	$390	$435	$505
2-BR Villas (8)	$545	$705	$890
Grand Villas (12)	$1,320	$1,510	$1,695
Disney's Old Key West			
Studios (4)	$254	$284	$329
1-BR Vacation Homes (4)	$340	$385	$445
2-BR Vacation Homes (8)	$479	$560	$680
3-BR Grand Villas (12)	$1,040	$1,160	$1,310
Saratoga Springs Resort & Spa			
Studios (5)	$254	$284	$329
1-BR Villas (4)	$340	$385	$445
2-BR Villas (8)	$479	$560	$680
Grand Villas (12)	$1,040	$1,160	$1,310

	Value	Regular	Peak*
HOME AWAY FROM HOME (continued)			
Fort Wilderness			
Cabins (6)	$229	$269	$299
The Villas at Wilderness Lodge			
Studios (4)	$279	$314	$370
1-BR Villas (4)	$380	$425	$495
2-BR Villas (8)	$535	$670	$810
MODERATE			
Caribbean Beach			
Rooms (4)	$133–$148	$144–$159	$169–$194
Coronado Springs			
Rooms (4)	$133–$148	$144–$159	$169–$194
Suites (4 to 6)	Call 407-934-7639 for suite prices		
Port Orleans French Quarter and Riverside			
Rooms (4)	$133–$148	$144–$159	$169–$194
VALUE			
All-Star Movies, All-Star Music, and All-Star Sports			
Rooms (4)	$77–$87	$99–$109	$109–$121
Pop Century			
Rooms (4)	$77–$87	$99–$109	$109–$121
CAMPGROUND			
Fort Wilderness Campsites			
Sites w/partial hookup (10)	$36	$52	$60
Sites w/full hookup (10)	$41	$62	$71
Preferred sites (10)	$49	$67	$76

Check-in time: 3 P.M. except at the Beach Club Villas, BoardWalk Villas, Wilderness Lodge Villas, Pop Century, All-Star resorts, and Old Key West, where check-in is at 4 P.M. and at Fort Wilderness Resort and Campground, where it's 1 P.M. **Check-out time:** 11 A.M. for Fort Wilderness and all hotels.

2004 Value rates apply: January 1 to February 11, August 29 to September 29, and October 31 to December 19 for all Value and Moderate resorts, Wilderness Lodge, Animal Kingdom Lodge, and Fort Wilderness Cabins; January 1 to February 11 and August 8 to November 18 for the Campground; January 1 to February 11, July 5 to September 29, and October 31 to December 19 for all other WDW properties.
2004 Regular rates apply: April 18 to August 28 and September 30 to October 30 for all Value and Moderate resorts, Wilderness Lodge, Animal Kingdom Lodge, and Fort Wilderness Cabins; April 18 to August 7 for the Campground; April 18 to July 4 and September 30 to October 30 for all other WDW properties (except Swan and Dolphin). **2004 Peak rates apply:** February 12 to April 17 for all WDW properties (except Swan and Dolphin). **2004 Pre-holiday rates apply:** November 19 to December 19 (Ft. Wilderness Cabins only) **2004 Holiday rates apply:** December 20–31. For updated Swan and Dolphin resort rates, call 800-527-1500.

Room capacity: Numbers in parentheses reflect maximum occupancy based on existing beds. A trundle bed (for one) can be rented at some properties for $15 a day. Cribs can be requested for free in most resorts. Rates include up to two adults. There is an additional charge for each extra adult in a room.

CALL 407-934-7639 FOR RESERVATIONS

Note: The prices provided here were correct at press time, but rates do change, so be sure to double-check with the hotels before setting your final budget. Charge is for one day, single or double occupancy.

*During holiday season, rates are higher. Call for information.

Magic Kingdom Area

Contemporary

Watching the monorail trains disappear into this hotel's enormous 15-story, A-frame tower never fails to amaze first-timers. The sleek trains look like long spaceships docking as they slide inside.

Passengers, for their part, are impressed by the cavernous lobby, with its tiers of balconies and, at its center, the soaring 90-foot-high, floor-to-ceiling tile mural depicting scenes from the Southwest. (Look carefully and you may spot the five-legged goat.)

This imposing structure has 1,007 rooms in its tower and the garden buildings that flank it on either side. There are six shops, three restaurants, three snack bars, two lounges, a marina, beach, health club, and more. The pool area incorporates two whirlpools, a water slide, and water jets. The Food and Fun Center—a vast area with an arcade and a snack bar—is open 24 hours. The large convention center offers business services. Perhaps the resort's most notable feature is its 15th-floor observation deck. From here guests dining at the resort's California Grill restaurant can enjoy a bird's-eye view of the Magic Kingdom.

A concierge package is available for guests who stay in the hotel's 14th-floor suites. Amenities include express check-in and check-out, complimentary continental breakfast, evening refreshments, and nightly turn-down service. The Tower Club also provides guests with special concierge privileges. To contact the Contemporary, call 407-824-1000.

ROOMS: Bold colors and wild patterns drive the quirky decor of these rooms, evenly apportioned among the tower and two garden buildings. Rooms located in the tower boast private balconies and views of Bay Lake or the Magic Kingdom. (Warning: Pop music blares from the pool area on the Bay Lake side. It often starts in the early morning and continues throughout the day. For maximum quiet, request the park view.) Most rooms can accommodate five guests (plus a child under 3). Typical units have a daybed and two queen-size beds; some rooms have a king-size bed and a daybed. The pillows are on the firm side. Connecting rooms may be requested. Bathrooms are spacious and well laid out. A variety of suites, consisting of a

living room and one or two bedrooms, can accommodate 4 to 8 people. There is free, weekday newspaper delivery.

WHERE TO EAT: In addition to the many restaurants and snack spots, 24-hour room service provides a wide range of offerings.

California Grill: On the 15th floor. The specialty is California fare—flatbread pizza, grilled meats, seafood, and market vegetables. An added treat: the spectacular view of the Magic Kingdom fireworks.

Chef Mickey's: Located on the fourth-floor concourse. Mickey and his friends host daily buffets. Breakfast features Mickey Mouse pancakes as well as more traditional items. Dinner offers carved meats, prime rib, nightly specials, a variety of entrées, plus a sundae and dessert bar. A true crowd pleaser.

Concourse Steakhouse: On the fourth-floor concourse. A full breakfast; burgers, salads, and sandwiches for lunch; steak, seafood, and pasta for dinner.

Food and Fun Center: On the first floor. Serves light fare 24 hours a day.

WHERE TO DRINK: The Magic Kingdom's no-alcohol policy doesn't trickle over to its nearest neighbor.

California Grill Lounge: On the resort's 15th floor, adjoining the California Grill. Picture windows provide a dramatic backdrop for sipping California wines and other drinks, and nibbling on appetizers. Seating is limited.

Contemporary Grounds: A lobby coffee bar, near the escalators. Serves cappuccino, espresso, latte, and other gourmet coffees, as well as biscotti.

Outer Rim: On the fourth-floor concourse, overlooking Bay Lake. Serves appetizers, cocktails, and specialty drinks.

Sand Bar: This poolside spot offers drinks, fruit plates, and light snacks from the grill.

WHAT TO DO: Volleyball nets are set up on the beach, and a basketball court is nearby. Waterskiing, parasailing, and fishing excursions may be arranged (see *Sports* for details).

Boating: Sailboats, canopy boats, Water Mouse, and other boats may be rented at the resort's marina.

Children's Program: The Mouseketeer Clubhouse is open from 4:30 P.M. to midnight for (potty-trained) kids ages 4 through 12 (two-hour minimum stay). Cost is $10 per hour per child. Reservations are necessary; call 407-824-1000, ext. 3038.

Health Club: The Olympiad health club has modern Cybex equipment, stair climbers, bicycles, a sauna, dry tanning beds, lockers, and massage (by appointment).

Parasailing: Supervised excursions are offered at the marina. Cost is about $75 per person, or $115 for two to ride tandem. Reservations are necessary; call 407-WDW-PLAY.

Salon: Contemporary Resort Salon on the third floor of the tower provides haircuts, facials, manicures, and other services.

Shopping: The fourth-floor concourse is home to first-class shops. Fantasia sells character merchandise, including plush animals and clothing for children and adults. Concourse Sundries & Spirits has newspapers, magazines, books, snacks, and liquor—just what's needed for a cocktail party on the terrace. Bay View Gifts (BVG) carries character merchandise and apparel for adults, items with the Contemporary Resort logo, jewelry, souvenirs, home decor items, kitchenware, and candy. There is also a pin-trading and purchasing station located on the concourse.

Swimming: In addition to a round, lakeside pool, the free-form pool features a 17-foot-high curving slide. Two large whirlpools have been added (one is located in the center of the pool, the other is tucked off to the side). Water jets shoot unexpectedly while smaller fountains spout randomly, delighting older and younger kids alike.

Tennis: Disney's Racquet Club, Walt Disney World's premier tennis center, is located near the north wing. It features six state-of-the-art hydrogrid clay courts. Private lessons are available (see *Sports* for details).

Video Arcade: On the first floor, the Food and Fun Center boasts everything from Skee-Ball to air hockey, and all the favorites of the pinball-

and-electronic-games-playing set. It's one of the best gamerooms at Walt Disney World.

Waterskiing, Wakeboarding, Tubing: Ski boats with instructors may be rented at the marina. Call 407-939-7529 for reservations and pricing information.

TRANSPORTATION: The Contemporary resort is connected to the Transportation and Ticket Center (TTC) and the Magic Kingdom by monorail. From the TTC, Epcot can be reached via monorail, and Typhoon Lagoon and Downtown Disney can be reached by bus. Buses also go to the Disney-MGM Studios, Animal Kingdom, and Blizzard Beach. Watercraft travel from the marina to Fort Wilderness and Wilderness Lodge.

Polynesian

The Polynesian resort is as close an approximation of the real thing as Walt Disney World's designers could create. The vegetation is lush, and the architecture summons the tropics. The mood is set by a three-story garden that occupies most of the lobby. Water cascades over craggy volcanic rocks, while coconut palms tower over about 75 different species of tropical and subtropical plants.

> ## Did You Know?
> The white sand on the beaches near the Polynesian and Grand Floridian resorts and along the Seven Seas Lagoon actually came from the bottom of Bay Lake, located behind the Contemporary resort.

The structure that contains this mass of greenery, the Great Ceremonial House, is the central building in the Polynesian complex. The front desk, shops, and most of the restaurants are located here. Flanking the Ceremonial House on either side are 11 two- and three-story village longhouses named for various Pacific islands. These structures house the resort's 853 rooms. The monorail stops at this hotel, making it a convenient place to stay; in fact, it's just a short ride to the Magic Kingdom.

Concierge service offers such amenities as express check-in, continental breakfast, cookies and soft drinks every afternoon, hors d'oeuvres and desserts in the evening, and a lounge with a prime view of the Seven Seas Lagoon and Cinderella Castle (not to mention the nightly

fireworks displays in the Magic Kingdom). Concierge rooms and suites are located in the Tonga and Hawaii buildings. The telephone number for the Polynesian is 407-824-2000.

ROOMS: Many of the rooms have balconies, and most have a view of the gardens, Seven Seas Lagoon, or one of the resort's swimming pools; rooms in the Tokelau, Tahiti, and Rapa Nui buildings are the largest. Most rooms have two queen-size beds and a daybed, and can accommodate five guests (plus a child under age 3). Adjoining rooms may be requested. The resort's suites—located exclusively in the Tonga building—can accommodate four to nine guests. Some have a king-size bed in the bedroom and one queen-size bed in the parlor.

WHERE TO EAT: A variety of specialties are available from room service between 6:30 A.M. and midnight. Also, some interesting eating spots are located here.

Captain Cook's Snack Company: On the lobby level of the Great Ceremonial House. This is a good spot for continental breakfast. Snacks are available 24 hours a day.

Kona Cafe: On the second floor of the Great Ceremonial House. This family restaurant serves lunch and dinner with an Asian flair, while the breakfast menu is filled with traditional American selections. A coffee bar provides the perfect capper to any meal.

'Ohana: On the second floor of the Great Ceremonial House. 'Ohana serves family-style dinners roasted in a large fire pit. Disney characters host a breakfast every morning.

WHERE TO DRINK: The Polynesian theme has inspired a whole raft of deceptively potent potables. As might be expected, both the drink offerings and the settings in which they are served are as tropical as they come.

Barefoot Bar: Adjoining the Swimming Pool Lagoon, and open seasonally.

Tambu: There's a tropical air about this lounge adjoining 'Ohana. The bar serves appetizers and exotic specialty drinks. Sporting events are shown on a large TV.

WHAT TO DO: A wide range of activities is available at the Polynesian, including a jogging path. Fishing excursions can also be arranged.

Boating: Several types of sailboats, Water Mouse boats, canopy boats, and pontoon boats are available for rent at the marina.

Children's Program: The Never Land Club is a supervised activity program for (potty-trained) kids ages 4 through 12. It's offered between 4 P.M. and midnight, with a kids' buffet from 6 P.M. to 8 P.M. The cost is $10 per hour. Reservations are necessary; call 407-824-2184.

Playground: The small playground near Swimming Pool Lagoon features equipment for climbing, swinging, and sliding.

Shopping: News from Polynesia is the locale for hotel and Polynesian items, as well as newspapers, magazines, film, sun care products, and gifts. Maui Mickey's sells character merchandise and clothing. Robinson Crusoe's sells resortwear and swimwear for men; the Polynesian Princess stocks resort fashions, bathing suits, and accessories for women. Trader Jack's sells Disney souvenirs, toys, fashions, and other items; Samoa Snacks is the place for food, spirits, soft drinks, snacks, and other fixings for an impromptu room party.

Swimming: There are two pools here: the elliptical East Pool, in the shadow of the Tokelau, Hawaii, Tuvalu, Rapa Nui, and Tahiti buildings, and the larger free-form Swimming Pool Lagoon, found closer to the marina and main beach. The popular volcano-themed watering hole, complete with slide, appeals to swimmers of all ages. It is often open late, with giddy guests getting water-logged into the wee hours of the morning. Toddlers have their own shallow wading pool to splash in nearby.

Video Arcade: Moana Mickey's Fun Hut has an assortment of current video games. It is located next to the Never Land Club.

TRANSPORTATION: The Polynesian resort is on the monorail line to the Magic Kingdom and the Transportation and Ticket Center (TTC). From the TTC, Epcot is accessible by another monorail, and Typhoon Lagoon and Downtown Disney can be reached by bus. Buses go to the Disney-MGM Studios, Animal Kingdom, and Blizzard Beach. Launches leave from the Polynesian dock for the Magic Kingdom and the Grand Floridian.

Grand Floridian Resort & Spa

At the turn of the century, Standard Oil magnate Henry M. Flagler saw the realization of his dream: The railroad he had built to "civilize" Florida had spawned along its right-of-way an empire of grand hotels, lavish estates, prominent families, and opulent lifestyles. High society blossomed in winter, as the likes of John D. Rockefeller and Teddy Roosevelt checked into the Royal Poinciana, in Palm Beach, enjoying the sea breezes from the oceanside suites.

The hotel later burned to the ground, and Florida's golden era faded with the Depression. But nearly a century after Flagler

first made Florida a fashionable resort destination, Walt Disney World opened a grand hotel—an 867-room Victorian structure with gabled roofs and carved moldings—on 40 acres of Seven Seas Lagoon shorefront, between the Magic Kingdom and the Polynesian.

Like its late-19th-century predecessors, the Grand Floridian resort boasts abundant verandas, ceiling fans, intricate latticework and balustrades, turrets, towers, and red-shingle roofs. And yet, it offers all the advantages of modern living, including monorail service. With five restaurants, two lounges, five shops, and an arcade, plus a child-care facility, convention center, swimming pool, marina, and full-service health club and spa, the Grand Floridian is not only a grand hotel but a complete resort.

The main building houses the Grand Lobby, a palatial space soaring five stories to a ceiling of stained-glass domes and glittering chandeliers. Palms and an aviary decorate the sitting area; an open-cage elevator carries guests to the shops and restaurants on the second floor. The turn-of-the-century theme is everywhere, from the costumes worn by the employees to the shop displays, restaurants, and room decor. The telephone number for the Grand Floridian resort is 407-824-3000.

ROOMS: The rooms are decorated as they might have been a century ago—with printed wall coverings, marble-topped sinks, ceiling fans, and Victorian woodwork. Amenities include hair dryers, bathrobes, mini-bars, nightly turndown service, and daily newspaper delivery.

The main building houses concierge rooms and suites; lodge buildings, each four and five stories high, contain standard rooms, slightly smaller "attic" chambers, and suites. Most rooms measure about 400 square feet and include two queen-size beds, plus a daybed, to accommodate up to five people. Many rooms have terraces. Suites include a parlor, plus one, two, or three bedrooms; there are king-size or queen-size beds in the bedrooms. Most of the 15 honeymoon rooms, located on the second, third, fourth, and fifth floors, enjoy wonderful views. In the main building, access to the upper three concierge-suite levels is restricted by private elevator.

On the third floor, the concierge desks offer such services as reservations and information. The fourth floor features a quiet seating area where continental breakfast and evening refreshments are served. Concierge service is also available in the Sugar Loaf building.

WHERE TO EAT: Most restaurants and lounges are located on the first two floors of the main building. Room service offers a wide assortment of items 24 hours a day.

Cítricos: The largest of the hotel's restaurants is also the newest. It features market-fresh cuisine from the south of France. Open for dinner, on select days. Some seating affords excellent views of the nightly fireworks presentation at the Magic Kingdom. Closed Monday and Tuesday.

Gasparilla Grill & Games: This 24-hour snack bar offers light items for all-day dining and snacking, plus a selection of video games.

Grand Floridian Cafe: Its peaches-and-cream color scheme and veranda-like feel make this a great place for a quick, sit-down meal. Lunch only.

Narcoossee's: This casual restaurant and bar has a romantic shoreline location. The ever-changing menu includes such staples as roast lamb chops and seafood. The partially open kitchen is the focal point of the restaurant. Guests may sip cocktails on the veranda.

1900 Park Fare: A buffet restaurant decorated with carousel horses, plants, and Big Bertha, the carnival organ. Characters host breakfast and dinner daily.

Victoria & Albert's: The eatery is named after the former queen and prince consort of England. Meals are served to no more than 60 guests. Jackets are required for men, and priority seating is a must.

WHERE TO DRINK: Guests will find the refined lounges here to be especially nice escapes. Cocktail service is provided in the lobby from 4 P.M. to 11 P.M. daily. Cítricos and Narcoossee's both have lounges, complete with scenic views of the Magic Kingdom.

Garden View: This pretty spot on the first floor offers a view of the hotel's lush, landscaped garden and pool area. Afternoon tea is served (as are finger sandwiches and small desserts).

Mizner's: Named after the eccentric, wildly prolific architect who defined much of the flavor of Palm Beach County, this bar is on the second floor.

Pool Bar: The place for pool and beachside refreshments, this spot features a variety of snacks and beverages.

WHAT TO DO: The Grand Floridian offers all the recreational facilities of a beach resort. Fishing excursions can be arranged (refer to the *Sports* chapter for details). Volleyball equipment is available.

Boating: Sailboats, canopy boats, pontoon boats, and Water Mouse boats are available for rent at Captain's Shipyard Marina. The *Grand 1* yacht (complete with a captain and first mate) can be rented for $350 an hour.

Children's Programs: The Mouseketeer Club is a supervised program for kids ages 4 through 12. It's open from 4:30 P.M. to midnight; the cost is $10 per hour for each child. There is a four-hour maximum. Reservations are required; call 407-827-5444. Kids ages 3 to 10 may also embark on a special Pirate Cruise and search for treasure near the Magic Kingdom. The 90-minute trip costs $25 per child. For information and to make reservations, call 407-WDW-DINE (939-3463).

Health Club: The health club has exercise machines, saunas, whirlpools, and steam rooms.

Playground: Adjacent to the Mouseketeer Clubhouse, the play area includes swings and climbing equipment.

Salon: The Ivy Trellis salon offers a full line of hair-care services.

Shopping: On the first floor of the main building is Summer Lace, specializing in women's resortwear and swimwear, and Sandy Cove, for gifts, sundries, and home decor. One level up is the M. Mouse Mercantile character shop, a Bally leather-goods store, and Commander Porter's, a men's shop.

Spa: The spa offers more than a dozen treatment rooms for massage, herbal wraps, and aromatherapy. There are some spa programs for children.

Swimming: There are two pools and a whirlpool for guests to splash in.

Tennis: There are two clay courts. There is no charge to play; available on a first-come, first-served basis.

Shades of Green

This 228-room resort is situated near the Grand Floridian but is not linked with the monorail system. Shades of Green is a recreational retreat for active and retired military personnel and their families, members of the reserves and the National Guard, and Department of Defense employees.

The resort features two tennis courts, two pools, a small health club, restaurant, bar and lounge, gift shop, arcade, laundry facilities, and free transportation around WDW.

Room rates are based on military or civilian grade. Select multi-day tickets are offered at a discount. The property's three golf courses—the Palm, the Magnolia, and Oak Trail—are open to all WDW guests (see *Sports* for details). All other activities are for hotel guests and their families only.

At press time, the resort was closed for renovation. It's scheduled to reopen in 2004. WDW is providing alternative accommodations for Shades of Green guests. The number for Shades of Green is 407-824-3400. For reservations, call 407-824-3600.

Video Arcade: Gasparilla Grill & Games is on the first floor of the main building.

TRANSPORTATION: The Grand Floridian is connected to the Transportation and Ticket Center (TTC) and the Magic Kingdom by monorail. From the TTC, Epcot is accessible by another monorail, and Typhoon Lagoon and Downtown Disney can be reached by bus. Buses travel to the Disney-MGM Studios, Animal Kingdom, and Blizzard Beach. Water launches go to the Magic Kingdom and the Polynesian resort.

Wilderness Lodge & Villas

This resort recalls the spirit of the early American West and the feeling of the National Park Service lodges built during the early 1900s. These grand structures architecturally unified the elements of the unspoiled wilderness parks, kept harmony with nature, and incorporated the culture of Native Americans. The Wilderness Lodge artfully recaptures this rustic charm.

The resort is located between the Contemporary resort and Fort Wilderness on Bay Lake. The lobby, which is shared by the lodge and villas, is in an eight-story, log-structured building. Massive bundled log columns support a series of trusses, while two Pacific Northwest totem poles soar 55 feet into the air. Four levels of corridors surround the lobby, providing access to guestrooms, sitting nooks, and terraces. The monorail does not stop here. Concierge service is available on the top floor. The telephone number for the Wilderness Lodge and Villas is 407-824-3200.

ROOMS: Most of the 728 guestrooms have two queen-size beds, a table and chairs, and a

balcony. Some have a queen-size bed and a bunk bed. The bathrooms have separate vanity areas with double sinks. The wallpaper has a Native American–motif border, and the colorful bedspreads and plaid curtains add to the decor. Images of wildlife complete the theme. Suite rooms include an iron (with board), hair dryer, and weekday newspaper delivery.

The 181 deluxe villas, which opened in late 2000, are housed in a five-story tower adjoining Disney's Wilderness Lodge. This tribute to turn-of-the-twentieth-century design is one of an ever-growing battery of Disney Vacation Club properties. The style of the villas building was inspired by the grandeur of Rocky Mountain geyser country. Units are available to all guests when not occupied by Vacation Club members.

Each studio has a queen-size bed and a double sleeper sofa, plus a kitchenette with microwave, coffeemaker, and refrigerator. Larger (one- and two-bedroom) villas sleep four to eight, and have dining areas, kitchens, laundry facilities, master baths with whirlpool tubs, and VCRs. They include king-size beds in the master bedroom, living rooms with queen sleeper sofas, and a queen-size bed in extra bedrooms. All rooms come with an iron (and board), folding crib, and hair dryer. Rooms in the Wilderness Lodge have daily newspaper delivery.

WHERE TO EAT: The Northwest theme is carried out with flair in the hotel's eateries. Room service runs from 7 A.M. to 11 A.M. and 4 P.M. to midnight.

Artist Point: Decorated with art representing painters who first chronicled the Northwest landscape, this fine dining spot features salmon, game, steak, seafood, and wines from the Pacific Northwest. (Be sure to ask if the tomato salad is in season—and order it if it is!)

Roaring Fork: Fast food is available here.

Whispering Canyon Cafe: A boisterous, family-style restaurant with all-day dining.

WHERE TO DRINK: Two spots are available for a relaxing break.

Territory: This lounge honors the survey parties who led the move westward. In addition to specialty drinks, microbrewed beer, and espresso, snacks are served.

Trout Pass: The poolside bar features a variety of specialty drinks and snacks.

WHAT TO DO: The resort offers many recreational activities. Teton Boat & Bike Rental is

in the Colonel's Cabin by the lake. Volleyball equipment is available. Fishing excursions may be arranged (see *Sports* for details). Or consider taking a free guided tour of the lodge.

Biking: Bikes may be rented for scenic rides around the resort. A three-quarter-mile path leads to Fort Wilderness.

Birthday parties: Children's birthday parties may be arranged by calling 407-939-7529. Each two-hour party includes lunch on the beach of the Wilderness Lodge resort, cake, decorations, prizes, and more. The cost is $20 per child. Hayrides, pony rides, and boat rides may be included for an additional charge.

Boating: A variety of watercraft, including Water Mouse boats, canopy boats, sailboats, and pontoon boats, may be rented for a trip around Bay Lake.

Children's Program: The Cubs Den is a supervised dining and entertainment club for (potty-trained) kids ages 4 through 12. Supervised activities, including Disney movies and Western-themed arts and crafts, keep kids entertained from 4 P.M. to midnight. Cost is $8 per hour per child. Dinner is included between 6:30 P.M. and 8 P.M. Call 407-939-3463 for reservations, which are required.

Health Club: The only thing rustic about the Sturdy Branches health club is the structure it's housed in. It features Cybex equipment, stair climbers, bicycles, sauna, and more. Massage therapy is available for a fee.

Iron Spike Room: A fireplace and railroad memorabilia add atmosphere to this relaxing room, equipped with comfy seating, tables, and games.

Shopping: Wilderness Lodge Mercantile stocks necessities and sundries as well as a line of clothing with the Wilderness Lodge logo and Disney character merchandise. There's also a pin-trading cart in the lobby.

Swimming: The main pool looks as if it were carved from the rockscape. A beach, a kiddie pool, two whirlpools, and a geyser complete the design. Fire Rock Geyser erupts on the hour from early morning until 10 P.M. The Hidden Springs pool near the Villas provides a quieter alternative.

Video Arcade: The Buttons and Bells Arcade has about 30 games to keep kids (and grown-ups) busy.

TRANSPORTATION: Boats go to the Magic Kingdom, Contemporary, and Fort Wilderness. Buses go to Epcot, the Disney-MGM Studios, Animal Kingdom, Blizzard Beach, and the

Transportation and Ticket Center (TTC). From the TTC, transfer to buses for Typhoon Lagoon and Downtown Disney.

Fort Wilderness Resort & Campground

The very existence of this canal-crossed expanse—with more than 700 acres of cypress and pine—always surprises visitors who come to Walt Disney World expecting to find nothing more than theme parks.

Tucked among the campsites are hundreds of air-conditioned Wilderness Cabins for rent, complete with housekeeping service. The cost is comparable to that of some of the more expensive rooms at Disney resorts. The phone number for the Fort Wilderness resort and campground is 407-824-2900.

CAMPSITES: Fort Wilderness has 784 traditional sites. They feature electricity hookups (30/50-amp), water, sanitary disposal, and cable television. (Note that the pet loops are not wired for cable.) Partial-hookup campsites supply electricity and water hookups only. All campsites feature a paved driveway pad, picnic table, and charcoal grill. Most loops have at least one air-conditioned comfort station equipped with restrooms, private showers, an ice machine, phones, and a laundry room. A site allows for occupancy by up to ten. Each site has room for one car (in addition to the camping vehicle). Other cars may be parked in the main lot.

The various campground areas are designated by numbers. The 100–500 loops are closest to the beach, the Settlement Trading Post, and Pioneer Hall. The 1500–2000 loops are farthest away from the beach and many other Fort Wilderness activities, but they are quieter and more private. Pets are welcome at certain campsites for a nightly charge of $3.

WILDERNESS CABINS: These woodland dwellings offer a rustic escape. The interiors of the six-person, log-cabin-like buildings are decorated with wilderness accents. Each one is shaded by a pine canopy. Cabins include a Television, a VCR (bring your own videos), full bath, hair dryer, iron, a deck, picnic table, and charcoal grill.

Note: No extra camping equipment is permitted; all guests must be accommodated in a cabin. (For prices, see pages 54–55.)

WHERE TO EAT: There are a couple of dining options, but many people cook here. A small selection of supplies is sold at the Meadow Trading Post and the Settlement Trading Post. Gooding's supermarket is located at the Crossroads of Lake Buena Vista. Ask about nearby grocery stores when you check in.

Trail's End Buffet: This log-walled spot in Pioneer Hall serves home-style fare three meals a day. Pizza is an option from 4:30 P.M. to 10 P.M. Spirits are are available. The breakfast buffet delivers a hefty bang for the buck.

WHERE TO DRINK: Cocktails are served at Crockett's Tavern in Pioneer Hall.

FAMILY ENTERTAINMENT AFTER DARK: The Hoop-Dee-Doo Musical Revue is quite popular with families. Reservations should be made in advance; call 407-939-3463. There's also a free nightly campfire program held near the Meadow Trading Post. (For details, see the *Everything Else in the World* and *Good Meals, Great Times* chapters.)

WHAT TO DO: There's a plethora of activities to choose from, including campfire sing-alongs and even a museum. Kids enjoy the petting farm. Activities are described in detail in *Everything Else in the World* and *Sports*.

TRANSPORTATION: Buses circulating at 20- to 30-minute intervals provide transportation within the campground, while buses and boats connect Fort Wilderness to the rest of the World. The Magic Kingdom, Contemporary, and Wilderness Lodge are most efficiently reached via watercraft that depart regularly from the marina. Buses make the trip from the Settlement Depot to Blizzard Beach.

Electric golf carts and bikes may be rented at the Bike Barn as an alternative means of getting around within the campground. Call 407-824-2742 for reservations.

Epcot Area

Caribbean Beach

This bright, colorful hotel is set on 200 acres southeast of Epcot and near the Disney-MGM Studios. It is composed of five brightly colored "villages" surrounding a 45-acre lake called Barefoot Bay. Each village is identified with a different Caribbean island—Martinique, Barbados, Trinidad, Aruba, and Jamaica—and features pastel walls, white railings, and vividly colored metal roofs. There are 2,112 rooms in all, making Caribbean Beach one of the largest hotels in the United States.

The villages consist of a cluster of two-story buildings, a swimming pool, a guest laundry, and a lakefront stretch of white-sand beach. Guests check in at the Custom House, a reception building that immediately projects the feeling of a tropical resort. Decor, furnishings, and staff costumes all reflect the Caribbean theme. Old Port Royale, a complex located near the center of the property, evokes images of an island market. Stone walls, pirates' cannons, and tropical birds and flowers add to the atmosphere. The area houses the resort's food court, restaurant and lounge, arcade, and two shops.

The port opens onto a lakeside recreation area that includes a pool with waterfalls and a slide; the main beach; the Barefoot Bay Boat Yard and Bike Works, where boats and bicycles may be rented; a 1.4-mile promenade around the lake that's perfect for biking, walking, or jogging; and Parrot Cay Island, an area in the middle of Barefoot Bay. It should come as no surprise that children love it here. The telephone number for the Caribbean Beach resort is 407-934-3400.

ROOMS: Rooms are located in two-story buildings in each island village. A typical 340-square-foot room has two double beds and can sleep up to four. The rooms here are a bit larger than standard rooms at Disney's other moderate resorts. Rooms are decorated in tones softer than the colors found on the exterior. Each room has a coffeemaker. A note for the budget-conscious: All rooms here are identical in terms of size and comfort, and the only difference between the most and least expensive is the view. To minimize time spent walking, request a room nearest the lobby or bus stop when you check in.

WHERE TO EAT: A full-service eatery called Shutters and a food court are located in Old Port Royale. Limited room service is available from 4 P.M. to 11:30 P.M.

Cinnamon Bay Bakery: Freshly baked rolls, croissants, and pastries are available in addition to ice cream and other treats.

Kingston Pasta Shop: Scads of savory pasta dishes are served.

Montego's Market Deli: Soups, salads, and cold sandwiches are offered.

Old Port Royale Burger Shop: Hot sandwiches and burgers are on the menu.

Royale Pizza Shop: Pizza is available in individual portions, along with pasta dishes and salads.

Shutters at Old Port Royale: The menu at this recently re-themed and refurbished Old Port Royale restaurant includes prime rib and a catch of the day. Cocktails are served.

WHERE TO DRINK: The tropical Caribbean theme is carried out in the specialty drinks found at Banana Cabana. Light snacks are also available at this poolside spot.

WHAT TO DO: There are many recreational opportunities here. The 1.4-mile promenade around the lake is ideal for walking, biking, or a morning jog.
   Biking: Bikes may be rented at the Barefoot Bay Boat Yard and Bike Works.
   Boating: Sailboats, Water Mouse boats, canopy boats, canoes, pontoon boats, and pedal boats are available for rent at the Barefoot Bay Boat Yard and Bike Works for use on the resort's scenic 45-acre lake.
   Playgrounds: Playgrounds are located on Parrot Cay Island, as well as on the Barbados, Jamaica, and Trinidad beaches.
   Shopping: At Old Port Royale, there's the Calypso Straw Market, which carries a slew of items with the resort logo and a variety of colorful, island-themed goods. Calypso Trading Post stocks Disney character merchandise and sundries.
   Swimming: Each village has its own pool, and the main pool has a waterfall and a slide in a Caribbean-themed setting, conjuring up images of swashbuckling adventures.
   Video Arcade: Goombay Games at Old Port Royale offers a selection of amusements.

TRANSPORTATION: Buses go to the Magic Kingdom, Epcot, the Studios, Animal Kingdom, and Blizzard Beach. Other bus routes lead to Downtown Disney and Typhoon Lagoon.

Yacht & Beach Club and Beach Club Villas

The New England seaside exists at Disney World in the form of the Yacht and Beach Club, and the Beach Club Villas. Situated beside Epcot, the resorts, designed by noted architect Robert A. M. Stern, are set around a 25-acre lake. The adjacent properties share most facilities—including a convention center offering access to business services—and transportation options.
   The Yacht Club's design evokes images of the New England seashore hotels of the 1880s. Guests enter the five-story beige clapboard building along a wooden-planked bridge. Hardwood floors and brass enhance the nautical theme. A lighthouse on the pier serves as a beacon to welcome guests back to the hotel from WDW attractions. To reach the Yacht Club by telephone, call 407-934-7000.
   Distance from the ocean is irrelevant over at the sand-and-surf-focused Beach Club resort, approached along an entrance drive flanked by oak trees. A walkway leads past a croquet court to beachside cabanas on the white-sand shore. Guests are met by hosts and hostesses dressed in colorful beach resort costumes of the 1870s. The telephone number for the Beach Club resort is 407-934-8000.

Meetings & Conventions

Convention centers at Walt Disney World range in size from 20,000 to 200,000 square feet. The Dolphin's center, featuring an exhibit hall and an executive boardroom, is the largest; the Swan provides additional space. The Contemporary has three ballrooms and a spacious pre-function area with lots of natural light. The convention center at the Yacht and Beach Club is reminiscent of a grand turn-of-the-century New England town-meeting hall. The Grand Floridian Resort and Spa has a lavish center with silk brocade walls. The BoardWalk offers a smaller conference area with a lakeside gazebo for outdoor events. And Coronado Springs, the first moderately priced Disney resort to offer convention facilities, boasts the largest hotel ballroom in the U.S.

Among the unique services available to Disney conventioneers is the use of Disney characters and performers for events. Special events can even be held in the parks. Resort business centers have clerical staffs and computers, in addition to faxing and photocopying equipment. (These services are available to all resort guests.)

Those interested in scheduling a convention should call 321-939-7221. Organizers are advised to book their events six months in advance, especially for large groups. Keep in mind that the busiest convention times are January, May, September, and October.

ROOMS: The rooms at the Yacht Club are decorated in a nautical motif. The Beach Club's rooms are also amply sized and, naturally, reflect a beach motif. In each room the furniture is white, and the headboard design on the one king-size bed or two queen-size beds incorporates small ship's wheels. Some rooms have daybeds. Most of the suites have a king-size bed as well as two sleeper sofas. In the bathrooms there is a separate vanity with double sinks and mirrors trimmed with brass. Each room has a ceiling fan, iron (with board), hair dryer, newspaper delivery, mini-bar, wall-mounted makeup mirror, small table (complete with a checkerboard top), and two chairs. Chess and checkers sets may be requested. Concierge rooms are available.

A five-story building beside the Beach Club is home to 225 Beach Club villas. The villas are available to Disney Vacation Club members. (They are available to all guests when not occupied by Vacation Club members.) Each studio has a queen-size bed and a double-sleeper sofa, plus a kitchenette with a microwave, coffeemaker, and fridge. Larger villas sleep four to eight, and all have a dining area, kitchen, laundry room, master bath with whirlpool tub, and a DVD player. They include a king-size bed in the master bedroom, living room with queen sleeper sofa, and a queen-size bed in the extra bedrooms.

WHERE TO EAT: The themes of yachting and the sea play an important role in the restaurants that are found at their respective resorts. A wide variety of menu items is available from room service 24 hours a day.

Beaches & Cream Soda Shop: A classic American soda fountain where shakes, malts, and sundaes are the prime lures. (The shop is located between the two resorts.)

Cape May Cafe: An indoor clambake is held here at the Beach Club each night. The varied and bountiful buffet features several types of clams and mussels, plus beef ribs and chicken. A character breakfast is presented daily.

Hurricane Hanna's Grill: Burgers, hot dogs, sausages, and other snacks are served at this spot. A full bar is also located here, and poolside beverage service is available.

Yacht Club Galley: The buffet breakfast is bountiful. Breakfast, lunch, and dinner are available from an à la carte menu.

Yachtsman Steakhouse: Select cuts of aged beef are the specialty of the house. Fresh seafood and poultry are also offered.

> ## Hot Tip!
> Cribs that accommodate one child under age 3 are available at all Disney resorts. Ask about them when you call to reserve your room. They're free. (If you'd like a more substantial sleeping apparatus for your toddler, refer to page 33 of the *Getting Ready to Go* chapter.)

WHERE TO DRINK: The lounges in both resorts offer a variety of specialty drinks in relaxing seaside settings.

Ale and Compass: This Yacht Club lobby lounge, featuring specialty coffees and drinks, provides a nice respite after a long day.

Crew's Cup: The place to try beers shipped in from the world's seaports before dining at Yachtsman Steakhouse next door.

Martha's Vineyard: This quiet lounge at the Beach Club offers selections from American and international vineyards, served in sample sizes and by the glass or bottle, as well as a full bar.

Rip Tide: The Beach Club lobby lounge features a variety of California wines, wine coolers, and frosty concoctions, plus beer and other cocktails.

WHAT TO DO: There is enough to do here to fill an entire vacation. A sand volleyball court and a croquet court may be found on the Beach Club side of the property. Equipment for both pursuits is available at no cost at the Ship Shape health club.

The Fantasia Gardens Miniature Golf complex is close at hand, and guided two-hour fishing excursions may be arranged (see *Sports* for details). Free garden tours are available throughout the week. And last but not least, the BoardWalk entertainment district is just a short walk around the lake.

Boating: Hydro Bikes and pedal, canopy, pontoon, and Water Mouse boats are available for rent at the Bayside Marina.

Children's Program: The Sandcastle Club, for potty-trained kids ages 4 through 12, is available from 4:30 P.M. to midnight. Cost is $10 per hour for each child. Reservations are required; call 407-939-3463. Toys, videos, games, and computers are on hand to keep children entertained. Dinner is included between 6 P.M. and 8 P.M.

Health Club: The Ship Shape health club features exercise machines, sauna, whirlpool, steam room, and massage (by appointment).

Special Room Requests

Central Reservations accepts requests for rooms with particular views or in certain locations. Agents will do their best to accommodate such requests, but cannot guarantee they will be able to fulfill every wish. Call 407-W-DISNEY (934-7639).

The health club is open to all Walt Disney World resort guests over the age of 13. Additional fees apply.

Playground: A small play area with a slide and climbing apparatus is located by the pool.

Salon: The Periwig salon for men and women is located in the central area.

Shopping: At the Yacht Club, Fittings & Fairings Clothes and Notions is an all-purpose shop offering nautical fashions, character merchandise, and sundries. At the Beach Club, Atlantic Wear and Wardrobe Emporium features a similar selection of goods (albeit with a beach theme).

Swimming: Between the marina and the beach is the centerpiece of the dual resort— Stormalong Bay, a three-acre pool that's really a mini water park. There is a lagoon expressly for relaxed bathing, and another with currents, jets, and sand-bottomed areas. Several whirlpools are scattered throughout the area. Adjacent to the main pool is a shipwreck, where guests can enjoy a water slide. There is one unguarded pool and whirlpool at the far end of each hotel. There is also an unguarded pool by the Beach Club villas. Guests may also opt to sunbathe on the beach.

Tennis: There is one lighted tennis court on the Yacht Club side of the property. Rental equipment is available at the Ship Shape health club.

Video Arcade: Lafferty Place Arcade, located in the central area, has about 60 video games and pinball machines.

TRANSPORTATION: Guests travel to Epcot and the Disney-MGM Studios via ferry boats or walkways. Buses go to the Magic Kingdom, Animal Kingdom, Downtown Disney, Typhoon Lagoon, and Blizzard Beach.

Swan & Dolphin

These sister resorts, situated on the shores of Crescent Lake, can easily be distinguished by the 47-foot swan and 56-foot dolphin statues that top them. The waterfalls, rows of palm trees, and beachfront location all reflect the tropical Florida landscape that was their inspiration. Both hotels were designed by noted architect Michael Graves as prime examples of "entertainment architecture." The turquoise waves on the colored facade of the Swan's 12-story main building and two 7-story wings are clearly evidence of this design, as is the Dolphin's exterior mural, which features a banana-leaf pattern. The soaring 27-story triangular tower at the center of the Dolphin is flanked by four 9-story guestroom wings.

The resorts share extensive convention facilities, many recreational options, and a host of restaurants. The Swan and Dolphin are operated by Westin and Sheraton, respectively, but are treated as Walt Disney World resorts; guests here enjoy most WDW resort

Hot Tip!
The Swan and Dolphin resorts run seasonal promotions throughout the year. For information, call 888-828-8850.

benefits. One notable difference involves room-key charging privileges: Guests cannot use their room keys to charge purchases on Walt Disney World property, with the exception of within the Swan and Dolphin resorts themselves. The telephone number for the Swan is 407-934-3000; for the Dolphin, it's 407-934-4000. Reservations for either resort may be made by calling 800-227-1500 or by visiting *www.swandolphin.com*.

Be aware that there is an automatic $10 room charge assessed per day to cover services such as newspaper delivery, local telephone calls (up to 60 minutes per day), coffee, use of

the health club, etc. Valet parking costs $10 per day. Free self-parking is also available.

ROOMS: The corridors outside the Swan guestrooms feature patterned carpets and murals on the walls that extend the wave theme from its exterior design. Inside, the recently redecorated rooms sport a contemporary look with soft colors. Each room has one king-size or two queen-size beds; safes and refrigerators are among the amenities. There are 54 concierge rooms on the 11th and 12th floors, and 55 suites.

The 1,509 rooms at the Dolphin, including 136 suites, have also been redecorated recently. All rooms feature two double beds or a king-size bed, as well as refrigerators, vanity dressing areas, irons and boards, and coffeemakers. Concierge rooms are located on the 12th through the 20th floors.. There are rooms equipped for guests with disabilities, and non-smoking rooms are available at both resorts. Unlike at most Walt Disney World resorts, the rooms here do not have ceiling fans.

WHERE TO EAT: In addition to many restaurant choices, 24-hour room service provides an extensive all-day dining menu. (The room service here is the best at Walt Disney World.)

Cabana Bar & Grill: This full-service poolside spot near the Dolphin serves burgers, sandwiches, yogurt, and fruit. The full bar serves specialty drinks.

Dolphin Fountain: Homemade ice cream is the specialty here. Huge sundaes, shakes, malts, and burgers are also offered.

Garden Grove Cafe: This Swan eatery, which features a greenhouse atmosphere, serves breakfast and lunch daily. At dinner,

the restaurant transforms into Gulliver's Grill. A buffet breakfast with the characters is held on Saturday, while a character dinner takes place several nights a week.

Palio: A fine Italian eatery, located at the Swan, featuring veal specialties, homemade pasta, and brick-oven pizza. There are daily specials and strolling musicians.

Shula's Steak House: A relative newcomer to the lineup of Dolphin eateries, Shula's is an upscale celebration of two American favorites: steak and football. It's a bit pricey, but the steaks are superb.

Splash Grill: A poolside cafe near the Swan serving lunch and snacks. A full-service bar is also located here.

Tubbi's: A snack bar with a little bit of flair. The checkerboard design makes this a pleasant place for a quick meal at the Dolphin resort. The 24-hour convenience store here sells snacks and sundries.

WHERE TO DRINK: It's easy to find a nice cocktail spot in this neck of the woods.

Kimonos: The Asian decor makes this Swan lounge an inviting place for sake, sushi, and other Japanese specialties. Karaoke is a house specialty. This place is generally hopping into the wee hours.

Lobby Court: This spot at the Swan offers a respite from the hubbub. Enjoy gourmet coffees with fresh pastries in the morning, and wine and specialty drinks at night in a European-style bistro setting.

Lobby Lounge: A cozy Dolphin area featuring wine and specialty drinks.

Shula's Steak House Lounge: Settle into a comfy chair, light up a stogie, and sip a cocktail in this cozy lounge adjacent to Shula's dining room.

WHAT TO DO: The Swan and Dolphin share many recreation options. Volleyball nets and hammocks are set up on the beach. The Fantasia Gardens Miniature Golf complex and BoardWalk are nearby (the proximity to BoardWalk and Epcot is a big plus). The Disney-MGM Studios are a short boat ride (or about a 20-minute walk) away.

Boating: Pedal boats are available for rent on the beach between the Swan and Dolphin.

Children's Program: Camp Dolphin welcomes children (potty-trained) ages 4 through 12 and offers supervised activities from 5:30 P.M. to midnight. The cost is $10 per child per hour.

Health Clubs: There is a fitness center near the pool area at the Dolphin. State-of-the-art equipment is available, as are personal trainers. There is a sauna, steam room, large whirlpool, and massage therapists. There's also a smaller health club with basic exercise equipment near Splash Grill at the Swan.

Playground: A play area with a slide, swings, chain bridge, sandbox, and several jungle gyms is located next to the Swan lap pool.

Salon: The Niki Bryan shop at the Dolphin resort provides a full battery of salon services, including hairstyling, manicures, and pedicures.

Shopping: Disney Cabanas, located in the lobby of the Swan, features men's and women's fashions, a line of character merchandise, and sundries. Four specialty shops are located at the Dolphin. A large selection of Cartier and other brand-name watches can be found at Brittany Jewels. Indulgences allows chocolate lovers the chance to sample some tasty concoctions. Statements of Fashion offers resortwear for men and women. Daisy's Garden is the place to find character goods at the Dolphin.

Swimming: In addition to a shared children's wading pool, there is a lap pool at each hotel and a lovely themed grotto pool with slides lies between the Swan and Dolphin. Several whirlpools are scattered around the area.

Tennis: Hard-surface tennis courts are located behind the pool area closest to the Dolphin resort. They are lighted for night play and are open 24 hours a day.

Video Arcades: A room full of video games is located near Tubbi's at the Dolphin. Another can be found adjacent to the pool.

TRANSPORTATION: Guests travel to Epcot and the Disney-MGM Studios via ferryboats or walkways. Buses go directly to the Magic Kingdom, Animal Kingdom, Downtown Disney, Typhoon Lagoon, and Blizzard Beach.

BoardWalk Inn & Villas

The enchantment of a bygone era is recaptured in the BoardWalk. The resort combines a waterside entertainment complex with deluxe hotel accommodations and vacation villas. Dining, recreation, shopping, and entertainment venues line the boardwalk, and twinkling lights trim the buildings. The ambience continues throughout, with detailed architecture featuring sherbet-colored facades, flagged turrets, and striped awnings, all reminiscent of the turn of the twentieth century. The BoardWalk resort

Resort Roundup

What's the best place to stay at Walt Disney World? It's a tough question–and one that Birnbaum editors are asked all the time. The answer? Well, it depends. Do you have a favorite park? What's your price range? Will a clown's tongue that doubles as a pool slide make your day? All factors to consider. That said, here are our favorites in each of Disney's price categories:

 DELUXE
Yacht and Beach Club: In addition to a picturesque setting and top-notch service, these sister resorts are all about location. For starters, you can walk to Epcot (and the Studios if you're feeling ambitious). Of course, you can always opt to take a water taxi. You're a stone's throw from the excitement of the bustling BoardWalk entertainment district, but get to enjoy the relative peace of life on the quieter side of Crescent Lake. Excellent dining options abound. And the pool area's to die for. We prefer to stay at the Yacht Club. *Very honorable mention: Grand Floridian*

 MODERATE
Port Orleans Riverside: One need not be a Southern aristocrat to live like one. Many of the guest buildings at this resort, formerly known as Dixie Landings, were designed to look like historic mansions. Even the food court has a certain Southern ambience. There's a table service restaurant, and a cozy lounge (which occasionally offers up live entertainment). Kids enjoy dropping their hooks in the fishing hole (strictly catch and release) and splashing in the free-form pool on Ol' Man Island. Pretty gardens and a relatively reasonable price add to the appeal. *Honorable mention: Caribbean Beach*

BIRNBAUM'S BEST VALUE
All Star Movies: This, the newest of the All Star properties, has some of the best theming around (i.e., *Toy Story* and *101 Dalmatians*), but what really sets it apart is the food court. It's bigger and brighter than its All Star counterparts, and as such, makes for a more pleasant and efficient dining experience. *Honorable mention: All Star Sports*

is adjacent to Epcot's International Gateway and connected to it via walkway. The phone number for BoardWalk is 407-939-5100.

ROOMS: Accommodations here evoke the charm of early Eastern seaboard inns. Most have private balconies or patios. The BoardWalk Inn has 378 deluxe hotel rooms decorated with cherry-wood furniture, board-walk postcard-print curtains, and light green accents. Guestrooms at the Inn sleep up to five, and feature two queen-size beds (or one king-size bed) and a child's daybed. Romantic two-story garden suites each have a private garden enclosed by a white picket fence. They sleep four, and have a living room on the first floor and a king-size bed in the bedroom loft. The Inn also has concierge rooms and suites.

The 520 vacation villas are collectively called Disney's BoardWalk Villas. These are Disney Vacation Club villas, available when not occupied by members. Each studio has a queen-size bed and double sleeper sofa, plus a kitchenette with microwave, coffeemaker, and small refrigerator. Larger (one-, two-, and three-bedroom) villas sleep 4 to 12 people, and feature dining areas, fully equipped kitchens, laundry facilities, master baths with whirlpool tubs, and VCRs. They also include king-size beds in the master bedroom, living rooms with queen sleeper sofas, and two queen-size beds (or one plus a double sleeper sofa) in any additional bedrooms. Rooms at the BoardWalk Inn include free newspaper delivery. All rooms have an iron (with board) and a hair dryer.

WHERE TO EAT: This resort has a wealth of dining and snacking options. A variety of

vendors along the boardwalk tempt with hot dogs, crêpes on a stick, gourmet coffee, and more. For those looking to eat in, 24-hour room service is available.

Big River Grille & Brewing Works: This working brewpub features a full menu, complemented by fresh specialty ales. View the on-site brewmaster through floor-to-ceiling glass walls.

BoardWalk Bakery: A popular stop that offers fresh baked goods, sandwiches, espresso, and cappuccino. Huge display windows allow passersby to watch bakers at work. "Bun rises" are held here every morning. Note that the line moves slowly.

BoardWalk Carts: Stands along the board-walk offer snacks and coffee.

ESPN Club: A serious sports bar for serious sports fans, it provides interactive sports video entertainment and all-day dining.

Flying Fish Cafe: This restaurant has a show kitchen, and its dinner menu emphasizes seafood, steak, and fresh seasonal items.

Seashore Sweets': An old-fashioned sweetshop serves candies, saltwater taffy, ice cream, frozen yogurt, and specialty coffees.

Spoodles: Mediterranean cuisine is the focus of this establishment geared toward families; the appetizers are meant for sharing.

WHERE TO DRINK: Guests have a multitude of options right in their backyard, with the BoardWalk's clubs and lounges on hand.

Atlantic Dance: This waterfront club is an elegantly designed dance spot. You must be 21 to enter. There usually isn't a cover charge, but that may change.

Belle Vue Room: Listen to old-time tunes on antique radios and play board games in this cocktail lounge near the lobby.

Jellyrolls: Dueling pianos provide live entertainment in a casual warehouse atmosphere. The cover charge is generally about $5 to $10 nightly. You must be 21 to enter.

Leaping Horse Libations: The carousel-themed pool bar at Luna Park serves a variety of cocktails, as well as snacks.

WHAT TO DO: The three-quarter-mile pathway encircling Crescent Lake (en route to Epcot) provides a ready venue for walkers and joggers. BoardWalk guests may rent boats from a neighboring resort's marina. The Fantasia Gardens Miniature Golf complex is nearby. At the resort itself, Ferris W. Eahlers Community Hall rents out equipment for many recreational pursuits, including croquet, shuffleboard, table tennis, pole fishing, badminton—even books and videos. Fishing excursions can be arranged.

Biking: Community Hall offers a variety of bicycles for rental. Surreys (canopied quadra-cycles for four) may also be rented.

Children's Program: The Harbor Club provides supervised activities for potty-trained kids ages 4 through 12 from 4:30 P.M. to 11:45 P.M. Cost is $10 per child per hour (with a one-hour minimum stay); dinner is included between 6:30 P.M. and 8 P.M. Call 407-939-3463 for necessary reservations.

Health Club: Muscles & Bustles health club offers steam rooms, tanning, Cybex machines, and circuit-training equipment, as well as massages (by appointment). Additional fees apply.

Midway Games: This area on the BoardWalk's WildWood Landing features games of luck and skill similar to those found along traditional boardwalks.

Playground: An amusement park-themed play area offers kids a pool to clown around in and other fun activities.

Shopping: Dundy's Sundries in the lobby is the source for basic necessities. Character Carnival on the boardwalk has children's apparel as well as character merchandise. Screen Door General Store stocks groceries, dry goods, snacks, and beverages. Thimbles & Threads, also on the boardwalk, carries apparel for men and women. Wyland Galleries features marine and environmental art.

Surrey Ride: A trip around Crescent Lake in a pedal-powered surrey is available for a fee.

Swimming: The BoardWalk's swimming area, Luna Park, features a large pool with a

200-foot water slide, "Keister Coaster," patterned after a wooden roller coaster (The pool slide is a clown's tongue.). A family of elephants is found posed throughout the area; their trunks act as a shower for adults on the pool deck or children in the wading pool. The resort has two unguarded pools. There are three whirlpools, one in each pool area.

Tennis: Two lighted soft-surface tennis courts are available for play.

Video Arcades: Side Show Games Arcade has video games, and a sports-themed arcade entertains at the ESPN Club.

TRANSPORTATION: Guests may travel to Epcot and the Disney-MGM Studios via ferry-boats or walkways. Buses transport guests to the Magic Kingdom, Animal Kingdom, Typhoon Lagoon, Blizzard Beach, and Downtown Disney.

Disney Vacation Club

The Disney Vacation Club grants members the convenience of flexible vacations from year to year, with the ability to choose when and where to visit, how long to stay, and the type of accommodations. It starts with the purchase of a real estate interest in a Disney Vacation Club property. For a one-time price and annual dues, members can enjoy vacation stays at Disney's Old Key West Resort, Disney's Beach Club Villas, Disney's BoardWalk Villas Resort, and The Villas at Disney's Wilderness Lodge at Walt Disney World; Disney's Vero Beach Resort in Florida; and Disney's Hilton Head Island Resort in South Carolina; plus access to additional destinations around the globe. Through "Member Getaways," members may also elect to stay at their choice of more than 300 resorts worldwide, including most Disney resorts and the Disney Cruise Line.

Disney's Vero Beach Resort is a two-hour drive from Walt Disney World. It has villa-type accommodations comparable to those at Disney's Old Key West Resort—with lush surroundings, beach, and lots of local sights. The proximity makes it easy to tack a beach vacation onto a WDW visit.

Disney Vacation Club information centers may be found at each of the Walt Disney World hotels and theme parks. For more information, call 800-800-9100, or visit *www.disneyvacationclub.com*.

Downtown Disney Area

Port Orleans French Quarter

This 1,008-room resort invites comparisons to the historic French Quarter of New Orleans. *(Although Port Orleans and Dixie Landings technically function as one resort—referred to as Port Orleans French Quarter and Riverside—we give them individual attention, to provide guests with the information necessary to select the area that works best for them.)*

Starting at the entrance gate, with its wrought-iron portal and overgrown landscape, the appeal of the Delta City surrounds arriving guests. The entry drive leads to the heart of the city, which is Port Orleans Square. The central building was based on a turn-of-the-twentieth-century mint. The Mint houses check-in facilities (for Port Orleans French Quarter *only*), a shop, food court, and arcade. It has a vaulted ceiling, and the check-in desks are designed as bank-teller windows. The musical notes in the mural are the notes to "When the Saints Go Marching In."

The phone number for Port Orleans French Quarter is 407-934-5000.

ROOMS: The guestrooms are located in seven 3-story buildings (with elevators). Each room has two double beds; some king-size beds are available. The rooms are a bit smaller than the standard rooms at the more expensive Disney hotels, but they are comfortable for a family of four. (The photos on the walls were donated by Disney employees.)

The buildings are painted cream, pink, blue, purple, and yellow, and feature wrought-iron railings of varying designs. Connecting rooms may be requested but can't be guaranteed. The least expensive rooms overlook gardens or parking areas, and the most expensive rooms offer water views.

WHERE TO EAT: A counter-service food court has a variety of dining options.

Sassagoula Floatworks & Food Factory: A variety of specialty foods is available in this food court, including gumbo, chicken with red beans and rice, fresh-baked beignets, and other traditional Creole dishes. Burgers, pizza, ice cream, and baked goods are also on the menu.

WHERE TO DRINK: A pool bar operates seasonally, and guests on a quest for a cocktail may head to Port Orleans Riverside—it's a short bus ride away. Of course, there's always Downtown Disney, or any theme park other than the Magic Kingdom.

WHAT TO DO: A themed pool is the highlight of the recreational opportunities here.

Biking: Bicycles are available for rent at Port Orleans Riverside.

Boating: Pedal boats, kayaks, canoes, rowboats, canopy boats, and pontoon boats are available for rent at nearby Port Orleans Riverside.

Playground: A small play area with slides is located across from the food court.

Shopping: Jackson Square Gifts & Desires, located at Port Orleans Square, features Disney character merchandise, clothing bearing the Port Orleans resort logo, and sundries.

Swimming: Doubloon Lagoon is a free-form pool built around a bright blue sea serpent. The water slide is actually the creature's tongue. A shower at the pool features an alligator's head, and there is a large clamshell where an all-gator band serves as the centerpiece of a fountain. There is a large whirlpool nearby. Port Orleans French Quarter guests are also invited to swim in the pool at Ol' Man Island at Port Orleans Riverside.

Video Arcade: South Quarter Games is located at Port Orleans Square. It features state-of-the-art video and arcade games.

TRANSPORTATION: Buses go to the Magic Kingdom, Transportation and Ticket Center (TTC), Epcot, the Disney-MGM Studios, Animal Kingdom, Typhoon Lagoon, Blizzard Beach, and Downtown Disney.

Port Orleans Riverside

This resort area used to be called Dixie Landings. Here, the city feel of the French Quarter gives way to the rural South. The resort is divided into "parishes." Closest to the "city," guestrooms are found in Mansion homes; farther upriver are the Bayou guestrooms, with a more rustic feel. The phone number for the Port Orleans Riverside resort is 407-934-6000.

ROOMS: The 2,048 Mansion and Bayou guestrooms are of the same size, and each room features two double beds (some king-size beds are available); 963 of the Bayou rooms have trundle beds (designed to sleep one child) as well. There is an additional fee of $15 per night for a trundle bed. The Magnolia Bend Mansion rooms, appointed with tapestries and cherry-wood furniture, are situated in sprawling, elegant manor homes with stately columns and grand staircases. The Alligator Bayou rooms are in rustic, weathered-wood buildings that are tucked among flora native to the area. Although all buildings have two to three floors, only the Magnolia Bend Mansions have elevators.

The Bayou rooms surround Ol' Man Island, a 3½-acre recreational area with a pool, playground, and fishing hole. Decorative touches in the rooms include wood and tin armoires and pedestal sinks with brass fittings. The beds have hickory bedposts. As is common with Disney's non-deluxe resorts, the closet space is not enclosed. The rooms are a bit on the small side, but they can accommodate a family of four.

WHERE TO EAT: In addition to a restaurant and food court, the hotel offers limited room service via Sassagoula Pizza Express, which delivers from 4 P.M. until midnight.

Boatright's Dining Hall: This 200-seat table-service eatery, next to Riverside Mill, serves Cajun specialties and American fare for dinner. Breakfast is also served.

Riverside Mill: This food court resembles an old-fashioned cotton mill with a working waterwheel that powers the cotton press inside.

The five counter-service stands here offer all sorts of choices. The basic selections are available for breakfast. **Acadian Pizza 'n' Pasta** has pasta dishes, pizza, and calzone. **Blue Bayou Burgers and Chicken** offers fried and grilled chicken and burgers. **Cajun Broiler** serves spit-roasted chicken and barbecued ribs. **Riverside Market and Deli** is a store that stocks snack foods, soda, salads, sandwiches, beer, and wine. **Southern Trace Bakery** serves pastries, pies, and sticky buns. Soft drinks may be refilled on a meal-by-meal basis.

WHERE TO DRINK: Two lounges possess an enticing degree of charm.

Muddy Rivers: The poolside bar serves cocktails, plus hot dogs, popcorn, and ice cream during pool hours. Seasonal.

River Roost: Situated in a room designed as a cotton exchange, this lounge features specialty drinks and light hors d'oeuvres.

WHAT TO DO: Many of the resort activities are at Ol' Man Island, a recreation center featuring a pool, whirlpool, wading pool, interactive fountains, playground, and fishing hole stocked with fish for catch and release.

Biking: Bicycles of all types can be rented.

Boating: Pedal boats, canoes, kayaks, canopy boats, and pontoon boats are available for rent.

Carriage rides: Horse-drawn carriages take guests for 30-minute rides throughout the grounds of the resort. Carriages hold up to 4 adults or 2 adults and 3 small kids. Tickets are sold by the driver. Each trip costs $30 and departs from Boatright's Dining Hall. Call 407-939-7529 for reservations.

Fishing: Two-hour guided fishing excursions are available (see *Sports*), and guests may fish on their own at the Ol' Fishin' Hole.

Playground: An elaborate play area is located on Ol' Man Island next to the pool.

Shopping: Fulton's General Store in the Riverside building stocks Disney character merchandise, clothing, and sundries.

Swimming: In addition to the main pool and kiddie pool at Ol' Man Island, there are

five unguarded pools at the resort. Guests may also swim the French Quarter pool.

Video Arcade: The Medicine Show Arcade features a small selection of games.

TRANSPORTATION: Buses go to the Magic Kingdom, Transportation and Ticket Center (TTC), Epcot, the Disney-MGM Studios, Animal Kingdom, Typhoon Lagoon, Blizzard Beach, and Downtown Disney.

Disney's Saratoga Springs Resort & Spa

Just across the lake from hustle and bustle of Downtown Disney, this new resort is a peaceful complement to its nearest neighbor. From the colorful Victorian architecture to the historic influence of horse racing, Disney's Saratoga Springs Resort & Spa aspires to recapture the heyday of upstate New York country retreats of the late 1800s. Set to open in phases beginning in late spring, 2004, the resort—which covers 65 acres formally occupied by the Disney Institute—is the newest and largest addition to the Disney Vacation Club. Guests may call for reservations in early 2004. To contact the resort, call 407-827-1100.

ROOMS: There are studios and villas with one, two, and three bedroms. A studio consists of a room with a queen-size bed and a full-size sofa bed, bathroom, kitchenette with wet bar, fridge, microwave, and coffee maker. All units have a porch or balcony and access to complimentary laundry facilities.

One-bedroom villas have a king-size bed in the master suite and a queen-size sleeper sofa in the living room. The one bathroom has a whirlpool tub. The full kitchen includes a fridge, stove, microwave, toaster, coffee maker, blender, dinnerware, and dishwasher. Each unit has a porch or balcony and a washer and dryer. Two-bedroom villas have an additional bathroom and bedroom, with two queen-size beds. The three-bedroom Grand Villa is similar to the two-bedroom models, but is about twice the size and has four bathrooms.

WHERE TO EAT: There is one source of sustenance at the resort, and dozens across the lake. There are two barbecue areas available to guests who want to have a cook-out.

ARTIST'S RENDERING

The Artist's Palette: Set in a converted artist's loft, this spot offers salads, sandwiches, lasagna, meatloaf, pizza, and more.

Groceries: In these parts, in-room grocery delivery is available from Artist's Palette, and many guests cook their own meals. The Earl of Sandwich at the Downtown Disney Marketplace has sandwiches. If you've got a car, ask for directions to a nearby grocery store.

WHERE TO DRINK: In addition to the onsite bar, many guests imbibe at Downtown Disney.

On the Rocks: A pool bar serving the usual battery of cocktails.

WHAT TO DO: In addition to the ever-popular spa, guests here rent bikes, swim, walk, swat some tennis balls, or just sit back and enjoy a prime view of the Downtown Disney fireworks.

Biking: Bicycles may be rented from Horsing Around Recreational Rentals.

Boating: Boats may be rented at nearby Downtown Disney.

Golf: The resort is adjacent to the Lake Buena Vista golf course.

Health Club: The fitness center features cardiovascular and weightlifting equipment.

Playground: A kids' play area is located by the resort's themed pool.

Shopping: The Artist's Palette stocks souvenirs and sundries.

Spa: The award-winning spa has ten treatment rooms for massage, manicures, facials, aromatherapy, and more.

Swimming: High Rock Spring cascades down rugged rockwork and feeds into a freeform, heated pool. The splash zone features a water slide, two whirlpools, and an interactive play area for kids.

Video Arcade: Expect to find the usual bells and whistles at "Win, Place, or Show."

TRANSPORTATION: Buses go to all theme and water parks. Boats ferry guests to Downtown Disney.

Disney's Old Key West Resort

Escape to the spirit of the Florida Keys. Disney's Old Key West Resort is the flagship Disney Vacation Club property, but villas not occupied by members are available for nightly rental. It has the laid-back feel of a resort community and all the amenities that go with resort life. The homey accommodations have lots of space and the convenience of kitchen facilities, making the resort especially comfortable for longer stays. The villas are designed in a Key West theme, with soothing color schemes. The telephone number for Disney's Old Key West resort is 407-827-7700.

VILLAS: There are studios and villas with one, two, or three bedrooms. A studio consists of a large room with two queen-size beds, a table and chairs, and a small fridge, coffeemaker, microwave, and sink. The bathrooms are spacious. Each of the one-bedroom villas has a king-size bed in the master bedroom and a queen-size sleeper sofa in the living room; the master bath has a whirlpool tub, sink, and shower.

The two-bedroom villa features a king-size bed in the master bedroom, two queen-size beds in the second bedroom, a living room with a queen-size sleeper sofa and a VCR, a dining room, and a kitchen with a refrigerator, dishwasher, toaster, and coffeemaker, plus dishes, flatware, cooking utensils, and more.

The master bathroom is divided into two rooms with an extra-large whirlpool tub and a sink in one and an oversize shower, sink and vanity, and toilet in the other. There's a porch or balcony off the living room and bedroom, and ceiling fans in each room. The configuration of the two-story, three-bedroom Grand

Villas is similar to that of the two-bedroom models, but adds a third bedroom with two double beds. As for capacity, the studios and one-bedroom villas sleep 4 people, the two-bedroom villas sleep 8 guests, and two-story three-bedroom villas accommodate 12.

WHERE TO EAT: In addition to the restaurant here, there are grills and picnic tables.

Good's Food to Go: The perfect place to pick up fixin's for a continental breakfast, this place also offers burgers, conch fritters, salads, sandwiches, and simple snacks.

Olivia's Cafe: This full-service restaurant serves Key West favorites, plus more traditional items, for breakfast, lunch, and dinner. Menus change seasonally.

WHERE TO DRINK: The watering holes at Old Key West are as laid-back as they come.

Gurgling Suitcase: This tiny bar serves specialty drinks, wine, beer, and soft drinks.

Turtle Shack: This poolside spot serves pizza, salads, sandwiches, and snacks. Open seasonally.

WHAT TO DO: At Conch Flats Community Hall, table tennis, board games, a large-screen television, video rentals, and planned activities are offered. There are basketball, shuffleboard, and volleyball courts, and equipment is available at Hank's Rent 'N Return.

Biking: Bikes may be rented from Hank's.

Boating: Pedal boats, rowboats, and pontoon boats are available for rent at Hank's.

Health Club: The R.E.S.T. health club features Nautilus and cardiovascular machines, a sauna, and massage (by appointment).

Playground: A kids' play area is located by each of the resort's swimming pools.

Shopping: Conch Flats General Store has groceries, books, sundries, and more.

Swimming: The sprawling main pool, with a large whirlpool nearby, is located behind the Hospitality House. The children's pool and play area looks like a big sandcastle. Additional pools are found around the resort.

Tennis: There are three courts (two lighted).

Video Arcade: The Electric Eel Arcade is in the Hospitality House; the Flying Fish arcade, by the Turtle Shack snack bar.

TRANSPORTATION: Buses go to the theme parks, water parks, and Downtown Disney. Water launches also make the trip between the resort and Downtown Disney.

Animal Kingdom Area

All-Star Movies, Music & Sports

The All-Star resorts are among the most brightly and boldly themed at Walt Disney World. Each resort has 1,920 rooms housed in ten buildings devoted to five Disney movies, types of music, and sports, respectively.

Sports fans will find themselves in a world of baseball, football, tennis, surfing, or basketball at the All-Star Sports resort. Brightly colored, larger-than-life football helmets, surfboards, tennis balls, basketball hoops, and baseball bats adorn the buildings.

At the All-Star Music resort, Broadway, country, jazz, rock, and calypso are the themes. A walk-through, neon-lit jukebox, a three-story pair of cowboy boots, and a Broadway theater marquee are among the giant icons.

The All-Star Movies resort celebrates five classic Disney films: *Toy Story*, *The Mighty Ducks*, *Fantasia*, *101 Dalmatians*, and *The Love Bug*. Buildings are adorned with such icons as 40-foot Dalmatians and wildly over-size versions of Buzz Lightyear and Woody.

As value resorts, the All-Star properties offer few frills, but the service and whimsical atmosphere are pure Disney.

Guests check in at Cinema Hall for All-Star Movies, Melody Hall for All-Star Music, or Stadium Hall for All-Star Sports. Each has a food court, arcade, shop, and Guest Services. To reach All-Star Movies, call 407-939-7000; to phone All-Star Music, call 407-939-6000; to contact All-Star Sports, call 407-939-5000.

ROOMS: The guestrooms, measuring 260 square feet, are rather small compared with those at Port Orleans, which are 314 square feet. Each room has two double beds (with the exception of rooms designed for travelers with disabilities, which have one king-size bed), a vanity area with a sink, a separate bathroom, a small dresser, and a small table with chairs.

WHERE TO EAT: Three food courts—**World Premiere** in Cinema Hall, **Intermission** in Melody Hall, and **End Zone** in Stadium Hall. Each features a bakery, convenience market, and several stands geared to barbecue, pizza and pasta, and burgers. Each food court has a seating area with a beverage bar.

For entertainment, the End Zone offers Disney movies during the day and showcases big games on its big-screen TV. The All-Star resorts all deliver pizza, salads, beer, and wine to rooms from 4 P.M. to midnight.

WHERE TO DRINK: There are no lounges at the All-Star resorts; however, the **Silver Screen Spirits**, **Singing Spirits**, and **Team Spirits** pool bars serve drinks throughout the day and evening. The bars are in the main pool areas.

WHAT TO DO: Guests may swim in any of the All-Star pools. All-Star guests may rent boating equipment at any WDW resort.

Playground: A playground is located in each hotel's courtyard area.

Shopping: Maestro Mickey's in Melody Hall, Sport Goofy's Gifts and Sundries in Stadium Hall, and Donald's Double Feature in Cinema Hall all have magazines, books, character merchandise, and sundries.

Swimming: Each hotel has two pools and one kiddie pool. The main pool at All-Star Movies has a *Fantasia* theme (look for Sorcerer Mickey). The smaller Duck Pond Pool is based on *The Mighty Ducks*. At the All-Star Music resort, the Calypso Pool is in the form of a giant guitar, while the Piano Pool bears a striking resemblance to a grand piano. At All-Star Sports, Surfboard Bay has a soothing ocean motif. The smaller Grand Slam Pool pays tribute to our national pastime—it's shaped like a baseball diamond (Goofy is on the mound).

Video Arcades: Each of the All-Star resorts boasts one video arcade.

TRANSPORTATION: Buses make pickups at Cinema Hall, Melody Hall, and Stadium Hall for trips to each of the four theme parks, Blizzard Beach, Typhoon Lagoon, and Downtown Disney. Each resort has its own bus line.

A word about All-Star resort transportation: The bus service at these "value" resorts tends to be slightly *more efficient* than at other locations. The combination of fewer stops and connections is a bonus for guests staying here.

Disney's Animal Kingdom Lodge

At first glance, Disney's Animal Kingdom Lodge, evokes images of a sleepy, little thatched-roof game lodge in the wilds of southern Africa. Upon closer examination, however, it's clear that the only things sleepy or little about this place are the small creatures that live in its shadow. Those animals, along with their more sizable cousins, inhabit the 33 acres of meticulously re-created African savanna that practically surround this 1,293-room resort. In all, more than 100 birds and hoofed animals, including giraffes, zebras, ostriches, and Thompson's gazelles, call Disney's newest wildlife reserve home. With the freedom to wander within a dozen or so yards of the lodge itself, these critters allow guests to go on safari without leaving their balconies.

The resort, located about a mile from Disney's Animal Kingdom park, opened in April 2001. The lobby is a huge, high-ceilinged room, richly appointed—as is the rest of the property—with colorful African artwork and artifacts. The biggest draw here is neither the large mud fireplace nor the suspension bridge spanning this cavernous chamber, but the four-story observation window overlooking the savanna. It's one of many portals through which to gaze upon meandering wildlife.

Like the African game lodges on which it is based, Disney's Animal Kingdom Lodge was constructed using a semicircular design. From overhead, it looks a bit like a horseshoe. This allows for maximum animal-viewing potential. Indeed, many of the resort's guestrooms have direct views of the savanna areas. Be sure to specify your viewing preference when you book a room. The telephone number for Disney's Animal Kingdom Lodge is 407-938-3000.

ROOMS: The 1,293 rooms, all finished in tapestries and vibrant colors, feature handcrafted dark-wood furniture, sand-colored walls, and earth-tone-patterned carpets. Deluxe rooms are a bit more spacious than their standard counterparts. Most rooms have two queen beds (some king-size beds are available), plus a daybed to accommodate up to five people; bunk beds are available in many rooms. All rooms have balconies. Suites include a parlor, plus one, two, or three bedrooms; there are king-size or queen-size beds in the bedrooms. Bathrooms have a separate vanity area with double sink. All rooms include an iron (with board), hair dryer, and newspaper delivery. Like at real African game lodges, some beds come draped with mosquito netting. Unlike in Africa, however, the nets here are purely decorative. Concierge service is available.

WHERE TO EAT: In addition to its restaurants, the hotel offers round-the-clock room service.

Boma—Flavors of Africa: Boma is modeled after a bustling African marketplace. This sprawling, popular family restaurant boasts many different types of cuisine in what chefs describe as a "global fusion" style. The cuisine, served buffet-style, is a blend of French, Malaysian, Indian, Chinese, and English.

Jiko—the Cooking Place: The colors of sunset are the backdrop for this sublime eatery with an African flair. Wines from South Africa are featured.

The Mara: A spacious fast-food restaurant serving such kid-pleasers as pizza, burgers, and chicken fingers.

WHERE TO DRINK: The lounges here are rustic and inviting. Some even offer the opportunity to sip cocktails while observing animals on the savanna.

Capetown Lounge and Wine Bar: Adjacent to Jiko—the Cooking Place, this spot features wines imported from South Africa.

Uzima Springs: The resort's poolside bar serves specialty and traditional drinks during regular pool hours.

Victoria Falls: Set alongside a soothing waterfall, this mezzanine-level lounge features coffee, tea, South African wines, and assorted cocktails.

WHAT TO DO: Spying on wildlife is the main event in these parts. However, if you can manage to pry yourself away from those hoofed exhibitionists for a bit, there are plenty of other diversions available. Note that guests are welcome to partake in activities offered at other Walt Disney World resorts.

Children's Programs: The Simba's Cubhouse play area, for (potty-trained) kids ages 4 through 12, is open in the evenings starting at 4:30 P.M. Reservations are required. Kids can learn about the wildlife surrounding the resort through nature-themed activities. For pricing information or to make reservations, call 407-939-3646.

Health Club: The Zahanati health club boasts state-of-the-art exercise equipment, a sauna and whirlpool, plus spa services, including massage (by appointment).

Playground: The Bana playground is located near the pool.

Shopping: Zawadi Marketplace stocks Africa-themed gifts, Disney character merchandise, clothing with the Animal Kingdom Lodge logo, and sundries.

Swimming: The resort has just one swimming pool, but it is huge. More impressive than its size, however, is the view from the pool deck. In addition to a kiddie pool, there are two whirlpools nearby.

Video Arcade: Pumbaa's Fun & Games features a selection of video games.

TRANSPORTATION: Buses go to the Magic Kingdom, Epcot, the Disney-MGM Studios, Animal Kingdom, Typhoon Lagoon, Blizzard Beach, and Downtown Disney.

Coronado Springs

This resort reveals its Southwestern U.S.-Mexican theme in such elements as a tiled stucco lobby with a fountain and a pyramid with water tumbling down from it that appears to have created the Mayan ruin-themed pool. The hotel's 1,921 rooms are found in three guest areas that stretch around Lago Dorado, a 15-acre lake. (It can take five minutes or more to walk to the farthest

rooms.) The food court, restaurant, and lounge are all near the lobby. A convention center offers access to business services. The telephone number for Coronado Springs is 407-939-1000.

ROOMS: Standard rooms are smaller than those at Disney's deluxe hotels, but adequate for a family of four; each has two double beds (some king-size beds are available). In-room amenities include a coffeemaker, hair dryer, and dataport. Decor varies in each section but is characterized by yellow, blue, and scarlet accents. In the Casitas area, where most of the suites are located, terra-cotta guest buildings occupy a citylike landscape. In the pueblo-style Ranchos, scattered along a dry stream bed, rooms have a rustic feel. Cabanas, located along the rocky palm-lined beach, reflect the casual feel of their namesake.

WHERE TO EAT: In addition to a full-service restaurant and food court, limited room service is available for breakfast and dinner.

Maya Grill: Open for breakfast and dinner, this spot offers seafood, steak, lamb, and pork cooked over an open-pit wood-fired grill.

Pepper Market: High ceilings make this nontraditional food court feel like an open-air market. The fare includes tacos, tostadas, pizza, pasta, and omelettes made to order. Note that there is an automatic 10 percent gratuity for dining in the Pepper Market.

WHERE TO DRINK: There are two places to wet your whistle at Coronado Springs.

Francisco's: This colorful lounge provides cocktails and evening entertainment and is located in the main building.

Siesta's: In the Dig Site area, this poolside bar lets swimmers and archaeologists enjoy a variety of cocktails and light snacks.

WHAT TO DO: There is an array of water sports in which to participate, as well as volleyball and a short nature trail.

Biking: Bikes may be rented at La Marina.

Boating: A variety of boating equipment is available for rent at La Marina.

Health Club: La Vida health club offers a full range of fitness equipment.

Playground: The Explorer's Playground is part of the Dig Site play area and includes a huge sandbox, complete with Mayan carvings waiting to be excavated.

Salon: The Casa de Belleza salon, located near La Vida health club, offers a large variety of spa services.

Shopping: Panchito's Gifts & Sundries is where to find items with a Southwestern flavor, Disney merchandise, film, and necessities.

Swimming: The main pool can be found in the Dig Site area. It surrounds a Mayan pyramid and features a towering water slide. There is a 22-person whirlpool and a kiddie pool nearby. Each of the guestroom areas features an unguarded quiet pool.

Video Arcades: The Jumping Bean Arcade is found in the main building, and the Iguana Arcade is in the Dig Site area.

TRANSPORTATION: Buses go to the Magic Kingdom, Epcot, the Disney-MGM Studios, Animal Kingdom, Typhoon Lagoon, Blizzard Beach, BoardWalk, and Downtown Disney.

Pop Century

What do you get when you mix a hundred years of American pop culture with a sprawling Disney resort? Pop Century. Like the All-Star Resorts, Pop Century is a vivid celebration of Americana. The 5,760-room resort has two major sections: the Legendary Years and the Classic Years, representing the first and second halves of the twentieth century, respectively. Each resort has 2,880 rooms housed in ten buildings. Call 407-934-7639 for up-to-the-minute information. Note that this resort may not be open for your visit.

The resort's larger-than-life "time capsules" represent the toys, fads, dance crazes, and catchphrases that swept the nation during the last century of the second millennium. It's meant to be groovy . . . you dig?

As value resorts, the Pop Century properties offer few frills, but the service is good, the atmosphere's colorful, and the transportation is efficient. Guests check in at Classic Hall for the Classic Years area, or Legendary Hall, for the Legendary Years area. Each section has a food court, an arcade, a shop, and a Guest Services desk. To reach Disney's Pop Century resort, call 407-938-3000.

ROOMS: The guestrooms, measuring 260 square feet, are a bit on the small side compared with those at Port Orleans, which are 314 square feet. Each room has two double beds (with the exception of guestrooms designed for travelers with disabilities, which have one king-size bed), a vanity area with a sink, a separate bathroom, a small dresser, a small table with chairs, voice mail, and a dataport.

WHERE TO EAT: The food court features a bakery, convenience market, plus several stands geared to pizza and pasta, and burgers. The Pop Century resort delivers pizza to guestrooms from about 4 P.M. to midnight.

WHERE TO DRINK: There are no traditional lounges at the resort; however, both the Classic and Legendary sections have pool bars serving drinks throughout the day. The bars are in the main pool areas.

WHAT TO DO: Guests may swim in any of the Pop Century resort pools. Guests may rent boating equipment at any WDW resorts.

Playground: There is a soft-surface playground with, among other compelling features, an interactive water fountain.

Shopping: There is a shop in Classic Hall and one in Legendary Hall. Each has books, character merchandise, sundries, and snacks.

Swimming: Each section of the hotel has three pools and a kiddie pool.

Video Arcades: Both the Legendary Years and Classic Years areas have an arcade.

TRANSPORTATION: Buses stop at Classic Hall and Legendary Hall for trips to each of the four theme parks, Blizzard Beach, Typhoon Lagoon, and Downtown Disney.

Disney Cruise Line

The *Disney Wonder* and its sister ship, the *Disney Magic*, rank among the world's finest oceangoing vessels. The onboard experience is essentially the same on both ships, but some restaurant names, entertainment, and theming differ. As do the length of the cruises, as well as the destinations. A *Disney Magic* voyage takes guests on a 7-night cruise to the Caribbean, while the *Wonder* journeys to the Bahamas (for three or four nights).

A Disney Cruise Line seven-night, land-and-sea vacation begins with a three- or four-night stay at a WDW resort. After that, guests (except those at the Swan and Dolphin) retain the same room keys for their staterooms aboard the *Disney Wonder*. There is no second check-in on the ship. Staterooms closely match the category of the resort accommodations, from moderate to deluxe. Guests may also opt for a seven-night cruise. This package does not include a stay at a WDW resort. All seven-night cruises take place on the *Disney Magic*.

When transfers are purchased, guests travel by bus to Port Canaveral, the departure point for all cruises. They then board a 2,400-passenger ship for their journey. From the ship design to entertainment options, families, teens, and adults without kids all have their own comfort zones—without ever having to say good-bye to Mickey. (In addition to the Mouse, the usual cast of characters is on board.) Three- and four-night cruises include a stop at Nassau in the Bahamas. The seven-night Caribbean cruise takes guests to

St. Thomas (including excursions to St. John) and St. Maarten. Another itinerary stops at Grand Cayman, Key West, and Cozumel. Each voyage includes a day at Castaway Cay. ID is required to enter the Bahamas—a passport or birth certificate will do.

The ships' classic exteriors recall the majesty of early ocean liners. For example, *Disney Magic* guests enter a three-story atrium, where traditional definitions of elegance expand to include a bronze statue of Mickey as helmsman and subtle cutout Disney character silhouettes along the grand staircase. There's even a 15-foot, topsy-turvy statue of a "goofy" painter hanging off the *Disney Magic's* stern.

Vacations can be booked through a travel agent or by calling 800-910-3659 or visiting *www.disneycruise.com*.

ROOMS: All 877 staterooms aboard both ships are a cut above the standard cruising cabin. On average, staterooms offer about 25 percent more space, most have a bath and a half, and 73 percent are outside rooms with ocean vistas—many with verandas. All feature telephones with "land lines," TVs, hair dryers, and safes. There are rooms equipped for guests with disabilities. All rooms are nonsmoking.

There are 12 stateroom categories that correspond to WDW resorts with comparable room rates. The seven-night vacations start at $829 for adults per person, double occupancy. (Packages for kids ages 3 through 12 who are the third or fourth person in a stateroom start at $399.) The seven-night land-sea package price includes Walt Disney World accommodations, admission to the theme and water parks, shipboard meals, cruise and port charges, and more. Depending on availability, guests may opt for a three- or four-night cruise.

WHERE TO EAT: There are three themed dining rooms (and one adults-only alternative), in addition to 24-hour room service, on each ship; guests dine in each of the three main rooms, enjoying a different culinary experience each night.

Note: The restaurants, clubs, and activities described on these pages focus on the *Disney Magic.* Their counterparts on the *Disney Wonder* deliver comparable experiences.

Animator's Palate: Here the restaurant and the food are works of art. As in the movie *The Wizard of Oz*, everything begins in black and white—from the floors to the waiters' attire to the food (to a degree). As the meal progresses, color creeps into the picture. When dessert arrives, the room is awash in brilliant hues.

Lumière's: Continental food, chandeliers, and *Beauty and the Beast* trompe l'oeil effects characterize this casually elegant dining room. An abundance of roses completes the theme.

Palo: A dining room reserved for adults, Palo is a romantic restaurant perched atop the vessel. Chefs prepare Italian cuisine in an exhibition kitchen. Reservations are required. Make arrangements as soon as possible, after boarding the ship. It's a popular spot.

Parrot Cay: In a colorful Caribbean setting complete with Sebastian wall sconces, this restaurant features tasty tropical cuisine.

Topsider Buffet: An indoor-outdoor cafe serving breakfast, lunch, snacks, and a buffet dinner for kids.

WHERE TO DRINK: Among the options are several lounges, including a small ESPN Skybox sports bar (with a big screen TV for the big game of the moment), and a number of other watering holes. Beat Street is a colorful, adults-only cluster of nighttime entertainment venues.

Offbeat: A boisterous dueling pianos bar.

Rockin' Bar D: A dance club with a live band and deejay.

Sessions: An intimate piano bar lounge.

WHAT TO DO: Recreational areas on each ship, as well as at its ports of call, are strategically located to attract families, teens, and

shopping fantasies while exploring the various ports of call. Shops on the ship are duty free.

Sports: Guests of all ages may play volleyball and basketball on the sports deck and at Castaway Cay.

Studio Sea: At this family lounge, guests participate in live entertainment, such as a family game show, in a TV studio setting.

Swimming: There are several whirlpools and three swimming pools on each ship: a family pool, a kids' pool, and an adults-only pool. Guests may also swim off the sandy shores and lagoon of Castaway Cay.

Teen Entertainment: In a coffee bar called Common Ground, teens (and teens only) may hang out, watch movies, and listen to music. There are also teen-oriented activities on the ship, as well as on Castaway Cay.

Vista Spa and Salon: Adult guests get in shipshape at this modern facility, which offers exercise equipment and spa treatments, educational and enrichment programs, sauna, steam room, whirlpool, and massage. The salon offers many services, including haircuts, manicures, and pedicures (for an extra fee). Note that spa appointments fill up fast—book yours as soon as possible once aboard the ship.

Walt Disney Theater: A tribute to the grand theatrical palaces of long ago. Guests see an original Disney production each night.

adults to different areas, with nearly an entire deck devoted to kids. A cruise director keeps guests apprised of the options. Off-shore excursions may be booked once on board.

Adult Activities: Adults-only activities range from wine tasting to guest lectures. There is an adults-only pool onboard and a secluded beach for grown-ups at Castaway Cay.

Biking: Bikes may be rented by the hour at Castaway Cay.

Buena Vista Theater: A 270-seat cinema, this movie theater offers feature films.

Children's Programs: A huge area dedicated exclusively to kids offers supervised, age-specific programs for kids ages 3 through 12 from 9 A.M. until midnight. The Oceaneer Club provides engaging activities for the 3- through 7-year-old set. The Oceaneer Lab, designed for children 8 through 12, is a science-based interactive play area. This area keeps older kids entertained for hours, too.

Deck Parties: Guests may dance to live music, sip cocktails, and nibble snacks at informal, yet swinging, shindigs at sea.

Internet Access: There are Internet stations in the Promenade Lounge and in Common Grounds. The cost is $.75 per minute, with a five-minute minimum. Packages are also available.

Shopping: In addition to the colorful shipboard shops—Mickey's Mates, Treasure Ketch, and Shutters—guests may indulge their

Hot Tip!

The Vista Spa Salon is wildly popular—and books up quickly. It's best to send a member of your party directly to the spa immediately after boarding. Even then, there's usually a line!

Castaway Cay

Every Disney Cruise Line trip includes a visit to Castaway Cay (pronounced *key*). Disney has maintained the island's natural beauty while providing a host of outdoor activities, including snorkeling, biking, and boating. The island has a beach for families, a beach for teens, and a mile-long stretch of sand—complete with massage cabanas—for adults seeking less action and more privacy.

As guests awaken at the island, they find their ship docked at Castaway Cay's private pier. The pier allows for easy access to and from the ship.

Castaway Cay, a 1,000-acre tropical island, is in the Bahamas, east of Fort Lauderdale. Trams are available for guests who wish to explore the island. All of the architecture, including a bar, restaurant, market, and even a post office, is in traditional Bahamian style.

Resorts on Hotel Plaza Blvd.

These seven hotels—Best Western Lake Buena Vista, Courtyard by Marriott, Doubletree Guest Suites, Grosvenor, Hilton, Royal Plaza, and Wyndham Palace Resort and Spa—though inside WDW boundaries, are neither owned nor operated by Disney. However, many have been here since the park opened in 1971 or soon thereafter (sometimes under different names), accommodating Mickey enthusiasts from the beginning. The hotels are not themed, but the three largest (the Hilton, Wyndham Palace, and Grosvenor) do have meals hosted by Disney characters.

Often referred to as the Downtown Disney Resort Area Hotels, they line the mile-long Hotel Plaza Boulevard. The Hilton, Wyndham Palace, and Grosvenor are across the street from the Marketplace, with its shops, restaurants, and nightlife. The other four properties are a 10- to 25-minute stroll away. They are also close to the Crossroads of Lake Buena Vista shopping center, home to inexpensive eateries and a 24-hour grocery. Privileges of staying in one of these hotels include:
• Guests are entitled to purchase "E-Ride" passes to the Magic Kingdom. (They must be used in conjunction with a multi-day park admission ticket. Ask at the front desk.)
• Car rental on the premises (at all but the Best Western Lake Buena Vista resort).

• Free bus service to the four theme parks, with limited service to Downtown Disney, Typhoon Lagoon, and Blizzard Beach. The buses, which are not part of the Disney transportation network, make up to two trips every hour; be sure to allow extra time for bus travel. One bus serves the Hilton and Wyndham Palace; another, the other hotels (it takes at least ten minutes to stop at all five). Buses stop in the middle of the parking lot at some parks.
• Flexibility to book tickets for both on- and off-WDW-property attractions.
• Preferred access to Disney golf courses.
• A 20 percent discount on Downtown Disney Pleasure Island admission when you present a receipt showing that you have eaten dinner at one of the hotels' restaurants on the same evening.
• Preferred seating at Planet Hollywood before 5 P.M.

Note that guests staying in the resorts on Hotel Plaza Boulevard do have to pay for parking at Disney parks and other Walt Disney World attractions, and they cannot charge purchases made at Disney World shops and restaurants with a resort ID or have purchases shipped to their rooms free of charge.

To book a room, call the individual hotel's toll-free number or WDW Central Reservations at 407-W-DISNEY (934-7639). The resors on Hotel Plaza Blvd. are included in several Walt Disney Travel Company packages. Internet users can get information via *www.downtowndisneyhotels.com*.

All of the hotels offer nonsmoking rooms and accommodations for travelers with disabilities. To get to the hotels from the airport, take Exit 27 off I-4.

PHOTO BY ALICE GARRARD

BEST WESTERN LAKE BUENA VISTA: This mostly leisure-oriented, 18-story hotel is surrounded by pines and has an entry lined with oaks draped in Spanish moss. Each of the 325 spacious rooms and suites has either one king-size bed and a queen sofa bed or two queen-size beds, as well as a balcony (floors 7 through 18 provide a panoramic Walt Disney World view). Rooms also come with voice mail, free coffee, safe, hair dryer, and iron with board. Baths have one sink and plenty of counter space. Small refrigerators may be rented for $10 a day.

Each of the four suites occupies a corner of the 18th floor and features a wet bar, two phones, two TVs, a whirlpool tub, and an impressive glassed-in porch with skylights and a ceiling fan; they offer fine views of the other resorts on Hotel Plaza Boulevard and, from the nonsmoking rooms, the (distant) fireworks at Disney theme parks.

The hotel also has a fitness center, business center, an arcade, a heated pool, kiddie pool, playground, sundries shop, and guest laundry facilities. Other amenities include room service and overnight film processing. Traders restaurant serves breakfast and dinner; the Parakeet Cafe offers breakfast, lunch, and dinner, as well as assorted snacks and pizza.

The hotel's lobby and restaurant area features the Flamingo Cove cocktail lounge and a game room. Rates range from $89 to $169 for

guestrooms; $199 to $399 for suites. Best Western Lake Buena Vista Resort, 2000 Hotel Plaza Blvd., Box 22205, Lake Buena Vista, FL 32830; 407-828-2424 or 800-348-3765; *www.orlandoresorthotel.com*.

COURTYARD BY MARRIOTT: The 323 guestrooms, some of the most spacious on Hotel Plaza Boulevard, are situated in a 14-story tower and a 6-story annex. They feature two double beds in most rooms, sitting areas, modem ports, high-speed Internet access, voice mail, movies and Nintendo (for a fee), coffeemakers with china mugs, irons (with boards), and safes. The bathrooms are small, but they have double vanities and hair dryers.

2 Go serves breakfast items, salads, sandwiches, frozen yogurt, and pizza. The Tipsy Parrot lounge offers cocktails and soft drinks. The Courtyard Cafe & Grille is a full-service restaurant with a breakfast buffet. Room service is available. There are three small heated pools, including one for young children; a whirlpool; playground; arcade; small exercise room; and guest laundry facilities. The pool bar is open seasonally.

There is a Dollar Rental Car desk near the lobby, as well as an ATM and a phone-card machine. Rates range from $99 to $219 year-round. Courtyard by Marriott, Box 22204, 1805 Hotel Plaza Blvd., Lake Buena Vista, FL 32830; 407-828-8888 or 800-223-9930; *www.courtyardorlando.com*.

DOUBLETREE GUEST SUITES: This 229-unit property has a stellar staff, homey atmosphere, low-slung facade reminiscent of WDW's Contemporary hotel, bright colors and whimsical patterns throughout, and an aviary in the lobby, where a child's check-in desk adjoins the one for grown-ups. Kids get a bag of goodies, and everyone gets cookies. The only all-suite hotel at Walt Disney World, it has roomy (625 square feet) units, each with a

PHOTO BY ALICE GARRARD

living room and sleeper sofa, dressing area, and separate bedroom. The one-bedroom suites sleep up to six ; there are five two-bedroom suites. Most of the bedrooms have two double beds; a few king beds are available.

The decor features vibrant blues, greens, and oranges, with plaid chairs and sofas. (More subdued surroundings are available.) Room amenities include two TVs, pay-per-view movies, wet bar, refrigerator, coffeemaker, microwave oven, hair dryer, and safe ($2.50 daily charge). The bathroom has a small TV.

Recreational facilities include a large heated pool and a whirlpool in a landscaped area with two hammocks, as well as a fitness room, sand volleyball court, two lighted tennis courts, and small playground. The Kids' Theater (children's playroom) has a big-screen TV, toys, games, popcorn, and seasonal activities. Streamers restaurant features American classics and a breakfast buffet; it's also the source for more of those cookies. Streamers Market sells snack items and groceries. There is a Budget Rental Car desk by the lobby, as well as stamp and phone-card machines.

Rates range from $119 to $299. DoubleTree Guest Suites, 2305 Hotel Plaza Blvd., Lake Buena Vista, FL 32830; 407-934-1000 or 800-222-8733; *www.doubletreeguestsuites.com.*

GROSVENOR: This hotel (the name is pronounced *GROVE*-nor) attracts many international guests. The 626 rooms are located in a 19-story tower and two wings framing two large courtyards with griffin centerpieces. Each room has voice mail, a coffeemaker, and a VCR; movie rentals are available. Most rooms have two double beds, though some 35 king rooms are available; 65 rooms also have daybeds and can sleep up to five. Bathrooms are small but stocked with toiletries.

Extensive recreational facilities—the hotel's appeal—include an exercise room, two lighted tennis courts, shuffleboard, basketball, volleyball, two heated pools, children's pool, play area, and arcade. Changing rooms with showers accommodate guests who check in or out early. Baskervilles restaurant incorporates a replica of Sherlock Holmes's office, and serves breakfast and dinner buffets; Disney characters come for breakfast on Tuesday, Thursday, and Saturday; Murder Watch Mystery Theatre takes place on Saturday at 6 P.M. and 8:45 P.M.

Crumpets Cafe, open 24 hours a day, serves continental breakfast and light fare. For

cocktails, there's Crickets lounge and Moriarty's pub. Rates range from $99 to $165 for two guests, year-round; suites are $345 to $480. Grosvenor, 1850 Hotel Plaza Blvd., Lake Buena Vista, FL 32830; 407-828-4444 or 800-624-4109; *www.grosvenorresort.com.*

HILTON: With a colorful facade and palm-lined drive, this hotel gets high marks for its 23 well-groomed acres, laid-back ambience, pool area, and upscale shops. The 814 rooms, all of which recently underwent extensive refurbishment, have mini-bars, phones with voice mail, and computer hookups.

Among the resort's seven restaurants and lounges, casual Finn's Grill offers dinners of seafood and steaks, wines by the glass, themed evenings, and creatively presented bread; Cape Cod–themed Covington Mill serves breakfast (with Disney characters in attendance on Sunday) and lunch only; Rum Largo Poolside Cafe serves burgers, sandwiches, salads, and tropical drinks alfresco. Mainstreet Market, open 24 hours, is part deli, part country store. For light meals, snacks, or cocktails, drop by John T's Lounge (off the lobby). After-dinner drinks, specialty coffees, beer, and wines by the glass are served at Mugs Coffee and Wine Bar.

Recreational facilities include two whirlpools, two heated swimming pools, a kiddie pool, fitness room, and large gameroom. There is an Avis Rental Car desk in the lobby. Rates range from $160 to $345; suites are $359 to $1,500. Hilton in the Walt Disney World Resort, 1751 Hotel Plaza Blvd., Lake Buena Vista, FL 32830; 407-827-4000 or 800-782-4414; *www.hilton-wdwv.com.*

Note: It is the *only* hotel on Hotel Plaza Boulevard to offer the "Extra Magic Hour." For details about this program (which, on select days, lets guests enter a theme park an hour before it officially opens), inquire at the front desk.

PHOTO BY ALICE GARRARD

ROYAL PLAZA: A subtle pineapple motif, a symbol of hospitality, permeates this property. The 394 guest units, including 22 suites, are divided between a 17-story main tower, with a glass-enclosed elevator scaling the facade, and two-story lanai wings with standard and superior rooms, and gated patios or small balconies. Each guestroom has a sitting area set off by shuttered partitions, a desk, dresser, double armoire with closet space, oversize bathtub, safe, and mini-bar. Baths have marble counters and corner tubs (whirlpools on the concierge level); baths in the spacious rooms with king-size beds have a separate glass-enclosed shower. All rooms are decorated in shades of coral, teal, and green; they have either two double beds or a king-size bed, ceiling fans, sofa beds, hair dryers, safes, mini-bars, and free coffee and tea.

Recreational facilities include a large heated pool, a whirlpool, fitness room (for guests 16 and older), gamerooms for adults and kids, and four lighted tennis courts. There is also a business center and a Disney merchandise shop.

The Giraffe Cafe offers all meals, including an ample breakfast buffet (kids under 12 eat for free); the Marketessen is open until 2 A.M. Rates range from $69 to $179 for up to five in a room; suites, $209 to $699. Royal Plaza, Box 22203, 1905 Hotel Plaza Blvd., Lake Buena Vista, FL 32830; 407-828-2828 or 800-248-7890; *www.royalplaza.com.*

WYNDHAM PALACE RESORT & SPA: The tallest resort in the Downtown Disney resort area and the largest of the resorts on Hotel Plaza Boulevard (it's actually at the intersection of Hotel Plaza Boulevard and Buena Vista Drive) is a cluster of towers set on 27 acres beside Lake Buena Vista. Each of the 1,014 rooms has a ceiling fan, two phones, including one cordless (with voice mail, speaker-

phone, and high-speed Internet access), two queen beds or a king, a coffeemaker, Sony PlayStation, and weekday newspaper delivery. Most rooms have a balcony or patio. There are also concierge accommodations, one- and two-bedroom suites (with coffeemakers, microwaves, refrigerators, mini-bars, and living rooms with queen sofas), and two-story penthouses. Safes are available free of charge.

The resort's European-style spa features myriad treatments and services, a full-service salon, fitness center, and private lap pool with a resistance jet stream. Recreation Island accommodates two swimming pools, a kiddie pool, whirlpool, sauna, three lighted tennis courts, sand volleyball court, and children's playground and arcade.

The hotel also provides 24-hour room service, and it has boutiques and a guest laundry. Dining spots include the lakeside Watercress Cafe, which serves breakfast and lunch only (Disney characters are in attendance Sunday morning); the Watercress Pastry Shop and Mini Market, open from 6 A.M. to midnight, for baked goods and sandwiches; Arthur's 27, upscale but austere; the Outback restaurant (not part of the chain) for seafood and steak.

The Laughing Kookaburra Good Time Bar, referred to by locals as "The Kook," features "Top 40" music and dancing. The Top of the Palace lounge provides the perfect perch to gaze at the sunset or fireworks over a glass of fine wine. For the allergy prone, 65 EverGreen Rooms provide filtered air and water. Rates for rooms range from $129 to $359 per night (no charge for kids under 18); suites, which sleep up to six, are $229 to $529. Rollaways cost $15 per night, cribs are free. Wyndham Palace Resort & Spa, 1900 Buena Vista Dr., Lake Buena Vista, FL 32830; 407-827-2727 or 800-996-3426; *www.wyndham.com/resorts/mcopv.*

PHOTO BY ALICE GARRARD

Magic Kingdom

The Magic Kingdom is the most enchanting part of the World. Few who visit it are disappointed, and even the most blasé travelers manage a smile. The sight of the soaring spires of Cinderella Castle, the gleaming woodwork of the Main Street shops, and the crescendo of music that follows the parades never fails to have its effect. Even when the crowds are large and the weather is hot, a visitor who has toured this wonderland dozens of times can still look around and think how satisfying this place is for the spirit.

What makes the Magic Kingdom timeless is its combination of the classic and the futuristic. Both childhood favorites and space-age creatures have a home here. Every "land" has a theme, carried through from the costumes worn by the hosts and hostesses and the food served in the restaurants to the merchandise sold in the shops, and even the design of the trash cans. Thousands of details contribute to the overall effect, and recognizing these touches makes any visit more enjoyable.

But the delight most guests experience upon first glimpse of the Magic Kingdom can disappear when disorientation sets in. There are so many bends to every pathway, so many sights and sounds clamoring for attention, it's too easy to wander aimlessly and miss the best the Magic Kingdom has to offer. So we earnestly suggest that you study this chapter before your visit.

LIBERTY SQUARE

16 The Hall of Presidents
17 The Haunted Mansion
18 Liberty Belle Riverboat

FANTASYLAND

19 Cinderella's Golden Carrousel
20 Dumbo the Flying Elephant
21 It's a Small World
22 Mad Tea Party
23 The Many Adventures of Winnie the Pooh
24 Peter Pan's Flight
25 Mickey's PhilharMagic
26 Snow White's Scary Adventures
27 Ariel's Grotto

MICKEY'S TOONTOWN FAIR

28 Donald's Boat
29 Mickey's Country House
30 Minnie's Country House
31 Toontown Hall of Fame
32 The Barnstormer
33 Walt Disney World Railroad Station

TOMORROWLAND

34 Astro Orbiter
35 Buzz Lightyear's Space Ranger Spin
36 The ExtraTERRORestrial Alien Encounter
37 Tomorrowland Indy Speedway
38 Space Mountain
39 Tomorrowland Transit Authority

MAIN STREET, U.S.A.

1 Main Street Vehicles
2 Walt Disney World Railroad
3 Main Street Exposition Hall

ADVENTURELAND

4 Jungle Cruise
5 Pirates of the Caribbean
6 Swiss Family Treehouse
7 The Enchanted Tiki Room—Under New Management
8 The Magic Carpets of Aladdin

FRONTIERLAND

9 Big Thunder Mountain Railroad
10 Country Bear Jamboree
11 Frontierland Shootin' Arcade
12 Splash Mountain
13 Tom Sawyer Island
14 Diamond Horseshoe
15 Walt Disney World Railroad Station

·········· Parade Route

Mickey's Toontown Fair

33
28
32
29
30
31

Fantasyland

27
20
26
19
25
24
21

Liberty Square

16
17
18
11
14

Frontierland

10
13
9
15
12
7
8
6
5
4

Adventureland

N ←

38

34
39
Tomorrowland
36
35
37
22
23

3

Main Street, U.S.A.

1
2

DISNEY RESORT BUS FACILITY

MONORAIL STATION

▼ BOAT LAUNCH

▼ FERRYBOAT LANDING

Getting Oriented

When you visit Walt Disney World's original theme park, it's vital to know the lay of the lands. The Magic Kingdom has seven "lands"—Main Street, U.S.A.; Adventureland; Frontierland; Liberty Square; Fantasyland; Mickey's Toontown Fair; and Tomorrowland. Main Street begins at Town Square, located just inside the park gates, and runs directly to Cinderella Castle. The area in front of the castle is known as the Central Plaza or, more aptly, the Hub. Bridges over the several narrow waterways here serve as passages to each of the lands.

As you enter the park, the first bridge on your left goes to Adventureland; the next, to Liberty Square and Frontierland. On your right, the first bridge heads to Tomorrowland, the second to Fantasyland and Mickey's Toontown Fair. The end points of the pathways leading to the lands are linked by a street that is roughly circular, so that the layout of the Magic Kingdom resembles a wheel. All attractions, restaurants, and shops are found along the wheel's rim and spokes.

Guidemaps and times guides are available at the turnstiles, at City Hall in Town Square, and at many shops.. Be sure to pick them up as soon as possible. You'll find them to be valuable navigational and scheduling resources.

HOW TO GET THERE

Take Exit 64B off I-4. Continue about four miles to the Auto Plaza and park; walk or take a tram to the main entrance complex, known as the Transportation and Ticket Center (TTC). Choose a seven-minute ferry ride or a slightly shorter trip by monorail for the last leg of an anticipation-filled journey.

By WDW Transportation: From the Grand Floridian and Polynesian: monorail or boat. Contemporary may be reached by monorail or walkway. (It is about a 10- to 15-minute stroll.) From Epcot: monorail to the TTC, then transfer to the Magic Kingdom monorail or ferry. From Disney-MGM Studios, Animal Kingdom, Downtown Disney, and the resorts on Hotel Plaza Boulevard: buses to the TTC, then transfer to ferry or monorail. From Fort Wilderness and the Wilderness Lodge: boat. From all other Walt Disney World resorts: buses.

PARKING

All-day parking at the Magic Kingdom is $7 for day visitors (free to Walt Disney World resort guests with presentation of a valid resort ID or an annual pass). Simply bear left after passing through the Auto Plaza; attendants will direct you into one of a dozen lots, all named after Disney characters. Minnie, Sleepy, and Dopey are within walking distance of the TTC; other lots are served by trams.

Be sure to note the section and aisle in which you park. Also, know that the parking ticket allows for re-entry to the parking area throughout the day.

HOURS

The Magic Kingdom is generally open from 9 A.M. to 7 P.M. However, during busy seasons, it's open later. It's best to reach the park entrance about a half hour before the opening time. To avoid the morning crush, consider postponing your visit until 1 P.M. or later.

Note that on select days, the Magic Kingdom opens one hour early for Walt Disney World resort guests only (this is known as the "Extra Magic Hour"). Call 407-824-4321 or visit *www.disneyworld.com* for details and current schedules. The park tends to be more crowded on such days, so consider starting here and "hopping" elsewhere later in the day.

GETTING AROUND

Walt Disney World Railroad steam trains make a 20-minute loop of the park, stopping to pick up and drop off passengers at stations on Main Street, Frontierland, and Mickey's Toontown Fair (It's an efficient way to travel when parades are being run or there's a lot of foot traffic). Horseless carriages, a fire engine, and horse-drawn trolleys take turns offering one-way trips down Main Street.

Park Primer

BABY FACILITIES

The best place in the Magic Kingdom to take care of little ones' needs is the Baby Care Center. This cheery site, equipped with changing tables and facilities for nursing mothers, is located next to the Crystal Palace restaurant. Disposable diapers are for sale at many Magic Kingdom shops (they're kept behind the counter, just ask). All park restrooms are equipped with changing facilities.

CAMERA NEEDS

The Camera Center in the Town Square Exposition Hall proffers disposable cameras as well as film and batteries. Two-hour film processing is available here and wherever you see a Photo Express sign. Film is also sold in most Magic Kingdom shops.

DISABILITY INFORMATION

Most Magic Kingdom shops and restaurants, and many attractions, are accessible to guests using wheelchairs. Additional services are available for guests with visual or hearing disabilities. The *Guidebook for Guests with Disabilities* provides an overview of all services available, including transportation, parking, and attraction access. For more information, refer to the "Travelers with Disabilities" section of the *Getting Ready to Go* chapter.

FERRY VERSUS MONORAIL

For guests arriving by car or bus, it's necessary to decide whether to travel to the Magic Kingdom by ferry or monorail. The monorail makes the trip from the Transportation and Ticket Center (TTC) in about five minutes while the ferry takes about seven. During busy seasons, the ferry will often get you there faster (long lines can form at the monorail and most people don't make the short walk to the

ferry landing). Vacationers who use wheelchairs should note that while the monorail platforms are accessible, the ramp leading to the boarding area is a bit on the steep side.

FIRST AID

A registered nurse tends to minor medical problems at the First Aid Center, located near the Crystal Palace restaurant.

INFORMATION

City Hall, just inside the park entrance, serves as the Magic Kingdom's information headquarters. Guest Relations representatives can answer questions. Guidemaps and times guides, updated weekly (including details about entertainment, as well as character greeting times and locations), are available here, and all kinds of arrangements can be made, including priority seating for restaurants. Should you have problems with your ticket or a question about the number of unused days remaining on a ticket, City Hall is the place to go.

LOCKERS

Attended lockers are located at Station Break, underneath the Main Street Railroad Station just inside the park entrance. Lockers are also available at the Transportation and Ticket Center (TTC). Cost is $5 per day (plus a $2 refundable deposit) for unlimited use. Certain oversize items can be checked at the Station Break desk (the spot where lockers are paid for).

LOST & FOUND

On the day of your visit, report lost articles at City Hall or at the TTC. Recovered items can also be claimed at these locations. After your visit, call 407-824-4245.

Hot Tip!

Certain attractions keep shorter hours than the Magic Kingdom itself (i.e., The Hall of Presidents and The Tomorrowland Transit Authority). To make sure you catch all your favorites, check a times guide when you enter the park.

Pal Mickey

He may look like just another plush toy, but Pal Mickey is a bit extraordinary. He's actually a high-tech theme park tour guide and companion. As guests stroll through the parks, Mickey shares helpful park-related advice, tells jokes and Disney fun facts, and plays games.

Pal Mickey may be rented for $8 (including tax) per day. For $50, you can take him home (where he will continue to amuse with interactive games). He's available in select shops at all four Disney theme parks, at Walt Disney World owned-and-operated resorts, and at the Once Upon a Toy shop at the Downtown Disney Marketplace (purchase only).

LOST CHILDREN

Report lost children at City Hall or the Baby Care Center, or alert the nearest Disney employee to the problem.

MONEY MATTERS

The Magic Kingdom has three ATMs: under Main Street's train station, near the Diamond Horseshoe Saloon in Frontierland, and at the Tomorrowland Light & Power Co. arcade (next to Space Mountain). Most foreign currency can be exchanged at City Hall.

Credit cards (American Express, Visa, MasterCard, JCB, Discover Card, Diner's Club, and the Disney Credit Card) are accepted as payment for admission, merchandise, and meals at all full-service restaurants and fast-food locations. Traveler's checks and Walt Disney World resort ID cards are also accepted in most places. Some food and souvenir carts accept cash only.

Disney Dollars are available at City Hall (as well as all Disney Stores) in $1, $5, and $10 denominations. They are accepted for dining and merchandise throughout Walt Disney World and can be exchanged at any time for U.S. currency.

PACKAGE PICKUP

Individual shops can arrange for large or heavy purchases to be transported to a location inside Town Square Exposition Hall for pickup between noon and park closing time. The service is free.

SAME-DAY RE-ENTRY

Be sure to have your hand stamped and to retain your ticket upon exiting the park if you plan to return later the same day.

STROLLERS & WHEELCHAIRS

Stroller and Wheelchair Rental, on the right, inside the Magic Kingdom entrance, offers one-day rentals of strollers, wheelchairs, and Electric Convenience Vehicles (ECVs). The cost for strollers and wheelchairs is $7, plus a $1 refundable deposit; $30 for ECVs, with a $10 refundable deposit. Quantities are limited. Hold onto your receipt; it can be used on the same day to get a replacement stroller or wheelchair at any of the theme parks.

Note that, during busy times, the park may offer "stroller express" service. Guests prepay for a stroller before passing through the turnstiles and bypass a potentially lengthy line once inside.

To prevent your stroller from getting lost in a sea of stroller clones, consider personalizing it with an item such as a ribbon or a balloon.

SECURITY CHECK

Guests entering Disney theme parks may be subject to a security check. Backpacks, parcels, purses, etc., may be searched by Disney security personnel before guests are permitted to pass through the turnstiles.

TIP BOARDS

Located at the end of Main Street, U.S.A., closest to Cinderella Castle and in Tomorrowland, Tip Boards are an excellent source of information on waiting times for attractions, as well as showtimes and other entertainment information. Check the boards throughout the day. The Main Street board is often overseen by a park-savvy Disney employee, ready and willing to answer guest questions.

Admission Prices

ONE-DAY TICKET
(Restricted to use only in the Magic Kingdom. Prices include sales tax and are likely to change in 2004.)

Adult	.$55.38
Child*	.$44.73

*3 through 9 years of age; children under 3 free

Main Street, U.S.A.

Most of the structures along the thorough-fare are given over to shops, and each one is different. Some emporiums are big and bustling, others are relatively quiet and orderly; some are spacious and airy, others are cozy and dark. Inside and out, maintenance and housekeeping are superb.

> ## Hot Tip!
> Plan to do your shopping in the early afternoon, rather than at day's end when the Main Street shops are normally jammed.

White-suited sanitation workers patrol the street to pick up litter and quickly shovel up any droppings from the horses that pull the trolley cars from Town Square to the Hub. As in the rest of the Magic Kingdom, the pavement here is washed down every night with fire hoses. There's one crew of maintenance workers whose sole job is to change the little white lights around the roofs; another crew devotes itself to keeping the woodwork painted. As soon as these people have worked their way as far as the Hub, they start all over again at Town Square. The greenish, horse-shaped, cast-iron hitching posts are repainted 20 times a year on average—and totally scraped down each time.

Stepping onto Main Street, U.S.A. is like jumping through a time portal. Welcome to turn-of-the-century America! Horse-drawn trolleys are the transportation of choice, peppy patriotic music underscores the bustle of merry, moving masses, and the tantalizing aroma of fresh-baked cookies constantly perfumes the air.

A rose-colored retrospective? Maybe. But this is Disney's version of a small-town Main Street—and the charm of this nostalgic land is lost on no one. Anchored by an old-fashioned train station at one end and a fairy-tale castle at the other, Main Street, U.S.A. whisks you from reality to fantasy in a few short blocks.

All of the addresses here feature just-dried coats of paint, curlicued gingerbread moldings, and pretty details. Add to that the baskets of hanging plants and genuine-looking gaslights, and Main Street, U.S.A. becomes a true showplace—both in the bright light of high noon and after nightfall, when the tiny lights edging all of the rooflines are flicked on.

The street represents an ideal American town. Although such a town never really existed, many claim to have served as the inspiration for it. Chances are Walt Disney got the idea from Marceline, Missouri, the tiny rural town that was his boyhood home.

The "attractions" along Main Street, U.S.A. are relatively minor compared to the really big deals such as Tomorrowland's Space Mountain, Frontierland's Splash Mountain, or The Haunted Mansion in Liberty Square. But each and every shop has its own quota of merchandise that is meant as much for show as for sale. It's almost as entertaining to watch the cooks stir up gooey batches of peanut brittle at the Main Street Confectionery as it is to actually savor a sweet sample. The shop windows, particularly at the Emporium, are also worth a look.

Once you start to meander along Main Street, be sure to notice the names on the second-story windows. Above the Uptown Jewelers store (near the Confectionery) is that of Walt's nephew, Roy E. Disney. And you'll see Walt's name above the ice cream parlor. Other names are those of people connected with The Walt Disney Company.

Note: Attractions in Main Street, U.S.A. are described in the order in which they are encountered upon entering the park.

WALT DISNEY WORLD RAILROAD: The best introduction to the Magic Kingdom, the 1½-mile journey on this rail line is as much a must for the first-time visitor as it is for railroad buffs. It offers an excellent orientation as it passes by most of the park's major lands.

The 1928 steam engine happens to be exactly the same age as Mickey Mouse. Walt Disney himself was a railroad aficionado. During the early years of television, viewers watched films of him circling his own backyard in a one-eighth-scale train, the *Lilly Belle* (named for his wife).

The Walt Disney World Railroad also has a *Lilly Belle* among its quartet of locomotives. The others are named *Roy O. Disney*, *Walter E. Disney*, and *Roger E. Broggie* (a Disney Imagineer who shared Walt Disney's enthusiasm for antique trains). All of them were built in the U.S. around the turn of the century and later taken to Mexico to haul freight and passengers in the Yucatán, where Disney scouts found them in 1969. The United Railways of Yucatán was using them to carry sugarcane. Brought north once again, they were completely overhauled, and even the smallest of parts were reworked or replaced.

The train circles the park in 20 minutes, making stops in Frontierland, Mickey's Toontown Fair, and Main Street, U.S.A. Trains arrive in each station every 4 to 10 minutes. The line is usually shortest in Toontown, but there's rarely a long wait at any of the stations. The train is the most efficient way to reach the exit when parades take over Main Street, U.S.A.

Hot Tip!

Guests staying at the Contemporary resort can walk to and from the Magic Kingdom's front gate. The trip takes about ten minutes. It's handy when there's a long line for the monorail.

Note: The Walt Disney World Railroad does not run during fireworks presentations.

MAIN STREET VEHICLES: A number of these can be seen traveling up and down Main Street—horseless carriages and jitneys patterned after turn-of-the-century vehicles (but fitted with Jeep transmissions and special mufflers that make a putt-putt-putting sound); a spiffy scarlet fire engine; and a troop of trolleys drawn by Belgians and Percherons, two strong breeds of horse that once pulled plows in Europe. These animals—weighing in at about a ton each and shod with plastic (easier on their hooves)—pull the trolley the length of Main Street about two dozen times during each of their working days. Between shifts, they can be seen resting inside Main Street's Car Barn. Feel free to stop by and say hello. At day's end they go home to their barn at Fort Wilderness (where you can also visit them). The horses are sometimes hosed down next to the Main Street firehouse. Youngsters love to watch.

TOWN SQUARE EXPOSITION HALL: A veritable shrine to photography, Town Square Exposition Hall does double duty as a museum and camera-supply shop. Engaging exhibits take guests on a voyage through time, connecting the high-tech cameras of today with their primitive cousins of yesteryear. The humble beginnings of Mickey Mouse are celebrated here, too. *Steamboat Willie* and other classic Mickey toons (previously shown at the Main Street Cinema) are screened throughout the day.

Be sure to take your own camera to the Exposition Hall—photo opportunities abound. You can also pay to have your image superimposed on a Disney background. Don't forget to say cheese.

Hot Tip!

Mondays tend to be the most crowded days at the Magic Kingdom.

Adventureland

Adventureland seems to have even more atmosphere than the other lands. That may be a result of its neat separation from the rest of the Magic Kingdom by the bridge over Main Street on one end and by a gallerylike structure (where it merges with Frontierland) on the other, or, possibly, it's because of the abundance of landscaping.

The centrally located attraction, The Magic Carpets of Aladdin, sets the tone for this recently refurbished corner of the Kingdom. Still surrounded by tropical splendor, the area has taken on the look and feel of a bustling marketplace—the likes of which one might stumble upon in Agrabah. The shops here offer imports from around the globe.

As guests stroll away from Main Street, U.S.A., they just may hear the sound of beating drums, the squawks of parrots, and the regular boom of a cannon. Paces quicken. And the wonders soon to be encountered do not disappoint.

SWISS FAMILY TREEHOUSE: "Everything we need is right at our fingertips," said the father in Disney's 1960 rendition of the classic story *Swiss Family Robinson*. He was describing the treehouse that he and his kids built for the family after their ship was wrecked in a storm. When given a chance—several adventures later—to leave the island, all but one son decided to stay on. That decision is not hard to understand after a tour of the Magic Kingdom's version of the Robinsons' banyan-tree home. This is everybody's idea of the perfect treehouse, with its many levels and comforts—patchwork quilts, lovely mahogany furniture, candles stuck in abalone shells, even running water in every room. (The system is rather ingenious.)

The Spanish moss draping the branches is real; the tree itself—unofficially christened *Disneyodendron eximus*, a genus that is translated roughly as "out-of-the-ordinary Disney tree"—was constructed entirely by the props department. Some statistics: The roots, which are made of concrete, poke 42 feet into the ground, and about 300,000 lifelike polyethylene leaves "grow" on the tree's 1,400 individual branches.

JUNGLE CRUISE: FP Inspired in part by the 1955 documentary film *The African Lion*, this ten-minute adventure is one of the crowning achievements of Magic Kingdom landscape artists for the way it takes guests through surroundings as diverse as a Southeast Asian jungle, the Nile Valley, and an Amazon rain forest. Along the way, passengers encounter zebras, giraffes, lions, headhunters, and more (all of the Audio-Animatronics variety); they also see elephants bathing, and tour a temple—while listening to an amusing, though corny, spiel delivered by the skipper. (Bet you didn't know that Schweitzer Falls was named after the famous doctor Albert . . . Falls.)

This adventure, which is best enjoyed by daylight, is one of the park's slower-moving attractions, and tends to be quite crowded from late morning until late afternoon.

THE ENCHANTED TIKI ROOM—UNDER NEW MANAGEMENT:

Though cherished for its historical significance (the Tiki Birds starred in the first Audio-Animatronics attraction ever), the Tiki show was growing a bit tiresome. Now, thanks to clever new co-stars and zippy new tunes, the Tiki Room is rockin' once again.

The nine-minute show still features Michael, Pierre, Fritz, and José (who is pining for his beloved Rosita)—plus some 200 birds, flowers, and tiki statues singing up a tropical storm. But before long, their sweet serenade is interrupted by an unimpressed Iago (Jafar's partner in crime from *Aladdin*).

It seems that Iago, along with Zazu from *The Lion King*, is a new owner of the Tiki Room—and he has big changes in store for the show. In a fractured version of "Friend Like Me," the bratty Iago warns the Tiki Birds that they'd "better get hip, or the audience will disappear." In a welcome twist, it is Iago who disappears, leaving the Tikis to prove just how hip they really are. While it helps to have seen the old show to appreciate all of the silly humor, veterans and newcomers alike are sure to get a kick out of The Enchanted Tiki Room—Under New Management.

THE MAGIC CARPETS OF ALADDIN:

Welcome to Agrabah! Adventureland's newest attraction is conveniently situated in the center of the action. It features not one, but 16 carpets that fly through the air in a fashion similar to those airborne elephants over in Fantasyland. Each flying carpet accommodates four guests at a time. Depending on where you sit, you'll have control of the carpet's vertical movement (the controls are in the front). Be prepared to dodge the occasional stream of liquid, courtesy of an expectorating camel.

PIRATES OF THE CARIBBEAN:

Quite simply, this is one of the very best of the Magic Kingdom's classic adventures. The beloved ten-minute cruise is a Disneyland original, added to Walt Disney World's Magic Kingdom (in slightly revised form) due to popular demand. Here, guests board a small boat and set sail for a series of scenes showing a pirate raid on a Caribbean island town, dodging cannon fire and weathering one small, though legitimate, watery dip along the way. There are singing marauders, plastered pigs, and wily wenches; the observant will note that the leg of one rum-swilling swashbuckler, dangled over the edge of a bridge, is actually hairy. What's not to love?

While it's by no means the most politically correct attraction on-property, the rendition of "Yo Ho, Yo Ho, a Pirate's Life for Me"—the attraction's theme song—makes what is actually a rather brutal scenario into something that comes across as good fun.

Before entering the queue area, stop and give a nod to the parrot dressed as a pirate, near the Pirates of the Caribbean sign. And, yes, this is the attraction that inspired the movie.

Frontierland

With the Rivers of America lapping at its borders and Big Thunder Mountain rising up in the rear, this re-creation of the American Frontier encompasses the area from New England to the Southwest, from the 1770s to the 1880s. In these parts, shops, restaurants, and attractions have unpainted barn siding or stone or clapboard walls, and outside there are several wooden sidewalks of the sort Marshal Matt Dillon used to stride along. The Walt Disney World Railroad makes a stop here.

GOOFY'S COUNTRY DANCIN' JAMBOREE: The Diamond Horseshoe Saloon is now the site of the rootin-tootin-est country dance party the Wild West has to offer. During each 18-minute audience-participation performance, Goofy and his pals (Chip, Dale, Woody, Jessie, and Bullseye) teach young'uns how to country line dance.

Note that the Diamond Horseshoe Saloon Revue has ridden off into the sunset.

FRONTIERLAND SHOOTIN' ARCADE: This arcade is set in an 1850s town in the Southwest Territory. Positions overlook Boothill, a town complete with bank, jail, hotel, and cemetery.

Genuine Hawkins .54-caliber buffalo rifles have been refitted, and when the infrared beam strikes any of the targets, an interesting result is triggered. Struck tombstones rise, sink, spin, or change their epitaphs; hit a cloud and a ghost rider gallops across the sky; a bull's-eye on a grave digger's shovel causes a skull to pop out of the grave. Sound effects—howling coyotes, creaking bridges, and shooting guns—are created by a digital audio system.

Admission tickets do not include use of the Frontierland Shootin' Arcade; there is an additional charge to play here.

COUNTRY BEAR JAMBOREE: The Country Bears may never make it to Broadway, but they don't seem to mind. Disney's brood of banjo-strummin' bruins has been playing to packed houses in Grizzly Hall for more than a quarter century. Judging by all the toe tappin' and hand clappin' that accompany each performance, the show remains a countrified crowd pleaser. As for the few folks who aren't charmed by the backwoods ballads and down-home humor, well, they just have to grin and *bear* it.

As guests are settling into their seats (all of which provide a decent view), Buff, Max, and Melvin are beginning to grumble. Despite their status as permanent fixtures in the theater, the mounted animal heads would rather not "hang around all day" waiting for the show to get going. The 17-minute review opens with a rousing ditty by the Five Bear Rugs. The wheels set in motion, the remaining songs come fast and furious. Together, they capture the spirit of a genre that has a tendency to celebrate and lampoon itself simultaneously.

For example, Bunny, Bubbles, and Beulah bemoan, "All the Guys That Turn Me On Turn Me Down"; Henry, the easy-going emcee who sports a coonskin cap (which is still attached to the 'coon), belts out "The Ballad of Davy Crockett"; and Big Al, the oversize tone-deaf fan-favorite, woefully croons "Blood on the Saddle," much to the delight of the giggle-prone audience.

The bears present a special Christmas concert during the holiday season.

Timing Tip: Lines can get long during busy periods. It's worth noting, however, that huge groups are admitted together—so once a line starts moving, it dwindles rather quickly.

TOM SAWYER ISLAND: This small patch of land in the middle of the Rivers of America has hills to scramble up; a working windmill, Harper's Mill, with an owl in the rafters and a perpetually creaky waterwheel; and a few pitch-black (and scary) caves. To reach the island, guests take a raft across the river. (It's the only way to get there and back.)

Paths wind this way and that, and it's easy to get disoriented, especially the first time around. Keep an eye out for the large mounted maps scattered about the island.

There are two bridges here—a suspension bridge and a barrel bridge, which floats atop some lashed-together wooden barrels. When one person bounces, everybody lurches—and all but the most chickenhearted laugh. Both of the bridges are easy to miss, so be sure to keep your eyes peeled.

Across the suspension bridge is Fort Langhorn. Poke around and you'll discover a twisting, dark, and occasionally scary escape tunnel. Walk along the pathway on the banks of the Rivers of America and you'll find your way back to the bridges.

The whole island seems as rugged as back-woods Missouri, and probably as a result, it actually feels a lot more remote than it is—enough to be able to provide some welcome respite from the bustle.

One particularly pleasant way to relax here is over lemonade and a snack at Aunt Polly's Dockside Inn. (The pickles are quite popular.) Restrooms are located at the main raft landing and inside Fort Langhorn.

Timing Tip: This attraction closes at dusk.

BIRNBAUM'S ★BEST★ **SPLASH MOUNTAIN:** FP On the day this attraction made its official 1992 Walt Disney World debut, *everyone* got soaked—thanks in part to a particularly potent Florida rain cloud. But the rain wasn't entirely responsible for the sea of soggy Magic Kingdom guests. The five-story drop into an aqueous briar patch was. And a steady stream of thrill seekers has been taking the plunge ever since.

In this guaranteed smile inducer, guests enjoy a waterborne journey through brightly colored swamps and bayous, and down waterfalls, and

> ## Hot Tip!
> If you'd like to get soaked on Splash Mountain, request a seat up front.

are finally hurtled from the peak of the mountain to a briar-laced pond five stories below.

Splash Mountain is based on the animated sequences in Walt Disney's 1946 film *Song of the South.* The scenery entertains as the story line follows Br'er Rabbit as he tries to reach his "laughin' place." It's tough for a first-time rider to take in all the details, since the tension of waiting for the big drop is all-consuming.

It is a bit terrifying at the top, but once back

on the ground, it seems most riders can't wait for another trip—even though they may get drenched. (Water-wary guests are often seen wearing rain ponchos on this attraction. On the other hand, if you *want* to get wet, try to sit up front or on the right; seats in the back receive a smaller splash.)

By the second or third time around, it's possible to relax a bit, enjoy the interior scenes, and take in the spectacular views of the Magic Kingdom from the top of the mountain. At this point you may even manage to keep your eyes open for the duration of the final fall—or at least part of it.

Splash Mountain's designers not only borrowed characters and color-saturated settings from *Song of the South,* but also used quite a bit of the film's Academy Award–winning music in this attraction. As a matter of fact, the song in Splash Mountain's final scene, "Zip-a-Dee-Doo-Dah," has become something of a Disney anthem over the years.

Note: You must be at least 40 inches tall to ride

Splash Mountain. (There is a small play area nearby to keep little ones occupied while older kids ride.) If you'd like to absorb as little precipitation as possible, sit on the left side of the log.

 BIG THUNDER MOUNTAIN RAILROAD: FP It's certainly not hard to spot Big Thunder, the lone red rock formation this side of the Mississippi. Even newcomers to the Magic Kingdom will be able to distinguish the landmark from its famed counterparts—Splash and Space mountains—because it's the only one that actually looks like a mountain range. The designers took Utah's Bryce Canyon as inspiration, and the resemblance is remarkable.

According to Disney legend, the 2.5-acre mountain is chock-full of gold. Unfortunately for the residents of Tumbleweed, the local mining town, a flood has ruined any chance of uncovering the remaining gold. Before these prospectors find drier land, they are having one last party at the saloon to celebrate their riches. Even though in danger of washing away, they don't seem too worried, and guests who decide to take a trip on the Big Thunder Mountain Railroad have nothing to worry about either.

As passengers board the 15-row train, they are advised to "hang on to your hats and glasses 'cause this here's the wildest ride in the wilderness." Do heed the warning, but

don't despair. The ride, though thrilling, is relatively tame, so relax and enjoy the sights. Note that passengers seated nearest the caboose experience more turbulence than those up front.

A bleating billy goat atop a peak, a family of opossums hanging overhead, and a dark cavern full of bats, not to mention chickens, donkeys, and washed-up miners, can be spotted along the way. Be sure to keep an eye out for the not-yet-sunken saloon—it's easy to miss the first time around.

A continuous string of curves and dips around Big Thunder's pinnacles and caverns is sure to please thrill seekers of all ages, but the adrenaline surge is caused by more than just the speed of the trip. The added sound of a rickety track, a steam whistle that blows right before the train accelerates into a curve, and an unexpected earthquake all compound the passengers' anticipation, making this attraction one of the Magic Kingdom's most popular. Note that you must be at least 40 inches tall and immune to motion sickness to experience the Big Thunder Mountain Railroad attraction.

Timing Tip: Plan to visit early in the morning, during a parade, or just before closing time. Of course, you can always plan ahead and get a Fastpass. If you plan to visit during a parade, consider taking the Walt Disney World Railroad to the Frontierland station.

Liberty Square

The transition between Frontierland on one side and Fantasyland on the other is so smooth that it's hard to say just when you arrive at Liberty Square, yet ultimately there's no mistaking the location. The small buildings are clapboard or brick and topped with weather vanes; the decorative moldings are Federal or Georgian in style; the glass is sometimes wavy, and there are flower boxes in shop windows, brightly colored gardens, neatly trimmed borders of Japanese yew, and masses of azaleas in a number of varieties and shades of white, pink, and red. There's a bounty of good shops, most notably The Yankee Trader and Ye Olde Christmas Shoppe; plus two of the park's most famous attractions, The Haunted Mansion and The Hall of Presidents; and the Liberty Tree Tavern, one of the few full-service restaurants in the Magic Kingdom.

Note: Attractions are described in the order they are reached upon entering the land from the Hub, heading away from the Castle.

THE HALL OF PRESIDENTS: This is not one of those laugh-a-minute attractions, like Splash Mountain or the Haunted Mansion; it's long on patriotism and short on silliness. But the detail of this classic 20-minute show certainly is fascinating. After a film (which is presented on a sweeping 70-mm screen) discusses the importance of the Constitution from the time of its framing through the dawn of the space age, the curtain goes up, revealing a cast of American leaders. All 42 chief executives are represented by lifelike Audio-Animatronic likenesses. (A small portion of the show was held over from the Disney-designed Illinois Pavilion's exhibition Great Moments with Mr. Lincoln, from New York's 1964–65 World's Fair.)

All of the chief executives are announced in a roll call and each President responds with a nod; careful observers will note the others swaying and nodding, fidgeting, and whispering to each other during the proceedings. Both Abraham Lincoln and George W. Bush have speaking roles. President Bush recorded his own speech, which addresses issues such as education and tolerance.

Costumes were created by two famous film tailors coaxed out of retirement. Not only are the styles those of the period in which each president lived but so are the tailoring techniques and the fabrics. Some had to be specially woven for the show. Each of the Audio-Animatronics figures has at least one change of clothes—jewelry, shoes, hair texture, and even George Washington's chair are re-created exactly as indicated by careful research of paintings, diaries, newspapers, and government archives. Perceptive viewers should be able to see the braces on Franklin Delano Roosevelt's legs. The effect is so lifelike that the figures look almost real, even at very close range.

Timing Tip: Planning to pop in on the presidents? Visit on the hour and the half hour. That's usually when the show starts.

LIBERTY BELLE RIVERBOAT: The *Liberty Belle*, built in dry dock at Walt Disney World, is a real steamboat. Its boiler turns water into steam, which is then piped to the engine, which drives the paddle wheel that propels the boat. It is not the real article in one respect, however: It moves through the nine-foot-deep Rivers of America on an underwater rail.

The pleasant ride, with narration by an actor playing Mark Twain, is a good way to beat the heat on steamy afternoons. En route, a variety of props create a sort of Wild West effect: moose, deer, a burning cabin, and the like. The tour is completed within 17 minutes.

THE HAUNTED MANSION: FP This eight-minute experience is among the Magic Kingdom's most enjoyable. However, guests who expect to be scared silly when they enter the big old house, modeled after those built in New York's Hudson River Valley in the 18th century, will be just a tad unfulfilled. This haunted house steers clear of anything too terrifying, and a good-spirited voice-over keeps the mood light.

Once you're inside the portrait hall, entered after passing through the front doors, it's amusing to speculate: Is the ceiling moving up, or is the floor dropping? It's also where you meet your "Ghost Host" and learn how he met his untimely demise.

The spooky journey through the mansion takes place in a "Doom Buggy." The attraction is full of tricks and treats for the eyes; just when you think you've seen it all, there's something new: bats' eyes on the wallpaper, a suit of armor that comes alive, a terrified

cemetery watchman and his mangy mutt, and the image of a creepy lady in a crystal ball.

One of the biggest jobs of the maintenance crews here is not cleaning up, but keeping things dirty. Since the mansion is littered with some 200 trunks, chairs, dress forms, harps, rugs, and assorted knickknacks, it requires a lot of dust. This is purchased by the five-pound bagful and distributed by a device that looks as if it were meant to spread grass seed—sort of a vacuum cleaner in reverse. Local legend has it that enough dust has been used since the park's 1971 opening to bury the mansion. (Which begs the question: Where did it all go?) Cobwebs are bought in liquid form and strung up by a secret process.

When waiting to enter, take note of the amusing inscriptions on the tombstones in the overgrown cemetery.

Fantasyland

Walt Disney called this a "timeless land of enchantment," and his successors termed it "the happiest land of all"—and it is, for some. It is the home of a number of rides that are particularly well liked by children.

CINDERELLA CASTLE: Just as Mickey stands for all the merriment in Walt Disney World, this storybook castle represents the hopes and dreams of childhood—a time in life when anything is possible.

At a height of about 190 feet, Cinderella Castle is nearly twice the height of Disneyland's Sleeping Beauty Castle. It was inspired by the architecture of 12th- and 13th-century France, the country where the classic fairy tale originated, as well as the Bavarian King Ludwig's fortress and designs prepared for Disney's 1950 classic, *Cinderella*.

Unlike real European castles, this one is made of steel and fiberglass; in lieu of dungeons, it has service tunnels. Its upper reaches contain security rooms; there's even

an apartment originally meant for the Disney family (but never occupied). From any vantage point, Cinderella Castle looks as if it came straight from the land of make-believe.

Mosaic Murals: The elaborate murals beneath the castle's archway rank among the true wonders of the World. They tell the story of the little cinder girl and one of childhood's happiest happily-ever-afters, using a million bits of glass in some 500 different colors, plus real silver and 14-karat gold.

Cinderella Wishing Well: This pleasant alcove, nestled along a path to Tomorrowland, is a nice spot from which to gaze at the castle. Any coins tossed into the water are donated to children's charities. Don't forget to make a wish as you part with your penny.

CINDERELLA'S GOLDEN CARROUSEL: Not everything in the Magic Kingdom is a Disney version of the real article. This carousel, discovered at the now-defunct Olympic Park in Maplewood, New Jersey, was built back in 1917. That was the end of the golden century of carousel building that began around 1825. During the Disney refurbishing, many of the original horses were replaced with horses made of fiberglass.

FAIRY TALE GARDEN: This special little corner of the Kingdom is tucked beside Cinderella Castle. Several times a day, Belle (from *Beauty and the Beast*) stops by to read a story and, afterward, mingle with guests. There is seating for about 20 at a time. Check a park guidemap for showtimes.

MICKEY'S PHILHARMAGIC: FP Mickey Mouse and a panoply of his pals (including Donald, Simba, and Ariel) strut their musical stuff in this ear- and eye-popping production.

The show, which marked its debut in late 2003, is an ambitious amalgam of music, puppetry, and animated film. Of course, this being Fantasyland, the film is by no means ordinary. It's crisp, colorful, and, to the delight of many a goggle-wearing guest, three-dimensional. The 3-D experience unfolds on a 150-foot-wide canvas, which is one of the largest screens ever created for a film of this kind. Special effects and surprises take place off-screen, too. Overall, the experience is intended to engage guests of any age.

The show is presented in the PhilharMagic Concert Hall, the venue that once hosted the Mickey Mouse Revue (a musical romp that ran from 1971 through 1980) and, most recently, The Legend of the Lion King. (*Lion King* devotees can get their fill by taking in the Festival of the Lion King stage show at Disney's Animal Kingdom park.)

As with many attractions, there may be occasional moments of darkness. If you're unsure as to whether your child might find this (or any attraction) unsettling, express your concern to an attendant. They'll help you make the right decision.

 PETER PAN'S FLIGHT: 🅵🅿 "Come on, everybody, here we go!" So says Peter Pan at the start of this nonstop flight to Never Land. The three-minute adventure, which takes you soaring in a pirate ship, fancifully retells the story of Peter Pan—a boy with a knack for flying and an immunity to maturity. The effects in this classic Fantasyland attraction are simple, but enchanting.

The journey starts in the Darling family nursery—which siblings Wendy, Michael, and John quickly abandon to follow Peter Pan on a trip to his homeland. As in Disney's animated feature, one of the most beautiful scenes—and one that makes this attraction a treat for grown-ups as well as smaller folk—is the sight of nighttime London, dark blue and speckled with twinkling lights. Keep your eyes peeled for such landmarks as Big Ben and London Bridge.

By the time you spot your first mermaid, you're deep in the heart of Never Land. Alas, something is terribly wrong—Captain Hook and his buccaneer buddies have taken the Darling kids captive. It's all really a trap for Peter (Hook is still peeved at Pan for serving his hand to a hungry crocodile). Does everyone live happily ever after? We'll *never* tell.

Timing Tip: The slow-moving lines for this popular attraction can be somewhat daunting.

> ## Hot Tip!
> Toddlers love to splash in the fountains near Ariel's Grotto (in Fantasyland) and Donald's Boat (in Toontown)—waterproof diapers are an absolute must.

Take advantage of the Fastpass option. Or plan to arrive close to when the park opens, late in the evening, or during any of the parades throughout the day.

IT'S A SMALL WORLD: *Hola! Guten Tag! Hello!* No matter what language you speak, what you look like, or where you live, you still have a lot in common with folks the world over (including an especially high tolerance for a singsong melody that repeatedly reminds us that it's a small world, after all). That's the message driving this ten-minute boat ride around the world.

Originally created for New York's 1964–65 World's Fair, the attraction is an oldie-but-goodie (and is quite popular with young children). The ride moves at slightly swifter than snail's pace, drifting past hundreds of colorfully costumed dolls from around the world—all of whom know all the words to the ride's infectious theme song.

A showcase of diversity, the attraction is a simple celebration of human similarities. It's also a relaxing alternative to many of the park's higher-tech, longer-line attractions.

DUMBO THE FLYING ELEPHANT: This is purely and simply a kiddie ride, though children of all ages have admitted to loving it. A beloved symbol of Fantasyland, the ride is most popular with the 2- to 7-year-old set. Inspired by the 1941 film classic *Dumbo*, the attraction lasts two memorable minutes. Consider stopping here first thing in the

Hot Tip!

Many of the Fantasyland attractions are dark, and in some cases special effects may be too intense for small children.

morning, or during the afternoon parade, when the line—which is often prohibitively long—thins a bit. Incidentally, the rodent in the center of the circle of flying elephants is Dumbo's faithful sidekick, Timothy Mouse.

MAD TEA PARTY: The theme of this two-minute ride—in a group of oversize pastel-colored teacups that whirl and spin wildly—was inspired by a scene in the Disney Studios' 1951 movie production of Lewis Carroll's novel *Alice in Wonderland*. During the sequence in question, the Mad Hatter hosts a tea party for his un-birthday.

Unlike many rides in Fantasyland, this is not just for younger kids; the 9-to-20 crowd seems to like it best. Keep in mind that when the cups stop spinning, your head may continue to do so. Skip this ride if you suffer from motion sickness or if you've recently enjoyed a snack. Don't miss the woozy mouse that pops out of the teapot at the center of the platform—he ignored our advice.

 THE MANY ADVENTURES OF WINNIE THE POOH: FP
Perhaps as a tribute to the mischievous Mr. Toad, the host of the attraction previously housed here, everyone's favorite honey-lovin' cub treats Magic Kingdom guests to a wild and whimsical 3½-minute tour of his home turf.

The attraction features a most unlikely form of transportation: honey pots! They whisk (and bounce) guests through the pages of a giant storybook and into the Hundred Acre

Wood, where the weather's most blustery. The wind is really ruffling the feathers of one of the locals. It seems Owl's treehouse has been shaken loose and just may topple to the ground—and onto the honey pots below. Similar sight gags abound, from a bubble-blowing Heffa-lump (hey, this is Fantasyland) to a treacherous flood that threatens to sweep Tigger, Piglet, and the rest of the gang away. When Pooh saves the day, it's time to celebrate—and everyone is invited to the party.

Note that, like other Fantasyland attractions, some parts of The Many Adventures of Winnie the Pooh take place in the dark. Timid youngsters may find the dark a bit unsettling.

SNOW WHITE'S SCARY ADVENTURES: This three-minute attraction takes guests on a twisting, turning journey through a few happy moments and several scary scenes from the Grimm brothers' fairy tale, which Walt Disney made into the world's first full-length animated feature in 1937. Snow White makes several appearances, as do the seven Audio-Animatronic dwarfs. But the wicked witch—evil, long-nosed, and practically toothless—shows up more than once with a suddenness that startles some youngsters (particularly those under the age of 5).

Ariel's Grotto

The Little Mermaid's Ariel doesn't greet Magic Kingdom guests in the traditional way, since mermaids, like most fish, find it difficult to walk around theme parks. Instead, she invites folks of all ages to stop by her Fantasyland home away from home—a colorful grotto surrounded by starfish, coral, and waterfalls. Here, guests can meet and pose for a picture with the ever-popular Disney heroine (don't forget to take your camera). The area, which is very popular with little ones, also features a soft-surface play zone filled with squirting fountains. Note that the line to meet Ariel is often long enough to scare Ursula herself.

Mickey's Toontown Fair

The newest neighborhood in the Magic Kingdom was built with little visitors in mind. Not only do Mickey, Minnie, and their pals keep homes here, but the county fair is always in town. Tucked away behind Fantasyland, the area can be reached by a path from the Mad Tea Party or Space Mountain and via the Walt Disney World Railroad. Guests who arrive by stroller are advised to park their vehicles in the lot across from Pete's Garage. Keep in mind that traffic here is heaviest early in the day.

Note: Attractions are described in the order in which they're encountered when the area is accessed from Fantasyland.

THE BARNSTORMER: At Goofy's Wiseacre Farm, guests of most sizes climb into crop dusters and follow the same fluky flight path taken by the Goof himself. The planes zip through the farm and crash through a barn, causing quite a ruckus among the chickens. Don't let the size fool you. This roller coaster proves that big thrills come in small packages. Although guests as young as three are allowed to ride, it may be too turbulent for some.

Hot Tip!

Toontown bustles with the most activity during the first half of the day. To avoid the biggest crowds, visit Mickey's country hideaway in the late afternoon or in the evening.

Explore Goofy's Wiseacre Farm before lining up for the ride. Cotton, tomatoes, and other real crops have been spotted growing here. The observant may notice the unconventional parking spot that Goofy found for his plane. (Hint: Look up.) Guests must be at least 35 inches tall to ride.

DONALD'S BOAT: If you want to cool off a bit, stop at Donald Duck's boat, the *Miss Daisy*. The vessel has sprung so many leaks, it looks like a fountain. It's almost impossible to walk across the "duck pond" without getting squirted. The ship's sparse interior includes a captain's wheel and a whistle—pull it and water shoots out the top. Tykes love it.

MICKEY'S COUNTRY HOUSE: Don't bother knocking—the door is always open. Guests are welcome to peer inside each of the cottage's rooms: bedroom, living room, kitchen, and gameroom. The kitchen is being remodeled, but it's worth a peek (after which you'll vow never to hire Donald Duck and Goofy to redecorate your own home). As the gameroom shows, the Mouse is quite an accomplished sportsman, dabbling in everything from Ping-Pong to football. (Is that a Heisman trophy on the shelf?!)

Despite all there is to see, one thing is conspicuously missing from Mickey Mouse's house . . . Mickey himself. Don't despair. The head judge of the county fair is in the Judge's Tent,

different rooms offer guests the opportunity to meet Disney characters.

There is a separate line for each room, and characters vary throughout the day. Signs indicate which characters are on hand at any given moment. It's best to have cameras (and autograph books) ready before entering the area.

MINNIE'S COUNTRY HOUSE: Since Minnie and Mickey are neighbors here in the country, Minnie's house is merely a hop, skip, and a jump from Mickey's. Young kids love it here because the special toon furniture is meant for climbing. As they explore, guests may push a button to listen to her answering-machine messages, open the refrigerator (Minnie has cheese-chip ice cream in the freezer, which is actually chilly inside), and try in vain to snatch some chocolate chip cookies (it's a mirror trick, courtesy of Minnie herself).

The screen porch is full of some very special plants. Don't miss the palm tree (it's made of hands), the Tiger Lilies (feline faces), and the Twolips (no explanation necessary).

PETE'S GARAGE: This cleverly disguised restroom is the only place to make a pit stop in Mickey's Toontown Fair. The toon vehicle, which is parked out front, makes for an excellent photo opportunity. The lot across from Pete's is zoned for stroller parking.

TOON PARK: Centrally located, this covered green provides a nice respite from the sun (or the rain). There are shaded benches surrounding a spongy, toddler-friendly play area.

where he greets guests all day long. (It's the best place to meet Mickey in all of Walt Disney World.) To get there, slip out the back door of the house and follow the path toward the tent. (Others can exit through the garage, which packs some surprises of its own.) It's fun to check out the backyard, where Mickey's award-winning garden is bursting with giant vegetables, many of which have mouse ears. This is also the spot to look at Pluto's doghouse.

JUDGE'S TENT: A must for fans of the Mouse, this place is all Mickey all the time. The waiting area (and there is always a significant wait) features a pre-show video that highlights all of his county fair successes. All guests are treated to a private meeting with the star, so have those cameras ready! To get to the Judge's Tent, take a trip through Mickey's Country House. The line is usually shortest late in the day or during a parade.

TOONTOWN HALL OF FAME: Just beyond Cornelius Coot Commons and across from Goofy's Wiseacre Farm is the Toontown Hall of Fame. The big tent is stocked with Disney souvenirs as well as some of the prize-winning entries from the Toontown Fair. (Only the former are for sale.) Beyond this area, three

Hot Tip!

The line to meet Mickey in the Judge's Tent can be quite lengthy. It's usually shorter late in the day and during parades.

Tomorrowland

The original Tomorrowland attempted a serious look at the future. But as Disney planners discovered, it isn't easy to portray a future that persists in becoming the present. So the old Tomorrowland has given way to a friendlier, space-age town whose neighborhood atmosphere is more in keeping with the other lands in the Magic Kingdom. This is the future that never was, the fantasy world imagined by the science-fiction writers and moviemakers of the 1920s and '30s. It's a land of sky-piercing beacons and glistening metal, where shiny robots do the work, whisper-quiet cars glide along an elevated highway, and even time travel is possible.

Note: Tomorrowland attractions are described in the order that they are encountered upon entering the land from the Hub and heading (counterclockwise) away from Cinderella Castle.

THE EXTRATERRORESTRIAL ALIEN ENCOUNTER: The Tomorrowland Interplanetary Convention Center has been the home of the Magic Kingdom's scariest attraction since 1995. It's scheduled to undergo some major changes in the near future. What follows is a description of the attraction guests were experiencing at press time. Your experience may be different. Keep in mind that the attraction may even be closed during your visit.

The ExtraTERRORestrial Alien Encounter was created by Disney Imagineers and motion picture director George Lucas. It features some of the most elaborate special effects ever employed by a theme park.

Hot Tip!
Big changes are possible for Alien Encounter. As a result, the attraction may be closed for several months at a time.

The premise: The Convention Center is hosting X-S Tech, a mysterious corporation from a distant planet. The goal is to impress earthlings with its high-tech products. After a preshow, guests are shown to a circular auditorium with a large teleporter (a machine that "beams" objects from place to place) in the center. Screens around the theater display a live transmission from their planet. Restraints are suddenly lowered onto guests' shoulders. (The experience isn't rough, just scary. Sit up straight as the restraint comes down. It will enhance your enjoyment of the show.) Just then, X-S Tech's Chairman Clench volunteers to be teleported to the Magic Kingdom.

Special effects abound as guests await the arrival of Chairman Clench. But something goes wrong, and an angry alien is transported into the audience as the theater goes black.

Next comes a series of creepy sensations designed to convince everyone that the monster has found its way to their side. And, no, you are not imagining it—something really is breathing down your neck.

Note: This 20-minute attraction may be too intense for some children. You must be at least 44 inches tall to enter Alien Encounter.

 BUZZ LIGHTYEAR'S SPACE RANGER SPIN: FP The Evil Emperor Zurg is up to no good. As soon as he swipes enough batteries to power his ultimate weapon of destruction—*KERPLOOEY!*—it's curtains for the toy universe as we know it. It's up to that Space Ranger extraordinaire Buzz Lightyear and his Junior Space Rangers (that means you) to save the day.

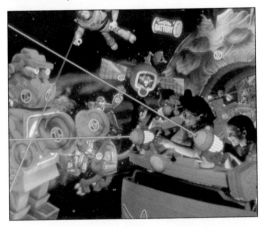

So goes the story line of Tomorrowland's video-game-inspired spin through toyland. The adventure is experienced from a toy's point of view. Guests begin their 4½-minute tour of duty as Space Rangers at Star Command Action Center. This is where Buzz gives his team a briefing on the mission that lies ahead. Then it's off to the Launch Bay to board the ride vehicles. The ships feature duel laser cannons, glowing lights, and a piloting joystick.

In addition to Buzz and the evil Emperor, you may recognize some other toy faces swirling about—the little green, multi-eyed alien squeaky toys, best known for their awe of "the claw." The squeakies have been enlisted to help in the fight against Zurg. (They and their counterparts were animated by Pixar, the creative team responsible for the groundbreaking set of *Toy Story* films. *Toy Story* director, John Lasseter, was also on board to shape the ride's story line.)

Once Junior Space Rangers blast off, they find themselves surrounded by Zurg's robots,

Hot Tip!

To up your score at Buzz Lightyear's Space Ranger Spin, keep the trigger depressed at all times. Also, be sure to aim for moving or distant targets—they provide the biggest point payoffs.

who are mercilessly ripping batteries from toys. As Rangers fire at targets, beams of light fill the air. For every target hit, you will be rewarded with sight gags, sound effects, and points. The points, which are tallied automatically, are accumulated throughout the journey. Although the vehicles follow a rigid flight path (they're on a track), the joystick allows riders to maneuver the ships, arcing from side to side or spinning in circles while taking aim at your surroundings.

When the star cruiser arrives at Zurg's spaceship, it's showdown time. Will good prevail over evil? Or has time run out for the toy universe? And will you score enough points to be a Galactic Hero? Most people improve their scores with a little practice.

TOMORROWLAND TRANSIT AUTHORITY: Boarded near Astro Orbiter, these trains (formerly known as the WEDway PeopleMover) move at a speed of about seven miles per hour along almost a mile of track, beside or through most of the attractions in Tomorrowland. They are operated by a linear induction motor that has no moving parts, uses little power, and emits no pollution.

The peaceful, breezy excursion through Tomorrowland takes about ten minutes. There is almost never a wait to board.

MAGIC KINGDOM

ASTRO ORBITER: Here, passengers fly around for two minutes in machine-age rockets designed to look more like oversize Buck Rogers toys than 21st-century space shuttles. Riders are surrounded by vibrantly colored, whirling planets as they get an astronaut's-eye view of Tomorrowland.

BIRNBAUM'S ★**BEST**★ **SPACE MOUNTAIN:** **FP** This attraction, which blasted onto the Magic Kingdom scene in 1975, is a can't-miss crowd pleaser for throngs of thrill seekers. Rising to a height of more than 180 feet, this gleaming steel and concrete cone houses an attraction that most people call a roller coaster. It's the Disney version—a roller coaster and then some.

The 2-minute, 38-second ride takes place in an outer-space-like darkness that gets inkier and scarier as the journey progresses.

The rockets that roar through this blackness attain a maximum speed of just over 28 miles per hour—but somehow it feels much faster.

The Space Mountain experience is wild enough to send eyeglasses, purses, wallets, and even an occasional set of false teeth plummeting to the bottom of the track, so be sure to find a safe place for your possessions before the ride starts. It's also turbulent enough to upset the sensitive stomachs of those so unwise as to ride it immediately after eating—but not so harrowing that knees shake for more than a minute or two after "touchdown." (Those who chicken out at the last minute have access to an exit.)

Note: Guests who are under 44 inches are not permitted to ride, and you must be in good health and free from heart conditions, motion sickness, back or neck problems, or other physical limitations to ride. Expectant mothers should skip the trip. Children under 7 must be accompanied by an adult. The Tomorrowland Light & Power Co., an arcade by Space Mountain's exit, is a good place to wait for your party if you skip the ride.

TOMORROWLAND INDY SPEEDWAY: Little cars that burn up the tracks at this attraction provide most of the background noise in Tomorrowland. Kids especially enjoy the driving experience.

Like true sports cars, the vehicles have rack-and-pinion steering and disc brakes, but unlike most cars, these run along a track. Yet, even expert drivers have trouble keeping them going in a straight line. (Don't panic when you notice the lack of a brake pedal—when you take your foot off the gas, the car comes to a quick, if not screeching, halt.) The one-lap trip takes about five minutes.

Note: You must be at least 52 inches tall to drive the cars by yourself. There is no height requirement to ride shotgun.

Shopping

No one travels all the way to the Magic Kingdom just to go shopping. But as many a first-time visitor has learned with some surprise, shopping is one of the most enjoyable pastimes here.

The Magic Kingdom's boutiques and stores stock much more than just Disneyana. Along with the more predictable items in Main Street shops, it's possible to find cookbooks and stoneware dishes, pirate hats and toy frontier rifles, 14-karat gold charms and filigreed costume jewelry. In Adventureland, shops boast many items imported from the exotic regions the area represents. Throughout the park, stores generally have merchandise that complements the themes of the various lands.

In some shops, you can watch people at work—a candy maker pouring peanut brittle in the Main Street Confectionery, a glassblower crafting wares in Main Street's Crystal Arts, and the like. And every store offers a selection of items from the inexpensive to the not-so-inexpensive.

Finally, some advice. We recommend shopping in the early afternoon, rather than at the end of the day, when the shops are more crowded. However, keep in mind that Main Street shops do stay open a half hour after park closing, in case you need any last-minute gifts on the way out of the park. Also note that purchases may be stored for the day in lockers under the Walt Disney World Railroad's depot or, in the case of very large items, sent to package pickup. WDW resort guests may arrange for purchases to be sent to their hotel rooms free of charge. Purchases may be shipped on request. Note that this service has been suspended in the past and may not be offered during your visit.

Main Street

THE CHAPEAU: This Town Square shop is the place to buy Mouse ears and have them monogrammed, and to shop for straw hats, baseball caps, and assorted other headgear.

CRYSTAL ARTS: Cut-glass bowls, vases, glasses, and plates glitter in the mirror-backed cases of this crystal-chandeliered emporium. An engraver or a glassblower is always at work by the bright light that floods through the big windows. There is a crystal castle on display in the window out front. Presented by the Arribas Brothers.

DISNEY & CO.: The wallpaper at this shop is Victorian and the woodwork elaborate; old-fashioned ceiling fans twirl slowly overhead. This store stocks a selection of intimate apparel. It also carries infant and toddler clothing and toys.

DISNEY CLOTHIERS: This shop features an array of clothing, including sweatshirts and flannel sleepwear, all of which incorporate Disney characters in some way. Bags, jewelry, watches, and other accessories round out the selection.

Where to Eat in the Magic Kingdom

A complete listing of all eateries—full-service restaurants, fast-food emporiums, and snack shops—can be found in the *Good Meals, Great Times* chapter. See the Magic Kingdom section beginning on page 214.

EMPORIUM: Framed by a two-story-high portico, the Magic Kingdom's largest gift shop (which recently expanded, taking over the space formerly occupied by the Center Street flower garden and the Harmony Barber Shop) stocks stuffed animals and toys, sundries, film, T-shirts, and more.

The cash registers always seem to be busy, especially toward the end of the afternoon and before park closing. Nearby lockers make for convenient storage of purchases.

Don't forget to peer into the windows, which usually feature elaborate displays ranging from seasonal themes to character tableaux from the latest Disney movie.

FIREHOUSE GIFT STATION: Authentic fire-fighting paraphernalia provides the backdrop for a variety of *101 Dalmatians* products, Mickey Mouse firefighter souvenirs, and reproductions of historical firefighting objects.

HARMONY BARBER SHOP: Situated next door to the Main Street Car Barn, the quaint, old-fashioned setting for this working shop (complete with occasional appearances by a harmonizing quartet) merits a peek even if you have no need for a trim. It's open from 9 A.M. to 5 P.M. daily.

MAIN STREET ATHLETIC CLUB: Sports-related gifts and apparel are the hallmarks of this shop. The merchandise features images of Disney characters pursuing their favorite sports. The shop also stocks golf shirts with a small Mickey embroidered on the pocket.

MAIN STREET CONFECTIONERY: Tasty chocolates are sold in this old-fashioned pink-and-white paradise. A delight at any time of day, but especially when the cooks in the shop's glass-walled kitchen are pouring peanut brittle onto a table to cool. Then the candy sends up clouds of aroma that you could

Let It Rain

The show doesn't stop just because of a storm. Instead, shops throughout the Magic Kingdom sell bright yellow Mickey ponchos to outfit guests who have left their own rain gear back home, at their hotel, or in the car.

swear were being fanned out onto the street. The peanut brittle is for sale in small bags, along with jelly beans, marshmallow crispy treats, and dozens of other confections that will satisfy any sweet tooth.

MAIN STREET GALLERY: The focus here is on Disneyana—including limited-edition Disney plates, cels from Disney movies, and other collectibles. The store is located in the building formerly occupied by the bank.

MAIN STREET MARKET HOUSE: An old-fashioned spot, with cookies, candy, and housewares, including specialty tins, napkin rings, and espresso cups.

NEWSSTAND: No newspapers are sold in the Magic Kingdom—even at its newsstand, which is near the park entrance. (It's to the left, just inside the turnstiles.) The stand sells a small selection of character merchandise and souvenirs.

THE SHADOW BOX: Watching Rubio Artist Co. silhouette cutters snip black paper into the likenesses of children is one of Main Street's more fascinating diversions.

STROLLER AND WHEELCHAIR RENTAL: Inside the turnstiles on the right as you enter the Magic Kingdom, this rental concession offers a limited number of strollers and wheel-chairs. They are available on a first-come, first-served basis. (Hold onto your receipt—it'll get you a replacement stroller should yours mysteriously disappear during the day.) Keep in mind that strollers and wheelchairs rented here cannot be taken outside the park. Souvenirs may also be purchased here.

TOWN SQUARE EXPOSITION HALL: A combination camera center and museum, Exposition Hall features exhibits celebrating the history of photography. This is the spot for film, batteries, collectible pins, photo albums, disposable cameras, two-hour film processing, and very minor camera repairs. It's also possible to have your photo snapped and superimposed onto a decidedly Disney background—be it in front of Cinderella Castle, beside Disney villains, or in the Hundred Acre Wood. These photos can be made into posters, plaques, or mouse pads.

UPTOWN JEWELERS: Designed to resemble a turn-of-the-century collectibles shop, this spiffy store specializes in jewelry and other gift items. One counter stocks souvenir charms in 14-karat gold and sterling silver, among them Tinker Bell, Cinderella Castle, and the Walt Disney World logo (a globe with mouse ears). There's also a selection of Disney character figurines. Clocks and watches in all shapes and sizes are available here, including Mickey Mouse watches in a wide variety of configurations.

Adventureland

ELEPHANT TALES: Clothing with a safari theme is featured at this shop. In addition, look for these handcrafted wood items imported from Kenya: giraffes, letter openers, salad spoons, wind chimes, rain sticks, and napkin holders. Fezzes, *Aladdin*-themed merchandise (including costumes), leather goods, drums, baskets, sandals, camel figures, and carpets are among the other wares available in this area.

ISLAND SUPPLY: This small tropical surf shop features a surprisingly large selection of surfing attire and accessories.

ZANZIBAR TRADING COMPANY: Across from Adventureland's famed "Egg Roll Wagon," this corner shop stocks souvenirs of the *Lion King, Jungle Book*, and *Winnie the Pooh* ilk—many with a safari theme.

Caribbean Plaza

HOUSE OF TREASURE: Ahoy there, maties! This is an excellent spot to pick up pirate hats and shirts. A swashbuckler's delight, the joint adjoining the Pirates of the Caribbean also stocks nautical gifts and other pirate booty, including, Jolly Roger flags, rings, dolls, sailing-ship models, ships in a bottle, and eye patches.

PLAZA DEL SOL CARIBE BAZAAR: Located next to the Pirates, this market sells candy and snacks, straw hats (including colorful oversize sombreros), piñatas, pottery, straw bags, clothing, and artificial flowers.

Frontierland

BIG AL'S: Named for the most popular (and least talented) member of the Country Bears, this riverfront shop is known for its Walt Disney World logo merchandise and candy.

BRIAR PATCH: Toys and cuddly creatures from the Hundred Acre Wood—Winnie the Pooh, Tigger, and their pals—are featured in the merchandise at this shop, located near the Splash Mountain exit.

FRONTIER TRADING POST: Yee-ha! This is the place to outfit a child as a youngster of the Great Frontier. Cowboy hats or feathered headdresses and moccasins, sleeve garters, sheriff's badges, and turquoise jewelry should do the trick.

FRONTIER WOOD CARVING: The spot for wooden gifts with personalized carvings. A small supply of leather jewelry is available. Some items can be personalized.

PRAIRIE OUTPOST & SUPPLY: Stop by this turn-of-the-century general store for candy, coffee, and cookies. Decorative items such as candles are also for sale.

TRAIL CREEK SHOP: An array of bean-bag toys and other items are for sale at this small shop near the Diamond Horseshoe.

Liberty Square

HERITAGE HOUSE: Early American reproductions predominate in the stock of this store next to The Hall of Presidents. Parchment copies of famous American documents are popular with youngsters. Collectors might be tempted to snap up busts of the presidents, souvenir spoons, or documents signed by famous figures from American history. Campaign buttons, flags, T-shirts, and Statue of Liberty items are also available.

LIBERTY SQUARE PORTRAIT GALLERY: In the midst of Liberty Square, next to The Hall of Presidents, guests may sit to have their portraits drawn in this open-air studio.

MADAME LEOTA'S CART: This shop gives guests on their way to The Haunted Mansion a taste of things to come, with horrific monster masks and ghoulish goodies. It's also the perfect place to pick up an invisible pooch. FYI: Madame Leota is the spirit featured in the crystal ball inside the Haunted Mansion.

THE YANKEE TRADER: This quaint little shop near The Haunted Mansion is filled with items for the kitchen. There are Mickey waffle irons and Mickey-shaped pasta, among other Disney-themed goods. The shop also stocks jams and jellies, cooking oils and sauces, pots, dishes, and other creative kitchenware.

YE OLDE CHRISTMAS SHOPPE: A wide variety of festive and decorative Christmas items, including tree-top dolls, automated display characters, angel figurines, and souvenir ornaments—Disney-themed and traditional—is available year-round.

Fantasyland

THE KING'S GALLERY: This shop inside Cinderella Castle features a line of knight-wear and other medieval items such as swords and shields. In addition, it stocks items related to Cinderella herself (including glass slippers), as well as her castle.

KODAK KIOSK: A convenient location to buy film and other photo supplies.

POOH'S THOTFUL SPOT: Located at the exit of The Many Adventures of Winnie the Pooh, this shop has wares featuring the folks from the Hundred Acre Wood. Oh, and it's not your imagination: This place really *does* smell like honey!

SEVEN DWARFS MINING CO.: This stand next to Snow White's Scary Adventures sells Disney-motif key chains, candies, and stuffed animals, plus a colorful collection of *Snow White and the Seven Dwarfs* merchandise.

SIR MICKEY'S: Expect to find all sorts of Disney souvenirs in this shop with a theme based on *The Brave Little Tailor*—the cartoon in which Mickey defeats a giant to win the hand of Princess Minnie. (It was one of the most elaborate and expensive Mickey Mouse cartoons ever made.) Notable items include embroidered denim jackets, character sweatshirts, hats, and videos.

TINKER BELL'S TREASURES: One of the more wonderful boutiques in the Magic Kingdom. For sale are character clothing and costumes for kids, stuffed animals, character toys, plus collector dolls.

Mickey's Toontown Fair

COUNTY BOUNTY: Disney character memorabilia, featuring all the favorites, can be found in this merchandise location under the big tent. Look for costumes, children's apparel, autograph books, key chains, candy, and more. Don't miss the doll-making exhibit or the winning entries from previous fairs, including the "most upside-down cake," baked by Daisy Duck.

Tomorrowland

GEIGER'S COUNTER: This small shop near the Tomorrowland Indy Speedway features a variety of souvenir hats. It also monograms Mouse ears.

MERCHANT OF VENUS: The kinds of collector items that sci-fi enthusiasts love can be found here: futuristic toys, games, clothing, and other such things. Also on hand are decorative items meant to grab the attention of the teen set.

MICKEY'S STAR TRADERS: This is one of the best places to go in the Magic Kingdom for Disney-themed items: plush toys, towels, hats, shirts, dishes, candy, etc. Film, sunglasses, and assorted sun-care products are also available.

Entertainment

In this most magical corner of the World, a tempting slate of live performances ranks among the more serendipitous discoveries. The Magic Kingdom's entertainment mix includes dazzling high-tech shows and old-fashioned numbers alike. To keep apprised of the offerings on any given day, stop at City Hall upon arrival at the park to pick up a current guidemap and times guide.

While specifics are subject to change, the following listing is a good indication of the Magic Kingdom's extensive repertoire. As always, we advise calling 407-824-4321 to confirm schedules. For information on special events at the Magic Kingdom, see the "Holidays & Special Events" section of *Getting Ready to Go*.

CASEY'S CORNER PIANO: A pianist tickles the ivories of a snow-white upright daily at the centrally located Casey's Corner restaurant on Main Street.

CINDERELLA'S SURPRISE CELEBRATION: Who better to host a party at Cinderella Castle than the princess herself? In this musical presentation, the hostess with the mostest steps onto the forecourt stage and welcomes guests with true royal flair. With a little help from her Fairy Godmother and the audience, Cinderella invites many of her friends, such as Mickey and Minnie, Peter Pan, and Mulan, to join her on the stage to sing songs, exchange presents, and interact with Magic Kingdom guests.

Be sure to have your camera ready, as many of the characters mix and mingle with guests after they take their bows.

DAPPER DANS: You just might encounter a barbershop quartet while strolling down Main Street. Conspicuously clad in straw hats and striped vests, the ever-so-jovial Dapper Dans tap-dance and let one-liners fly during their short four-part-harmony performances.

FIREWORKS: A brand-new, state-of-the-art pyrotechnic extravaganza is presented on all nights when the Magic Kingdom stays open after dark. The show, which made its debut in the fall of 2003, is ideally viewed from Main Street, but there are good viewing locations throughout the park. It is presented rain or shine. The Magic Kingdom fireworks display is often presented at 10 P.M. during peak periods, earlier during the rest of the year. Check a park times guide for specifics.

FLAG RETREAT: At about 5:10 P.M. each day (check a current times guide), patriotic music fills the air as a color guard marches to Town Square, in Main Street, U.S.A. and takes down the American flag that flies from the flagpole. On special occasions, a band plays live music. WDW veterans should know that the doves that used to take part in the ceremony are enjoying a hard-earned retirement.

SHARE A DREAM COME TRUE PARADE: This parade, created especially for the Magic Kingdom park, invites guests to celebrate Disney magic and "share a dream come true." The interactive parade, which has floats shaped like oversize snowglobes, as well as every Disney character imaginable, begins in Frontierland and winds its way up Main Street, U.S.A. Check a times guide for the schedule.

SWORD IN THE STONE CEREMONY: Several times each day, a child is appointed temporary ruler of the realm by pulling the magical sword, Excalibur, from the stone in front of Cinderella's Golden Carrousel. Merlin the Magician presides over the ceremony. Note a park times guide for the schedule.

Holiday Happenings

It's a rare holiday that passes quietly in the Magic Kingdom. During certain holidays, such as Christmas, New Year's Eve, and the Fourth of July, this Kingdom usually breaks curfew, staying open extra late and stepping up its nighttime entertainment. On these occasions, special performances of the SpectroMagic parade and the fireworks are often in store. Of course, entertainment plans are subject to change, so it's important to call 407-824-4321 for current schedules.

EASTER: Easter is a delightful, if a bit crowded, time to visit the Magic Kingdom. Mr. and Mrs. Easter Bunny have been known to appear in the park to help guests celebrate the occasion.

FOURTH OF JULY: The busiest day of the summer—and with good reason: There's a double-size fireworks extravaganza whose explosions light up the skies not only above Cinderella Castle, but also over Seven Seas Lagoon. It's a thrilling display.

HALLOWEEN: This most spooky of holidays is generally celebrated on several nights in October (though not necessarily on Halloween itself) with a special-ticket event: Mickey's Not-So-Scary Halloween Party. The park closes a bit early on nights when the party takes place.

(Guests bearing tickets to the party can stay in the park.) Mickey's Not-So-Scary Halloween Parade winds its way through the Kingdom during this event, too. Call 401-824-4321 or visit *www.disneyworld.com* to order tickets to the Halloween party.

CHRISTMAS: A towering Christmas tree goes up in Town Square, and the Magic Kingdom is decked out as only Disney can do it. On select nights, the Magic Kingdom hosts a special-admission celebration known as Mickey's Very Merry Christmas Party.

The festivities, complete with complimentary hot chocolate and snow flurries on Main Street, include a running (or two) of Mickey's Very Merry Christmas Parade and other shows. There are also special performances during the day—even the Country Bears have been known to get into the act. Disney characters are on hand, too.

The Christmas party is a very popular (and enjoyable) event. Plan to purchase tickets way ahead of time. And don't forget to wear your red and green!

NEW YEAR'S EVE: It has always been true that on December 31 the throngs here are body to body. Expect a dazzling, super-size fireworks display and oodles of happy holiday decorations. There's plenty of nip in the air as the evening goes on, so dress accordingly.

Where to Find the Characters

Mickey's pals make appearances throughout the day. Alice and her Wonderland friends show up in Fantasyland, as does Ariel. Belle reads stories to guests in Fairy Tale Garden, near the Castle. The Fantasyland Character Festival is an excellent spot to see characters, as is the Diamond Horseshoe Saloon. Character meals at Crystal Palace, Cinderella's Royal Table, and Liberty Tree Tavern offer guests a chance to meet their favorites. But the best place is at Toontown Fair, where guests can meet Mickey and his buddies. Characters may greet guests in Town Square at park opening time. Check a times guide for updated information.

SpectroMagic Lights Up the Park

SpectroMagic, the dazzling parade which first premiered during Disney World's 20th anniversary celebration, has gotten rave reviews and taken its place among Disney's must-sees. (Its beloved predecessor, the Main Street Electrical Parade, can currently be seen at Disney's California Adventure, in Anaheim, California.)

Fiber-optic cable and threads are the conduits for shimmering lights that create everything from the "hair" on King Triton's beard on one float to daisy petals on another. Some 600,000 miniature bulbs light up in wild, changing patterns, moving in perfect concert with sound effects and musical score.

SpectroMagic follows the Magic Kingdom's traditional parade route (heading from Main Street, U.S.A. to Frontierland and vice versa). There are excellent viewing locations throughout the route, with many along the curbs of Main Street. It gets very crowded there, so you must plan to claim your foot of curb as much as an hour and a half ahead of time (particularly for the earlier running).

The parade lights up the Magic Kingdom during all peak seasons and select evenings throughout the year.

Timing tip: When the parade runs twice a night, the earlier presentation is always significantly more crowded than the later one. So, if your family hasn't collectively run out of steam, stick around for the late show. You'll be glad you did.

Note: Some performances may be canceled due to inclement weather.

Hot Tips

- Start the day by picking up a Fastpass assignment for your favorite attraction.

- If the weather's steamy, dress toddlers in waterproof diapers. Then they'll be free to frolic in the fountains in Fantasyland and Mickey's Toontown Fair.

- If there are two performances of the evening parade, the later one tends to draw smaller crowds.

- If you're driving to the park, start out very early. Most people arrive between 9:30 A.M. and 11:30 A.M., and the roads and parking lots are jammed. If you're coming at Easter, Christmas, or in summer, arrive before 8:30 A.M. or wait until later in the afternoon, when things are less hectic. Plan to be at the gates to the Magic Kingdom before they open, and then be at the end of Main Street when the rest of the park opens.

- Wear very comfortable shoes: You'll be spending a lot of time on your feet. (Note that no bare feet are permitted in the park.)

- Dying to meet Mickey Mouse? Head for the Judge's Tent in Mickey's Toontown Fair. (You have to go through his house to get there.) He greets visitors all day, every day.

- You can usually get in line for an attraction right up until the minute the park closes.

- Avoid the mealtime rush hours by eating early or late: before 11 A.M. or after 2 P.M., and before 5 P.M. or after 8 P.M.

- At busy times, take in these not-so-packed attractions: Walt Disney World Railroad, Liberty Belle Riverboat, Hall of Presidents, and Tomorrowland Transit Authority.

- Check the Tip Boards for information on the wait times for popular attractions.

- Break up your day. Consider heading back to your hotel (if it's not too far) for some swimming. Be sure to have your hand stamped, and hold on to your admission pass and your parking stub, so that you can re-enter the Magic Kingdom.

- If your party decides to split up, set a meeting place and time. Avoid meeting in front of Cinderella Castle, since this area can become quite congested.

- Many Magic Kingdom attractions have two lines. The one on the left usually will be shorter, since most visitors automatically head for the one on the right.

- For a full-service meal in the Magic Kingdom, make advance priority seating arrangements by calling 407-WDW-DINE (939-3463).

- There are picnic facilities at the Transportation and Ticket Center (TTC).

- Disney park guests have the right to chicken out at any time. In other words, should you or a member of your party have second thoughts about soaring on Space Mountain, visiting with the grinning ghosts of the Haunted Mansion, or another attraction, simply inform an attendant and you'll be discreetly whisked out a special exit.

- If you've rented a stroller, consider returning it just before the night's fireworks presentation. That way, after the show, you'll be able to make a beeline for your bed rather than stand in a line to return your stroller.

- Merchandise found in shops at Walt Didsney World is also available through mail order. Call 407-363-6200 for info.

Epcot

EPCOT

Imagine a place whose entertainment inventory includes both a rich sampling of world cultures and a fun, enlightening journey to the technological frontier. You now have an inkling of the eye-opening and mind-broadening potential of Epcot—a place that's evolved most imaginatively in each of the twenty years it's been open.

Walt Disney suggested the idea back in 1966: "Epcot will be an experimental prototype community of tomorrow that will take its cue from the new ideas and technologies that are emerging from the creative center of American industry." It would never be completed, he said, but would "always be introducing and testing and demonstrating new materials and systems." Now, Walt Disney's dream is a reality. Test Track puts guests on the thrilling inside track of the fast and perilous world of automobile testing. Mission: SPACE delivers the breathtaking sensation of space travel. And classics like The Universe of Energy and The Wonders of Life continue to ignite the creative forces within us all.

The park consists of two areas of exploration: Future World and World Showcase. The former examines ideas in science and technology in ways that make them seem not only comprehensible but downright irresistible. The latter celebrates the diversity of the world's peoples, portraying a stunning array of nations, with extraordinary devotion to detail.

Think of Epcot as Disney's playground for the curious and the thoughtful. The experiences it delivers—all of them wonders of the real world— continue to amaze, educate, inspire, and (rest assured) entertain.

EPCOT

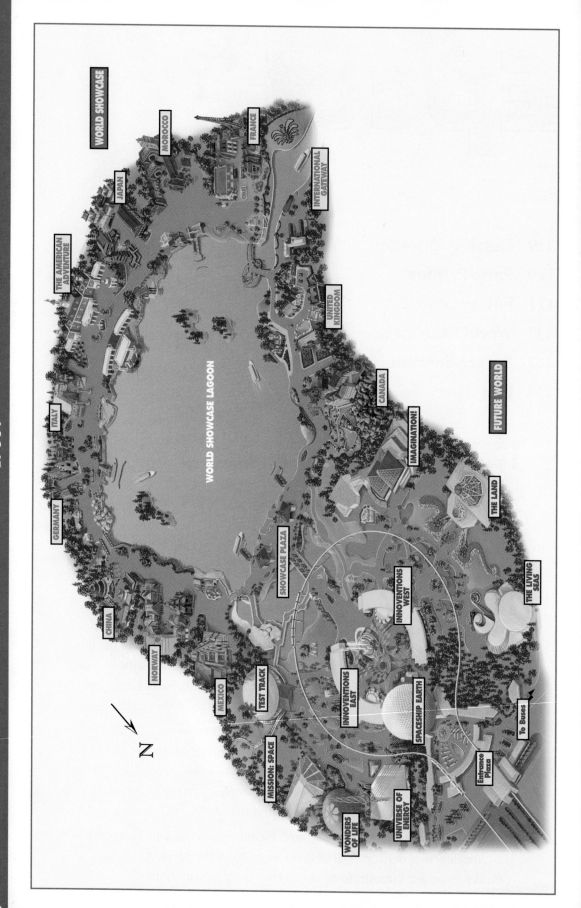

WORLD SHOWCASE

FUTURE WORLD

MOROCCO

FRANCE

JAPAN

INTERNATIONAL GATEWAY

THE AMERICAN ADVENTURE

UNITED KINGDOM

ITALY

CANADA

GERMANY

IMAGINATION!

WORLD SHOWCASE LAGOON

THE LAND

CHINA

THE LIVING SEAS

NORWAY

SHOWCASE PLAZA

INNOVENTIONS WEST

MEXICO

TEST TRACK

INNOVENTIONS EAST

SPACESHIP EARTH

MISSION: SPACE

To Buses

Entrance Plaza

WONDERS OF LIFE

UNIVERSE OF ENERGY

N

Getting Oriented

Double the Magic Kingdom park and you have an idea of the size of Epcot. As for layout, the park is shaped something like a giant hourglass. The pavilions of Future World fill the northern bulb, while the international potpourri called World Showcase occupies the southern bulb. Future World is anchored on the north by the imposing silver "geosphere," dubbed Spaceship Earth.

As you pass through Epcot's main Entrance Plaza, Spaceship Earth looms straight ahead. Pathways curve around the 180-foot-tall geosphere, winding up at Innoventions Plaza. Here, in addition to a huge show fountain, you'll see signposts for Innoventions, whose two buildings cradle the east and west sides of the plaza. Beyond this central area, there are two roughly symmetrical north-south avenues; these are dotted with the six pavilions that form the outer perimeter of Future World. Mission: SPACE, Test Track, Wonders of Life, and Universe of Energy flank Spaceship Earth on the east, while Imagination!, The Land, and The Living Seas lie to the west.

In World Showcase, the international pavilions are arranged around the edge of sparkling World Showcase Lagoon, with The American Adventure directly south of Spaceship Earth on the lake's southernmost shore. A walkway from Future World leads to the World Showcase Promenade, a 1.2-mile thoroughfare that wraps around the lagoon, winding past each World Showcase pavilion in the process.

HOW TO GET THERE

Take Exit 67 off I-4. Continue along to the Epcot Auto Plaza; if you park in a distant lot, take a tram from the parking lot to the park's main entrance.

By WDW Transportation: From the Grand Floridian, Contemporary, and Polynesian: hotel monorail to the Transportation and Ticket Center (TTC), then switch to the TTC-Epcot monorail. From the Magic Kingdom: express monorail to the TTC, then switch to the TTC-Epcot monorail. From Fort Wilderness and Downtown Disney: buses to the TTC, then change to the TTC-Epcot monorail. From the Disney-MGM Studios, Animal Kingdom, all other Walt Disney World resorts, and the resorts on Hotel Plaza Boulevard: buses.

Note: A second Epcot entrance, called International Gateway, provides entry directly to World Showcase. It may be reached via walkways and the *FriendShip* water launches from the Swan, Dolphin, Yacht and Beach Club, and BoardWalk resorts. The boat deposits guests between the France and United Kingdom pavilions. It is possible to purchase theme park admission here, at Epcot's "back door."

PARKING

All-day parking at Epcot is $7 for day visitors (free to Disney resort guests with a resort ID, as well as annual pass-holders). Attendants will direct you to park in one of several lots named for steps in the creative process, such as Discover and Imagine. Trams circulate regularly, providing transportation between the distant lots and the main entrance. Be sure to note the section and aisle in which you park. Parking tickets allow for re-entry to the area (and the other theme parks) throughout the day.

HOURS

Future World is usually open from about 9 A.M. to 7 P.M. World Showcase hours are about 11 A.M. to 9 P.M. During certain holiday periods and the summer months, hours are extended. It's best to arrive at least a half hour before the posted opening time, particularly during these busy seasons. On select days, the park opens one hour early for Disney resort guests only. Call 407-824-4321 for current schedules, or visit *www.disneyworld.com*.

GETTING AROUND

Water taxis, called *FriendShip* launches, ferry guests across the World Showcase Lagoon. Docks are located near Mexico, Canada, Germany, and Morocco. (The only other way to traverse the vast area is on foot.)

Admission Prices

ONE-DAY TICKET
(Restricted to use only in Epcot. Prices include sales tax and are subject to change.)
Adult $55.38
Child* $44.73
*3 through 9 years of age; children under 3 free

Park Primer

BABY FACILITIES

There are changing tables and facilities for nursing mothers at the Baby Care Center in the Odyssey Center, between Test Track and Mexico. Disposable diapers are kept behind the counter at many Epcot shops; just ask.

CAMERA NEEDS

The Camera Center in Entrance Plaza and World Traveler at International Gateway stock film, batteries, camera straps, and disposable cameras. Film processing is available wherever you see a Photo Express sign. There is an additional camera shop inside the Imagination! pavilion.

DISABILITY INFORMATION

Nearly all attractions, shops, and restaurants are accessible to guests using wheelchairs. Parking for guests with disabilities is available. Additional services are available for guests with visual and hearing disabilities. The *Guidebook for Guests with Disabilities* is available at Guest Relations. It provides a detailed overview of all services. For more information, turn to the *Getting Ready to Go* chapter of this book.

FIRST AID

Minor medical problems can be handled at the First Aid Center, in the Odyssey Center, between Test Track and Mexico. Keep in mind that many guests could avoid a trip to First Aid simply by staying well hydrated. If you have an emergency, notify an employee.

INFORMATION

Guest Relations, which is located next to Spaceship Earth, is equipped with guidemaps, times guides, and a helpful staff.

LOCKERS

Lockers are found immediately west of Spaceship Earth. Cost is $5, plus a $2 refundable deposit for unlimited use all day.

LOST AND FOUND

Lost and Found is located at Guest Relations in Innoventions East. To report any lost items after your visit, call 407-560-7500. If you find an item, present it to a park employee.

LOST CHILDREN

Report lost children at Guest Relations or the Baby Care Center, or alert the nearest Disney employee.

MONEY MATTERS

There are ATMs at the main entrance, on the path between Future World and World Showcase, and at The American Adventure. Some foreign currency may be exchanged at Guest Relations. Credit cards (American Express, JCB, Discover, Diner's Club, Visa, MasterCard, and The Disney Visa Card), traveler's checks, Disney Dollars, and WDW resort IDs are accepted for admission and merchandise, as well as meals at most restaurants.

PACKAGE PICKUP

Epcot shops can arrange for most purchases to be transported (for free) to the Gift Stop in Entrance Plaza or International Gateway in World Showcase for later pickup.

SAME-DAY RE-ENTRY

Be sure to have your hand stamped upon exiting the park and to retain your ticket if you plan to return later the same day.

SECURITY CHECK

Guests entering Disney theme parks may be subject to a security check. Backpacks, parcels, purses, etc., may be searched by security personnel before guests are permitted to enter.

STROLLERS & WHEELCHAIRS

Strollers, wheelchairs, and Electric Convenience Vehicles (ECVs) may be rented from venues at both park entrances. Wheelchairs are also available at the Gift Stop. Cost is $7 for strollers and wheelchairs, plus a $1 refundable deposit; and $30 for ECVs, plus a $10 refundable deposit. Quantities are limited. ECVs tend to sell out early. Keep your rental receipt; it can be used that same day to get a replacement at Epcot or at any of the other theme parks.

TIP BOARD

Check this digital board in Innoventions Plaza throughout the day to learn current waiting times for the most popular attractions.

Future World

A mere listing of the basic themes covered by the pavilions at Future World—agriculture, communications, car safety, the ocean, energy, health, imagination, and space—tends to sound a tad academic. But when these serious topics are presented with a special flair, they become part of an experience that ranks among Disney's most entertaining.

Some of these subjects are explored in the course of lively and unusual Disney "adventures," involving a whole arsenal of remarkable motion pictures, special effects, and Audio-Animatronics figures so lifelike that it is hard to remain unmoved. And the new Innoventions offers an invitation to sample cutting-edge technology. The basic elements are also appealing in their own right, from the palm-dotted Entrance Plaza and the massive buildings of Innoventions to the stupendous fountain just past Spaceship Earth, the many-faceted "geosphere" that has become the universal symbol of Epcot.

There is so much to see and enjoy that it's hard to know just what to do first. Many guests simply stop at Spaceship Earth on their way into Future World. As a result, they end up spending more time waiting in line than they need to. A wise alternative is to save Spaceship Earth for later in the day (when the lines inevitably thin out), and head for Mission: SPACE and Test Track as soon as the park opens (the lines tends to stay long throughout the day). If you have young children, consider kicking things off with a visit to the colorful Wonders of Life pavilion. Then take in as many Future World attractions as time allows, making sure to see the Image Works playground in the Imagination! pavilion, and save World Showcase for the evening hours. This strategy works well for families. (Refer to page 26 for a detailed version of this recommended plan of attack.)

Another alternative—one that requires quite a bit of extra walking, but can help skirt a long line or two—is to explore Future World until World Showcase opens at noon. Then, in the afternoon, when many guests have shifted over to World Showcase, return to the Future World area. Innoventions is not only a fascinating spot to pass the busy hours after lunch, but also a pleasantly cool refuge when uncomfortably high temperatures prevail outdoors.

(Refer to page 26 for a detailed version of this recommended plan of attack.)

Hot Tip!

If you've got small children in your party, be sure to visit The Living Seas and the Wonders of Life pavilions in Epcot's Future World and the Kidcot Fun Stop craft areas in World Showcase.

And although queues can be found during peak seasons at Mission: SPACE, Test Track, Imagination!, The Land, and Wonders of Life throughout most of the late morning and afternoon, the period from late afternoon until park closing is usually less hectic. But don't forget to make it back to World Showcase in time to see the nighttime spectacular, IllumiNations: Reflections of Earth.

Spaceship Earth

As it looms impressively just above the Earth, this great faceted silver structure looks a little bit like a spaceship ready to blast off. It appears large from a distance, and it seems even more immense when viewed from directly underneath. It's no surprise that some visitors simply stop beneath it and gawk.

The show inside, which explores the continuing search by human beings for ever more efficient means of communication, remains one of Epcot's most compelling.

A common misconception about Spaceship Earth is that it is a geodesic dome. Not so. It is

Leave a Legacy

The Leave a Legacy program, held over from Disney's Millennium Celebration, invites guests to leave their mark on the park. This cluster of odd monoliths inside Epcot's main entrance is covered with images of Walt Disney World guests etched on one-inch square tiles on massive stone walls.

To purchase a tile, inquire at the kiosk within the Leave a Legacy vicinity (near the Spaceship Earth entrance) between 10 A.M. and 7 P.M. One tile costs $25. Each additional tile costs $20. Note that this exhibit may not be a permanent one.

a geosphere. A geodesic dome is only half a sphere, while Spaceship Earth is almost completely round. Affectionately known to many simply as "the Ball," Spaceship Earth is indeed a sight to behold.

The noted science-fiction writer Ray Bradbury, together with consultants from the Smithsonian Institution, the Los Angeles area's prestigious Huntington Library, the University of Southern California, and (among others) the University of Chicago, collaborated with Disney in developing this memorable 14-minute journey. It begins in an inky black time tunnel, complete with a musty smell that suggests the dust of ages, and continues through history from the days of Cro-Magnon man (30,000 or 40,000 years ago) to the future.

The attraction features remarkable special effects, such as the flickering candles in the scene where a monk has nodded off and the smell of smoke coming from the fall of Rome. Every scene is executed in exquisite detail. The symbols on the wall of that Egyptian temple really are hieroglyphics, and the content of the letter being dictated by the pharaoh was excerpted from a missive actually received by an agent of a ruler of the period.

All of these sights are enough to keep heads turning as the "time machines" wend their

> ## Hot Tip!
> The line for Spaceship Earth is usually quite long during the early morning hours and relatively short in the late afternoon and evening.

way upward. The most dazzling scene is saved for the ride's finale, when the audience is placed in the heart of a communications revolution amid interactive global networks that tie all the peoples of the world together.

In the Global Neighborhood exhibit at the end of the journey, guests interact with emerging technologies such as voice-activated TV and telephones with wacky sound effects. (The phones are real—so make sure the booth is vacant before you go inside.)

GATEWAY GIFTS AND CAMERA CENTER: These two shops are located near the entrance to Spaceship Earth. The former sells Epcot souvenirs—shirts, mugs, toys, etc.—as well as sunscreen, tissues, and the like. Film and various other Kodak products, including disposable cameras, are sold at the Camera Center. Film processing is available.

Innoventions

Where else but Disney World would the information superhighway intersect with The Road to Tomorrow? It does at Innoventions, a forward-thinking showplace that encourages guests to experience futuristic technologies today. It's an opportunity to test products that may soon change the way we live and work. Equally important, Innoventions offers an unintimidating environment where you don't need to know how to program a VCR to be able to try out supercomputers or send video e-mail messages.

> ## Hot Tip!
> Keep an eye (or ear) out for a talking trash can inside the Electric Umbrella restaurant and a talking drinking fountain near the Imagination! pavilion.

An introduction hosted by Tom Morrow 2.0, a mini-robot and "a friend to technology," provides an overview of the new Innoventions experience, as well as some navigational tips. Once Tom's had his say, it's time to follow The Road to Tomorrow, a long, winding thoroughfare that snakes throughout Innoventions, and along which the exhibits are found.

The displays change often, making one of Walt Disney's original dreams for Epcot a reality. Employees will answer questions from curious—or skeptical—visitors.

Hot Tip!

Innoventions Plaza is home to Pin Central. This area, between Innoventions East and West, is the pin-trading headquarters for Epcot. (Of course, there are many other pin-trading locations throughout Walt Disney World.)

Innoventions covers two buildings, referred to as Innoventions East and West. The outside area between the pavilions is filled with color, light, spinning mobiles, and sidewalks glistening with fiber-optic lighting effects.

Above all, count on spending time exploring the exhibit areas (at least an hour or two). There's so much to see and do that curiosity will often get the better of any schedule here.

MOUSE GEAR: This enormous shop used to be called the Centorium. Though the name has changed, the selection remains top-notch. Mouse Gear stocks Disney character memorabilia, key chains, T-shirts, hats, books, candy, mugs, photo albums, jewelry, towels, footwear, Figment (the purple dragon from Epcot's Imagination! pavilion) toys, and much more—making this the best source for character merchandise in Epcot. There are also items related to the park itself, along with Disney-themed apparel and children's clothing. It is one of the best shops at Disney, and it stays open at least a half hour longer than the park does. It's a nice place to browse as the crowds exit the park after IllumiNations.

THE ART OF DISNEY EPCOT GALLERY: This is Epcot's spot for a unique assortment of Disney collectibles. The store showcases a wide variety of Disney animation art, including production cels, hand-painted limited-edition cels, character figurines, fine-art serigraphs, and lithographs.

The Living Seas

The Living Seas is the largest facility ever dedicated to humanity's relationship with the ocean. It was designed by Disney Imagineers, in cooperation with distinguished oceanographic experts and scientists.

The show also features a seven-minute film about how Earth's oceans were formed and about the tremendous diversity of the life that calls them home.

Under the Sea

Three behind-the-scenes tours offer guests a closer look at life in The Living Seas under-water environs. DiveQuest gives certified scuba divers the opportunity to explore one of the world's largest aquariums. Epcot Seas lets guests snorkel the Living Seas. Dolphins in Depth offers guests the chance to learn about dolphin behavior as they closely observe researchers and trainers interacting with dolphins. Reservations for either tour can be made by calling 407-WDW-TOUR (939-8687). For more information on both of these programs, turn to page 200 of the *Everything Else in the World* chapter.

From there, a look at a simulated Caribbean coral reef environment and the hands-on activities of Sea Base Alpha combine to prolong a visitor's stay.

CARIBBEAN CORAL REEF: To reach the coral reef, visitors enter "hydrolators," special elevator-like capsules that create the illusion of diving deep under the sea while actually descending only about an inch. The man-made reef exists in an enormous tank that holds about six million gallons of water and more than 60 species of sea life. Among the 2,000 or so inhabitants are turtles, angelfish, sharks, dolphins, and diamond rays. It's worth it to stop by as the park opens—that's usually when breakfast is served to the fish!

Guests sometimes get to see scuba divers testing and demonstrating the newest diving gear and underwater monitoring equipment as they carry on training experiments with

dolphins. After the three-minute ride, guests are deposited at Sea Base Alpha. This pavilion is an especially big hit with young guests.

SEA BASE ALPHA: This prototype undersea research facility, spread over two levels, includes a visitors center and six rooms, each dedicated to a specific subject. One focuses on ocean ecosystems and shows various forms of adaptation, including camouflage and symbiosis.

A tremendous tank displays another coral reef in which a staggering variety of fish swim about. Another room is dedicated to the study of porpoises and manatees. A tank features a step-in port, where guests can see the manatees up close.

Guests can try a cutaway suit and test its maneuverability. There are also video screens to test and expand your knowledge of oceanography. Adjacent to Sea Base Alpha, the concourse has several interesting displays.

The Land

Occupying six acres, this enormous skylighted pavilion examines the nature of one of everybody's favorite topics—food. A film, *The Circle of Life*, uses characters from *The Lion King* to deliver an entertaining yet inspirational message about humanity and the environment. A boat ride explores farming in the past and future.

Guided tours give visitors the chance to learn about the experimental agricultural techniques being practiced in the pavilion. In addition, the subject of nutrition is touched upon in one of Epcot's wackiest attractions, a musical show called Food Rocks.

Timing Tip: During peak seasons, lengthy queues build up for the boat ride and *The Circle of Life* movie. It's best to visit early in the morning and have a quick breakfast at the food court. Or wait until later in the afternoon, when many people have moved on to World Showcase.

BEHIND THE SEEDS: For guests interested in a more detailed look at the growing areas at The Land, one-hour guided tours take place throughout the day. Tours travel through four greenhouses where plants are grown hydroponically (without soil).

Different areas of the greenhouses showcase pioneering research projects undertaken in cooperation with NASA and the U.S. Departments of Agriculture and Energy. Because this walking tour is an expanded version of the Living with the Land boat ride, the ride is suggested as a prerequisite.

Reservations, which are required, can be made in person on the day of the tour, inside the Green Thumb Emporium, or by calling 407-939-8687. Cost is $6 for adults and $4 for kids ages 3 through 9. The first tour of the day starts at about 11 A.M. The reservations desk opens at 10 A.M. Book your tour as early as possible.

LIVING WITH THE LAND: FP The 13½-minute boat ride through the rain forest and greenhouses in this pavilion opens with a dramatic storm scene. Guests sail through tropical rain forests, prairie grain fields, and a family farm. As the boat passes through each realistic setting, the guide offers commentary on humanity's ongoing struggle to cultivate and live in harmony with the land. Note the details that make each setting so convincing, such as

sand blowing over the desert and light flickering from the TV in the farmhouse window.

In the next segment, guests enter a plant research laboratory and solarium. Here, our planet's major food crops are being grown in research projects, along with rare new crops that may someday help meet Earth's ever-growing dietary needs.

The guide on each boat provides information on the crops being grown. Also of interest are the experiments being conducted to explore the practice of farming fish, and a desert farm area, where plants get nutrients through a drip irrigation system that delivers just the right amount of water—important in a dry climate.

As unreal as they appear, all the plants on view in the experimental greenhouses are living. In contrast, those in the biomes (the ecological communities viewed from the boat ride) were made in Disney studios out of lightweight plastic that simulates the cellulose found in real trees. The trunks and branches were molded from live specimens; the sycamore in the farmhouse's front yard, for example, duplicates one that stands outside a Burbank, California, car wash. Thousands of polyethylene leaves were snapped on.

FOOD ROCKS: Classic songs have been humorously altered to deliver a nutritional message at this 15-minute mock rock concert. The show is set in a kitchen of cartoonish proportions, and life-size characters make this an entertaining show. It is hosted by Füd Wrapper, who was inspired by rapper Tone Loc.

The opening number, performed by a "heavy metal" group—giant kitchen utensils atop a cartoon stove—is Queen's "Bohemian Rhapsody" with new lyrics. Musical guests include the Peach Boys, Neil Moussaka, Chubby Cheddar, the Get-the-Point Sisters, and (Little) Richard. (Some less-savory types try to sell audience members on the concept of excess and the wonders of junk food, but rest assured: they're quickly canned.)

It's interesting to note that Tone Loc, Chubby Checker, Neil Sedaka, Little Richard, and the Pointer Sisters actually recorded the parodies of their music.

The show is simple, but sweet. And there's rarely a long wait to get in.

CIRCLE OF LIFE: This 20-minute film uses animation and live action to illustrate some of the dangers to our environment, as well as potential solutions. Presented as a fable featuring *The Lion King* favorites Simba, Timon, and Pumbaa, the film takes an optimistic approach to a serious subject. It is shown in the Harvest Theater, just inside the entrance to The Land.

Soon after the film begins, Simba's startled by the exuberant shout of "Timber!" and is drenched by the splash of a fallen tree in the water. The culprits are none other than his friends Timon and Pumbaa, who are clearing the savanna for the development of the Hakuna Matata Lakeside Village. Simba seizes the opportunity to tell them a tale about creatures who sometimes forget that everything is connected in the Circle of Life: humans.

Ice Station Cool

Future World's Ice Station Cool is a great place to beat the heat. Located near Innoventions, it bears a striking resemblance to an iceberg—with one major difference: It has a door. Inside, an ice tunnel (with an average temperature of 32 degrees and constant snowfall) leads to Coca-Cola's International Tasting Station. Here, you can sample eight different soft drinks from around the world, some tastier than others.

After you've quenched your thirst, courtesy of the Coca-Cola Company, you may have a desire to do some shopping. Not coincidentally, there's plenty of Coke merchandise available to choose from (at this point, you will have to open your wallet if you'd like a souvenir).

At press time, Ice Station Cool was open for business during Future World's regular operating hours.

Simba demonstrates to Timon and Pumbaa the consequences of progress, as his lessons are driven home by visual evidence of humans' mistreatment of the air, water, and land. (Timon: "And everybody was *okay* with this?") The effect is a mix of entertainment and a message about responsibility.

GREEN THUMB EMPORIUM: This little shop between Sunshine Season Food Fair and Food Rocks stocks land-related merchandise, such as hydroponic plants, seeds, and gardening books, as well as kitchen accessories, candy, and home products.

Imagination!

The oddly shaped pyramids that house the Imagination! pavilion are quite striking to behold. They certainly set the stage for the engaging experiences inside, some of which are among the most whimsical at Epcot. The undisputed crown jewel here is a dazzling 3-D movie called Honey, I Shrunk the Audience. Guests are also invited behind the scenes of the Imagination Institute in an attraction known as Journey Into Imagination with Figment.

Another pavilion highlight is the pair of quirky fountains outside—the Jellyfish Fountains, which spurt streams of water that spread out at the top, looking for an instant

like their namesake sea creature, and the Leap Frog Fountains, which send out smooth streams of water that arc from one garden plot to another in the most astonishing fashion. Kids just can't get enough of them.

Timing Tip: During peak seasons, the queue outside seems to be longest from about 10 A.M. to noon and remains fairly lengthy throughout most of the day. Count on spending up to an hour at this pavilion.

JOURNEY INTO IMAGINATION WITH FIGMENT: He's back! Figment, the tiny purple dragon with the orange wings and yellow eyes, is on hand to guide guests on an imaginative quest. The goal? To figure out, once and for all, the best way to capture your imagination.

The journey takes place at Imagination Institute, where guests are invited to step behind the scenes and get a peek at its latest groundbreaking project: The Imagination Scanner. It seems the prototype is nearly ready, save for a bit of testing. Fortunately,

there's no shortage of test subjects at Epcot. Guests are literally lining up for the chance to serve as human guinea pigs. All in all, it's a tame experience, save for the occasional blast of air or flashing lights.

The Imagination Scanner–induced sensory experiences begin soon after test subjects board their ride vehicle. Special effects and optical illusions are combined to create intriguing images. (Pay attention as the ride vehicle glides past the birdcage in which an enormous butterfly mysteriously disappears. It's an impressive illusion.) Expect all of your senses to get a workout during this colorful, eight-minute trip.

Nostalgia buffs, take note: The classic song "One Little Spark," which made its debut with the original incarnation of this attraction, underscores the show once more.

IMAGEWORKS: "WHAT IF" LABS: It's a rare ImageWorks visitor who doesn't experience at least some of the emotion felt by the little kid who cried when her parents tried to tear her away. That's not surprising, because the area is filled with activities that give every visitor the chance to have some fun while stretching the imagination.

Although this interactive wonderland recently underwent extensive refurbishment, it has retained some old favorites. A true highlight for youngsters (though guests of all ages appreciate it) is an area called Stepping Tones. It's hopscotch with a musical twist. Another popular attraction invites guests to wave their arms conductor style and, by doing so, trigger a cacophony of sounds, some more melodious than others.

A recent addition to this imaginative playground encourages guests to morph pictures of themselves into flowers, puppies, and even cartoon characters. Once you've been transformed into a daisy or a superhero, you can send the image to friends (or even yourself) via the Internet.

Plan to spend up to an hour exploring these entertaining labs.

IMAGEWORKS SHOP: This spot at the exit to the ImageWorks: "What If" Labs offers merchandise themed to the Imagination! pavilion (including the ever-popular Figment). It also provides a service whereby your image can be captured by computer and reproduced onto items such as ornaments and crystal cubes. You can have your mug slapped onto a poster, or a variety of other accessories. Film, disposable cameras, and other photographic essentials are available, too.

 HONEY, I SHRUNK THE AUDIENCE: FP Welcome to the Imagination Institute, workplace of Professor Wayne Szalinski, the featured character in the three "Honey" movies: *Honey, I Shrunk the Kids*; *Honey, I Blew Up the Kid*; and *Honey, We Shrunk Ourselves*. Rick Moranis, Marcia Strassman, and the kids reprise their familiar film roles at this 25-minute attraction.

In the pre-show area, guests see a movie about imagination. Then they are welcomed to the Imagination Institute and given an overview of what they will see inside the theater. Professor Szalinski is to be presented with the Inventor of the Year Award, and will demonstrate several of his inventions. On the way into the theater, guests are provided with "protective goggles" (3-D glasses), to shield their eyes from the flying debris that can come loose during new-product demonstrations.

Once the audience is seated, Szalinski is nowhere to be found. Then he suddenly zooms off the screen in his new HoverPod, out of control and miniaturized by his shrinking machine. Szalinski's son Nick steps in to

FP = Fastpass attraction (see page 19)

> ### Hot Tip!
> Early mornings and late evenings are the least congested times to visit Epcot's Imagination! pavilion.

demonstrate the "Dimensional Duplicator," a machine that can make copies of anything. As Nick switches on the machine, his brother drops a pet mouse into the duplicating chamber and hits the number 999. Suddenly hundreds of sqeaking mice pour out of the screen in an effect that leaves guests squirming.

Nick quickly gets rid of the mice with Professor Szalinski's No-Mess Holographic Pet System, which projects a 3-D cat out into the audience to scare away the mice. The cat morphs into a lynx and a ferocious lion before overheating and exploding. Just then, Szalinski returns, blows himself up to normal size, and demonstrates his new, more powerful, shrinking machine.

Of course, the machine spins out of control and accidentally shrinks the audience and Nick. While the audience is miniaturized, the theater shakes with every on-screen footstep. When apparent giants crouch down to ogle guests in the theater, it's a rare person who doesn't feel diminished to ant proportions. The effects are believable, particularly when Adam picks up the theater and shows it to his

Hot Tip!

Honey, I Shrunk the Audience is known to frighten small children and more than the occasional grown-up (especially those afraid of snakes or mice).

mom. Motion effects in the theater add to the realism, as does the pet snake that gets loose. The audience is eventually brought back to normal size, of course, although not without incident. The attraction has one last surprise in store, which we won't divulge.

Note: The effects in this attraction give some guests the heebie-jeebies, especially those afraid of snakes or mice. If you suspect that you or any of your kids will have an adverse reaction, consider skipping the movie and heading to ImageWorks while the rest of your party watches the movie.

Timing Tip: This attraction tends to be less crowded later in the day.

Test Track FP

Fasten your safety belt! This industrial-looking pavilion puts guests through the frenetic motions of automobile testing. As vehicles progress along the track, they whiz down

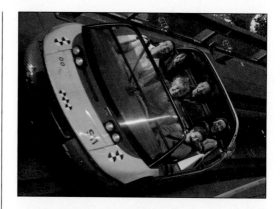

straightaways, hug hairpin turns, and face near-collisions—and not always in ideal road conditions. En route, riders learn how tests are performed in real facilities (called proving grounds) and discover why certain procedures are crucial to car safety.

Before developing the attraction, Disney Imagineers toured GM proving grounds around the country. The result: From the steely facade to the rows of authentic testing equipment inside, Test Track bears more than a passing resemblance to the real thing.

The experience begins with a pre-show walking tour of the plant that reveals the incredible amount of component testing performed before automakers commit to production. Guests witness automotive testing vignettes, with everything from human interface (our courageous, crash-prone counterparts) to tires, brakes, air bags, and even seats being put through their paces.

The computer-controlled, six-seater vehicles are equipped with video and audio, but no steering wheels or brake pedals. The roads bear the familiar lines and signage of the real world, adding to the attraction's realism.

The five-minute ride begins with an uphill acceleration test. Then the suspension gets a workout, as vehicles descend over a bumpy surface that puts the wheels at odds with one another. During environmental testing, riders feel the heat and get the shivers as vehicles pass first through a radiant heat chamber, then a cold chamber. Roadside robots pitch in by spraying the fenders and door panels with water to test for corrosion.

Hot Tip!

If you don't mind splitting up your party, head for Test Track's "single rider" line. It moves faster than the standby line. (See if they offer it at Mission: SPACE, too.)

The ride takes a dramatic turn during the road-handling segment. Vehicles course along a winding road, complete with mountain scenery, and into a darkened tunnel. Passengers hear a horn blast, see the high beams of a tractor trailer, and swerve to avoid the truck. As they emerge, there is a crash; guests round a corner to witness a barrier crash test. Their own vehicles then accelerate toward the barrier.

A long straightaway feeds into a series of banked turns and another straight shot that sends vehicles rocketing around the pavilion at top speed (up to 65 miles per hour).

Note: Kids under 7 must be accompanied by an adult; guests under 40 inches cannot ride; passengers must be free of back problems, heart conditions, motion sickness, and other physical limitations. Pregnant women are advised to sit this one out.

Mission: SPACE FP

BIRNBAUM'S **BEST** Think you've got "the right stuff?" Well, this is your chance to prove it. Epcot's newest attraction, which touched down in Future World in the fall of 2003, has a bold mission—to give you a chance to experience the excitement and intensity of space travel without acutally leaving the planet.

Hot Tip!

Epcot is bigger than it seems, so allow yourself plenty of time to get from place to place. (It takes about a half hour to walk from Spaceship Earth to The American Adventure in World Showcase.) Keep this in mind if you have made priority seating arrangements at a restaurant or hope to secure a nice fireworks veiwing location on the World Showcase promenade.

Mission: SPACE aspires to provide a galaxy of thrills. The adventure begins with a white-knuckle blast-off of a spacecraft (which has rather snug seating for four) on a secret mission. The sustained G-force during the launch is intended to be most realistic. Once en route, expect to experience a rather strange sensation. It's not quite weightlessness, but according to astronauts who've felt the real thing, it's pretty darn close.

Throughout the journey, you will work with your fellow crew members (assuming the roles of captain, engineer, navigator, and pilot) to accomplish your mission.

Note: To experience this attraction, guests must be at least 44 inches tall and free of back and heart problems, motion sickness, and other physical limitations. Pregnant women should skip the trip, as should anyone with claustrophobic tendencies. And don't eat before riding!

EPCOT

Wonders of Life

The 72-foot-tall steel DNA molecule at the entrance to this popular pavilion beckons guests to humorous and informative experiences related to health. Housed in a geodesic dome and two attached buildings, this pavilion allows guests to enjoy both a serious and an amusing look at health, fitness, and modern lifestyles. Wonders of Life also boasts Body Wars, Epcot's dramatic simulator ride — a fast and furious (and bloody) journey through the human body.

Once inside the building, guests find themselves at the Fitness Fairgrounds. At the Fairgrounds, a variety of shows and activities for both children and adults are offered. *Goofy About Health* is an eight-minute multi-screen montage that sees Goofy go from a sloppy-living guy to a health-conscious fellow. Using old Goofy cartoons that haven't been seen for many years, the show traces Goofy's ups and downs, and winds up with new footage of Goofy at his doctor's office. The film is shown in an open theater where visitors may come and go as they please.

The third theater at the Fitness Fairgrounds is enclosed. The 14-minute film shown here, *The Making of Me*, is a story starring Martin Short as a man who wonders how he came into existence. To find out, he travels back in time to the birth of his parents, their first few years together, and their decision to have a child—him. Footage from an actual delivery is part of the film; it is sensitively presented and provides an accessible and touching view of childbirth. It was written and directed by Glenn Gordon Caron, who directed the TV show *Moonlighting*.

Parents should be aware that the film is a bit graphic and may not be suitable for some children. It also leaves a few key questions unanswered, thereby allowing parents to satiate their kids' appetite for knowledge on a case-by-case basis.

There are plenty of hands-on activities in areas surrounding the theaters. Guests may ride Wonder Cycles, computerized stationary bicycles that enable guests to pedal through a variety of locales, including Disneyland and the Rose Bowl Parade. The Sensory Funhouse offers hands-on activities for the young and young at heart. It's the Disney version of a children's museum, where education and entertainment go hand in hand.

At the Lifestyle Revue, guests punch in such information as age, weight, height, exercise habits, whether they smoke, and perceived stress levels at an interactive computer terminal. The computer then processes the information and offers some advice on how to lead a healthier and less stressful existence.

Frontiers of Medicine, located toward the back of the Fitness Fairgrounds, features the only completely serious segment of Wonders of Life. Here, guests can see scientific and educational exhibits of leading developments in medicine and health sciences. The exhibits change regularly.

WELL & GOODS LIMITED: Located near Body Wars, this shop offers a selection of athletic wear, most of which features classic Disney characters participating in sporting activities, as well as educational materials.

CRANIUM COMMAND: This area of the Wonders of Life pavilion welcomes guests into the mind of a 12-year-old kid. The pre-show sets the mood as a brief animated film explains what you are about to see. General

Knowledge is recruiting pilots for an assortment of new brains. There are jokes aplenty, many of which go right over the heads of young kids. Buzzy, our star pilot, fumbles through basic training and gets assigned to one of the most volatile brains of them all, that of an adolescent boy.

Inside a 200-seat theater, the enormously exaggerated head of our 12-year-old subject

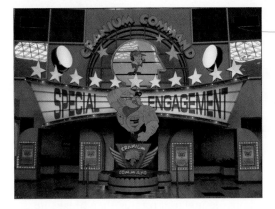

is piloted by Buzzy, a delightfully goofy Audio-Animatronics figure. The two large eyes are actually rear-projection video screens, and it is through them that the audience gets an idea of how a young boy thinks and reacts. The other animated participant, General Knowledge, helps Buzzy learn which portion of the mind is required for a particular situation.

The right and left sides of the brain, the stomach, the heart, and the adrenal gland are all represented by perfectly cast celebrities. One such actor is George Wendt (Norm from *Cheers*), operating the stomach. Other characters include Bobcat Goldthwait as the adrenal gland, Dana Carvey and Kevin Nealon (Hans and Franz of *Saturday Night Live* fame) as the heart, Charles Grodin as the left brain, and Jon Lovitz as the right brain.

Cranium Command is an altogether whimsical and entertaining (not to mention educational) show—one of Epcot's best. This 17-minute presentation is fast-paced and packed with so many details that you'll notice new things even after seeing it many times.

 BODY WARS: The same state-of-the-art technology that sends guests on a rollicking ride through outer space at the Star Tours attraction at the Disney-MGM Studios also exists at Wonders of Life in the form of this five-minute thrill ride. After boarding the

vehicles, which are actually the same type of flight simulators employed by military and commercial airlines in pilot training, guests are whisked away on a rough and exciting ride through the human body. Movie buffs will think immediately of the films *Fantastic Voyage* and *Inner Space*.

The queue area features exhibits from a fictional company specializing in the latest technology in the miniaturization of human beings. Park guests pass through two special-effects portals and are ready to do a routine medical probe of the human body—from the inside.

During the course of this bumpy trip, a scientist is dispatched to remove a splinter that has made its way beneath the patient's skin. Guests go along for the ride but end up on a rescue mission when the scientist is attacked by a white blood cell. Of course, there are some problems along the way, making this trip seem out of control.

Note: This is a somewhat rougher ride than Star Tours, its simulator-ride counterpart at the Disney-MGM Studios. Signs posted outside Body Wars warn that passengers must be free of back problems, neck problems, heart conditions, motion sickness, and other such physical limitations. Pregnant women should not ride Body Wars. Children must be at least 40 inches tall to ride. Finally, if the sight of blood makes you woozy, this attraction is probably not for you.

Universe of Energy

 Although it's easy to spot this pavilion's mirrored pyramid, the facade doesn't provide any clue at all to the 45 minutes of surprises in store. One of the most technologically complex experiences at Epcot, the show consists of several movies and a ride-through segment. None of these is exactly what guests might expect. This is especially true after the pavilion's 1996 major renovation, which repackaged the attraction, placing its legendary

Hot Tip!

As home to a 45-minute attraction, the Universe of Energy is a great place to take a load off your feet and give your body a chance to cool off. And it's funny, to boot!

Audio-Animatronics dinosaurs and lofty environmental message in a decidedly funny and much more personal context.

The show begins with a film (featuring a few familiar faces). In it, a character named Ellen is watching *Jeopardy!* One of the contestants is Ellen's annoying college roommate, Judy.

Ellen plays along but keeps striking out, particularly in the ENERGY category. As she watches, her neighbor Bill Nye, the Science Guy, pops in and is aghast at Ellen's ignorance. Shortly thereafter, Ellen falls asleep.

Ellen dreams she is a contestant on the show, competing against her former friend Judy and Albert Einstein. This time, all of the questions are about energy. As Einstein ponders and Ellen fumbles, Judy is racking up points. Ellen, who has a negative score ("this nightmare game is a lot harder than the home version"), decides to freeze her dream and ask Bill Nye, the Science Guy, for some help.

The second segment leads guests into a theater, where Bill vows to educate Ellen about the importance of energy. He persuades her to travel back in time to see where some of

our energy sources came from. Suddenly, the whole seating area rotates, then breaks up into six sections that move slowly forward. The vehicles embark with Ellen upon an odyssey through the primeval world. Enormous prehistoric trees crowd the forest. Apatosauruses wallow in the lagoon out front. A lofty allosaurus battles with an armored stegosaurus, and an elasmosaurus bursts out of a tide pool with frightening suddenness—all under the watchful gaze of winged pteranodons.

Next, guests move out of the forest and view a montage of pictures capturing the history of civilization, from cave dwellers to the present. (Keep your eyes peeled for the wacky caveman who discovers fire—chances are, you'll recognize him.) The issue of alternative-energy sources is raised, and the message is that there is no save-all source, but rather there are many possibilities with promise.

The attraction winds up with Ellen returning to the game show of her dreams. This time, she's beating her friend Judy, who is not at all happy about how much Ellen has learned during the commercial break. To win, she must name the one energy source that will never be depleted. (We won't reveal the answer, but we're not too proud to brag about getting it right!)

Almost as intriguing as the attraction is the technology behind it. The vehicles weigh about 30,000 pounds when fully loaded with passengers, yet are guided along the floor by a wire that is only *one-eighth inch thick*.

World Showcase

Noble sentiments about humanity and the fellowship of nations, which have motivated so many world's fairs in the past, also inhabit World Showcase. But make no mistake about it: This area of Epcot is unlike any previous international exposition.

The group of pavilions that encircles World Showcase Lagoon (a body of water that is about the size of 85 football fields, with a perimeter of about 1.2 miles) demonstrates Disney conceptions about participating countries in remarkably realistic, consistently entertaining styles. You won't find the real Germany here—rather, the country's essence, much as a traveler returning from a visit might remember what he or she saw.

Shops, restaurants, and attractions are housed in a group of structures that is an artful pastiche of all the elements that give that nation's countryside and towns their distinctive flavor. Although occasional liberties have been taken when scale and proportion required them, careful research governed the design of every nook and cranny.

Equally impressive is the cuisine. With no fewer than eleven upscale eateries to choose from, it's no wonder some guests here do nothing but nosh. (That is especially true during Epcot's popular Food and Wine Festival, a time when dozens more nations contribute to an already fortified international menu. See page 10 for additional information.)

In the shops, many of the wares represent the country in whose pavilion they are sold. Craftspeople are occasionally on hand to demonstrate their arts. Thanks to special cultural exchange programs and recruiting efforts, many World Showcase staffers hail from the countries the pavilions represent.

A diverse lineup of entertainment ensures that all visitors experience more than a little culture, foreign or otherwise. The entertainment is as authentic as the Disney casting directors can make it, with native performers commonly featured and new festivities always in the works.

Hot Tip!

World Showcase pavilions may open at 11 A.M. or later. However, guests may use the International Gateway entrance as much as a half hour prior to Future World's official opening time.

Pavilions are described in the order in which they would be encountered while moving counterclockwise around the World Showcase Lagoon after crossing the bridge from Future World.

Canada

Celebrating the many beauties of the U.S.A.'s neighbor to the north, the area devoted to the Western Hemisphere's largest nation is complete with its own mountain, waterfall, rushing stream, rocky canyon, mine, and splendid garden massed with colorful flowers. There's even a totem pole, a trading post, and an elaborate, mansard-roofed hotel similar to ones built by Canadian railroad companies as they pushed west around the turn of the 20th century. All this is imaginatively arranged somewhat like a split-level house, with the section representing French Canada on top, and another devoted to the mountains alongside it and below. From a distance, the Hôtel du Canada, the main building here, looks like little more than a bump on the landscape—as does Epcot's single Canadian Rocky Mountain. But up close they both seem to tower as high as the real thing.

The gardens were inspired by the Butchart Gardens, in Victoria, British Columbia, a famous park created on the site of a limestone quarry. The hotel is modeled after Ottawa's Victorian-style Château Laurier. Entertainment may be provided by a troupe of Celtic rock musicians, called "Off-Kilter." They perform on a stage facing the promenade.

O CANADA!: This 17-minute motion picture, presented in Circle-Vision 360 inside Canada's mountain, portrays the Canadian confederation in all its coast-to-coast splendor—the prairies and plains, sparkling shorelines and

rivers, and the untouched snowfields and rocky mountainsides surround you. The Royal Canadian Mounted Police also put in an appearance. All the maritime provinces are pictured, with their covered bridges and sailing ships, as is Montreal, with its old-world cafes and churches; the scene in the Notre Dame Basilica, with its organ booming and choirboys in attendance, is particularly stirring.

The great outdoors gets equal play. In one scene, snow geese take off all around the screen, and the beating of their wings is positively thunderous. Eagles, possums, mallards, bobcats, wolves, bears, deer, bison, and herds of reindeer can also be seen.

Filmed, too, were steers being roped at a rodeo and the chuck wagon race that takes place every year at that great provincial fair known as the Calgary Stampede. Skiers in the vast and empty Bugaboos, dogsledders, and ice-skaters are featured in the winter scenes; in a hockey game, the sound system almost perfectly conveys the scratch of skates on ice and the sharp whack of sticks slamming against the puck. And throughout, the motion picture provides a you-are-there feeling that makes all of this spectacular scenery still more memorable. Note that there are no seats in this theater.

NORTHWEST MERCANTILE: The first shop to the left upon entering the pavilion's plaza features merchandise by Roots, a Canadian apparel label. The Roots line features athletic attire, shoes, and fragrances. The shop also stocks plush toys, maple syrup, and other Canada-themed collectibles. Skeins of rope, tin scoops, lanterns, and antique ice skates hanging from the long beams overhead set the mood, together with the structure itself.

LA BOUTIQUE DES PROVINCES: This small shop inside Hôtel du Canada, which features a variety of items with an *Anne of Green Gables* theme, also proffers Linda Edgington decoupage, pewter, and other items crafted by Canadian artists.

United Kingdom

In the space of only a few hundred feet, visitors to this pavilion stroll from an elegant London square to the edge of a canal in the rural countryside—via a bustling urban English street framed by buildings that constitute a veritable rhapsody of historic architectural styles. But one scene leads to the next so

smoothly that nothing ever seems amiss. Here again, note the attention to detail: the half-timbered High Street structure that leans a bit, the hand-painted "smoke" stains that make the chimneys look as if they had been there for centuries. When a thatched roof is required, it's right where it should be—though the roof may be made of plastic broom bristles because fire regulations prohibit the real thing. Off to the side is a pair of scarlet phone booths identical to those that used to be found all around the United Kingdom. And there are eight architectural styles characteristic of the streetscapes, from English Tudor to Georgian and English Victorian.

There is no major attraction in this pavilion; instead, it features half a dozen shops and a pub that serves a selection of beers and ales that would be the toast of any "local" in London itself. There's also plenty of entertainment, including a group of comedians called the World Showcase Players, who, when not engaged in general clowning on the World Showcase Promenade, coax audience members into participating in their farcical playlets. In the pub, a pianist has been known to play late into the evening. A mop-topped quartet known as the British Invasion occasionally plays Beatles tunes in the garden courtyard.

They're a true crowd pleaser. Entertainment is subject to change.

THE CROWN & CREST: This shop looks like a backdrop for a child's fantasy of the days of King Arthur, with its high rafters decked out with bright banners, vast fireplace (and crossed swords above), and wrought-iron chandelier. "Pub mugs," glasses that serve yards of beer, limited-edition chess sets, and passport stamp sets are the stock-in-trade at this emporium adjoining the Sportsman Shoppe. Name histories and family crests are also available.

SPORTSMAN SHOPPE: Head here for clothing and accessories centered on uniquely British locales and events. You can expect to find an assortment of Wimbledon tennis garb,

Hot Tip!

A great place to watch IllumiNations is from the Rose & Crown Pub in the United Kingdom pavilion. Try to snag a lagoon-side table—whether within the pub's boundaries or in the self-serve sitting area nearby—about 30 minutes before the show is set to begin.

golf items from Scotland's Royal and Ancient Golf Club at Saint Andrews, plus Rugby shirts. Don't miss the tartan map on the wall opposite The Crown & Crest; it identifies plaids from Glen Burn and Gordon to Langtree and St. Lawrence. Outside, the shop resembles a stone manor built during the last half of the 16th century.

THE TEA CADDY: Fitted out with heavy wooden beams and a broad fireplace to resemble the Stratford-upon-Avon cottage of William Shakespeare's wife, Anne Hathaway, this shop stocks English teas, both loose and in bags, in a wide variety of flavors. Other items include teapots, china, biscuits, and assorted candies.

THE TOY SOLDIER: This shop presents a nice selection of British toys, as well as a rather extensive selection of merchandise featuring the gang from the Hundred Acre Wood: Winnie the Pooh, Piglet, Eeyore, and Tigger, too.

THE QUEEN'S TABLE: This shop (opposite the Sportsman Shoppe) may be one of the loveliest in Epcot. This is particularly true of the store's elegant Adams Room, embellished with elaborate moldings, hung with a crystal chandelier, and painted in cream and robin's-egg blue. The setting is a lovely background for the perfumes, soaps, and other fragrant items that are available.

Don't neglect to inspect small, serene Britannia Square outside the shop farthest from the promenade. But for its small size and the Florida climate, it feels like London itself.

THE MAGIC OF WALES: This small emporium offers pottery, jewelry, souvenirs, and hand-crafted gifts.

International Gateway

International Gateway, informally known as Epcot's back door, is located between the United Kingdom and France pavilions. Here you'll find:

FRIENDSHIP LANDING: Disney's water taxis, known as *FriendShip* boats, ferry guests from this point to the Yacht and Beach club, the BoardWalk, and the Swan and Dolphin Resorts. It's also possible to transfer and cruise over to the Disney-MGM Studios. Note that the dock is located outside the International Gateway turnstiles.

GATEWAY GIFTS: Candy, convenience items, souvenirs, and a package pickup depot are located at this spot near the France entrance.

Where to Eat in Epcot

A complete listing of all eateries—full-service restaurants, fast-food emporiums, and snack shops—can be found in the *Good Meals, Great Times* chapter. See the Epcot section beginning on page 219.

WORLD TRAVELER: Disney fashions, home items, and character merchandise, plus film and a drop-off for two-hour film processing are located here.

STROLLER AND WHEELCHAIR RENTAL: Strollers and wheelchairs are available for rent at this location. Remember to keep your rental receipt; it can be used on the same day in the Magic Kingdom, the Disney-MGM Studios, Animal Kingdom, or again in Epcot, should you leave and return later on. It is also possible to get a replacement stroller here.

France

The buildings here have mansard roofs and casement windows so Gallic in appearance that you may expect to see some sad Bohemian poet looking down from above. A canal-like offshoot of the lagoon seems like the Seine itself; the footbridge that spans it recalls the old Pont des Arts. There's a kiosk nearby like those that punctuate the streets of Paris and a bakery whose heavenly rich aromas announce its presence long before it's visible.

Shops sell perfumes and other items. Their roofs are of real copper or slate, and the cabinetry is finely crafted. Galérie des Halles—the iron-and-glass-ceilinged market that Paris once counted as one of its most beloved institutions—lives again. But perhaps most special of all are the people. Hosts and hostesses who hail from Paris and the French provinces answer questions in French-accented English. It's fun to take in the shows put on by Imaginum. It's a statue act featuring amazing white-robed actors who seem to be statues, but change poses when you least expect it. (The entertainment may change unexpectedly, too.)

Some interesting background notes: The dusty rose-colored, lace-trimmed costumes that the hostesses wear were inspired by the dresses in *Le Bar aux Folies-Bergère* by the Impressionist painter Edouard Manet, and the main entrance to the pavilion recalls the architecture of Paris, most of which was built during the Belle Epoque ("beautiful age"), the last decades of the 19th century.

Don't miss the garden on the opposite side of this arcade. It is one of the most peaceful spots in World Showcase.

BIRNBAUM'S BEST | IMPRESSIONS DE FRANCE: Shown in the Palais du Cinéma, a little theater that's not unlike the one at Fontainebleau, this enchanting 18-minute film takes viewers on a trip through France.

The film shows off a beautiful tree-dotted estate, fields and vineyards at harvest time, a flower market and a pastry shop, a glacier, and a harbor full of squawking gulls. Viewers visit the Eiffel Tower; Versailles and its gilt Hall of Mirrors (just outside Paris); Mont Saint Michel; the French Alps; and Cannes, the star-studded resort city on the Mediterranean coast. All this is even more appealing thanks to a superb sound track, consisting almost entirely of the music of French classical composers.

The exceptionally wide screen adds yet another dimension. This is not a Circle-Vision 360 film like the movies shown at China and Canada. The France film used only five cameras, and it is shown on five large projection surfaces—200 degrees around. It's a beautiful film, one of the park's best. We recommend stopping for a French pastry break after the show.

PLUME ET PALETTE: This is one of the loveliest shops in World Showcase. The Art Nouveau style is reflected in the curves that embellish the wrought-iron balustrade edging the mezzanine and the moldings that decorate cherry-wood cabinets and shelves. Among the wares are French fragrances and soaps.

LA SIGNATURE: Another beautiful spot, this boutique features a selection of Guerlain cosmetics and fragrances.

L'ESPRIT DE PROVENCE: This little shop stocks a selection of dinnerware and kitchen accessories from the Provence region of Southern France.

LES VINS DE FRANCE: Selections in this lovely wine shop range from the inexpensive to the pricey, from *vin ordinaire* going for

several dollars to upward of $99 for a rare vintage. Wine tastings are held here to sample the offerings (note that a charge is levied for each taste). Those who don't want to carry their purchases may have them dispatched to a package pickup location (either at the Park's Future World entrance or at the International Gateway entrance in World Showcase) for retrieval later in the day (be sure to allow at least two hours for packages to make it to their destination).

SOUVENIRS DE FRANCE: Everything from Eiffel Tower statues to CDs with music by French composers is the stock-in-trade at this location near the exit of the cinema. Gifts are themed to the artwork of renowned French artists, such as Monet and Renoir. Mugs, tote bags, umbrellas, and picture frames are among the offerings available. The area is based on Paris's now-demolished Les Halles, the city's old fruit and vegetable market.

Morocco

Nine tons of tile were handmade, hand cut, and shipped to Epcot to create this World Showcase pavilion. To capture the unique quality of this North African country's architecture, Moroccan artisans came to Epcot to practice the mosaic art that has been a part of their homeland for thousands of years. Koutoubia Minaret, a detailed replica of the famous prayer tower in Marrakesh, stands guard at the entrance. A courtyard with a

Hot Tip!
Don't try to fit all of the World Showcase movies into one day, especially if you are traveling with kids.

fountain at the center leads to the Medina (Old City). Between the traditional alleyways and the more modern sections are the pointed arches and swirling patterns of the Bab Boujouloud gate, a replica of the one that stands in the city of Fez. An ancient working waterwheel irrigates the gardens, and the motifs repeated throughout the buildings include carved plaster and wood, tile, and brass. Mo'rockin takes over the courtyard, with musicians playing Western music with an Arabic twist. (Entertainment may change.)

MOROCCAN NATIONAL TOURIST OFFICE: An information center offering literature useful in planning a visit to Morocco, this is also the place to inquire about experiencing a "Morocco Tour." The guided tour of the pavilion includes an in-depth description of the culture, history, and architecture of Morocco. Tours are held daily at 1 P.M., 3 P.M., and 5 P.M. They are free to all Epcot park guests and last from about 20 to 45 minutes.

TANGIER TRADERS: This is the place to shop if you're in the market for a fez, woven belts, leather sandals and purses, and other traditional Moroccan clothing and accessories.

MARKETPLACE IN THE MEDINA: Hand-woven baskets, sheepskin wallets and bags, assorted straw hats, drums, *Aladdin* merchandise, sandals, postcards, scarves, and small carpets are among the available wares.

THE BRASS BAZAAR: Interspersed among the decorative brass plates in this store are ceramic pitchers, planters, pots, ornate bottles of rosewater, serving sets, soapstone carvings, wooden collectibles, books, framed prints, and other Moroccan wares.

SOUK AL MAGREB: This small waterside enclave located on the World Showcase promenade spills over with crafted brass work. Moroccan baskets and leather goods also abound. In addition to henna tattoos (provided by a resident tattoo artist), one can also pick up toy camels, hats, and shirts.

Japan

Serenity rules in Japan. Except, of course, when the pavilion resounds with traditional music performed by a drum-playing duo or group.

The landscaping, designed in accordance with traditional symbolic and aesthetic values, contributes to the pavilion's peaceful mood. Rocks, which in Japan represent the enduring nature of the Earth, were brought from North Carolina and Georgia (since boulders are scarce in the Sunshine State). Water, symbolizing the sea (which the Japanese consider a life source), is abundant; the Japan pavilion garden has a stream and pools inhabited by *koi* (fish). Evergreen trees, which in Japan are symbols of eternal life, are here in force.

Disney horticulturists created this very Japanese landscape using few plants native to that country because the climate there is so different from that of Florida. Among the few trees here native to Japan are the *sago*, near the courtyard entrance to the Yakitori House; the two Japanese maple trees, identifiable by their small leaves, not far away (near the first stairway from the promenade on the left side of the courtyard as you face it); and the prickly monkey-puzzle trees, near the walkway to the promenade, on

The American Adventure side of the pagoda. Needle-sharp thorns make the latter the only species of tree that monkeys cannot climb.

The pagoda was modeled after an eighth-century structure located in the Horyuji Temple, in Nara, Japan. The striking *torii* gate on the shore of World Showcase Lagoon derives from the design of the one at the Itsukushima shrine in Hiroshima Bay.

BIJUTSU-KAN GALLERY: Housing a changing cultural display, this small museum has offered, among other exhibitions, "Netsuke— Historic Carvings of Old Japan," a showcase of traditional Japanese art forms, and, more recently, "Diamond Warriors: Traditions in Japanese Baseball."

MITSUKOSHI DEPARTMENT STORE: There are kimonos, T-shirts bearing Japanese characters, traditional headdresses, and a selection of bowls and vases meant for flower arranging for sale at this spacious store set up by Mitsukoshi—a four-century-old retail firm.

The shop features a large selection of kimonos, as well as chopsticks, bonsai, jewelry, china, paper fans, and origami products. There is also a bounty of snacks, candies, and tea. The pleasant atmosphere and wide variety of merchandise make this establishment a most rewarding experience for both the casual browser and the serious shopper.

The building's design was inspired by the Gosho Imperial Palace, which was constructed in Kyoto in A.D. 794.

The American Adventure

BIRNBAUM'S BEST When it came to creating The American Adventure, the centerpiece of World Showcase, Disney Imagineers were given relatively free rein. So the 110,000 bricks of the imposing Colonial-style structure that houses a spectacular show, fast-food restaurant, and souvenir shop are the real thing—patiently crafted *by hand* from soft Georgia clay.

The show inside stands out because of its wonderfully evocative settings, its detailed sets, and the 35 superb Audio-Animatronics players, some of the most lifelike ever created by the Disney organization. Stellar a cappella vocal groups called Voices of Liberty and American Vybe periodically serenade guests in the building's foyer. By all means, catch a performance.

THE AMERICAN ADVENTURE SHOW: One of the truly outstanding Epcot attractions, this 26-minute presentation celebrates the American spirit from our nation's earliest years right up to the present. Beginning with the arrival of the Pilgrims at Plymouth Rock and their hard first winter on the western shore of the Atlantic, the Audio-Animatronics narrators—an amazingly lifelike Ben Franklin and a convincing, cigar-puffing Mark Twain—recall key people and events in American history: the Boston Tea Party, George Washington and the grueling winter at Valley Forge, the influential abolitionist Frederick Douglass, the celebrated 19th-century Nez Percé chief Joseph, and many more. The Philadelphia Centennial Exposition is remembered, along with women's rights campaigner Susan B. Anthony, telephone inventor Alexander Graham Bell, and the steel giant and philanthropist Andrew Carnegie. Naturalist John Muir converses onstage with Teddy Roosevelt. Charles Lindbergh, Rosie the Riveter, Jackie Robinson, Marilyn Monroe, and Walt Disney are represented. So are John Wayne, Lucille Ball, Margaret Mead, John F. Kennedy, Martin Luther King, Jr., and Billie Jean King.

The idea is to recall episodes in history, both negative and positive, that contributed to the growth of the spirit of America, either by engendering "a new burst of creativity," (in the designers' words) "or a better understanding of ourselves as partners in the American experience."

For information about how each of the many featured historical figures spoke during his or her lifetime, researchers contacted historians and cultural institutions—the Philadelphia Historical Commission, Harvard's Carpenter Center of Visual Arts, the State Historical Society of Missouri, the Department of the Navy's Ships Historical Branch, and others. When recordings were not available, educated guesses were made: Alexander Graham Bell's voice was created on the basis of contemporary comments about his voice's clarity, expressiveness, and crisp articulation, combined with the fact that his father taught elocution.

A special highlight of the show is the majestic music played throughout by the Philadelphia Symphony Orchestra.

Seats toward the front of the house give the best view of the Audio-Animatronics figures. If you have some extra time before the show, be sure to read the inspirational quotes on the walls—Jane Addams, Charles Lindbergh, Herman Melville, and Ayn Rand are among the Americans who are quoted.

Hot Tip!
While all of the seats in the American Adventure theater provide good views, the sound quality is best in the middle and toward the front.

HERITAGE MANOR GIFTS: Visit this shop to find authentic Americana in all of its red-white-and-blue glory. Gifts include patriotic clothing, flags, autographs of famous Americans, and books about American history.

AMERICA GARDENS THEATRE: An ever-changing slate of entertainment is presented throughout the week in this lakeside amphitheater in front of The American Adventure pavilion. Check your park guidemap and times guide for details and exact times. Showtimes are also posted on the promenade at the east and west entrances to the theater.

Be sure to note the pruning of the western sycamores overhead: The old-fashioned pollarding method used, which involves trimming the treetops flat and allowing the lower branches to interlock, produces a thick canopy. The flower beds are planted appropriately with red, white, and blue blossoms.

Italy

The arches and cutout motifs that adorn the World Showcase reproduction of the Doge's Palace in Venice are just the more obvious examples of the attention to detail lavished on the individual structures in this relatively small pavilion. The angel perched atop the scaled-down campanile was sculpted on the model of the original right down to the curls on the back of its head. It was then covered with real gold leaf, despite the fact that it was destined to be set almost 100 feet in the air.

The other statues in the complex, including the sea god Neptune presiding over the fountain in the rear of the piazza, are similarly exact. And the pavilion even has an island like Venice's own, its seawall appropriately stained with age, plus moorings that look like barber poles, with several distinctively Venetian gondolas tied to them. St. Mark the Evangelist is also remembered, together with the lion that is the saint's companion and Venice's guardian; these can be seen atop the two massive columns that flank the small arched footbridge that connects the island to the mainland. The only deviation from Venetian reality is the alteration of the site of the Doge's Palace in reference to the real St. Mark's Square.

The quaint pavilion is equally interesting from a horticultural point of view. The island boasts kumquat trees, citrus plants typical of the Mediterranean, and a couple of olive trees that can be seen on both sidewalls of the Delizie Italiane. Originally located in a Sacramento, California, grove, the olive trees arrived in Florida via flatbed truck a bit slimmer than when they started out. (Arizona border inspectors decreed that the trees be trimmed to the ten-foot width required by state law; therefore, the ancient olives were shorn en route. The hardy trees survived, leaving only their scars to remind visitors of the ordeal; the darker bark is what remains of the original, while the lighter areas are new growth.) The tall, narrow trees that stand like dark columns are Italian cypresses, which are extremely common in their native country.

ENOTECA CASTELLO: This shop on the edge of the piazza features a selection of red and white Italian wines. Items such as chocolate, espresso, cookbooks, and decorative bottle toppers are also on hand.

IL BEL CRISTALLO: There is an abundance of fine leather goods, including purses, wallets, and bags inside this shop (just off the promenade on the Germany side of the piazza). Delicate Armani porcelain figurines are also on display. Other featured wares include scarves, ties, fragrances, and jewelry.

LA BOTTEGA ITALIANA: This shop sells an eclectic blend of decorative ceramics and glassware, plus an assortment of masks.

Germany

There are no villages in Germany quite like this one. Inspired by various towns in the Rhine region, Bavaria, and the German north, it boasts structures reminiscent of those found in urban enclaves as diverse as Frankfurt, Freiburg, and Rothenburg. There are stair-stepped rooflines and towers, balconies and arcaded walkways, and so much overall charm that the scene seems to come straight out of a fairy tale. The beer hall to the rear is almost as lively as the one at Munich's famed Oktoberfest, especially late in the evening. The shops, which offer a range of merchandise from wine and sweets to ceramics and cuckoo clocks, toys, and books—and even art—are so tempting that it's hard to leave the area empty-handed.

The elements that constitute the Germany pavilion are described here as they would be encountered walking from west to east (counterclockwise) around the cobblestone-paved central plaza, which is known as the St. Georgsplatz, after the statue at its center. St. George, the patron saint of soldiers, is depicted with a dragon that legend says he slew during a pilgrimage to the Middle East.

Try to time your World Showcase peregrinations to take you to Germany on the hour, when the handsome, specially designed glockenspiel at the plaza's rear can be heard chiming in a melody composed specifically for the pavilion.

DAS KAUFHAUS: This two-story structure, whose exterior is patterned after a merchants' hall known as the Kaufhaus (located in the German town of Freiburg in Breisgau), stocks hand-painted eggs (some painted on the premises), glassware, and housewares. Film and sundries are also available.

VOLKSKUNST: Small and exceptionally appealing, this establishment is filled with a burgher's bounty of German timepieces, plus a smattering of other items made by hand in the rural corners of the nation. As for cuckoo clocks, some are small and unobtrusive, while others are so immense that they'd look appropriate only in some cathedral-ceilinged hunting lodge. This is also the place to pick up a traditional German beer stein.

DER TEDDYBAR: Located adjacent to Volkskunst, this toy shop would be a delight if only for the lively mechanized displays: Some of the stuffed lambs and the dolls wearing folk dresses (called *dirndls*) have been animated so that tails wag and skirts swirl in time to German folk tunes. The shop is also home to one of Walt Disney World's best selections of toys, including an assortment of expensive stuffed keepsakes from Steiff. Last but not least, the dolls are simply wonderful—you can even have one created to your personal specifications.

KUNSTARBEIT IN KRISTALL: This shop to the left of the Biergarten features Austrian and crystal jewelry, tall beer mugs, wineglasses in traditional German tints of green and amber, and crystal decanters. Guests may have glassware etched on the spot.

SUSSIGKEITEN: It's a mistake to visit this tiny confectionery shop on an empty stomach: Chocolate cookies, butter cookies, and almond biscuits mix with caramels, nuts, and pretzels on the shelves, and there are boxes upon boxes of *lebkuchen*, the spicy chewy cookies traditionally baked in Germany at Christmas, not to mention Gummy Bears (which the packages announce as *Gummibaeren*). Be sure to note the attractive display of old Bahlsen sweets by the door.

WEINKELLER: The Germany pavilion's wine shop, situated between the cookie shop and the crystal shop toward the rear of St. Georgsplatz, offers about 50 varieties of German wine. Wine tastings are held here daily. The selection includes not only those vintages meant for everyday consumption, but also fine estate wines. These are white (with a few exceptions), because white wine constitutes the bulk of Germany's vinicultural output. (Only 20 percent of all German bottlings are red.) The setting itself is quite attractive—low-ceilinged and cozy, and full of cabinets embellished with carvings of vines and bunches of grapes.

DIE WEIHNACHTS ECKE: This is a shop that can set a visitor's mind to thoughts of Christmas—even in the hottest dog days of summer. Ornaments, decorations, and gifts manufactured by various German companies line the shelves of this store. Among them are wood carvings made in the German town of Oberammergau, nutcrackers, and a whole collection of "smokers" (carved wooden dolls with a receptacle for incense and a hollow pipe for the smoke to escape).

GLAS UND PORZELLAN: Featuring glass and porcelain items made by the German firm of Goebel, this is an attractive establishment with rope-turned columns, curved moldings, delicate scrollwork, and tiny carved rosettes. But no matter how attractive the background, the stars of the show are the M. I. Hummel figurines that Goebel makes. Cherubic, rosy-cheeked children, shown carrying baskets, trays, umbrellas, and other items—depicted as in the drawings of a young German nun named Berta Hummel—are favorites of collectors around the world. There is always an elaborate showpiece at the center of the shop, and a Goebel artist is here to demonstrate the process by which Hummel creations are painted and finished.

China

Dominated by the Disney equivalent of Beijing's Temple of Heaven and announced by a pair of banners that offer good wishes to passersby (the Chinese characters translate to: "May good fortune follow you on your path through life" and "May virtue be your neighbor"), this pavilion conveys a level of serenity that offers an appealing contrast to the hearty merriment of the

bordering Germany and the gaiety of nearby Mexico. Part of this quiet environment is the by-product of the soothing, traditional Chinese music. Live flute, zither, or dulcimer music is performed inside the Temple of Heaven, while agile acrobats do tricks in the courtyard. The gardens also make a major contribution. They are full of rosebushes native to China, and there is a century-old mulberry tree (to the left of the main walkway into the pavilion), with a pomegranate tree and a wiggly-looking Florida native known as a water oak nearby.

The number of stones in the floor of the pavilion's main structure is not random; the center stone is surrounded by nine stones because nine is considered a lucky number in China. Around the edge of the outer room rise 12 columns—because 12 is the number of months in the year and the number of years in a full cycle of the Chinese calendar. Be sure to stand on the round stone in the center: Every whisper is amplified.

Village Traders

Located between the Germany and China pavilions, this open-air shop sports a selection of gift items from Africa, India, and Australia. Browse through such souvenirs as wind chimes, handbags, hats, and, of course, T-shirts.

A spacious emporium is devoted to Chinese wares, and two restaurants add to the overall atmosphere. However, all this is secondary to the motion picture shown inside the Temple of Heaven—a Circle-Vision 360 film that is one of the most diverting World Showcase attractions. Keep in mind that this is a standing-room-only experience.

REFLECTIONS OF CHINA: This new presentation shows the beauties of a land that few Epcot visitors have seen firsthand—and does it so vividly that it's possible to see the film twice and still not fully absorb all the wonderful sights.

The film replaces "Wonders of China," the Circle-Vision 360 movie that played at Epcot's China pavilion since 1982. Just as with the original, filmmakers used nine cameras to capture cultural and scenic images that will wrap completely around viewers. The tour includes stops in Hong Kong, Macau, Beijing, and Shanghai.

This updated film includes footage of many landmarks, such as the 2,400-year-old Great Wall and Tian'anmen Square, as well as some newer cultural developments. Overall, it showcases the majesty of this ancient country and highlights some of the more dramatic changes that have taken place over the past 20 years. Note that the theater has no seats.

HOUSE OF WHISPERING WILLOWS: When exiting, pass by the House of Whispering Willows, an exhibit of ancient Chinese art and artifacts. Changed about every six months, it invariably includes fine pieces from well-known collections.

YONG FENG SHANGDIAN: This vast Chinese emporium, located off the narrow, charming Street of Good Fortune, offers a huge assortment of merchandise—silk robes, prints, paper umbrellas, embroidered items, and more. Trinkets, moderately priced items, and expensive antiques are available. The calligraphy on the curtains wishes passersby good fortune, long life, prosperity, and happiness.

Norway

Set between Mexico and China is Norway, a pavilion added to the World Showcase mix in 1988. Built in conjunction with many Norwegian companies, the pavilion celebrates the rich history, folklore, and culture of one of the Western world's oldest countries.

The cobblestone town square is an architectural showcase of the styles of such Norwegian towns as Bergen, Alesund, and Oslo. There's also a Norwegian castle fashioned after Akershus, a 14th-century fortress still standing in Oslo's harbor; the castle here houses the Akershus restaurant. Few can resist walking into the bakery for a taste of its treats. In a show of modernity, a statue of Norway's living legend, marathoner Grete Waitz, stands behind the bakery. Shops stock handicrafts and folk items: hand-knit woolens, wood carvings, and glass and metal artwork.

For a free guided tour of the pavilion in addition to a crash course in Norwegian culture and architecture, stop by the Norway Tourism desk. Consult a park guidemap for tour times.

MAELSTROM FP: Visitors tour Norway by boat—16-passenger, dragon-headed longboats inspired by those Eric the Red and other Vikings used a thousand years ago. The five-minute voyage begins in a tenth-century Viking village, where a ship is being readied to head out to sea. Seafarers then find themselves in a mythical Norwegian forest, populated by trolls who cause the boats to plummet backward, through a maelstrom, to the grandeur of the Geiranger fjord, where the

EPCOT

vessel nearly spills over a waterfall. After a plunge through a rocky passage, the boats wind up in the stormy North Sea. As the boats pass the legs of an oil rig, the storm calms and a coastal village appears on the horizon.

Survivors disembark and enter a movie theater, where the journey continues on-screen for five more minutes. If you wish to skip the flick, walk straight through the theater to exit.

STAVE CHURCH GALLERY: Inside the wooden stave church, there is a small exhibit that explores Norwegian culture. It's interesting (and sad) to note that only 28 stave churches remain in Norway today.

THE PUFFIN'S ROOST: Norwegian gifts, sweaters, activewear, fragrances, jewelry, Christmas items, pewter, candy, toys, and trolls are the wares for sale at this shop.

Mexico

The tangle of tropical vegetation surrounding the great pyramid that encloses this pavilion and the Mexican restaurant at the lagoon's edge on the promenade provide only the barest suggestion of the charming area inside.

Dominated by a re-creation of a quaint plaza at dusk, the pyramid's interior is rimmed by balconied, tile-roofed, colonial-style structures. Crowding a pretty fountain area is a quartet of stands selling Mexican handicrafts, and to the left is a shop stocked with other handsome wares. The Mariachi Cobre band keeps things lively. To the rear, the San Angel Inn, a corporate cousin of the famous Mexico City restaurant, serves authentic Mexican fare. Behind it, the pavilion's main show chronicles Mexican culture from earliest times right up to the present.

Take a look at the cultural exhibit inside the pyramid entrance on the way in. Note that the

pyramid itself was inspired by Meso-American structures dating from the third century A.D.

EL RIO DEL TIEMPO: THE RIVER OF TIME: Over the course of this simple six-minute boat trip, sprinkled with vignettes of pre-Columbian, Spanish colonial, and modern Mexican life, visitors greet a Mayan high priest, watch performers dance, and are assailed by vendors at a market. A band dressed to look like skeletons entertains at one juncture (in a reference to the Day of the Dead, a holiday celebrated in Mexico with candies and sweets shaped like skulls and skeletons). The cheery montage of film, props, and Audio-Animatronics figures is reminiscent of It's a Small World, though on a decidedly smaller scale.

PLAZA DE LOS AMIGOS: Even if you're not in a buying mood, make a point of stopping by to take a look at this bustling marketplace. Brightly colored paper flowers, sombreros, malachite, baskets, mariachi music (available on CD), and pottery make this *mercado* (market) at the plaza's center as bright and almost as lively as one in Mexico itself. The brilliantly hued papier-mâché piñatas that figure strongly in the scenery here are quite popular. Authentic pre-Colombian figures are on display. Also available for purchase are spices, salsa, liquors (emphasis on tequila), cocktail accessories, candy, film, and Mexican musical instruments.

EL RANCHITO DEL NORTE: Located on the lagoon side of World Showcase Promenade, this spot features gifts and souvenirs from Mexico.

LA FAMILIA FASHIONS: Traditional and modern Mexican accessories for everyone in the family; the handcrafted silver jewelry is a major draw.

Showcase Plaza

PORT OF ENTRY: A children's shop carrying infants' and kids' clothing, girls' character dresses, plush dolls, and toys.

DISNEY TRADERS: Merchandise combining the charms of classic Disney characters and World Showcase themes is the primary stock-in-trade. Sunglasses, film, and sundries are also available.

Entertainment

Epcot presents an intriguing array of live performances each day, making it very important to consult an entertainment schedule when they arrive. For up-to-the-minute schedules and information, call 407-824-4321.

AMERICA GARDENS THEATRE: The venue alongside the lagoon at The American Adventure pavilion hosts an ever-changing program of live entertainment. Top name performers may appear during the summer. Check a park guidemap for current offerings.

ILLUMINATIONS: REFLECTIONS OF EARTH: This nighttime spectacular presents the entire history of our planet in 13 minutes—from its creation to the present and a look toward the future. A dazzling mix of lasers, fireworks, fountains, and music, this show is a highlight of any Epcot visit.

The extravaganza, visible from anywhere on the World Showcase Promenade, takes place nightly at closing time. There are excellent viewing locations all around the World Showcase lagoon. Note that additional viewing areas have been added to the stretch between the Germany and China pavilions.

KIDCOT FUN STOPS: There is an activity area in each of the countries of World Showcase. These spots allow young guests to play games and make crafts that are native to each country's culture. Note that these areas are best enjoyed by small children.

WORLD SHOWCASE PERFORMERS: It's all but impossible to complete a circuit of World Showcase without catching a few performances en route. Keep an eye on the schedule to take in live entertainment at each pavilion, often performed by natives of the country represented. Among the possibilities: worldly comedians, a Mexican mariachi band, Moroccan belly dancers, Chinese acrobats, Canadian rock band, African storytellers, and more.

Holiday Happenings

During certain holidays, such as the Fourth of July, Christmas, and New Year's Eve, Epcot usually stays open extra late and presents added entertainment for the occasion. Call 407-824-4321 for details about any celebrations that may be planned during your visit.

CHRISTMAS: Epcot celebrates this holiday with a nightly tree-lighting ceremony, a lighted archway that hugs the path to Showcase Plaza, and a candlelight choral processional.

The Candlelight Processional, a stirring presentation of traditional holiday songs, features a reading of the Christmas story by a celebrity narrator. This is a very popular event (and one of our favorites!).

Hot Tips

- On your way into the park, pick up a free guidemap and a times guide. Consult the entertainment schedule first thing.

- Lines throughout Epcot are longest at mid-day and shortest in the early evening.

- During peak seasons, preferred priority seating times at Epcot's table-service restaurants book quickly—arrange for priority seating as far in advance as possible. However, some tables may be available on a first-come, first-served basis (with a bit of a wait).

- Most World Showcase restaurants seat guests until park closing. To make advance plans, call 407-WDW-DINE (939-3463).

- Check the Tip Board in Innoventions Plaza for wait times at the most popular attractions and adjust your plans accordingly.

- Several interactive fountain areas at Epcot provide guests of all ages with an opportunity to cool off. Be sure to pack swimsuits (or waterproof diapers) for little ones who will undoubtedly spend time splashing in the water.

- If you plan to play at Image Works, the delightful interactive play area inside Imagination!, take along the e-mail address of a friend. It may come in handy.

- Allow plenty of time to explore the hands-on exhibits at Innoventions East and West, and Image Works in Imagination!, as well as Fitness Fairgrounds inside the Wonders of Life pavilion.

- When it comes to park-hopping, Epcot is an ideal park to hop to. It's usually open late.

- Although a *FriendShip* water taxi is unlikely to transport you across World Showcase Lagoon any faster than a brisk walk would, it is a peaceful, foot-friendly way to make the half-mile-plus journey.

Where to Find the Characters

Classic Disney characters, such as Mickey Mouse, Chip, and Dale, host all meals served at the Garden Grill restaurant in The Land pavilion in Future World. The Disney princesses invite you to join them for breakfast at Norway's Restaurant Akershus. Characters also appear at World Showcase by the busload. Each day, after traveling around the promenade, characters spill out of a double-decker bus and interact with guests. Check a times guide for exact times and greeting locations.

EPCOT

Disney-MGM Studios

Welcome to "the Hollywood that never was and always will be." So said Walt Disney Company chairman Michael Eisner when he officially opened the Disney-MGM Studios in April 1989. A bit hokey—but also true. Enter the gates and the mosaic of flashy neon, chromed Art Deco, and streamlined architecture, and star-gazing street characters immediately plunge you into the Hollywood of the 1940s. A nostalgic view of the movie-making capital has been combined with revealing backstage tours, a variety of TV- and movie-themed attractions, and a delightful selection of eateries to create this Walt Disney World enclave. Throw in a character-laden motorcade parade, and the result is an entertainment wallop worthy of a rave review.

The Studios' water tower, known to punsters (for obvious reasons) as the "Earffel Tower," is reminiscent of the structures looming over Hollywood studios of the Golden Age. Here, however, it gets that special Disney touch— it's capped by a Mouseketeer-style hat. In true Hollywood style, this established star is somewhat upstaged by a relative newcomer: a towering Sorcerer Mickey hat, stationed at the far end of Hollywood Boulevard.

Since opening, the park continues to expand and evolve. Its eclectic lineup of classic attractions is joined by a trio of thrilling newcomers: an enhanced (and scarier) Tower of Terror, the rollicking Rock 'n' Roller Coaster, and an explosive struggle between good and evil in Fantasmic! Each adds a whole new dimension to the Hollywood term *action*.

A Beauty and the Beast — Live on Stage

B Fantasmic!

C The Twilight Zone Tower of Terror

D Rock 'n' Roller Coaster

E The Magic of Disney Animation

F Playhouse Disney — Live on Stage!

G Walt Disney: One Man's Dream

H Voyage of The Little Mermaid

I Who Wants to Be a Millionaire — Play It!

J Disney-MGM Studios Backlot Tour

K American Film Institute Showcase

L Honey, I Shrunk the Kids Movie Set Adventure

M Jim Henson's Muppet★Vision 3-D

N Star Tours

O Indiana Jones Epic Stunt Spectacular

P Sounds Dangerous starring Drew Carey

Q The Great Movie Ride

••••••••• Parade Route

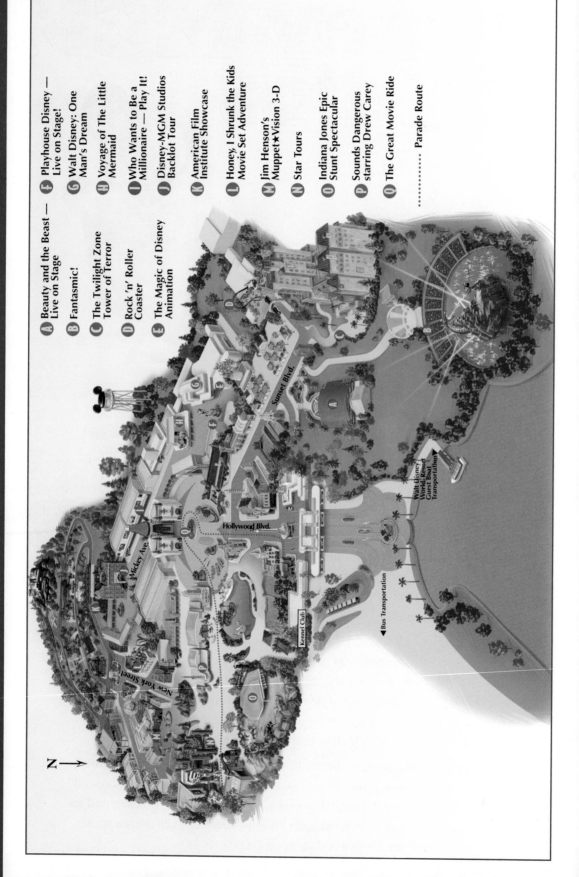

Sunset Blvd.

Hollywood Blvd.

Mickey Ave.

New York Street

Kennel Club

▶ Bus Transportation

Walt Disney World Resort Guest Boat Transportation ▶

N →

Getting Oriented

While the Disney-MGM Studios is much smaller than Epcot, the park has a sprawling layout with no distinctive shape or main thoroughfare. As such, the Studios can be a bit of a challenge to navigate. Be sure to study a guidemap as you enter.

The park entrance is at Hollywood Boulevard. This shop-lined avenue leads straight to Hollywood Plaza, address of the Studios' Chinese Theater, a replica of Mann's Theatre that doubles as the site of The Great Movie Ride (it's hidden behind the giant Sorcerer Mickey hat). Walking along Hollywood Boulevard, toward the plaza, you'll come to Hollywood Junction. Here, a wide, palm-fringed thoroughfare known as Sunset Boulevard branches off to the right.

Stroll down Sunset Boulevard and you'll come across The Hollywood Hills amphitheater, home of Fantasmic! and Rock 'n' Roller Coaster, starring Aerosmith. At the street's far end is The Hollywood Tower Hotel, home of The Twilight Zone Tower of Terror. The strip is also graced with shops, the Sunset Ranch Market, and the Theater of the Stars amphitheater, where Beauty and the Beast—Live on Stage is performed daily.

Stand in Hollywood Plaza, facing the Chinese Theater, and you'll notice an archway just off to your right. This leads to Animation Courtyard. Mickey Avenue, the street veering off to the left of Animation Courtyard, leads to The Disney-MGM Studios Backlot Tour, and Who Wants to Be a Millionaire—Play It! If you turn left off Hollywood Boulevard and go past Echo Lake, you're on course for such attractions as Sounds Dangerous starring Drew Carey, Indiana Jones Epic Stunt Spectacular, and Star Tours. Just beyond Star Tours there is another entertainment zone, near New York Street. The biggies to see here: Jim Henson's Muppet*Vision 3-D, and the Honey, I Shrunk the Kids Movie Set Adventure.

HOW TO GET THERE

Take Exit 64B off I-4. Continue about a half mile to reach the parking area. Take a tram to the park entrance.

By WDW Transportation: From the Swan, Dolphin, Yacht and Beach Club, and BoardWalk: boat or walkway. From Fort Wilderness and Downtown Disney: bus to the Transportation and Ticket Center (TTC), then transfer to the Disney-MGM Studios bus. From the Magic Kingdom, ferry or monorail to the TTC, then bus to the Studios, Epcot, Animal Kingdom, all other WDW resorts, and the resorts on Hotel Plaza Blvd.: bus.

PARKING

All-day parking at the Studios is $7 for day visitors (free to WDW resort guests and annual passholders). Trams circulate regularly, providing transportation from the parking area to the park entrance. Be sure to note the section and the aisle in which you park. The parking ticket you receive allows for re-entry to the parking area throughout the day.

HOURS

The Disney-MGM Studios is usually open from 9 A.M. until about one hour after sunset. During certain holiday periods and summer months, hours are extended. It's best to arrive about 20 minutes before the posted opening time—guests are often let in early. Depending on the season, some stage shows do not open until late in the morning.

Admission Prices

ONE-DAY TICKET
(Restricted to use only in the Disney-MGM Studios. Prices include sales tax and are subject to change.)
Adult $55.38
Child* $44.73
*3 through 9 years of age; children under 3 free

Park Primer

BABY FACILITIES

Changing tables and facilities for nursing mothers can be found at the Baby Care Center at Guest Relations near the park entrance.

CAMERA NEEDS

The Darkroom on Hollywood Boulevard stocks film, batteries, and disposable cameras. Film processing is offered here and wherever you see a Photo Express sign. Film is sold in most Studios shops.

DISABILITY INFORMATION

Most Disney World attractions, restaurants, shops, and shows are accessible to guests using wheelchairs. Additional services are available for guests with visual or hearing disabilities. For a detailed overview of the services offered, including transportation, parking, attraction access, and more, pick up a copy of the *Guidebook for Guests with Disabilities* at Guest Relations. For more information, refer to the *Getting Ready to Go* chapter.

FIRST AID

Minor medical problems can be handled at the First Aid Center, located next to Guest Relations at the park entrance.

INFORMATION

Guest Relations, located just inside the park entrance, has free guidemaps and times guides and an ever-resourceful staff. To make same-day dining arrangements for certain Studios eateries, head over to the booth at the junction of Hollywood and Sunset boulevards.

LOCKERS

Lockers, found by Oscar's Super Service, near the entrance, cost $5 per day (plus a $2 refundable deposit) for unlimited use. They may be rented from the Crossroads of the World kiosk, directly across from Oscar's classic pick-up truck. Your receipt entitles you to a locker at any other theme park on the same day (not including the deposit).

LOST & FOUND

Located near the park entrance, past the turnstiles on the right. To report lost items after your visit, call 407-824-4245.

LOST CHILDREN

Report lost children at Guest Relations, or alert a Disney employee to the problem.

MONEY MATTERS

There is an ATM just outside the park entrance, and one inside Toy Story Pizza Planet Arcade. In addition to cash, credit cards (American Express, Visa, Discover, JCB, Diner's Club, the Disney Visa Card, and MasterCard), traveler's checks, and Walt Disney World resort IDs are accepted for admission, merchandise, and meals at all restaurants. Most snack carts and souvenir stands accept cash only.

PACKAGE PICKUP

Shops can arrange for cumbersome purchases to be transported to package pickup at the Lost and Found (near the park entrance), where they can be picked up later. There is no charge for this service.

SAME DAY RE-ENTRY

Be sure to have your hand stamped upon exiting the park and to retain your ticket if you plan to return later the same day.

SECURITY CHECK

Guests entering Disney theme parks may be subject to a security check. Bags may be searched by Disney security personnel before guests are permitted to enter the park.

STROLLERS & WHEELCHAIRS

Strollers, wheelchairs, and Electric Convenience Vehicles (ECVs) may be rented from Oscar's Super Service, inside the park entrance on the right. Cost for strollers and wheelchairs is $7, plus a $1 refundable deposit. Cost for ECVs is $30, plus a $10 refundable deposit. Keep your receipt—it can be used on the same day for a replacement at any theme park. Quantities are limited.

TIP BOARDS

Check the Tip Boards at the junction of Hollywood and Sunset boulevards and on New York Street to learn the current waiting times for the most popular attractions in the park. Attendants can answer questions, too.

The Main Attractions

The Disney-MGM Studios has a brand of attractions altogether unique. Some offer guests behind-the-scenes looks at the creative and technical processes that generate television, movies, and animation. Others go so far as to allow guests to gain a bit of showbiz experience along with the insight. Still others resurrect popular characters and stories in new forms—from stage shows to thrill rides.

Many shows and attractions are presented at scheduled times, or keep shorter hours than the park itself—consult a times guide or the park's Tip Board for starting times.

The Twilight Zone Tower of Terror FP

The Hollywood Tower Hotel is the creepy home of a spectacular thrill ride. On the facade of the 199-foot-tall building hangs a sparking electric sign. As the legend goes, lightning struck the building on Halloween night in 1939. An entire guest wing disappeared, along with an elevator carrying five people.

The line for the ride runs through the lobby, where dusty furniture, cobwebs, and old newspapers add to the eerie atmosphere. As guests enter the library, they see a TV brought to life by a bolt of lightning. Rod Serling invites them to enter The Twilight Zone.

Guests are led toward the boiler room to enter the ride elevator. (This is your chance to change your mind about riding. Simply ask the attendant to direct you toward the "chicken exit.") Once you take a seat in the elevator, the doors close and the room begins its ascent. At the first stop, the doors open and guests have a view down a corridor. Among the many effects is a ghostly visit by the hotel guests who vanished. The doors close again and you continue your trip skyward.

At the next stop, you enter another dimension, a combination of sights and sounds reminiscent of *The Twilight Zone* TV series. In fact, Disney Imagineers watched each of the 156 original *Twilight Zone* episodes at least twice for inspiration. This part of the ride is a disorienting experience, in part because the elevator moves horizontally.

What happens next depends upon the whim of Disney Imagineers, who have programmed the ride so that the drop sequence is chillingly random. At the top (about 157 feet up), passengers can look out at the Studios below. Once the doors shut, you plummet 13 stories. The drop lasts about two seconds, but it seems a whole lot longer.

Just when you think it's over, the elevator launches skyward, barely stopping before it plunges again. And again. As you exit, Rod Serling claims this is the kind of thing "they don't tell you about in any guidebook." It's been our privilege to prove him wrong.

From the time you are seated, the trip takes about five minutes. Note that you must be at least 40 inches tall to ride. It is not recommended for pregnant women, those with a heart condition, or people with back and neck problems. Though thrilling (and scary), the drops are surprisingly smooth. Still, if you'd rather not experience the sensation of being a human yo-yo, sit this one out.

Rock 'n' Roller Coaster starring Aerosmith FP

 The newest and fastest roller coaster in Walt Disney World history is guaranteed to rock your world. Open since summer 1999, it's ideally suited for those who consider the Tower of Terror a little on the tame side.

The indoor attraction reaches a speed of 60 miles per hour—in 2.8 seconds flat. Other twists include two loops and a corkscrew—marking the first time Disney has ever turned guests upside down on American soil.

The ride's premise is this: The rock band Aerosmith has invited you to a backstage party. The only thing standing between you and the big bash is a classically chaotic Los Angeles freeway.

Hot Tip!

You'll need to stop at a locker (near the park entrance) before riding Rock 'n' Roller Coaster—there's no place to store loose articles in the ride vehicles.

To get to the party on time, you'll have to zip through the nighttime L.A. streets in a stretch limo. The ride vehicles (designed to resemble limousines) are equipped with a high-tech sound system (five speakers per seat make for a mega-decibel ride), and the remainder of the journey features rockin' synchronized sound—adding a dramatic dimension to the roller coaster experience most daredevils have come to expect.

You must be free of back, neck, and heart problems to experience this topsy-turvy tour. Expectant mothers should sit this one out. Guests must be at least 48 inches tall to ride.

Beauty and the Beast —Live on Stage

Here's the show that gave birth to the Broadway musical. Several times each day, Belle, Gaston, Mrs. Potts, and the rest of the cast of the Disney film *Beauty and the Beast* come to life at the 1,500-seat Theater of the Stars, near the Tower of Terror, on Sunset Boulevard.

The 20-minute show is as entertaining as they come. The staging's just right and the music simply addictive as it traces the classic tale—from Belle's dissatisfaction with her life in a small French town to the climactic battle between the staff of the Beast's castle and Gaston and the townspeople. Lumière and friends perform the song "Be Our Guest" with a delightful display of dancing flatware.

Although showtimes vary, the first performance of the day usually takes place in the morning hours.

The Magic of Disney Animation

This tour gives guests an insider look at the creative process behind Disney's many animated blockbusters. In each 35-minute tour (which run continuously), guests learn about animation and watch Disney animators at work. (They are generally on duty weekdays until about 5 P.M.)

The fun begins with a film featuring Robin Williams and Walter Cronkite. It offers a lesson in the basics of animation. The film is followed by a meeting with a Disney artist. Feel free to ask questions—this is an interactive presentation.

Next stop: the animation studio. Once inside the studio, guests see the story room, where plot lines are developed for animated features. Then it's off to the drawing boards, where characters undergo the metamorphosis from pencil sketch to moving picture. Working at their desks in full view of visitors, Disney animators are seen creating the drawings that will later appear in real films. A tour guide describes what the artists are doing.

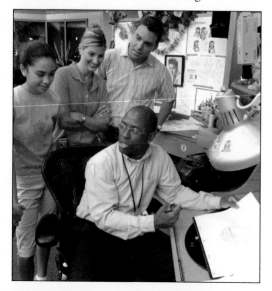

There's a special treat at the end of the tour: Copies of some of the Academy Awards won by the Disney animation team are on display, along with drawings from famous films.

Before moving on, spend some time browsing at the Animation Gallery, where Disney animation cels, exclusive limited-edition reproductions, books, figurines, and many other collectibles are for sale.

Voyage of The Little Mermaid [FP]

One of the Disney-MGM Studios' most popular attractions, this is a 15-minute live musical production, adapted from the Disney animated classic. The show is presented in a theater with an underwater feel. In it, many of the film's beloved animated characters, such as Flounder and Sebastian, are brought to life by puppeteers. The show opens with a lively rendition of "Under the Sea," then animated clips from the movie are shown as people join the puppets onstage.

Ariel is the star and performs songs from the film. Prince Eric makes an appearance, and an enormous Ursula glides across the stage to steal Ariel's voice. Of course, as in the movie, the happy ending prevails. The story line is a little bit disjointed, hopping from scene to scene, and some of the signature songs are missing. However, most viewers are familiar with the plot of the film, so this choppiness doesn't detract much from the show.

There are many special effects, including cascading water, lasers, and a lightning storm that may be a bit intense for very young children. Note that many of the effects are best enjoyed from the middle to the rear of the theater. Keep in mind that, although this is a Fastpass attraction, performances are still presented at scheduled times throughout the day. Current showtimes are always listed on the times guide (available at many locations throughout the park).

Playhouse Disney— Live on Stage!

Put on your dancing shoes! Bear, Tutter, Pip, Pop, and the rest of the gang will be disappointed if you don't join in the fun as they perform playful ditties from their Disney Channel show. Most popular with preschoolers, this stage show gets off to a bit of a slow start: Bear is sound asleep. Once audience members rouse him from his nap (no easy task), he bursts into song, welcoming one and all to his big blue

house. Later, Bear invites his new friends to investigate the day's mail, pay tribute to his beloved home, search for Shadow, and, of course, do the Bear Cha Cha.

The performance space, which resembles a working TV studio, holds large crowds (of mostly tiny people) at a time. There are no seats, but there's plenty of room to sprawl out on the carpeted floor. This show is presented at Playhouse Disney in the Animation Courtyard area of the theme park. Expect to see characters from *Rolie Polie Olie, Stanley, Book of Pooh*, and other Disney Channel favorites. Times guides list performance times.

[FP] = Fastpass attraction (see page 19)

Disney-MGM Studios Backlot Tour

Guests go backstage to see and experience some little-known aspects of TV and movie production on a tour of sets and prop stations. The 35-minute tour runs throughout the day.

The first stop is a large, outdoor special-effects area. This zone features a water tank, and teaches guests how special effects-laden waterborne scenes can be created on a set.

Guests then board the trams and travel to the backlot. Trips begin with a look at the vast wardrobe department. More than 100 designers create costumes for Disney's movie, TV, and other entertainment projects—and with 2.5 million garments for its workers, Disney World has the planet's largest working wardrobe. Famous costumes are on display.

The tram then passes through the camera, props, and lighting departments. A look into the scene shop reveals carpenters at work on sets that will later be finished on the soundstages.

Hot Tip!

Guests on the left side of the tram may get wet at Catastrophe Canyon, while those on the right stay dry. Choose accordingly.

Where in Central Florida can you find an active oil field in the middle of a dry, rocky, barren desert canyon prone to flash floods? In Catastrophe Canyon! As the guide will tell you, crews are filming a movie in which a backstage tram gets stuck in the canyon during a flash flood. But supposedly it's safe to go in because they're not filming today.

In a series of special effects, a rainstorm begins. Then there's an explosion, complete with flames that are so hot even riders on the right side of the tram feel them, followed by a flash flood that is so convincing, it forces everyone to lean the other way. The road underneath the tram shifts and dips, lending even more reality to the adventure.

From Catastrophe Canyon, the tram rides by New York Street, where reproduced building facades line the urban street. Though the brickwork looks authentic, these backless facades are constructed mostly of fiberglass and Styrofoam. The skyscrapers, including the Empire State Building and the Chrysler Building, are actually painted flats. Forced perspective (the same technique that makes Cinderella Castle appear

taller than it is) makes the four-story Empire State Building appear as if it were the actual 104-story structure. After the tour, if crews are not filming, guests may explore New York Street on foot. (It is possible to visit New York Street without experiencing the backlot tour.)

Hot Tip!

At press time, demolition had begun on Residential Street, so don't expect to see it on the Backlot Tour. The lots won't be vacant for long—a new "E-Ticket" stunt show attraction is planned for 2005.

Timing Tip: Early morning tends to be the best time to visit this attraction.

Who Wants to Be a Millionaire—Play It! FP

BIRNBAUM'S **BEST** Think you're ready for the hot seat? Then this just might be your lucky day. This attraction invites you to join the studio audience of the Disney-MGM Studios' version of the game show *Who Wants to Be a Millionaire*. You may also get the opportunity to jump into the famous hot seat and play for fabulous prizes. (Sorry, there are no million-dollar prizes up for grabs—just Disney stuff.)

Here's how it works: The hot seat contestant is chosen from an audience of more than 600 guests. He or she who has the "fastest finger" wins the right to play for points (as opposed to dollars). The more trivia questions answered correctly, the more points earned. (At press time, the million-point-prize was a Disney Cruise Line trip.)

Just as the design of the studio mirrors the actual set (right down to the dramatic music and lighting), so do the rules of the game—with a couple of notable exceptions. The most interesting new twist? While the contestant plays onstage, audience members play along on individual keypads. If the contestant hits a million points or leaves the hot seat, the audience member with the highest score will be the next contestant.

Of course, prior to coughing up your final answer to any question, you'll have a chance to use your lifelines. Polling the audience takes place just as it does on the actual show, as does the 50/50. You'll have the chance to phone someone for help, too—but it won't be a friend (that'd be a logistical nightmare). Instead, you'll get to phone a complete stranger (a random guest meandering on Mickey Avenue).

Each show lasts about 25 minutes. Note that employees of the Disney company are permitted to play along as audience members—but they are not allowed to compete for prizes.

American Film Institute Showcase

Though it is the final stop on the Backlot Tour, it is possible to visit this treasure chest of Hollywood memorabilia without taking the tour itself. Costumes, props, and set pieces used in recent, as well as classic, movies and

Hot Tip!
Don't miss the special tribute to the man who started it all: Walt Disney himself. The exhibit, entitled "Walt Disney: One Man's Dream" is housed in a theater on Mickey Avenue.

television programs are on display in this ever-changing exhibit.

Although showcased items will be different when you visit (most recently, there was a preponderance of paraphernalia paying tribute to Hollywood villains), displays have included Barbara Stanwyck's costume from *Sorry, Wrong Number*, the police car from *Dick Tracy*, an Academy Award won by the film *My Fair Lady*, concept artwork from *Toy Story*, and live-action sets and stop-motion puppets from *James and the Giant Peach*.

The Great Movie Ride

Housed in a full-scale reproduction of historic Mann's Chinese Theatre, this 22-minute attraction captivates guests' imaginations from the get-go. The queue area winds through a lobby and into the heart of filmmaking, where movie scenes are shown on a large screen.

The guided tour begins in an area reminiscent of the hills of Hollywood (which, as the famous, now abbreviated, sign indicates, was once known as Hollywoodland) in its heyday. As a ride vehicle whisks guests under a vibrant marquee, they are transported to the celluloid world of yesteryear. More than 60 dancing mannequins atop a cake greet guests in a replay of the "By a Waterfall" scene from the Busby Berkeley musical *Footlight Parade*.

Gene Kelly's memorable performance from *Singin' in the Rain* is the next scene, in which rain seems to drench the soundstage but does not dampen the spirits of the Audio-Animatronics representation of Mr. Kelly. (Gene Kelly personally inspected his likeness.) Then Mary Poppins and Bert the chimney sweep entertain (Julie Andrews and Dick Van Dyke, respectively), as Mary floats from above via her magical umbrella and Bert sings "Chim Chim Cher-ee" from a rooftop.

From the world of musical entertainment, guests segue to adventure. James Cagney recreates his role from *Public Enemy* as the ride proceeds along Gangster Alley. A mob shootout begins and puts guests in the midst of an ambush. An alternate route leads to a western town, where John Wayne can be seen on horseback eyeing some would-be bank robbers. When the thieves blow up the safe and flames pour from the building, heat can be felt from the trams.

As the ride vehicle glides into the spaceship from *Alien*, Officer Ripley guards the corridor while a slimy monster threatens riders from overhead. (Note that this and other scenes may upset young children.)

The legendary farewell from *Casablanca* is also depicted, complete with a lifelike Rick and Ilsa. (Ingrid Bergman's daughter Isabella Rossellini has brought her kids here to "see Grandma.") Guests are moved from the airfield to the swirling winds of Munchkinland, where a house has just fallen on the Wicked Witch of the East. Her sister, as portrayed by Margaret Hamilton, appears in a burst of smoke. This Audio-Animatronics figure is impressively realistic (and scary). But happy endings prevail, and guests follow Dorothy and company along the Yellow Brick Road to the Emerald City of Oz. As the ride draws to a close, guests view a montage of memorable moments from classic films.

Timing Tip: If the queue extends outside the building, you're in for a long wait. It takes about 25 minutes to reach the ride vehicles once you've entered the theater.

Sounds Dangerous starring Drew Carey

As you streak around a hairpin curve, precariously positioned in the driver's seat of a speeding car, you may want to check the security of your safety belt. Don't bother. There are no seat belts. Why? As its name indicates, this attraction only *sounds* dangerous. The majority of the action takes place in your head, thanks to a personal headset and some remarkably convincing stereo sound effects.

This 3-D audio adventure occurs inside a television soundstage. Audience members (that's you) are on hand to watch a new show being filmed. The program, *Undercover Live*, follows a detective (played by Drew Carey) as he attempts to solve cases in the real world. Drew sports a tiny camera on his tie, so the audience can see and hear all the action.

Initially, all goes according to plan. Drew infiltrates a warehouse owned by the United Snowglobe Company. He suspects they are smuggling something, though he can't put his finger on exactly what the contraband is. (Nor does he catch on after brushing past a box labeled SMUGGLED DIAMONDS, KEEP CLEAR.)

As Drew breaks into a suspect's office, he pulls the camera out of his tie tack, to give the audience a closer look at his lock-picking prowess. The unexpected appearance of a security guard sends a wave of panic over our hero, and he quickly hides the camera . . . in his mouth. Snap, crackle, blackout—the camera's video feed shorts out. Fortunately, the audio is unaffected, so it's on with the show!

From here on in, it's all about 3-D sound. (Drew Carey actually wore tiny microphones on his ears to achieve this effect.) Drew's mad pursuit to catch the bad guys takes audience members everywhere from a room full of buzzing honeybees to a barber shop for a quick trim and blow-dry. The case is finally resolved at the circus, but not before a close encounter with a prancing pachyderm.

The show, which runs continuously, lasts about 12 minutes. Generally fun for everyone, it does have its dark and intense (remember the bees?) moments. It may be a bit unsettling for kids under the age of 7.

Indiana Jones Epic Stunt Spectacular FP

Earthquakes, fiery explosions, and assorted other dramatic events give guests some insight into the science of movie stunts and special effects at this 2,000-seat amphitheater. Stunt people re-create scenes from Indiana Jones films to demonstrate the skill required to keep audiences on the edge of their seats. Show director Glenn Randall, who served as stunt coordinator of such films as *Raiders of the Lost Ark*, *Poltergeist*, *E.T.*, and *Jewel of the Nile*, calls the show "big visual excitement."

But the 30-minute show isn't all flying leaps. Guests also see how the elaborate stunts are pulled off—safely—while the crew and an assistant director explain what goes on both in front of and behind the camera.

In one segment, a scene from *Raiders of the Lost Ark* is staged. A 12-foot-tall rolling ball chases a Harrison Ford look-alike out of the temple. The steam and flames are so intense that the audience can feel the heat. The crew then dismantles the set, revealing the remarkable lightness of movie props, as assistants roll the ball uphill for the next show.

In a scene at a busy "Cairo" street market, "extras" chosen from the audience play the famous scene in which Indiana Jones pulls a gun while others are fighting with swords. The explosive action continues and leads to a desert finale in which the hero and his sweetheart make a death-defying escape.

There are moments during this show when audience members might wonder if something has actually gone wrong. But by revealing tricks of the trade, the directors and stars show that what appears to be dangerous is actually a safe, controlled bit of movie magic.

Star Tours FP

BIRNBAUM'S ★BEST★ This attraction, which was inspired by George Lucas's series of *Star Wars* movies, offers guests a chance to board StarSpeeders that are the same type of flight simulators regularly employed by the military and commercial airlines to train pilots. By synchronizing a stunning film with the virtually limitless motion of the simulator, the ride allows guests to truly feel what they see.

Visitors enter an area where the famed *Star Wars* characters R2-D2 and C-3PO are working for a galactic travel agency. They spend their time in a bustling hangar area servicing the Star Tours fleet of spacecraft. Riders board the craft for what is intended to be a

leisurely trip to the Moon of Endor, but the five-minute ride quickly develops into a harrowing flight into the depths of space, including encounters with giant ice crystals and laser-blasting fighters. The flight is out of control from the start, as the rookie pilot comically proves that Murphy's Law applies to the entire universe.

This is a very turbulent trip through the galaxy. Passengers must be free of back problems, heart conditions, motion sickness (do not ride on a full stomach!), and other physical limitations. Pregnant women are not permitted to board. Guests must be at least 40 inches tall, and children under 7 must be accompanied by an adult; kids under 3 are not allowed to ride.

DISNEY-MGM STUDIOS

FP = Fastpass attraction (see page 19)

Jim Henson's
Muppet*Vision 3-D FP

BIRNBAUM'S ★BEST★ One of the most entertaining attractions at the Studios, this 3-D movie is quite remarkable. As with so many other Disney theme park attractions, much of the appeal is in the details. A funny 12-minute pre-show gives clues about what's to come. Once inside the theater, many will notice that it looks just like the one from the classic television series *The Muppet Show*. Even the two curmudgeonly fellows, Statler and Waldorf, are sitting in the balcony, bantering with each other and offering their typically critical commentary on the show.

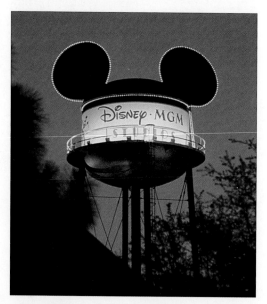

The production comes directly from Muppet Labs, presided over by Dr. Bunsen Honeydew—and his long-suffering assistant, Beaker—and introduces a new character, Waldo, the "Spirit of 3-D." Among the highlights is Miss Piggy's solo, which Bean Bunny turns into quite a fiasco. Sam Eagle's grand finale leads to trouble as a veritable war breaks out, culminating with a cannon blast to the screen from the rear balcony, courtesy of everyone's favorite Swedish Chef.

The 3-D effects, spectacular as they may be, are only part of the show: There are appearances by live Muppet characters, fireworks, and lots of funny details built into the walls of the huge theater. Including the pre-show, expect to spend about 25 minutes with Kermit and company. Shows run continuously throughout the day.

Honey, I Shrunk the Kids
Movie Set Adventure

The set for the backyard scenes of the popular Disney movie has been re-created as an oversize, soft-surface playground. Enter it and experience the world from an ant's perspective.

Blades of grass soar 30 feet high, paper clips are as tall as trees, and Lego toys are practically big enough to live in. There are caves to explore (under the giant mushrooms) and many climbing opportunities (tremendous tree stumps and sprawling spiderwebs are among the better ones). Kids love to crawl into the discarded film canister and slide out along an oversize piece of film.

A leaky hose also provides entertainment as it squirts in a slightly different location each time. The props make everyone look and feel as though they were, indeed, shrunk by *Honey, I Shrunk the Kids*' Professor Wayne Szalinski.

FP = Fastpass attraction (see page 19)

Shopping

Hollywood Boulevard

CELEBRITY 5 & 10: Modeled after a 1940s Woolworth's, this large shop carries Disney-MGM Studios logo merchandise, frames, clothing, and backpacks.

COVER STORY: A small area located just through The Darkroom, this is the place to pick up your picture if you've had it taken by any of the park photographers.

CROSSROADS OF THE WORLD: In the middle of the entrance plaza, Mickey Mouse keeps watch from atop this Hollywood Boulevard landmark. The kiosk deals in souvenirs, film, rain gear, sundries, and guidemaps. This is also the place to stop if you'd like to rent a locker.

THE DARKROOM: The Art Deco facade of this shop allows guests to peer through an aperture-like window. Cameras (including the disposable kind), film, and camera accessories are sold.

KEYSTONE CLOTHIERS: Women's and men's fashions and accessories are the specialties of the house.

L.A. PROP CINEMA STORAGE: A great source for kids' stuff, with a nice variety of clothing and toys for infants, toddlers, and small children. Many items feature classic Disney characters, including Mickey, Minnie, Donald, Goofy, and the like.

MICKEY'S OF HOLLYWOOD: The place to find character T-shirts, sweatshirts, hats, plush toys, watches, socks, wallets, bags, books, and sunglasses, plus items emblazoned with the Walt Disney Studios logo.

MOVIELAND MEMORABILIA: This kiosk, located just to the left of the Studios main entrance, stocks stuffed toys, hats, sunglasses, film, key chains, and other souvenirs.

SID CAHUENGA'S ONE-OF-A-KIND: Unique antiques and curios are the stock-in-trade here. Autographed photos of past and present matinee idols and sports stars, old movie magazines and posters, and assorted Hollywood memorabilia, such as Clark Gable's pants, Barbra Streisand's purse, Susan Lucci's dress, and baubles once owned by Cher, have been among the many celebrity-oriented collectibles with which Sid's been willing to part—for a price.

Sunset Boulevard

THE BEVERLY SUNSET: This shop has a super selection of candy, plus Fantasmic! merchandise and items featuring classic Disney villains. The caramel apples are to die for.

LEGENDS OF HOLLYWOOD: A tribute to Disney's animated legend, Winnie the Pooh. Expect to find an abundance of shirts, hats, and other colorful merchandise featuring everyone's favorite chubby little cubby—plus his pals from the Hundred Acre Wood.

MOUSE ABOUT TOWN: The best source for men's sports apparel featuring the famed mouse subtly embroidered onto sportswear, sweatshirts, and jackets. The Mouse also purveys golf-related apparel and accessories.

ONCE UPON A TIME: The exterior of this shop replicates the Carthay Circle Theatre, in Hollywood, where *Snow White and the Seven Dwarfs* premiered in 1937. The shop specializes in decorative gifts and Disney houseware items. For a fee, a Disney artist will customize a character sketch for you.

ROCK AROUND THE SHOP: Survive the Rock 'n' Roller Coaster and earn the right to shop here (okay, you can sneak into the shop from the outside, too). Expect to find music-related items such as drumsticks and CDs.

SUNSET CLUB COUTURE: A sophisticated selection of jewelry and mostly Mickey watches includes limited-edition pieces and pocket watches. A Disney artist can customize character watches on the spot.

SUNSET RANCH: This open-air shop carries Disney character hats, totes, and apparel, plus sunscreen, film, and sundries.

TOWER OF TERROR SHOP: Inside the Hollywood Tower hotel, near the ride exit (but accessible from the outside), this spot specializes in merchandise from the infamous Hollywood Tower Hotel.

Beyond the Boulevards

AMERICAN FILM INSTITUTE SHOWCASE: Looking for items featuring the likes of Betty Boop, Abbott and Costello, or Lucille Ball? Head here. There is also a nice supply of Three Stooges stuff. Nyuk, nyuk, nyuk.

ANIMATION GALLERY: Don't overlook this shop in the Animation Building, where limited-edition figurines, Disney animation cels, books, statues, and other collectibles ensure great browsing, even if buying isn't on your mind.

GOLDEN AGE SOUVENIRS: Located beside Sounds Dangerous starring Drew Carey, this tiny shop stocks items such as hats, sunglasses, film, and souvenirs.

IN CHARACTER: In front of the Voyage of The Little Mermaid, this costume shop has everything a child needs to dress like a Disney prince or princess.

INDIANA JONES ADVENTURE OUTPOST: Next to the Indiana Jones attraction, you'll discover adventure clothing, as well as memorabilia emblazoned with the Indy insignia.

IT'S A WONDERFUL SHOP: Tucked away behind Jim Henson's Muppet*Vision 3-D, this "snow-covered" shop makes it feel like Christmastime all year round. Look for items such as tree ornaments and stockings.

STAGE 1 COMPANY STORE: Near the exit of Jim Henson's Muppet*Vision 3-D, guests can find toys, shirts, and other merchandise with the likenesses of Muppet characters.

THE STUDIO STORE: Expect to find T-shirts, hats, and accessories inspired by Disney films at this Animation Courtyard shop. Items featuring the park's logo are available, too.

TATOOINE TRADERS: This shop near the exit of the Star Tours attraction offers intergalactic souvenirs tied to the ever-growing family of *Star Wars* films, as well as the ever-popular Disney-MGM Studios' Star Tours attraction.

THE WRITER'S STOP: This cozy nook next to the Sci-Fi Dine-In Theater has coffee, stationery, and a small selection of reading material—plus cookies!

Where to Eat at the Studios

A complete listing of eateries at the Studios—full-service restaurants, fast-food emporiums, and snack shops—can be found in the *Good Meals, Great Times* chapter. See the Disney-MGM Studios section beginning on page 226.

Entertainment

As you might expect from a park fashioned in the image of Hollywood's heyday, the Disney-MGM Studios knows how to put on a show. Celebrity appearances are a distinct possibility as well. Basically, in these parts, it's always showtime. So be sure to pick up a free guide-map and times guide (at Guest Relations or any shop), not only to check attraction starting times but also to find out what other entertainment is on tap.

While specifics may change, the following list is a good indication of the Studios' stage presence. As always, we advise calling 407-824-4321 for entertainment schedules.

DISNEY STARS AND MOTOR CARS PARADE: The Disney-MGM Studios celebrates Hollywood's golden era with a cavalcade of stars. This processional, presented as an old-fashioned motorcade, features souped-up cars occupied by super stars. Classic Disney characters are joined by friends from Disney Channel shows, not to mention members of the Muppets and *Star Wars* crews.

STREETMOSPHERE CHARACTERS: This troupe of performers infuses Hollywood Boulevard with old-time Tinseltown ambience. Would-be starlets searching for their big break, fans seeking guests' autographs, and gossip columnists chasing leads entertain daily.

Holiday Happenings

The park usually stays open extra late to mark holidays such as New Year's Eve, the Fourth of July, and Christmas. During these times, lots of special entertainment is often in store. Call 407-824-4321 for up-to-the-minute schedules.

CHRISTMAS: The Osborne Family Spectacle of Lights is the Studios' brilliant, twinkling homage to the season. At press time, the extraordinary display featuring about five million lights (provided by Little Rock businessman Jennings Osborne and his family) was looking for a new home. For updates on the status and location of this popular presentation, visit *www.disneyworld.com*.

Trip the Light Fantasmic!

BIRNBAUM'S ★BEST★ Fantasmic!, a lavish musical production, plays nightly at The Hollywood Hills Amphitheater on Sunset Boulevard. A dramatic mix of fireworks, fountains, lasers, special effects, and Disney characters, it invites guests to take a peek into the dream world of Mickey Mouse.

Though similar to its Disneyland counterpart, half of this 26-minute production is original. The action follows Mickey through a series of dreams. In the first dream, he appears on a mountain, shoots fireworks from his fingertips, and conducts an orchestra of colorful fountains. (Guests seated up front get spritzed.) Soon Mickey is plagued by nightmares as Disney villains take over his dreams. (This part has been known to scare small children.) In the end, the Mouse and his pals prevail (of course!).

Seating begins about 90 minutes before showtime—though some guests line up even earlier. Check a times guide for the schedule.

We recommend sitting toward the back—the view is good and it's easier to get out after the show. There is standing room, too.

After the finale, plan to sit for a bit. It can take 20 minutes for the crowd to exit the theater.

Timing Tip: On nights when Fantasmic! is presented twice, see the last show. Afterward, as the masses exit the park, take some time to browse the shops that keep their doors open after hours.

Hot Tips

- Some attractions keep shorter hours than the park itself. Check a times guide when you arrive. It lists current hours and schedules.

- Check the Studios Tip Board often to get an idea of showtimes and crowds.

- See Rock 'n' Roller Coaster, Voyage of The Little Mermaid, and Star Tours early in the day, before crowds build up.

- Snag a spot along Hollywood Boulevard about 20 to 30 minutes before the parade.

- Tower of Terror is a popular attraction with long lines. Use Fastpass whenever possible. And never ride immediately after a meal!

- The line for The Great Movie Ride is generally the longest early in the morning and immediately following the afternoon parade.

- For a full-service meal, make priority seating arrangements when you arrive, at either Hollywood Junction or the eatery: 50's Prime Time Cafe, Hollywood Brown Derby, Sci-Fi Dine-In Theater, Hollywood & Vine, or Mama Melrose's Ristorante Italiano. For reservations, call 407-WDW-DINE (939-3463) up to four months ahead.

- The shops on Hollywood Boulevard are open a half hour past park closing.

- Park hoppers take note: There is a water taxi link between the Disney-MGM Studios and Epcot. The boat docks to the left as you exit the Studios. You may also reach Epcot, as well as all other parks, by bus. Ambitious athletes may choose to walk. (It'll take you at least 20 to 30 minutes to make the trip.)

- The Hollywood Brown Derby, Hollywood and Vine, and Mama Melrose's Ristorante Italiano offer a dinner-and-show combination: a meal followed by Fantasmic!, complete with V.I.P. seating. It's a great way to avoid the time-consuming hassle of waiting for the show. Reservations must be made in person, within seven days of the show.

- Many attractions and shows stop admitting guests prior to the park's closing time. (Check a guidemap and times guide for schedules.) Attractions that you may enter up until the very last minute include Rock 'n' Roller Coaster, The Twilight Zone Tower of Terror, The Great Movie Ride, Jim Henson's Muppet*Vision 3-D, and Star Tours.

- If you choose to skip Fantasmic!, keep an eye on your watch and plan to exit the park before the show ends. This way, you'll avoid the inevitable bottleneck at the exit. If you're watching the show, consider making your exit before the big finale.

Where to Find the Characters

You'll find Disney characters—such as Buzz Lightyear and Woody from *Toy Story*—by Al's Toy Barn. They may be joined by Jessie, Bullseye, or some other *Toy Story* friends. Tigger hangs out in his trailer on Mickey Avenue. Mickey himself makes frequent appearances in the park, but specific locations were not available at press time.

   Another way to meet characters is to eat breakfast or lunch at the Hollywood & Vine restaurant. As always, check a guidemap or ask a park employee for current details.

Disney's Animal Kingdom

With a mix of lush landscapes, thrilling attractions, and spine-tingling encounters with exotic animals, this is clearly a theme park raised to another level of excitement. Here, guests do more than just watch the action— they live it. They become paleontologists, explorers, and students of nature. And if, by doing so, they leave with nothing more than a great big smile, Disney will have accomplished one of its major goals. But many guests come away with a little bit more: a renewed sense of respect for our planet and for the life-forms we share it with (not to mention a few boffo souvenirs).

The attractions at Disney's Animal Kingdom are meant to engage, entertain, and inspire. They immerse guests in a tropical landscape and introduce them to wondrous creatures from the past and present—as well as a few that exist only in our collective imagination.

The park, which is accredited by the American Zoo and Aquarium Association, is home to more than 1,700 animals representing 250 different species. Most of the creatures are of the animate variety, as opposed to the Audio-Animatronics kind. Despite that, you won't see many beasts behind bars here. Instead, you'll go on safari and see a menagerie of wild critters living in spacious habitats, with remarkably few separations visible to the naked eye.

The following pages will help you get the most out of your visit to Disney's Animal Kingdom. It is, after all, a jungle out there.

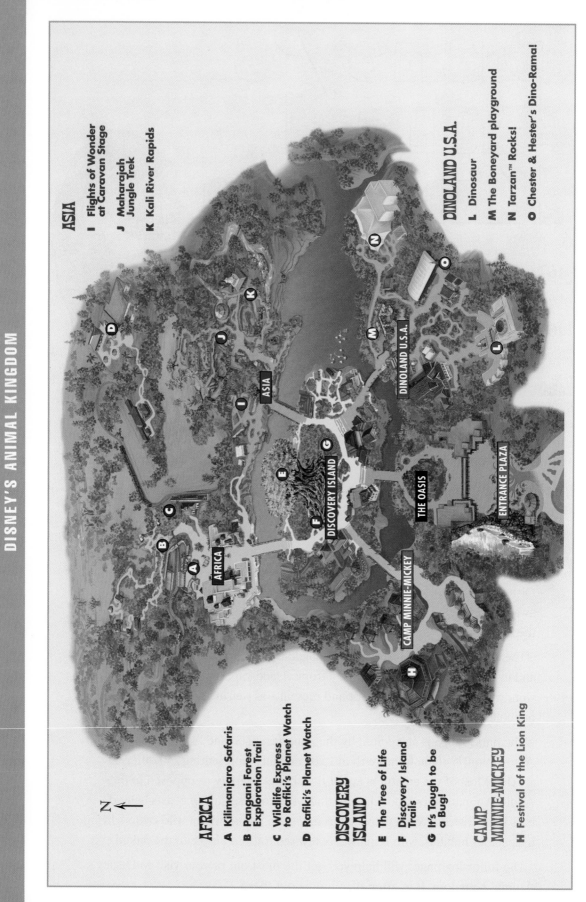

N ←

ASIA

I Flights of Wonder at Caravan Stage

J Maharajah Jungle Trek

K Kali River Rapids

DINOLAND U.S.A.

L Dinosaur

M The Boneyard playground

N Tarzan™ Rocks!

O Chester & Hester's Dino-Rama!

AFRICA

A Kilimanjaro Safaris

B Pangani Forest Exploration Trail

C Wildlife Express to Rafiki's Planet Watch

D Rafiki's Planet Watch

DISCOVERY ISLAND

E The Tree of Life

F Discovery Island Trails

G It's Tough to be a Bug!

CAMP MINNIE-MICKEY

H Festival of the Lion King

Getting Oriented

Though Disney's Animal Kingdom encompasses about five times the area of its Magic counterpart, one need not be in training for the Olympics to tackle it. By all estimates, pedestrians rack up about the same mileage in one day here as they do in a day at Epcot. (If you *want* to pack the hiking boots, by all means do—there's plenty of ground to cover.)

The park's layout is relatively simple: a series of sections, or "lands," connected to a central hub. In this case, the hub is Discovery Island (formerly known as Safari Village), an island surrounded by a river, and home to The Tree of Life, the park's icon. A set of bridges connects Discovery Island with other lands: the Oasis, DinoLand U.S.A., Asia, Africa, and Camp Minnie-Mickey.

As you pass through Animal Kingdom's entrance plaza, you approach the Oasis. Feel free to meander at a leisurely pace, absorbing the soothing ambience of a thick, elaborate jungle, or you can proceed more quickly and plan to revisit this relaxing region later on. Each of several pathways deposits you at the foot of a bridge leading to Discovery Island. As you emerge from the Oasis, you'll see the awe-inspiring Tree of Life, a 14-story Disney-made tree, looming ahead. The tree, which stands near the middle of the island, is surrounded by Discovery Island Trails. Off to the southwest is the character-laden land known as Camp Minnie-Mickey.

To the southeast lies DinoLand U.S.A., home of countless prehistoric animals, a fossil dig, and an attraction that's sure to induce a mammoth adrenaline surge: Dinosaur. Behind Discovery Island and to the northwest is Africa, where guests may go on an African safari, explore a nature trail, and take a train to Rafiki's Planet Watch, the park's research and education center.

The park's newest land, Asia, is northeast of Discovery Island. Here, guests may encounter tigers on the exotic Maharajah Jungle Trek, and take a daring journey through the rain forest on a raft at the splashy Kali River Rapids.

HOW TO GET THERE

Take Exit 65 off I-4. Then follow the signs to Disney's Animal Kingdom. Trams run between the parking lot and the main entrance.

By WDW Transportation: From all Walt Disney World resorts: buses. From Downtown Disney: bus to the Transportation and Ticket Center (TTC), then transfer to the bus for Animal Kingdom. From the Magic Kingdom, ferry or monorail to the TTC, then bus to Animal Kingdom. From Epcot, the Disney-MGM Studios, and the resorts on Hotel Plaza Blvd.: buses.

PARKING

All-day parking at Animal Kingdom is $7 for day visitors (free to Walt Disney World resort guests with presentation of resort ID). Trams circulate regularly, providing transportation from the parking area to the park entrance. Be sure to note the section and aisle in which you park. Also, be aware that the parking ticket allows for re-entry to the parking area throughout the day.

HOURS

Although hours are subject to change, the gates are generally open daily from about 8 A.M. until about an hour after dusk (at press time, there was a possibility that the park opening time would change to 9 A.M.). During certain holiday periods and the summer months, hours may change. It's best to arrive up to a half hour before the official opening time. For current schedules, call 407-824-4321 or visit *www.disneyworld.com*.

Admission Prices

ONE-DAY TICKET
(Restricted to use only in Disney's Animal Kingdom. Prices include sales tax and are subject to change.)
Adult $55.38
Child* $44.73
*3 through 9 years of age; children under 3 free

Park Primer

BABY FACILITIES

Changing tables and facilities for nursing mothers can be found at the Baby Care Center on Discovery Island, adjacent to Creature Comforts. It's also possible to purchase certain necessities, such as formula and diapers, at this facility.

CAMERA NEEDS

Film may be left for processing at Garden Gate Gifts, near the Oasis, the Disney Outfitters shop on Discovery Island, Duka La Filimu and Mombasa Marketplace in Harambe, and Chester and Hester's Dinosaur Treasures in DinoLand U.S.A. The photo pickup location is at Garden Gate Gifts. Film is sold in most shops.

DISABILITY INFORMATION

Nearly all of the Animal Kingdom attractions, shops, and restaurants are accessible to guests using wheelchairs. Additional services are available for guests with visual or hearing disabilities. The *Guidebook for Guests with Disabilities* provides a detailed overview of the services available, including transportation, parking, and attraction access. (For additional information, refer to the *Getting Ready to Go* chapter.)

FIRST AID

Minor medical problems can be handled at the First Aid Center, located on Discovery Island on the northwest side of The Tree of Life, near Creature Comforts.

INFORMATION

Guest Relations, located just inside the park entrance, is equipped with guidemaps, times guides, and a helpful staff. Free guidemaps are also available in many shops.

LOCKERS

Lockers are found just inside the main entrance area, near Guest Relations. Cost is $5 (plus a $2 refundable deposit) for unlimited use all day.

LOST & FOUND

The department is located at Guest Relations, just inside the park entrance. To report lost items after your visit, call 407-824-4245.

LOST CHILDREN

Report lost children at the park's Baby Services, next door to Creature Comforts on Discovery Island, or alert the closest Disney employee to the matter.

MONEY MATTERS

There is an ATM at the entrance to the park. Currency exchange can be handled at Guest Relations. Disney Dollars, in $1, $5, and $10 denominations, are also available at Guest Relations. In addition to cash, credit cards (American Express, Diner's Club, Discover Card, JCB, Visa, MasterCard, and the Disney Credit Card), traveler's checks, and Disney resort IDs are accepted for admission and merchandise, and for meals at most restaurants. Many snack carts accept cash only.

PACKAGE PICKUP

Shops can arrange for purchases to be sent to Garden Gate Gifts for later pickup (packages should be ready for pickup about three hours after purchase). The service is free.

SAME-DAY RE-ENTRY

Be sure to have your hand stamped upon exiting the park and to retain your ticket if you plan to return later the same day.

SECURITY CHECK

Guests entering Disney theme parks may be subject to a security check. Expect backpacks, parcels, purses, etc., to be searched.

STROLLERS & WHEELCHAIRS

Strollers, wheelchairs, and Electric Convenience Vehicles (ECVs) may be rented at Garden Gate Gifts. The cost is $7 for strollers and wheelchairs, plus a $1 refundable deposit (double strollers cost $14 plus $1 deposit); $30 for ECVs, plus a $10 refundable deposit. Quantities are limited (and they run out early in the day). Keep your receipt; it may be used the same day to get a replacement here or at the other theme parks.

TIP BOARD

There is a Tip Board on Discovery Island. Check it to learn the current wait times for popular park attractions.

The Oasis

Traditionally, one has to travel across a long, sunbaked stretch of desert in order to experience the soothing atmosphere of a tropical oasis. With that in mind, think of the Animal Kingdom parking lot as a concrete version of the Sahara. Once you've trekked across it, your journey takes you through the park's front gate and entrance plaza. What's that up ahead? Could it be a towering African tree? Here in Central Florida? It must be a mirage.

But, no. Within seconds you arrive at the Oasis, a thriving tropical garden filled with waterfalls, running streams, and lush vegetation. The transition is by no means a subtle one. Guests are immediately enveloped in a world of nature. The peaceful setting is most idyllic.

Though not a full-fledged "land" per se, this small jungle simply oozes atmosphere. It is thick and elaborate and crawling with critters. (Some are more difficult to spot than others. When searching for the naturally camouflaged creatures, remember to look up occasionally.) As park visitors walk along the pathways, they may catch glimpses of different kinds of animals, from deer and iguanas to anteaters and birds. As in the rest of

Animal Kingdom, there is the illusion that guests are walking among the wildlife.

The Oasis is at once an exciting and calming experience. It sets the stage for what's to come. Guests have several options once they've entered the Oasis. They can continue on a northerly path, making tracks toward The Tree of Life and across a bridge to Discovery Island. They can proceed at a more snail-friendly pace, keeping a tally of the various life-forms that slither by. Or they can simply take time to stop and smell the flowers.

> **"I have learned from the animal world. And what everyone will learn who studies it is a renewed sense of kinship with the Earth and all of its inhabitants."**
> **— Walt Disney**

Timing Tip: Making a trip through the Oasis is the only way to get in (and out of) Animal Kingdom. Some paths can become congested during the hours closest to opening and closing times. To beat the crowds, use a path to the left when you enter and exit the park.

Discovery Island

Once you've passed through the Oasis, you will come to a bridge spanning a peaceful river. The bridge leads to Discovery Island, an area at the center of Animal Kingdom and the hub from which all other realms of the park may be reached.

Discovery Island is defined by the brilliant colors, tropical surroundings, and equatorial architecture of Africa and the South Pacific. The facades of the buildings are all carved and painted based on the art of nations from around the world. Don't fail to notice all the bright, whimsical folk-art images representing various members of the animal kingdom.

This island is the shopping and dining center of Animal Kingdom. Many of the park's fast-food restaurants can be found here, including Pizzafari and Flame Tree Barbecue.

Hot Tip!

Take a moment to study a guidemap as you enter Animal Kingdom. It will give you a sense of the park's layout. The park times guide provides information about showtimes for Festival of the Lion King and other attractions.

By far the most striking element on Discovery Island is The Tree of Life. It is on the map, but chances are you'll have no trouble finding it. Rising from the middle of the island and as tall as a 14-story building, The Tree of Life is hard to miss.

The Tree of Life

The majestic Tree of Life is the dramatic 145-foot icon of Disney's Animal Kingdom. The imposing tree, with its swaying limbs and gnarled trunk, looks an awful lot like the real thing—from a distance. Up close, it's apparent that this is a most unusual bit of greenery. Covered with more than 325 animal images, it is a swirling tapestry of carved figures, painstakingly assembled by a team of artisans. The tree, though inorganic, stands as a symbol of the connected nature of life on Earth. We think Joyce Kilmer would have approved.

DISCOVERY ISLAND TRAILS: Walkways that snake around The Tree of Life allow guests to get a close-up view of the trunk and even play a game of "spot the animals." (The spiraling animal images go all the way to the top of the tree. You'll need binoculars if you hope to see them all.) Scattered about the tree's base is a variety of animal habitats. Animals can be seen in a very open, somewhat traditional parklike setting, with lush grass, trees, and other vegetation. Among the creatures you may recognize are macaws, flamingos, and deer. Others to which you may be introduced for the very first time as you meander through the exhibits include capybaras (huge rodents with an affinity for swimming) and ringtailed lemurs (not quite monkeys' uncles, more like cousins). The trails are accessible from several points around the tree.

Hot Tip!

Children under age 4 may have loved the film *A Bug's Life*, but few of them fancy It's Tough to be a Bug! As a matter of fact, it terrifies them.

BIRNBAUM'S ★BEST **IT'S TOUGH TO BE A BUG!:** FP Inside the trunk of The Tree of Life is a 430-seat auditorium featuring an eight-minute, animated 3-D movie augmented by some surprising "4-D" effects. The stars of the show are the world's most abundant inhabitants—insects. They creep, crawl, and demonstrate why, someday, they just might inherit the earth. It's a bug's-eye view of the trials and tribulations of their multi-legged world.

As guests enter "The Tree of Life Repertory Theater," the orchestra can be heard warming

up amid the sounds of chirping crickets. When Flik, the emcee (and star of *A Bug's Life*), makes his first appearance, he dubs audience members honorary bugs and instructs them to don their bug eyes (3-D glasses). Then the mild-mannered ant introduces some of his not-so-mild-mannered cronies, including a Chilean tarantula, dung beetles, and "the silent but deadly member of the bug world"—the stink bug. What follows is a manic, often hilarious, revue.

Note: The combination of intense special effects and frequent darkness tends to frighten toddlers and young children. In addition, anyone leery of spiders, roaches, and their ilk is advised to skip the performance, or risk being seriously bugged.

DISNEY'S ANIMAL KINGDOM

Africa

The largest section of Animal Kingdom, Africa is bigger than the Magic Kingdom all by itself. This 110-acre, truer-than-life replica of an African savanna is packed with pachyderms, giraffes, hippos, and other wild beasts. All guests enter Africa through Harambe, a village based on a modern East African coastal town. It is the dining and shopping center of Animal Kingdom's Africa.

The instant you walk across the bridge to Harambe, you are transported to Africa. Everything here is authentic, from the architecture to the landscaping to the merchandise in the marketplace. The result was achieved after Disney Imagineers made countless trips to the continent. After seven years of observing, filming, and photographing the real thing, they re-created it here in North America.

The animals that live here, however, are not re-creations. They are quite real, most varied, and extremely abundant. In fact, this chunk of land puts the *animal* in Disney's Animal Kingdom.

Kilimanjaro Safaris FP

BIRNBAUM'S ★BEST★ The Kilimanjaro Safaris has something for everyone: beautiful landscapes, majestic, free-roaming animals, and a thrilling adventure. It is everything you may expect from a trip to Africa, and a whole lot more.

The 20-minute safari begins with a brief introduction from a guide who does double duty as your driver.

Once you climb aboard the ride vehicle, look at the plates above the seat in front of you. They will help you identify the animals you see. And have those cameras ready!

As the vehicle travels along dirt roads, you'll spot free-roaming wild animals: zebras, gazelles, hippos, elephants, warthogs, rhinos, lions, and more. Some animals wander near your vehicle, and others cross its path. (Relax. Only the harmless critters will approach. Others, such as lions and cheetahs, only *appear* to invade your safe, personal space.)

The majesty of the Serengeti may lull you into a state of serenity, but it's merely the calm before the storm. You'll soon be jostled and jolted as the vehicle crosses pothole-filled terrain and rickety bridges—one of which puts you close to a horde of sunbathing crocodiles.

The safari experience takes a dramatic turn when a band of renegade ivory poachers is discovered hunting for elephants. Your guide chases the outlaws and takes you along for the ride. If you're prone to motion sickness, back trouble, or have other physical limitations, you may want to sit this one out. The ride is a rather bumpy one.

Pangani Forest Exploration Trail

This self-guided walking trail winds past communities of gorillas and other rare African animals. Access it at the end of the Kilimanjaro Safaris or by the entrance in Harambe.

The first major stop on the trail, the name of which translates to "place of enchantment" in Swahili, is the Research Station. The station contains exhibits, including naked mole rats. Just outside are a free-flight aviary and an aquarium teeming with fish. Not far away is the hippo exhibit, which provides close-up views of hippopotamuses both in and out of water.

Farther along the trail there is a scenic over-look point, where you can get an unobstructed view of the African savanna. This is also known as the "Timon" exhibit, featuring a family of perky meerkats. Afterward, you may catch an up-close glimpse (through a glass wall) of a cavorting gorilla or two.

As you come to the end of the suspension bridge, you'll find yourself in a beautiful green valley. Congratulations! You've finally reached the gorilla area—an experience well worth the wait. (Note that you may have to wait a little bit longer for that first gorilla sighting. Our evolutionary cousins have been known to play hide-and-seek in the lush vegetation.)

Rafiki's Planet Watch

On the east side of the village of Harambe is the Harambe Train Station. That's where you board the Wildlife Express and experience a behind-the-scenes look at a Disney park while en route to Rafiki's Planet Watch.

As part of the 5½-minute trip, you'll glide past the buildings where elephants, rhinos, and giraffes sleep at night. A guide narrates throughout the trip. All guests disembark at the Rafiki's Planet Watch station. (You must reboard the train to return to Harambe.)

While Animal Kingdom's stories often carry a conservation theme, this part really brings the message home. This area is the park's con-servation headquarters. It's also a veterinary lab, as well as the research and education hub. Here, guests get a look at the way animals are cared for.

"Much of the world's wildlife is in imminent danger," says Judson Green, former chairman of Walt Disney Attractions. "Disney is working to save endangered animals, but we also hope to motivate our guests to support wildlife pro-grams that are in urgent need of support." After spending some time at Rafiki's Planet Watch, visitors just might have the motivation they need. Exhibits are geared to spark curiosity and awe about wildlife and conservation efforts around the world. Here are a few highlights:

Affection Section: An animal encounter area with critters to see and touch. Most of the animals are exotic breeds of familiar petting-zoo types: goats, sheep, pigs, etc. However, this is still an enjoyable experience for young guests. So is the elephant fountain just outside the gate. It's an entertaining way to rinse little hands after frolicking with the fauna.

Animal Cams: Guest-operated video cameras that observe animals throughout Animal Kingdom as they go about their daily business.

Animal Health & Care: A tour of veteri-nary labs and research facilities.

Eco Heroes: A set of touch-sensitive video kiosks that allow guests to interact with famous biologists and conservationists.

EcoWeb: A computer link to conservation organizations around the world.

Rafiki's Planet Watch Video: An interac-tive video, hosted Rafiki, that connects guests to information about endangered animals.

Song of the Rainforest: A thoroughly entertaining "3-D" audio show that surrounds guests with sounds of the rain forest.

Rafiki's Planet Watch is about a five-minute walk from the train depot. In addition to its educational appeal, this is also one of the best places to cool off at Animal Kingdom.

Coming Attraction

Walt Disney World's mountain range is about to get a bit more intense, as the world's tallest mountain—Everest—rises from the peaceful villiage of Anandapur in Animal Kingdom's Asia. Like it's sister peaks, Space, Splash, and Big Thunder, this E-ticket precipice promises thrills, spills, and, chills.

The new Expedition: EVEREST attraction will involve an old mountain train chugging into bamboo forests, past waterfalls, and along glacier fields as it climbs up and around snow-capped peaks. Suddenly, the track comes to an end in a gnarled mess of twisted metal. Lurching forward and back-ward, the train hurtles through caverns and icy canyons before depositing guests in the presence of the legendary yeti (aka The Abominable Snowman)—who's not too happy that you've scaled the mountain he so fiercely protects.

Feeling up to the challenge of a dramatic, high-speed train ride? Plan to visit in 2006. That's when Expedition: EVEREST is scheduled to open.

Asia

On the far side of a Himalayan-style bridge, beyond an ancient temple, lies the tranquil village of Anandapur (Sanskrit for "place of delight"). The buildings' design was inspired by structures in Thailand, Indonesia, and other Asian countries known for their rich architectural history.

A product of Disney Imagineering, the village epitomizes the complex, enduring relationship between the animals and ecosystems of the Asian continent. The tiny village borders an elaborate re-creation of a Southeast Asian rain forest. As such, Disney's Asia is an ideal location for trekking through the lush jungle, shooting the rapids on a raging river, and gazing upon the multi-hued inhabitants of this treasured terrain.

Kali River Rapids FP

Before guests board rafts at Kali (pronounced *KAH-lee*) River Rapids, a wise voice admonishes that "the river is like life itself, full of mysterious twists and turns." What the voice *doesn't* say is that this particular river is also full of splashing water and a blazing inferno. This may be business as usual for some daring souls, but for most of us, these elements make for one dramatic, drenching adventure.

All guests begin the journey in the offices of Kali River Rapids Expeditions, a river rafting company. A slide show offers information on the sometimes unscrupulous business of logging—how it has ravaged the rain forest and deprived animals of their habitats. However, thanks to ecotourism (among other things), there is hope. Peaceful voyages give people a new appreciation and sense of responsibility for this endangered land.

A 12-seater raft whisks "ecotourists" up a watery ramp and through an arching tunnel of bamboo. It proceeds onward, through a hazy mist and past remnants of an ancient shrine. As the raft moves along curves of the river, guests enjoy spectacular views of undisturbed rain forest.

The tranquility is shattered by a startling sight. A huge chunk of forest has been gutted by loggers. On both sides of the river, the

174

forest has vanished. As guests absorb the image, they are besieged by more disturbing sights and sounds. Straight ahead, the river is choked with a tangled arch of burning logs—and the raft is headed straight for it. Suddenly, the rain forest isn't the only thing endangered.

Kali River Rapids is an especially soggy experience. It is the rare guest who leaves the ride without a thorough soaking. Should you wish to repel as much precipitation as possible, plan on purchasing a plastic poncho at the ride's entrance.

Hot Tip!

Everyone and everything gets wet on Kali River Rapids. Any items that simply must stay dry should be stored in a locker or with a non-riding member of your party.

Note: This is a bumpy adventure. In order to experience it, you must be at least 38 inches tall. It is not recommended for pregnant women, those with a heart condition, people with back or neck problems, or anyone who wishes to stay dry.

Maharajah Jungle Trek FP

BIRNBAUM'S BEST Welcome to the jungle! The Maharajah Jungle Trek is a self-guided walking tour of a tropical paradise, complete with roaming tigers, gushing waterfalls, and dense greenery. Throughout the expedition, trekkers encounter a deluge of flora and fauna typically found in the rain forests of Southeast Asia. Tapirs, Komodo dragons, and a conglomeration of colorful birds call this corner of Animal Kingdom home. Majestic Asian tigers can be spotted stalking ancient ruins, strategically separated from would-be prey. Deer and antelope graze and frolic nearby, blissfully oblivious of their fearsome neighbors' proximity.

Approximately midway through the thicket stands a rustic, tin-roofed assembly hall. Step inside to witness the breathtaking sight of giant fruit bats showing off their six-foot wingspans. As you look through the windows, thinking that the crystal-clear glass was cleaned by a super-diligent window washer, think again. There is no glass in some of the windows—and, therefore, *nothing*

separating you from the giant creatures fluttering about on the other side. What keeps the big bats from getting up close and personal with guests? They're a lot less interested in humans than humans are in them. (Can't say that we blame them.) Note that some viewing areas are adorned with wire or glass—for guests who are more comfortable with a bat buffer.

Flights of Wonder

A 1,000-seat, open-air theater, the Caravan Stage features performances by actors wearing nothing but feathers and the occasional crown. Members of more than 20 different bird species have starring roles in Flights of Wonder, a high-flying celebration of the winged wonders of the world. Hawks, falcons, and even chickens awe spectators as they swoop, soar, and strut their stuff in each 20-minute performance. Some demonstrate how they hunt. Others, such as Sluggo the Red-legged Seriema, display the fine points of pulverizing prey. And a few simply show off. Check a park times guide for the schedule. Note that this show may undergo substantial changes by the time you visit.

DinoLand U.S.A.

If the look and feel of DinoLand U.S.A. seems familiar, there's a reason: It was designed to capture the flavor of roadside America. It is a mixture of culture and kitsch—the likes of which you might stumble upon during a cross-country road trip. Here, you'll come face-to-face with fossil fanatics, jump into gigantic footprints, and browse through a typically tacky roadside souvenir stand, where you can pick up some dinosaur mementos for the folks back home.

This corner of Animal Kingdom comes complete with its own dramatic entrance: a 50-foot skeleton of a brachiosaurus. As guests stroll beneath the bones, they find themselves smack in the middle of a paleontological dig. Here, guests of all ages (especially little ones) have the chance to play paleontologist as they dig through a fossil-packed pocket of dino discovery.

The dinosaurs that dwell here, though often quite animated, are all of the inanimate variety. But do keep your eyes peeled for the prehistoric life-forms that actually *live* in this land. That is, for real creatures that exist in the here and now, but whose ancestors kept company with the likes of the carnotaurus and its cousins from the Cretaceous Era.

The Boneyard

The Boneyard gives guests—especially the very young ones—an opportunity to dig for fossils in a discovery-oriented playground. They will excavate the ancient bones of a mammoth in this re-creation of a paleontological dig (think huge sandbox). They will also unearth clues that may help them solve the mystery of how and when the creature met its untimely demise.

For serious "boneheads" who just aren't satisfied with simple digging, there are plenty of other bone-related activities here. You can bang out a primitive tune on a bony xylophone (it's located near the car; to make a sound, simply press on a rib), zip down prehistoric slides, and work your way through a fossil-filled maze. While exploring, watch your step: If you accidentally wander into a giant

dinosaur footprint, you'll be greeted with an ominous roar.

While in DinoLand, be sure to check out the OldenGate Bridge. It's a gateway structure made from a dinosaur skeleton. The bridge links one end of The Boneyard with the other. This is a good place to take young kids while other members of your party ride Dinosaur.

Chester & Hester's Dino-Rama!

A colorful land-within-a-land, Chester and Hester's is an area ideally suited for small thrill seekers. Located just beyond The Boneyard playground, this wild-and-woolly, carnival-like zone features old-fashioned midway games and two rides: Primeval Whirl and TriceraTop Spin.

PRIMEVAL WHIRL: A small roller coaster (with spinning cars) that seems to have been plucked from a traveling fair, this ride has a familiar feel to it. By all means, give it a whirl—it's a truly wild ride. You must be at least 48 inches tall to ride. **FP**

TRICERATOP SPIN: The ride is apt to please fans of the Magic Kingdom's Dumbo, the Flying Elephant and the Magic Carpets of Aladdin. Guests ride in one of the 16 flying dinos, each of which resembles an oversize tin toy. It's tame when compared to its Dinosaur attraction neighbor, but worth checking out—especially for young dinosaur groupies.

Dinosaur FP

BIRNBAUM'S ★BEST★ This thrilling attraction is dramatic with a capital D. The dizzying adventure begins with guests being strapped into vehicles and catapulted back in time to complete a dangerous, albeit noble, mission: to rescue the last iguanodon—a 16-foot plant-eating dinosaur that you may recognize from the Disney film *Dinosaur*—and bring him back to the present. The iguanodon, which lived more than 65 million years ago (during the Cretaceous Period), just might hold the answer to the mysterious disappearance of his dino brethren.

Hot Tip!

For a slightly less turbulent experience on the Dinosaur attraction, request an inside seat near the front of the ride vehicle.

Throughout the frenetic quest to locate the elusive iguanodon, you cling to an out-of-control vehicle while dodging blazing meteors and a mix of friendly and ferocious dinosaurs. Soon you encounter the carnotaurus—a fearsome, carnivorous dinosaur. The carnotaurus, which has horns like a bull and a face like a toad, is an unsightly specimen.

All of the dinosaurs are especially fierce-looking and move as though they were alive. Even their nostrils move as they "breathe."

This 3½-minute attraction offers more than a thrill a minute. You rocket through time, are practically pelted by meteors, and

Did You Know?

Many of the benches in Disney's Animal Kingdom are made of recycled plastic milk jugs. It takes 1,350 jugs to make a single bench!

narrowly escape becoming a dino dinner as the carnotaurus suddenly turns the tables and chases after *you*.

Guests reach the attraction through the Dino Institute, a museum-like building deep in the heart of DinoLand. Here, you'll be treated to a pre-show by Bill Nye, the Science Guy (audio only) and see a dinosaur skeleton and an assortment of fossils and other artifacts.

This is an extremely intense attraction. You must be at least 40 inches tall to experience it. It is not recommended for pregnant women, those with a heart condition, or people with back or neck problems. Small kids will certainly be frightened.

Tarzan™ Rocks!

The covered Theater in the Wild seats 1,500 guests at a time. Here, audiences experience a 30-minute rock concert featuring songs, dances, and characters based on those made famous by Disney's animated feature *Tarzan*.

This energetic, artistic interpretation of the Disney film includes appearances by Tarzan, Jane, and Terk, plus a cast of jungle gymnasts and other rock 'n' roll animals.

Like Animal Kingdom's other big-ticket performance, the Festival of the Lion King, the show aspires to dazzle guests with aerial spectacles, acrobatic stunts, and stirring sound. Tarzan Rocks! runs throughout the day, on most days. Check a times guide for exact showtimes.

Camp Minnie-Mickey

What would a theme park be without a gregarious cast of handshaking characters? You will find the patented Disney character experience in all of its animated glory in Camp Minnie-Mickey. Set deep in a dense forest, this land is really a summer camp frequented by Mickey Mouse and all of his pals.

To find the characters, guests follow one of four short trails. Each one leads to an open-air hut, occupied by the likes of Mickey Mouse, Minnie Mouse, Donald Duck, Daisy Duck, or Goofy. Different Disney characters make appearances at these meet-and-greet pavilions throughout the day.

Keep in mind that this is the best place in the park to schmooze with the characters. Therefore, if you are traveling with small children, this area is not to be missed. Be sure to have the autograph books and cameras ready.

Camp Minnie-Mickey is also the home of an engaging theater show, starring the cast of *The Lion King*. Check a times guide for schedules.

Festival of the Lion King

BIRNBAUM'S BEST In addition to rustling up grubs in Camp Minnie-Mickey, the talented cast of *The Lion King* performs a 30-minute stage show in the Lion King Theater.

Presented in the round, this lavish outdoor revue is as bright and boisterous as they come. The dramatic opening features a parade of performers in colorful animal costumes. What follows is an intriguing, energetic interpretation of the film, including songs, dances, and acrobatics. With the exception of Timon, who plays himself, lead characters are portrayed by humans draped in bold African costumes.

Songs include Scar's nasty version of "Be Prepared," as well as "Can You Feel the Love Tonight?," "The Circle of Life," and a rousing audience-participation rendition of "The Lion Sleeps Tonight."

Timing Tip: Although this covered theater accommodates 1,400 guests at a time, we recommend arriving at least 45 minutes before the performance time, since the show is extremely popular. Take our word for it: It's worth the wait. Check a times guide for a performance schedule.

Get Involved

When it comes to conservation efforts, the folks at the Walt Disney Company want you to do as they say—and as they do: The Disney Wildlife Conservation Fund helps non-profit groups protect and study endangered and threatened animals and their habitats. Among those groups are the ASPCA, Dian Fossey Gorilla Fund, Jane Goodall Institute, and the Wildlife Conservation Society. And guests who "Add a Dollar" help, too.

Of course, as a trip to Animal Kingdom makes clear, there are many ways to help our planet's wild inhabitants. Stop by Rafiki's Planet Watch during your visit. There, you can get information about conservation efforts in your neck of the woods. Don't leave your enthusiasm behind when you leave the park!

Shopping

Entrance Area

GARDEN GATE GIFTS: Located near the entrance to the Oasis, this is the place to rent strollers and wheelchairs. Film and disposable cameras are for sale, as is a selection of shirts, hats, and other merchandise. This is also the park's package-pickup location.

OUTPOST: This small shop, located just outside the park's entrance, features a variety of character merchandise and Animal Kingdom souvenirs.

Discovery Island

BEASTLY BAZAAR: Safari hats with Mickey, Pooh, or Pluto ears; Disney's Animal Kingdom logo watches; character figurines; and plush toys clad in safari garb are among the wares offered in this shop, designed as a celebration of aquatic animals. There's a selection of kitchen, bath, and home decor items.

CREATURE COMFORTS: This shop offers items for kids—toys, clothes, costumes, hats, and more.

DISNEY OUTFITTERS: Nature-themed gifts and apparel are the stock-in-trade here. In addition to men's and women's clothing, you'll discover many items with a Winnie the Pooh theme. Make a point of checking out the authentic carved animal totem poles in the center room—they are most impressive.

ISLAND MERCANTILE: This sprawling shop is themed as a shipping company that celebrates working animals—camels, elephants, beavers, and others. Here, you'll find character merchandise, clothing, candy, and Disney paraphernalia. Note that it stays open about a half hour after the park closes for the day.

Africa

DUKA LA FILIMU: Situated near the entrance to Kilimanjaro Safaris, this is an ideal place to load up on film for your trip. You will find it comes in handy when you need to develop the film after your visit to the African savanna, too.

MOMBASA MARKETPLACE AND ZIWANI TRADERS: An African marketplace and trading company, these connected shops feature animal toys, safari clothing, T-shirts, books, and Africa-themed gifts such as pottery, masks, and musical instruments.

OUT OF THE WILD: Located just outside the exit of Rafiki's Planet Watch, this open-air shop stocks a variety of souvenirs with a nature theme, including shirts, hats, notebooks, and toys.

DinoLand U.S.A.

CHESTER & HESTER'S DINOSAUR TREASURES: Themed as an American roadside souvenir stand, this shop pays homage to all reptiles and prehistoric animals. Its focus is reflected in an assortment of wacky items strewn about the shop.

Entertainment

AFRICAN ENTERTAINMENT: Contemporary sounds of Africa often fill the air as bands serenade guests passing through the village of Harambe. Storytellers have been known to perform animal tales from time to time.

ANIMAL ENCOUNTERS: Enjoy up-close encounters with some of the smaller members of the animal kingdom as they wander the park with their human keepers.

MICKEY'S JAMMIN' JUNGLE PARADE: Animal Kingdom celebrates the wonders of the natural world in this peppy parade. It features familiar Disney characters—including Mickey Mouse, Minnie Mouse, Goofy, Donald Duck, and Rafiki—cruising in jazzy jalopies. Stilt-walkers and puppets put in appearances, too. Check a times guide for the parade schedule.

Hot Tips

- Arrive at the park 15 to 30 minutes before park opening time. Animal Kingdom often kicks off the day with "The Awakening"—a character-laden musical celebration. It's a very Disney way to start the day.

- Island Mercantile on Discovery Island stays open a half hour after the park closes.

- Most of Animal Kingdom's attractions take place outdoors. Don't become overheated! Make a point of slipping into an air-conditioned shop or restaurant from time to time to cool off.

- Narrow, winding paths; grooved pavement; and hilly terrain make this the most challenging Disney theme park in which to navigate a wheelchair.

- Check the Animal Kingdom Tip Board often to get an idea of showtimes and crowds.

- The line for Kilimanjaro Safaris tends to dwindle a bit by midday. See it then (the experience is enjoyable at any time of day).

- Make priority seating arrangements in advance for the character breakfast at Restaurantosaurus in DinoLand U.S.A.

- Rainforest Cafe generally keeps longer hours than the park does.

- When the weather gets steamy, keep a refillable water bottle with you at all times.

- If you plan to park hop, Animal Kingdom is a good park at which to begin the day.

Where to Eat in Animal Kingdom

A complete listing of eateries at Disney's Animal Kingdom—table-service restaurants, fast-food spots, and snack stands—can be found in the *Good Meals, Great Times* chapter. See the Animal Kingdom section beginning on page 229.

Everything Else in the World

While the total turf of the World encompasses 47 square miles, the theme parks cover less than 1,000 acres. Much of the remaining Walt Disney World terrain is crammed with irresistible activities of a variety and quality seldom found anywhere else.

There's superb golf and tennis, beaches for sunbathing, lakes for speed-boating and sailing, canoes to rent and winding streams to paddle along, bicycles for hire, campfire sites, horseback riding, race-car driving, nature trails, and picnic grounds. The recreation options continue with Typhoon Lagoon, a lushly landscaped, state-of-the-art water park complete with surfing lagoon; and Blizzard Beach, a thrilling watery wonderland that translates the hallmarks of a ski resort to the realm of swimming.

A triumvirate of lavish spas provides guests with ample opportunity to pamper themselves silly. Intriguing "backstage" programs invite the curious to slip behind the scenes and learn about the workings of Walt Disney World. Add to all that Downtown Disney, a dining, shopping, and amusement district encompassing Pleasure Island, an after-dark entertainment complex; the Marketplace, a colorful assortment of shops and restaurants; and the West Side, a cluster of themed eateries, unique shops, and interactive entertainment experiences. It seems this really is a World without end.

Downtown Disney

Sprinkled across 120 waterfront acres are the shops, nightclubs, restaurants, and entertainment sites that collectively make up Downtown Disney. Like the downtown area of any thriving metropolis, Disney's Downtown consists of several distinct neighborhoods. In this case, they are known as the Marketplace, Pleasure Island, and the West Side. Unlike a typical downtown, however, the Disney depiction dispenses with the downside. You won't see litter on the streets, unsightly storefronts, or weary workers rushing home at 5 o'clock. You *will* see a series of spirited spots designed solely for your dining, shopping, and partying pleasure.

Judging by the throngs that descend upon this place, Downtown Disney is *the* place to be after dark. That said, it can get a tad congested—especially on the roads leading here. However you're traveling, allow plenty of extra time to get to and from this fun zone. Note that all sections are connected by walking paths. For information, visit *www.disneyworld.com*, or call 407-939-2648

Downtown Disney Essentials

GUEST SERVICES: Across from Once Upon a Toy in the Marketplace, and across from Wetzel's Pretzels on the West Side, these information centers are also the place to go for priority seating help, Lost and Found, stroller and wheelchair rental, theme park tickets, and more. There is an ATM near Guest Services in the Marketplace, next to Wetzel's Pretzels on the West Side, and near the Rock N Roll Beach Club at Pleasure Island.

HOW TO GET THERE: Downtown Disney is accessible from exits 67 and 68 off I-4.

By WDW Transportation: From Old Key West: boats or buses. From the Magic Kingdom, Epcot, Grand Floridian, Contemporary, and Polynesian: monorail to the Transportation and Ticket Center (TTC), then transfer to a Downtown Disney bus. From all other Walt Disney World resorts: buses. After 4 P.M., there is direct bus service from the Grand Floridian, Contemporary, Polynesian, Wilderness Lodge, and the Disney-MGM Studios. For more information, turn to the *Transportation & Accommodations* chapter.

By Taxi: Yellow cabs, operated by several different companies, service the Downtown Disney area. The cost to most WDW resorts is usually $5 to $15.

Note: Stick with authorized cabs, and avoid independent cabs. Their fees aren't regulated and are often outrageous.

West Side

Pleasure Island

Marketplace

Located on the shores of Lake Buena Vista, the Marketplace is a relaxing setting for shopping, dining, and much more. The waterside enclave is sprinkled with gardens featuring whimsical topiaries. Kids are fond of the Downtown Disney Marketplace Carousel (tucked between Pooh Corner and Earl of Sandwich). And adults may enjoy a drink at the area known as Sunset Cove.

While many guests opt to eat in a restaurant, others grab a bite from the Earl of Sandwich and sit at waterfront tables. (Refer to *Good Meals, Great Times* for restaurant information.) Afterward, some gravitate toward the marina for boating or fishing. (Turn to the *Sports* chapter for details.) There is no admission charge to visit the Marketplace.

Shopping

The descriptions below suggest the types of wares each store offers. Most shops in the Downtown Disney Marketplace are open daily from 9:30 A.M. to 11 P.M.

THE ART OF DISNEY: Disney animation cels, porcelain figures, ceramics, posters, and other collectibles are the goods available at this engaging gallery.

BASIN: Products designed to clean you up and calm you down are the stock in trade at this soothing new Marketplace establishment. Candles, soaps, and bath crystals are just some of the wares on hand. A sampling area allows shoppers to try before they buy.

DISNEY AT HOME: You'll find an eclectic selection of items for the bedroom and bath here. Among the wares once on display were Pooh sheets, bathroom carpets shaped like Mickey's head, and lamps, rocking chairs, and even beds with a Mickey theme (some designs are more subtle than others).

DISNEY'S DAYS OF CHRISTMAS: Here is the best place to deck the halls Disney-style — it's the largest Christmas shop on Disney property. In addition to many character items, the shop, which smells of cinnamon, boasts a large assortment of handcrafted ornaments. Other items to look for: Christmas cards, candles, Santa hats with Mouse ears, and books. Many items can be personalized.

DISNEY'S PIN TRADERS: This shop boasts a nice selection of Disney merchandise, as well as a tremendous assortment of collector pins. In fact, this is Walt Disney World's largest pin-trading center.

DISNEY'S WONDERFUL WORLD OF MEMORIES: Housed in the spot that was once 2 R's Reading and Riting, this shop is now scrapbook central. In addition to pre-packaged kits and other scrapbooking supplies, several stations allow guests to create their own scrapbook pages and postcards.

EARL OF SANDWICH: This new shop specializes in sandwiches and freshly-made potato chips. (It stands on the site formerly occupied by Gourmet Pantry.)

Marketplace

EUROSPAIN: This shop sells handcrafted items from Spanish artisans and designers. Large cut-glass bowls and vases are available, along with mugs, sculptures, and other wares, all of which can be engraved.

LEGO IMAGINATION CENTER: World of Disney's next-door neighbor, this shop is a showcase for larger-than-life Lego models, including dinosaurs and scary aliens. It also invites guests to flaunt their creativity in an outdoor play area. The store stocks a wide variety of Lego products and educational toys. By the way, that fire-breathing sea serpent in Lake Buena Vista is also made of Legos.

ONCE UPON A TOY: A sprawling toy box of a store, this site features colorful displays and an outdoor interactive play area.

POOH CORNER: Searching for that perfect plush Pooh? You'll find him here, along with his pals from the Hundred Acre Wood. Also on hand are kitchen items, stationery, books,

sweatshirts, T-shirts, and other clothing. This spot is pleasing to the nose as well as the eye—the aromatically aware may get a whiff of apple pie or honey.

TEAM MICKEY'S ATHLETIC CLUB: A cavernous store with a locker-room motif, this shop is the perfect setting for sports clothing, active-wear, and sports equipment. You'll find many items with Disney characters in sporting poses emblazoned on them. There is also a large selection of men's and women's golf apparel.

WORLD OF DISNEY: A gigantic retail space stuffed with a tremendous selection of Disney merchandise, this is the place for one-stop shopping. Twelve themed rooms provide the backdrop for the huge array of goods. The enchanted dining room from *Beauty and the Beast* was the inspiration for the culinary section; Disney villains are celebrated in a room that's filled with items such as clocks, watches, candles, and frames; and fairies from *Cinderella* and *Sleeping Beauty* can be seen floating through the intimate apparel department. Disney characters are available on everything from hats and shirts to sleepwear and bags.

Where to Eat at Downtown Disney

A complete listing of restaurants, bars, and snack spots can be found in the *Good Meals, Great Times* chapter. See the Downtown Disney restaurant listing, beginning on page 231. Most restaurants here are open from about 11:30 A.M. to midnight. Planet Hollywood serves until 1 A.M. West Side spots serve as late as 2 A.M.

Pleasure Island

A six-acre nighttime entertainment complex, Pleasure Island delivers a wealth of options that nicely top off a day in the parks. In addition to clubs, there are several restaurants and shops here in the central area of Downtown Disney.

Most clubs open at 8 P.M. and don't close until 2 A.M. There is no fee to explore Pleasure Island before clubs open. A single admission of $21 (including tax) allows access to the clubs and nightly street party. Ultimate Park Hopper Tickets include Pleasure Island admission. It's also an option with a Park Hopper Plus Ticket. An annual pass costs $58.25 ($47.65 to renew). Guests under age 18 must be accompanied by a parent or guardian.

Cocktails and soft drinks are available at all of the clubs. The drinking age in Florida is 21. Guests who are 18, 19, and 20 will be admitted to the clubs (except Mannequins and BET SoundStage Club) but will not be served alcohol. A valid U.S., foreign, or international driver's license with a photo, an active U.S. military identification card, or a passport must be presented as proof of age.

Hot Tip!

Drivers take note: In order to prove that you are 21 years old, you must present an official photo ID. So if your mug is not emblazoned on your license, be sure to bring it *and* a photo ID. Otherwise, you will not be allowed to imbibe—even though your driver's license is indeed the real McCoy.

Clubs

ADVENTURERS CLUB: "Explore the unknown, discover the impossible" states the credo posted at the entrance. The place is modeled after the paneled libraries and elegant salons of similar clubs of the 19th century and is packed with memorabilia. Most of the items on display were collected at garage sales, antiques shows, and shops from around the world by Disney Imagineers.

The two-story club is littered with "stuff," so stroll around and snoop all you like. If you have a seat at the bar, ask the bartender to

work some magic; your stool may slowly sink toward the floor. In the library, a haunted organ sets the scene for outrageous storytellers. The show is a little silly, but fun.

MANNEQUINS: This is the place to head to dance the night away. Guests enter through an elevator that rises to the third floor. Lights, contemporary dance music, and an overall exuberant atmosphere dominate the scene. The name of the club comes from the many mannequins serving as props.

The main dance floor is actually a big turntable, and the music is provided by a deejay. The lighting is a major attraction, with 60 robotically controlled lighting instruments and a matrix of lights behind the stage.

Note that guests must be at least 21 years old (with valid proof of age) to enter Mannequins. As the most intense of Pleasure Island's nightclubs, this spot draws quite a few young adults, of both the guest and local resident varieties.

BET SOUNDSTAGE CLUB: Dancing and other audience-engaging activities combine to make BET SoundStage Club a unique entertainment experience. The club welcomed its first visitors in 1998. (It's operated by BET Holdings, Inc., which owns Black Entertainment Television.)

In keeping with the BET musical tradition, the club features the best in rhythm and blues and hip-hop. Early in the evening, a veejay cues up videos by contemporary urban artists and encourages everyone to take to the dance floor. A tempting selection of appetizers is available.

Admission is included with a Pleasure Island ticket. Call 407-WDW-2648 for show information. BET SoundStage is restricted to guests 21 and older.

COMEDY WAREHOUSE: A comedy troupe performs five times each evening from 7 P.M. to 1 A.M. There are five comedians and one musician. It's a show that features improvisational comedy based on audience suggestions. Every seat offers a good view, even if the stools are a little tough on bad backs. Popcorn is the snack of choice.

8TRAX: Got a penchant for the Partridge Family? Does Abba have a special place in your heart? If so, make tracks for 8TRAX. Music from the early seventies and the disco era fills this dance spot. To keep things in a nostalgic mode, the staff even dresses in polyester. The club also features eighties music for the seventies-challenged.

PLEASURE ISLAND JAZZ COMPANY: Reminiscent of jazz clubs from the 1930s, the interior of this spot resembles an old warehouse. There is live entertainment nightly, featuring jazz from the 1930s to the present. Guests sit at tables.

ROCK N ROLL BEACH CLUB: A combination of dancing and surfer-style decor awaits guests here. The dance floor is on the lowest level of the building, and there are billiard tables and games on the other two floors. Live bands perform hits from the 1960s to the present. The atmosphere is a little frenetic but nonetheless exciting. Light snacks are available. There are now two stairways for entering and exiting the venue.

Entertainment

LATE NIGHT STREET PARTY: There's a fireworks display and outdoor entertainment on a nightly basis.

WEST END STAGE: Bands perform here nightly. The outdoor stage is located between Comedy Warehouse and BET SoundStage. Check at guest relations for schedules.

Shopping

The following Pleasure Island shops generally keep the same hours as the clubs.

Hot Tip!

While the Wildhorse Saloon has moseyed off into the sunset, a new nighttime dance spot called Motion has taken its place on Pleasure Island. Call 407-824-4321 for current information. (And if it's a country music fix you're after, you'll have to settle for the Magic Kingdom's Country Bear Jamboree— it's the only country venue in town.)

CHANGING ATTITUDES: This shop reveals its hip young style with an assortment of shirts, jewelry, bags, and other goods.

DTV: A collection of fun and colorful contemporary fashions featuring Mickey Mouse and his friends is available here.

ISLAND DEPOT: The shop has a nice selection of surfwear and activewear, including shirts, shorts, backpacks, and hats, plus wristwatches and jewelry.

REEL FINDS: Movie- and television-themed memorabilia constitute the stock here. Items once owned by celebrities are also for sale.

SUSPENDED ANIMATION: Posters, prints, lithographs, cels, and original Disney animation art are sold here.

ZEN ZONE: This tranquil shop proffers a variety of relaxation products, such as herbal packs and massage-related products.

Shopping at Crossroads

Constructed by the WDW folks, the Crossroads of Lake Buena Vista shopping center, near the resorts on Hotel Plaza Boulevard, is a convenient dining and shopping area. The center is anchored by a Gooding's supermarket, which is open 24 hours a day.

West Side

When Disney's shopping and entertainment district underwent its latest growth spurt, it did so in true American style: It went west. The West Side boasts a wide variety of restaurants, shops, movies, and clubs. Although it does not have an admission fee, some venues may charge a cover.

AMC THEATRES: The most popular multi-screen movie theater complex in the state of Florida is also one of the largest. The 24 screens show an impressive selection of current movie releases. The seats are roomy and comfortable, and the sound system is first-rate. (It was developed by George Lucas, the creative force behind the series of *Star Wars* blockbusters.) For current schedules, call 407-298-4488.

BONGOS CUBAN CAFE: Situated across from the AMC Theatres on the edge of Lake Buena Vista, Bongos echoes the style of clubs in Miami's South Beach. Created by Gloria Estefan and her husband, it features the flavors and rhythms of Cuba and other Latin American countries. The bold design is dramatic, yet whimsical. Guests dine and, if the mood strikes, even dance amid the colorful, tropical decor (and one remarkably oversized pineapple, which houses a multi-level cocktail lounge).

The food here moves to a Latin beat as well, with its slate of traditional and nouvelle Cuban dishes. There is entertainment on Friday and Saturday nights.

CIRQUE DU SOLEIL: The building that towers over all the others at Downtown Disney West Side is actually a tent—a circus tent. It's the home of a most extraordinary entertainment experience: Cirque du Soleil. This original show, titled La Nouba, is a Walt Disney World exclusive.

Known for its high energy and artistic performances, Cirque du Soleil shows feature a mix of acrobatics and modern dance combined with colorful costumes and dramatic original music. A cast of more than 70 international performers showcase their physical talents twice a day, five days a week.

Tickets for the show may be purchased up to six months in advance. Call 407-939-7600 for information or to order tickets. If you have not already purchased tickets to La Nouba,

consider stopping by the Cirque du Soleil box office at Downtown Disney West Side—some seats may be available at the last minute. Note that the show is quite popular.

DISNEYQUEST: This imaginative entertainment complex features high-tech activities that engage kids and grown-ups alike. Sometimes described as a self-contained, interactive theme park, the five floors under the DisneyQuest roof are divided into four "zones": Explore, Score, Create, and Replay.

Each zone features rides and games from the simple (classic video games like Asteroids, in Replay) to some of the more technologically advanced (e.g., Create's CyberSpace Mountain, in which guests not only design gravity-defying roller coasters but get to ride their creations in a simulator).

Other stops on the tour include Buzz Lightyear's AstroBlaster (bumper cars that let you shoot balls at other drivers), Mighty Ducks Pinball Slam (which turns players into human joysticks), Sid's Create-a-Toy (a computer terminal that allows guests to assemble their own twisted toys), the family-oriented Virtual Jungle Cruise (a turbulent river-raft ride into a primeval world), and Pirates of the Caribbean: Battle for Buccaneer Gold (a swashbuckling shipboard adventure).

Expect to be fully engaged for two to three hours (or until sensory overload sets in). DisneyQuest is open daily from late morning till midnight. Admission is included with the Premium Annual Pass and the Ultimate Park Hopper. (If admission isn't included with your pass, pay at the entrance.)

HOUSE OF BLUES: A huge, combination restaurant-music hall with room for 2,000 (most of it is standing room), House of Blues was inspired by one of America's most celebrated musical traditions. Lest too much of the blues bring you down, there is a lively dose of jazz and country, plus a little bit of R&B and some rock 'n' roll thrown into the music mix. The old-fashioned southern cooking lures diners here—especially on Sunday mornings, when the chefs prepare an all-you-can-eat buffet feast, complemented by live gospel music. Tickets can be purchased through Ticket Master (407-839-3900; *www.ticketmaster.com*) or the House of Blues box office (407-934-2583). Concert prices range from about $5 to $30, depending on the performer.

The House of Blues restaurant features a mélange of Delta-inspired cuisine, including jambalaya, étouffée, and bread pudding.

WOLFGANG PUCK CAFE: There are three dining areas in this two-story restaurant—an express counter, a cafe, and a more formal dining room on the second floor—plus a sushi bar. All feature the celebrated chef's signature pizzas, rotisserie chicken, and other specialties.

Shopping

CANDY CAULDRON: Stop here for some homemade southern-style sweets in an open candy kitchen.

CELEBRITY EYEWORKS STUDIO: Looking to change your eyeglass image? Slip on shades that have been sported by the stars—or at least replicas of their shades.

GUITAR GALLERY: Whether you prefer it plugged or unplugged, this spot can satisfy all of your guitar needs. A vintage guitar display entices buyers and browsers alike.

HOYPOLOI: The glass, ceramics, sculpture, jewelry, and other eclectic, decorative items on display here make this shop seem more like an art gallery. Designed as a "soothing retreat," it is meant to communicate an ambience of harmony, balance, and serenity. It's worth a peek.

MAGIC MASTERS: You won't believe your eyes when you enter this mysterious little shop. There's no merchandise on display. There is simply a list of magical items, from crystal balls to linking handcuffs to a "wizard and book" (whatever that means). The cashier does double duty as the in-house magician. Feel free to ask for a demonstration. It's one of the more entertaining shops at WDW.

MAGNETRON: Your fridge will never be the same once you've paid a visit to this specialty magnet shop with its eclectic assortment of 50,000 magnets.

MICKEY'S GROOVE: This is trend central. Look for accessories, bags, jewelry, and make-up for today's tweens.

PLANET HOLLYWOOD ON LOCATION: This shop specializes in Planet Hollywood–brand merchandise.

SOSA FAMILY CIGARS: In addition to offering premium cigars, this shop showcases the art of hand-rolling.

STARABILIAS: The spotlight here is on memorabilia—music, television, movie—allowing you to bring a piece of Hollywood to the folks back home.

VIRGIN MEGASTORE: This store has a huge selection of music, from classical to contemporary. DVDs and books are also available.

BoardWalk

A stroll at Disney's BoardWalk is a journey back in time. Inspired by the Middle Atlantic seaside attractions of the early 1900s, BoardWalk recaptures the carefree atmosphere of that bygone era. The resort is surrounded by restaurants, clubs, and amusements similar to those enjoyed by beachgoers of yesteryear. It's bordered by a wood-planked walkway, which hugs the shore of Crescent Lake. By day, BoardWalk is a peaceful place to soak up sun, enjoy lunch, or simply walk the boards. After dark, the place turns into a twinkling center of nighttime activity—some of it elegant, some of it downright raucous.

Wyland Galleries, which features the world's foremost marine environmental art, is one of the more calming diversions. WildWood Landing challenges onlookers to test their luck and skill at a collection of classic carnival games. And strolling performers enchant passersby of all ages with magic shows, balloon tricks, or other antics.

BoardWalk is open to everyone. Although there is no admission price, individual venues may charge a cover. There is a $6 charge for valet parking after 5 P.M. (even for guests who are staying at a Disney resort). Self-parking is free. For more restaurant information, refer to *Good Meals, Great Times*.

Clubs

ATLANTIC DANCE: This is a lovely atmosphere in which to dance the night away. A deejay cranks up tunes, tempting guests to twist and shout on the spacious dance floor. Live bands, some big, some small, play on select occasions.

In addition to traditional cocktails, the club serves specialty drinks. Sample one in the "big room" or on the waterfront balcony.

Guests must be 21 or older, with a legal photo ID, to enter. There was no cover charge at press time, but that could change. Hours are generally 8 P.M. until 2 A.M., Thursday through Monday.

This club is known for reinventing itself: specifics may be different during your visit.

ESPN CLUB: This club aims to please sports enthusiasts of all kinds, from the casual armchair quarterback to the most rabid fanatic. It includes a broadcasting facility, arcade, and table-service restaurant and bar.

More than 100 televisions broadcast live sports events, so guests always know the score. (Need to make a pit stop at a crucial moment of the game? Don't sweat it . . . there are even TVs in the bathrooms.)

The ESPN Club has three sections. As you enter, you're on the 50-yard line at The Sidelines. You can catch a game on a television monitor above the "penalty box" bar or sit at a nearby table. Beer, wine, and soft drinks are available, as is the usual pub fare.

Sports Central, the main dining area, has a big screen, showing—what else?—the big game. The kitchen is open until 11:30 P.M. for meals, 1 A.M. for appetizers.

The Yard Arcade, a gameroom with an "urban playground" motif, lets you play the latest sports-themed video games while listening to the big game of the moment.

Big-name athletes often drop by for a little Q&A session with diners. The appearances aren't publicized, but it can't hurt to stop in and ask if any VIP visits are scheduled for your stay.

JELLYROLLS: You might want to warm up your vocal cords before crossing the threshold. They don't call it a sing-along bar for nothing: Guests are expected to sing, clap, and join in the fun at this warehouse home of dueling pianos. You'll hear everything from Gershwin to *Grease*. The piano players take requests, so plan ahead. Write the request—a cocktail napkin will do—and slip it onto the piano. (Although it's not required, we recommend slipping a tip along, too. It will increase the odds of your hearing the request *and* help the musicians pay their rent.)

Jellyrolls is open from 7 P.M. until 2 A.M. nightly. There is sometimes a $5-10 cover charge to enter. (Note that the cover charge may vary.) To get in, you must be at least 21 years old and willing to prove it.

Water Parks
Typhoon Lagoon

> *A furious storm once roared 'cross the sea,*
> *Catching ships in its path, helpless to flee.*
> *Instead of a certain and watery doom,*
> *The winds swept them here to Typhoon Lagoon!*

So reads the legend that guests see as they approach Typhoon Lagoon. The watery playground was inspired by an imagined legend: A typhoon hit a tiny resort village many years ago, and the storm—plus an ensuing earthquake and volcanic eruption—left the village in ruins. The locals, however, were resourceful and rebuilt their town as this "wateropolis."

The centerpiece of Typhoon Lagoon is a huge watershed mountain known as Mount Mayday. Perched atop its peak is the *Miss Tilly*, a marooned shrimp boat originally from Safen Sound, Florida. *Miss Tilly*'s smokestack erupts every half hour, shooting a 50-foot flume of water into the air.

The surf lagoon is huge: Thrilling slides snake through caves, tamer ones offer twisting journeys, and tiny slides entertain small kids. Note that children under 10 must be accompanied by an adult.

SURF POOL: The main swimming area contains nearly three million gallons of water, making it one of the world's largest wave pools. The Caribbean-blue lagoon is surrounded by a white-sand beach, and its main attraction is the waves that come crashing to the shore every 90 seconds. The less adventurous can loll about in two relatively calm tide pools, Whitecap Cove and Blustery Bay.

CASTAWAY CREEK: This 2,100-foot circular river that winds through the park offers a lazy, relaxing orientation to Typhoon Lagoon. Tubes may be borrowed for free and are the most enjoyable way to make the trip along the three-foot-deep waterway. The ride takes guests through a rain forest, where they are cooled by mists and spray; through caves and grottoes that provide welcome shade on hot summer days; and through an area known as Water Works, where "broken" pipes from a

water tower unleash showers on helpless passersby. The current is calm, and aside from a few floating props and the occasional whirlpool, the journey is unimpeded. There are exits along the way, where guests can hop out for a while and do something else, or just dry off a bit and then jump right back into the water. It takes 20 to 35 minutes to ride around the park without taking a break.

GANGPLANK FALLS, KEELHAUL FALLS, AND MAYDAY FALLS: These white-water rides offer guests a variety of slippery trips, two of them in inner tubes. All of the slides course through caves and waterfalls, and past rockwork, making the scenery an attraction in itself. Gangplank Falls gives families a chance to ride together in a three- to five-passenger craft.

HUMUNGA KOWABUNGA: These three speed slides, reported to have been carved into the landscape by the historic earthquake, will send guests zooming through caverns at speeds of 30 miles per hour. The 214-foot slides each offer a 51-foot drop, and the view from the top is a little scary. But it's over before you know it, and once-wary guests hurry back for another try. Guests are also warned that they should be free of back trouble, heart conditions, and other physical limitations to take the trip. Guests must be at least four feet tall to ride any of the Humunga Kowabunga speed slides. Pregnant women are not permitted to ride.

STORM SLIDES: The Jib Jammer, Rudder Buster, and Stern Burner body slides send guests off at about 30 miles per hour down winding fiberglass slides, in and out of rock formations and caves and through waterfalls. It's a somewhat tamer ride than Humunga Kowabunga, but still offers a speedy descent. The slides run about 300 feet, and each offers a different view and experience.

SHARK REEF: Guests obtain free snorkel equipment for a swim through a coral reef, where they come face-to-face with sharks and tropical fish. The reef is built around a sunken tanker (where non-swimming guests can get a close look from the portholes). The sharks, by the way, leopard and bonnethead, are passive members of the species. All guests must shower before entering. Kids must be at least 10 years old to experience Shark Reef.

KETCHAKIDDEE CREEK: Open only to those four feet tall or under, this area has small rides for pint-size visitors. Children must be accompanied by an adult. There are slides, fountains, waterfalls, squirting whales and seals, a mini-rapids ride, an interactive tug-boat, and a grotto with a veil of water that kids love to run through.

SURFING: Surf clinics are offered on select mornings before the park opens. For information, call 407-WDW-SURF (939-7873).

Essentials

WHEN TO GO: Typhoon Lagoon gets very crowded early in the day. When the park reaches peak capacity, no one will be admitted until crowds subside (usually after 3 P.M.). Hours vary seasonally, but the park is generally open from 10 A.M. to 5 P.M., with extended hours in the summer months. All of the pools are heated in the winter. Note that Typhoon Lagoon is usually closed for refurbishment during certain winter months, typically November and December. The park may also close due to inclement weather. Call 407-WDW-PLAY (939-7529) for schedules.

HOW TO GET THERE: Buses from the Transportation and Ticket Center (TTC) and all Walt Disney World resorts, except the Grand Floridian, Contemporary, Polynesian, Wilderness Lodge, and Fort Wilderness (which require a transfer at the TTC). Parking is free.

LOCKER ROOMS: Restrooms with showers and lockers are located close to the entrance. Other restrooms are available farther into the park. These are labeled "Buoys" and "Gulls." Small lockers cost $5 plus a $2 deposit to rent for the day, while large lockers cost $7 plus a $2 deposit. Towels rent for $1; life jackets and tubes are available free of charge.

WHERE TO EAT: Both Typhoon Lagoon restaurants offer similar fare and outdoor seating. Leaning Palms, which was known as Placid Palms before the typhoon hit, was renamed to fit its somewhat unorthodox architecture. Burgers, pizza, salads, ice cream, and assorted snacks are sold here. Typhoon Tilly's Snack Shack serves fish-and-chips and has a separate area just for ice cream treats. Let's Go Slurpin offers a selection of frozen drink specialties and spirits. Also on hand are picnic areas, where guests may bring their own food or enjoy a sampling from the restaurants. No alcoholic beverages, glass containers, or coolers may be brought into the park.

FIRST AID: A first-aid station capable of handling minor medical problems is located just to the left of Leaning Palms.

BEACH SHOP: Singapore Sal's, located to the right of the park's main entrance, is set in a ramshackle building left a bit battered by the typhoon. Bathing suits, sunglasses, hats, towels, sunscreen, souvenirs, water shoes, and Typhoon Lagoon products are available.

Admission Prices

Prices include sales tax and are subject to change. **Note:** Admission is included with an Ultimate Park Hopper Ticket or Premium Annual Pass. It is an option with a Park Hopper Plus Ticket.

	Adults	Children*
One-Day Ticket	$31.75	$25.44
Annual Pass	$105.95	$85.33

*3 through 9 years of age; children under 3 free

Blizzard Beach

A wintry, watery wonderland, Blizzard Beach is said to be the result of a freak storm that dropped a mountain of snow onto Walt Disney World, prompting the quick construction of Florida's first ski resort. When temperatures soared and the snow began to melt, designers prepared to close the resort. But when they spotted an alligator sliding down the slopes, they realized that they had created an exhilarating water adventure park. The slalom and bobsled runs became downhill water slides. The ski jump is one of the world's tallest (120 feet) and fastest (60 miles per hour) free-fall speed slides.

The centerpiece of Blizzard Beach is the snow-capped Mt. Gushmore and its Summit Plummet. Most of the more thrilling runs are found on the slopes of this mountain, which tops out at 90 feet. At the summit, swimmers have a choice of speed slides, flumes, a whitewater raft ride, and an inner-tube run. Guests may reach the top of Mt. Gushmore via chairlift. The lift has a gondola for guests with disabilities. There are stairs, too.

This is the most action-packed Disney water park yet, with enough activities for the entire family to fill at least a day. Note that kids under 10 must be accompanied by an adult.

MELT-AWAY BAY: This one-acre pool at the base of Mt. Gushmore is equipped with its own wave machine. No tsunamis here, however— just a pleasant bobbing wave.

CROSS COUNTRY CREEK: This meandering 3,000-foot waterway circles the entire park. A slow current keeps visitors moving merrily along. Inner tubes, which are free, are the most pleasant way to travel. The ride includes a trip through a bone-chilling ice cave, where guests are splashed with the "melting ice" from overhead.

SUMMIT PLUMMET: The thrilling ride begins 120 feet in the air on a platform 30 feet above the top of Mt. Gushmore. Brave souls travel about 60 miles per hour down a 350-foot slide. Near the top, guests pass through a ski chalet. To those watching from below, riders seem to disappear into an explosion of mist. You must be at least four feet tall to take the plunge.

SLUSH GUSHER: This relatively tame, double-humped water slide offers a brisk journey through a snow-banked mountain gully. Topping out at 90 feet, Slush Gusher is the tallest slide of its kind. You'll find it on Mt. Gushmore, next to Summit Plummet. Guests must be at least four feet tall to ride.

TEAMBOAT SPRINGS: The longest family white-water raft ride in the world takes five-passenger rafts down a twisting, 1,200-foot series of rushing waterfalls.

TOBOGGAN RACERS: An eight-lane water slide sends guests racing over a number of dips. They lie on their stomachs on a mat and travel headfirst down the 250-foot route.

SNOW STORMERS: A trio of flumes descends from the top of the mountain. Guests race down on a switchback course that includes ski-type slalom gates.

RUNOFF RAPIDS: On this inner-tube run, guests careen down three twisting, turning flumes in a single, double, or triple tube.

DOWNHILL DOUBLE DIPPER: Guests travel down these two parallel 230-foot-long racing slides at speeds of up to 25 miles per hour. The partially enclosed water runs feature ski-racing graphics, flags, and time clocks. You must be 48 inches tall to ride.

SKI PATROL TRAINING CAMP: An area designed specifically for preteens, Frozen Pipe Springs looks like an old pipe and drops sliders into eight feet of water. The Thin Ice Training Course tests agility as kids try to walk along broken "icebergs" without falling into the water. Snow Falls' "wide" slides allow a parent and child to ride together. At the Ski Patrol Shelter, guests grab on to a T-bar for an airborne trip. At any point in the ride they can drop into the water below. Ski patrol participants also experience Cool Runners, where riders can count on hurtling and whirling over lots of moguls on twin inner-tube slides. No bunny slopes for these brave daredevils.

TIKE'S PEAK: A kid-size variation of Blizzard Beach, this attraction features miniature versions of Mt. Gushmore's slides and a snow-castle fountain play area. Adults must be accompanied by a child to enter this zone.

Essentials

WHEN TO GO: As a guest favorite, Blizzard Beach tends to get very crowded early in the day. When the park reaches peak capacity, no one is admitted until crowds subside (usually after 3 P.M.). Hours vary seasonally, but the park is generally open from 10 A.M. to 5 P.M., with extended hours in summer. All pools are heated in winter. Blizzard Beach is often closed for refurbishment during certain winter months, typically January and February. It may also close due to inclement weather. For schedules, call 407-WDW-PLAY (939-7529).

HOW TO GET THERE: Buses are available from the Disney-MGM Studios and all Walt Disney World resorts. Parking is free.

LOCKER ROOMS: There are restrooms with showers near the main entrance. Other restrooms and dressing rooms are located around the park. Small lockers cost $5 plus a $2 deposit for the day, while large lockers cost $7 plus a $2 deposit. Towels rent for $1, and life jackets and tubes may be used for free.

WHERE TO EAT: Burgers, hot dogs, fruit salads, and drinks are available at Lottawatta Lodge, in the main village area. Two snack stands with limited offerings are located in more remote areas: Avalunch and The Warming Hut. Polar Pub offers drink specialties and spirits. There are picnic areas for those who prefer to pack their own food. No alcoholic beverages, glass containers, or coolers are permitted in the park.

FIRST AID: Minor medical problems are handled at this station near the main entrance.

BEACH SHOP: The Beach Haus stocks bathing suits, T-shirts, shorts, sunglasses, hats, sunscreen, beach towels, and more.

Admission Prices

Prices include sales tax and are subject to change. **Note:** Admission is included with an Ultimate Park Hopper Ticket or Premium Annual Pass. It is an option with a Park Hopper Plus Ticket.

	Adults	Children*
One-Day Ticket	$31.75	$25.44
Annual Pass	$105.95	$85.33
Combo Ticket	$39.17	$31.75

(Includes one-day admission to Blizzard Beach and Disney's Winter Summerland miniature-golf course.)

*3 through 9 years of age; children under 3 free

Daredevil Disney

You've catapulted through the galaxy on Space Mountain, survived the role of crash dummy on Test Track, and become something of a human yo-yo on the Twilight Zone Tower of Terror. Now what? Believe it or not, there are plenty of thrills awaiting you outside the theme park turnstiles. Some of them, such as the wedgie-inducing slides at the water parks, are well known. Others may be lower key, but they're definitely high octane. Here's a rundown of our favorite theme-park-alternative thrill rides.

PARASAILING: Even if you've never had the urge to be a human kite, consider giving this a whirl. After a simple lift-off from the back of a boat, you and your parachute gradually climb skyward. Before you know it, you're eye level with the roof of the Contemporary resort hotel. A few peaceful minutes later, the hotel and the nearby Magic Kingdom appear to have shrunk considerably. It's not unlike the illusion of flying over London in Peter Pan's Flight. Only this flight's no illusion: You're really 500 or so feet above it all. And don't worry about the landing. It's as smooth as the trip itself. The attendants simply reel you in for a soft touchdown on the back of the boat.

For information on prices and reservations, turn to page 207.

STOCK CAR RACING: Few people can say they've ridden shotgun in a race car, let alone driven one. And this is the real deal. Whether you do it as a driver or a passenger, the Richard Petty Driving Experience is guaranteed to deliver the adrenaline surge of a

lifetime. The track is off the beaten path, so some Disney guests fail to notice it. Those who do tend to come back for more.

For the ride-along experience, you'll don a helmet and climb through the window into the passenger seat. Buckle up and . . . you're off! The big challenges here: (1) not obsessing over the speedometer (it may reach 145 mph) and (2) keeping your head straight (the force from the extreme velocity tends to push noggins to the right).

The expert driver will take you inches from the wall and zip in and out of traffic. (Yes, there are other cars on the track at the same time.) If you're in the driver's seat, you'll have an expert driver to follow. Tailgate at your own risk.

For details on pricing (it's not cheap) and reservations, turn to page 212.

SURFING: When the sun comes up, so does the surf at Disney's Typhoon Lagoon. On select days, guests can take part in a surf clinic taught by competitive surfers. Instructors control the height of the waves—and they give Mother Nature a run for her money.

If you've never hung ten before, know this: It's not easy. But once you've managed to get up on a board, it's a blast.

For more information, call 407-939-7873.

WATERSKIING: Florida weather being what it is (hot!), waterskiing never really goes out of season. It's a refreshing way to see the sights of Disney's Bay Lake—and a serious workout to boot. Sammy Duvall instructors are on hand to assist. For additional information, turn to page 208.

SPEEDBOATING: If you've been to Walt Disney World before, you've no doubt seen folks tooling about in zippy, little speedboats. But have you ever actually given them a try? It's an experience we highly recommend.

For starters, the watercraft known as Water Mouse boats are much speedier than their Water Sprite predecessors. And it's an experience everyone in the family can enjoy (though guests need to be at least 14 years old to drive). Expect to pay about $20 for a half hour. And be sure to wear a watch—as you're apt to lose track of time. For more information, turn to page 208.

Fort Wilderness

In a part of the state where campgrounds tend to look like dried pastures—barren and very hot—the Fort Wilderness Resort and Campground, located almost due east of the Contemporary resort, is an anomaly—a forested, 700-acre wonder of tall slash pines, white-flowering bay trees, and ancient cypresses hung with Spanish moss. Seminole Indians once hunted and fished here.

There are more than a thousand campsites arranged in several campground loops; among them, Wilderness Cabins are available for rent, completely furnished and fitted with all the comforts of home. For information about lodging options, see *Transportation & Accommodations*.

Scattered throughout the campground loops are sporting facilities, including two tennis courts and many tetherball, basketball, and volleyball courts. Fort Wilderness has riding stables, two swimming pools, a marina full of boats, a canoe livery, a beach, bikes and golf carts for rent, and a nature trail. Some facilities are available to campground guests only; some are open to guests at Walt Disney World-owned resort hotels and villas as well; some may also be enjoyed by guests lodging at any of the resorts on Hotel Plaza Boulevard as well as off Disney property.

There's a petting farm and a barn that's home to the horses that pull the Magic Kingdom's Main Street trolleys. The barn houses a small museum that celebrates horses and the cherished role they've played in Disney history.

Two stores—the Settlement Trading Post and the Meadow Trading Post—stock campers' necessities, a limited supply of groceries, and souvenirs. And then there's Pioneer Hall, the home of the Hoop-Dee-Doo Musical Revue dinner show (described in the *Good Meals, Great Times* chapter). This rustic structure (made of white pine shipped from Montana) also has a buffet restaurant and a small lounge area.

BEACHES AND SWIMMING: The beach on the shore of Bay Lake is a good spot for sunning or snoozing in a hammock. There are also two pools for campers' use. Note that the beaches and pools are open to Fort Wilderness guests only.

BIKE RENTALS: A variety of bikes may be rented at the Bike Barn for trips along the bike paths and roadways of Fort Wilderness—or just for getting around. Bikes cost about $8 per hour or $22 per day.

BLACKSMITH SHOP: The pleasant fellow who shoes the draft horses that pull trolleys in the Magic Kingdom is on hand most mornings to answer questions and talk about his job; occasionally, guests may watch him at work, fitting the big animals with the special polyurethane-covered, steel-cored horseshoes that are used to protect the horses' hooves. This shop is located at the Tri-Circle-D Ranch.

BOATING: Fort Wilderness is ribboned with tranquil canals that make for delightful canoe trips of one to three hours—or longer if you take fishing gear and elect to wet your line. Canoe rentals are available at the Bike Barn for about $7 per half hour or $11 per hour. Pedal boats (about $7 per half hour or $11 per hour) may also be rented here for use in the canals. For a trip around Bay Lake, zippy little Water Mouse boats, canopy boats, and pontoon boats are available for rent at the marina, at the north end of the campground. (Refer to the *Sports* chapter for additional details and pricing information.)

CAMPFIRE PROGRAM: Held nightly (weather permitting) near the Meadow Trading Post at the center of the campground, this evening program features Disney movies, a sing-along, and cartoons. Chip and Dale often put in an appearance. It's open to WDW resort guests only (no charge).

CARRIAGE RIDES: Guests may enjoy a relaxing and intimate carriage ride through the picturesque grounds of Fort Wilderness. The rate for each 30-minute ride is $30.

Small carriages can hold up to two adults and a small child. Larger carriages fit 4 adults or 2 adults and up to 3 small kids. Reservations are a must. Rides are offered nightly. Call 407-824-2734 for information or to make a reservation. Same-day reservations are walk-up only. (Ask the driver about buying tickets. If they're available, expect to pay with cash or a Disney Resort ID card. Credit cards are not accepted.) Rides may be canceled due to inclement weather. Cancellations must be made at least 24 hours ahead to avoid paying full price.

Note that guests are picked up in front of Crockett's Tavern at Pioneer Hall. Feel free to bring your own liquid refreshments.

ELECTRIC CART RENTALS: Available at the Bike Barn (about $46 for 24 hours) for sightseeing or transportation. Renters must be 18 years old and have a valid driver's license. Reservations are necessary; call 407-824-2742 for reservations and additional information.

ELECTRICAL WATER PAGEANT: This cavalcade of lights (described in more detail in *Good Meals, Great Times*) can be seen from the beach here nightly at 9:45 P.M.

FISHING EXCURSIONS ON BAY LAKE: Walt Disney World's restrictive fishing policy means plenty of angling action—largemouth bass weighing two to eight pounds, mainly— for those who sign up for fishing excursions.

The fee ranges from about $180–$210 for up to five people for a two-hour excursion (one additional hour is about $80) and includes gear, a guide, and soft drinks; no license is required. The price varies based on time of day, with the early morning trips commanding the highest rate.

Note that all fishing is strictly catch-and-release. Call 407-WDW-PLAY (939-7529) for exact times and to make reservations.

FISHING IN THE CANALS: In addition to largemouth bass, catfish and panfish can be caught here as well. Those without their own gear will find cane poles and lures for sale at the trading posts; equipment is also available for rent at the Bike Barn. Cane poles are about $6 per hour or $8 for the whole day. Rods and reels are about $7 per hour or $10 per day. Bait costs about $3.50. No license is required. Fort Wilderness resort guests may toss their lines in right from the shore.

LAWN MOWER TREE: The tree that mysteriously grew around a lawn mower is a Fort Wilderness point of interest worth seeking out. It's just off the path leading to the marina, across the way from the Meadow Trading Post.

PETTING FARM: This enclave just behind Pioneer Hall is home to some friendly goats, sheep, rabbits, chickens, and other barnyard critters. (A colony of prairie dogs didn't work out because its members kept burrowing out of their compound; no sooner would their Disney caretakers try to thwart them—by digging a bigger hole and installing a below-ground-level wire fence—than the little creatures would gnaw through it.)

Pony rides, offered seasonally, are available between 10 A.M. and 5 P.M. for $3. (The pony-ride weight limit is 80 pounds.) The Petting Farm is a good place to visit before the Hoop-Dee-Doo Musical Revue.

TENNIS: Two tennis courts are available; play is on a first-come, first-served basis.

TRAIL RIDES: Guided horseback trips depart four times daily from the Trail Blaze Corral and take riders on a leisurely, meandering ride through the Florida wilderness, where it is not uncommon to see birds, deer, and even an occasional alligator. Galloping is not part of the experience, so you don't need riding know-how to sign up. Cost is about $32 per

person. No children under 9 are permitted to ride. There is a weight limit of 250 pounds. Reservations are necessary; call 407-WDW-PLAY (939-7529) up to 30 days in advance.

TRI-CIRCLE-D RANCH: This corner of Fort Wilderness is the place that the world champion Percherons and the draft horses that pull trolleys down Main Street in the Magic Kingdom call home. You may watch them chomping on their food and occasionally see young colts and fillies as well. The Tri-Circle-D insignia above the barn door—two small circles atop a large one with the letter *D* inside—is the WDW brand. The barn is also the site of a museum that pays tribute to horses and their role in Disney history.

VOLLEYBALL, TETHERBALL, AND BASKETBALL COURTS: These are scattered throughout the camping loops. There is no charge to use the courts.

WAGON RIDES: The wagon departs from Pioneer Hall at 7 P.M. and 9:30 P.M. and carries guests on a trip through wooded areas near Bay Lake. Each ride lasts about 45 minutes and concludes at Pioneer Hall.

Purchase tickets from the wagon ride host: $8 for adults, $4 for children 3 through 9. Children under 12 must be accompanied by an adult.

On nights when the Magic Kingdom offers a fireworks presentation, Fort Wilderness offers "fireworks wagon rides." These excursions are in addition to those regularly scheduled. Expect fireworks wagon rides to depart at 8:30 P.M. for a 9 P.M. fireworks show. The fireworks are viewed from a distance, but the experience is made special by plugging into the show's audio soundtrack.

Group wagon rides are available by calling 407-824-2734 (24 hours in advance). The price is $125 per hour.

WILDERNESS SWAMP TRAIL: A three-quarter-mile trail, this smooth footpath into the woods skirts the marshes along the shore of Bay Lake, then plunges into a forest thick with tall, straight-standing cypress trees. It is near Marshmallow Marsh, at the northern end of the campground.

Essentials

HOW TO GET THERE: From outside the World, take Magic Kingdom Exit 64B off I-4 onto US 192, go through the Magic Kingdom Auto Plaza, and, bearing to your right, follow the Fort Wilderness signs. This is the most expeditious way to go, even for WDW resort guests.

By WDW Transportation: Buses or boats. Buses can get you just about anywhere, but allow yourself plenty of time—the system, while efficient, is time-consuming.

Boats are also available from Magic Kingdom marinas (about a 30-minute ride) and from the Contemporary and Wilderness Lodge resorts (about a 25-minute ride). For details about WDW Transportation, see the *Transportation & Accommodations* chapter.

WHERE TO EAT: For a description of the Trail's End Buffet at Fort Wilderness, refer to the *Good Meals, Great Times* chapter.

The Settlement Trading Post, located not far from the beach at the north end of the campground, and the Meadow Trading Post, located near the center of Fort Wilderness, also offer a limited supply of food staples. For serious grocery-shopping, head to Goodings at Crossroads or another nearby supermarket. Ask for directions at Guest Relations.

> ## Hot Tip!
> River Country, Walt Disney World's original water park, was closed indefinitely when this book went to press. It is not expected to be open in 2004.

WDW Spas

For many guests, a day at the theme parks is an exciting test of physical endurance—complete with sprinting (say, from Dumbo to Space Mountain before that Fastpass time expires), weight lifting (toting tired toddlers), and long-distance hiking (covering more than a mile to reach the American Adventure pavilion from Epcot's front gate—and back again!). Fortunately, there are many ways to rest and rejuvenate weary bones, throbbing feet, and noise-addled noggins. Chief among them is a visit to a soothing spa (ahhhh). There are three such spots on Disney property, all open to WDW resort guests and day visitors alike.

GRAND FLORIDIAN SPA: A short walk from the Grand Floridian Resort, this relaxing retreat is located right next to the health club (across from the wedding pavilion). With saunas, steam rooms, and whirlpools, even the locker rooms promote pampering. Specialties of the house include baths steeped in flowers, a deluxe facial, complete with hand and foot massage, and a cooling lavender oil wrap, guaranteed to take the sting out of any sunburn. Other services include hydrotherapy, aroma-therapy, and massage (including shiatsu, Swedish, sports, and one specially designed for expectant mothers). Manicures, pedicures, and other hand and foot treatments are also available.

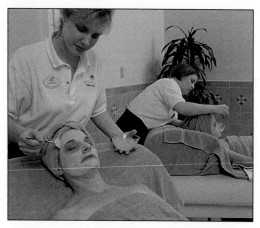

Hours are generally from 6 A.M. to 9 P.M., but vary seasonally. Prices (which include 18 percent gratuity) run about $57 for a 25-minute massage and about $110 for a facial. Full- and half-day packages are available. For additional information, call 407-824-2332. Reservations are accepted up to one year in advance.

THE SPA AT DISNEY'S SARATOGA SPRINGS: Terra-cotta-colored tiles and teal towels accent this spa's ten treatment rooms. Signature services include the Warm Seafoam Mud Wrap and Seaweed Hydro-Massage. Also on tap: aromatherapy, reflexology, sports and Swedish massage, and hydrotherapy, plus a variety of body wraps and scrubs. Manicures, pedicures, and facials are also options. The locker rooms are equipped with a steam room, sauna, and whirlpool.

Located on the shore of Lake Buena Vista, the spa is inside the Fitness Center at Disney's Saratoga Springs resort. Hours are generally from 8 A.M. to 8 P.M., but vary seasonally. A 25-minute massage costs about $57, with facials going for about $100 (plus gratuity). Full- and half-day packages are available. For information, call 407-827-4455. Reservations are taken up to six months ahead.

THE SPA AT WYNDHAM PALACE: A plush, peaceful place, this spa is as well equipped as they come. One-way glass provides natural, picture-window views from (but not into) the 14 treatment rooms. High-tech chairs with whirlpool foot baths and back massage capability make getting a pedicure a real event. And a cool-mud Theme Park Leg Relief Wrap can put the spring back in the step of even the most labored lower limbs. Landscaped, outdoor whirlpools, plus locker room saunas and steam rooms, are there to aid the relaxation process.

Among the many treatments from which to choose are aromatherapy and massage, including sports, shiatsu, Swedish, deep-tissue, reflexology, and hydrotherapy. A variety of special facials (including one for sun-stressed skin), baths (herbal, mud, mineral, and seaweed), scrubs, and wraps are available. An adjacent salon offers the usual lineup of services.

The Wyndham Palace Resort & Spa is situated opposite the Downtown Disney Marketplace, on Buena Vista Drive. Hours are usually 6 A.M. to 9 P.M., but vary seasonally. A 25-minute massage costs about $60, and facials are about $92 (including 18 percent gratuity). Full- and half-day packages are available, as are custom packages. For information, call 800-981-1472. Reservations are accepted up to one month in advance.

Specialty Cruises

At Walt Disney World, every evening ends with a bang—which comes in the form of elaborate pyrotechnic displays. Two such presentations, the Magic Kingdom's fireworks and Epcot's IllumiNations: Reflections of Earth, are seen by thousands of park-goers on a nightly basis. However, these dazzling displays are also enjoyed by a privileged few, far removed from the hubbub of the theme park crowds, yet close enough to marvel at the subtleties of each brilliant burst. These are the guests who chose to book a boat for a specialty cruise. This vintage vantage point is available to everyone, provided that the rates don't break the budget and that reservations are made in advance. Of course, there is the other extreme: a peaceful, moonlit cruise on the quiet waterways of the World. This option is also available to guests who book a specialty cruise.

Reservations are accepted up to 24 hours ahead; advance reservations, accepted up to 90 days ahead, are strongly recommended. While specifics may change, the following is a good indication of what was available at press time.

> ## Hot Tip!
> If you plan to enjoy a scenic fireworks cruise, pack a sweater. It can get chilly out there on the open seas—even during summer.

THE GRAND 1: This striking 45-foot Sea Ray escorts up to 12 guests at a time. A private tour of the Seven Seas Lagoon and Bay Lake culminates with a front-row seat for the Magic Kingdom's fireworks, when possible. (The vessel drops anchor in the vicinity of the park entrance, aligning itself as closely with Cinderella Castle as possible.)

The *Grand 1* departs from the Grand Floridian, but stops at the Polynesian, Contemporary, Wilderness Lodge, or Fort Wilderness Lodge on request. It costs about $350 per hour to rent, with the per-boatload fee covering up to 12 guests, plus a driver and a deckhand. Call 407-824-2439 to reserve it.

PONTOON BOATS: More practical than luxurious, Disney's fleet of pontoon boats still deliver a crowd-pleasing cruise experience.

The boats, which accommodate up to ten, take guests on tours of the Seven Seas Lagoon and Bay Lake, near the Magic Kingdom, as well as Crescent Lake, near Epcot's World Showcase. Those in the Magic Kingdom area are treated to VIP viewing of that park's fireworks, while Epcot-area cruisers take in IllumiNations: Reflections of Earth, when available.

Pontoon cruises last about one hour. Magic Kingdom fireworks excursions depart from the Grand Floridian, Polynesian, Contemporary, Wilderness Lodge, and Fort Wilderness marinas. IllumiNations cruises leave from BoardWalk and Yacht and Beach Club marinas. The cost (which includes a driver) starts at about $120 per boatload. Call 407-WDW-PLAY (939-7529) for reservations.

THE BREATHLESS: This elegant, open-air motorboat, is a sleek 24-foot reproduction of a 1930s mahogany runabout. Named after the Dick Tracy character, the vessel is equipped with bench seats and fits up to seven guests.

Moored at the Yacht and Beach Club marina, the *Breathless* escorts private parties around Crescent Lake and adjoining waterways by day and night. All cruises depart from a dock at the Yacht and Beach Club, but requests for pickups at the BoardWalk resort marina will be honored.

The one-hour IllumiNations cruise costs about $175. Prices are per boatload (for up to seven passengers) and include a driver. Call 407-WDW-PLAY (939-7529) for reservations.

Behind-the-Scenes Tours

Disney Adult Discoveries programs offer the chance to experience Walt Disney World from the inside out. Most of the guided behind-the-scenes tours are only open to visitors 16 and older. Guests are required to carry a photo ID when attending backstage programs. Many tours are offered as "flex" options with vacation packages. Tours and prices (which include tax) are subject to change; for information or to make reservations, call 407-WDW-TOUR (939-8687).

BACKSTAGE MAGIC (Monday through Friday): This is one of Walt Disney World's best programs. Highlighting the 7-hour exploration of the Magic Kingdom, Disney-MGM Studios, and Epcot is an underground tour of the Magic Kingdom's Utilidors—Disney's tunnel system. Lunch is included, as are a few special surprises. Cost is $199 per person. Theme park admission is not required or included.

BACKSTAGE SAFARI (Monday, Wednesday, Thursday, Friday): This 3-hour tour takes guests through backstage animal facilities, such as the veterinary hospital and elephant barn at Disney's Animal Kingdom. The cost is $65, plus theme park admission.

DISNEY'S FAMILY MAGIC TOUR (daily): Families may participate in this 2-hour, scavenger hunt through the Magic Kingdom. The cost is $25 per guest (above age 3). Park admission is not included, but is required.

DIVEQUEST (daily): The highlight of the 2½-hour program is a 40-minute underwater adventure—complete with sharks, turtles, rays, and other fish—in The Living Seas aquarium. Participants must present proof of current scuba certification. Cost is $140. Guests between the ages of 10 and 14 must dive with a parent or guardian. Gear is provided. Park admission is not required or included.

DOLPHINS IN DEPTH (weekdays at 9:45 A.M.): This 3½–hour program teaches guests about dolphin behavior as they interact with the animals and observe researchers and trainers working with them. Cost is $150 and includes a souvenir T-shirt. Park admission is not required or included. Wetsuits are provided; wear your own swimsuit.

EPCOT SEAS AQUA TOUR (weekdays at 12:30 P.M.): A new 2½-hour program that lets guests learn about and interact with ocean life in the Living Seas pavilion. First, guests watch a video about sea creatures, then they join them in their habitat using a Supplied-Air Snorkel system. Cost is $100 (all profits go to the Disney Wildlife Conservation fund). Gear is included, as are refreshments, a T-shirt, and a group photo of the experience. Guests must wear a bathing suit. Park admission is not required or included.

GARDENS OF THE WORLD (Tuesday, Thursday): Hosted by a horticulturist, this 3-hour program guides guests through a study of plants, flowers, and trees at Epcot's World Showcase. Cost is $59, plus park admission.

HIDDEN TREASURES OF WORLD SHOWCASE (Tuesday, Thursday): This 3-hour tour takes guests to the international pavilions at Epcot. The focus is on international art, architecture, and traditions. Cost is $59, plus park admission.

KEYS TO THE KINGDOM (daily): A 4½-hour tour that offers an on-site orientation to the history and workings of Walt Disney World's original theme park, the Magic Kingdom. Guests visit an attraction (waiting in the regular attraction line) and take a peek at the Production Center and the Utilidors (the legendary tunnels underneath the park). Cost is $58, plus theme park admission.

THE MAGIC BEHIND OUR STEAM TRAINS (Monday, Thursday): A 2-hour tour that gives guests an inside look at the Walt Disney World Railroad. In addition to an exploration of Walt Disney's passion for steam trains, guests visit the backstage "roundhouse" where the steam trains are stored, and join the opening crew as they prepare for the daily railroad operation in the Magic Kingdom.

Guests must be at least 10 to take the tour. Cost is $30 per person. Theme park admission is required, but not included.

THE UNDISCOVERED FUTURE WORLD

(Monday, Tuesday, Friday, Saturday at 10:30 A.M.): Walt Disney dreamed about making the world a better place. In this 4-hour tour, guests are taken back to the creation of Epcot and learn about Walt's lofty ambitions and his legacy.

Guests walk to all Future World pavilions and learn how each area celebrates humanity's accomplishments and challenges. The goal is to share the vision behind the park.

Cost is $49 per person. Guests must be at least 16 years old to attend this walking program. It is offered as a "flex" option with several vacation packages. Theme park admission is required, but not included.

WELCOME TO THE MAGIC KINGDOM

(Sunday through Wednesday, Friday): Think of it as "Magic Kingdom 101." This 90-minute walking tour of Walt Disney World's original kingdom is an informative overview, taking guests to each of the park's seven themed lands.

Guests of all ages may experience the tour. Those under age 10 can do so for free, while those 10 and up pay $20 per person. It is offered as a "flex" option with several vacation packages. Theme park admission is required, but not included. The tour is offered in several languages.

WILD BY DESIGN (Tuesday, Thursday, Friday at 8:30 A.M.): A 3-hour experience that invites guests to learn how art, architecture, historical artifacts, and storytelling were combined to create Disney's Animal Kingdom. The tour takes place in the park itself, not behind the scenes. As guests explore various lands, a guide offers insight into the complexities of caring for wild animals and their habitats.

A light continental breakfast is served at the halfway point of the tour. Cost is $58 per person. It is offered as a "flex" option with several vacation packages. Theme park admission is required, but not included. Guests must be at least 14 years old to attend the program. Given prior notice, this outdoor walking tour can accommodate guests with special needs.

YULETIDE FANTASY (Seasonal): A festive 3½–hour experience, this program showcases the way Disney weaves stories and folklore into decorations found in the theme parks and resorts. It offers a unique perspective on how colors, textures, architecture, and illusions help WDW deck the halls for the holidays.

Cost is $59 per person. Theme park admission is not included or required. Guests must be at least 16 years old to participate. All guests must present a photo ID.

VIP Tours

Though Disney technically regards every guest as a VIP, you can knock your status up a notch by booking a special VIP Tour. In addition to a knowledgeable guide (one of those cheerful people in the plaid vests) who will help you navigate Walt Disney World, you'll have access to preferred VIP seating for many of the live stage shows, parades, and nighttime spectaculars.

The VIP Tours, which can be customized, may even include such services as private transportation to and from the airport and among various destinations throughout Walt Disney World Property.

Tour requests may be made up to 90 days in advance. Disney recommends calling at least 3 days ahead to ensure availability. If you have to cancel, do so at least 48 hours before. Otherwise, cancellation fees apply. For details and pricing information, or to make reservations, call Disney Special Activities at 407-560-4033.

It's a Celebration

What happens when a little bit of Disney magic spills into the real world? A town called Celebration, Florida. Founded in 1996 by a subsidiary of the Walt Disney Company, the town is surrounded by 4,700 acres of protected greenland.

The homes, with their front porches and picket fences, hark back to a much simpler time in American history. Built along a scenic lakeside promenade, downtown Celebration is a pleasant place to relax outdoors.

With the addition of the Celebration Hotel, which opened in fall 1999, guests can do more than just visit this quaint little town— they can move in! (If temporarily.)

The 115-room, four-star hotel is situated lakeside in downtown Celebration. Guest accommodations include an environmental sound and music system, phone with dataport, hair dryer, iron with board, and a safe. There is ample meeting space in addition to a pool, whirlpool, fitness center, lobby bar, and breakfast buffet.

Note that Plantation is the only restaurant here—but guests need only cross the street to find additional spots in which to dine.

Architect Graham Gund based the design of the hotel on a 1920s Florida wood-frame look. With its big roofs, low eaves and dormers, and wraparound porches, the hotel reinforces the small town theme of Celebration.

Guests can shop, stroll, skate, or simply enjoy a picnic by the lake. There are several village parks, miles of nature trails, and the Celebration Golf Club's 18-hole public golf course (rates range from $55 to $115). Near the par-72 course is a 3-hole youth course where the Tiger Woods of tomorrow can practice their golf swings today.

The community's retail and business district invites visitors to enjoy a variety of dining, shopping, and entertainment spots, including a bookstore, antiques shop, ice cream parlor, diner, and movie theater.

Located southeast of the intersection of U.S. 192 and I-4 near Kissimmee, Celebration is about a ten-minute drive from Walt Disney World. For information, call 407-566-2200, or write: Celebration Information; 610 Sycamore Street, Suite 310; Celebration, FL 34747. Or visit *www.celebrationfl.com* to see what's happening during your visit.

Sports

SPORTS

Many first-time visitors don't realize that Disney World provides a plethora of sporting opportunities. Within WDW's 27,000-plus acres there are more tennis courts than at most tennis resorts, and more holes of championship-caliber golf than at most golf centers, plus so many other diversions—from fishing and biking to boating, swimming, parasailing, and horseback riding—that the quantity and variety are matched by few other vacation destinations.

So while the family golfers are pursuing a perfect swing on one of five first-rate, 18-hole courses, tennis buffs can be wearing themselves out on the courts, sailors can be sailing, water-skiers can be skimming back and forth across powerboat wakes, and anglers can be dangling a cane pole in hopes of hooking a big bream. Those who prefer to spectate rather than participate can visit a virtual sports mecca at Disney's Wide World of Sports complex, an enormous state-of-the-art facility that hosts a staggering array of sporting events, both amateur and professional.

Instruction, as well as guides, drivers, and assorted supervisors, makes every sport as much fun for beginners as for hard-core aficionados. Moreover, the ready accessibility of WDW sporting activities—via an excellent system of public transportation (see *Transportation & Accommodations*)—means that no family member need curtail playtime to chauffeur others around.

Note: All prices are subject to change.

A Matter of Courses

Most people don't immediately think of Walt Disney World when they contemplate a golf vacation. Yet there are six superb courses here: The Magnolia, the Palm, and the Oak Trail are situated across from the Polynesian resort and extend nearly to the borders of the Magic Kingdom. Just a short drive away is the Lake Buena Vista course, whose fairways are framed by the Disney Institute and Old Key West resort. Osprey Ridge and Eagle Pines play from the Bonnet Creek Golf Club near Fort Wilderness.

While the original Joe Lee–designed courses (the Palm, Magnolia, and Lake Buena Vista) won't set anyone's knees to knocking in terror from the regular tees, all three are demanding enough to have merited the status of a stop on the PGA Tour tournament trail.

Tom Fazio designed Osprey Ridge to offer a reasonable challenge for beginners as well as more advanced players. Eagle Pines, designed by Pete Dye, is a low-profile layout built level with, or lower than, the surrounding land.

Depending on the tee from which a golfer plays, Disney courses will prove challenging and/or fun, and all are constructed to be especially forgiving for the midhandicap player.

PALM & MAGNOLIA: The wide-open, tree-dotted Magnolia measures 5,232 yards from the front tees, 6,642 from the middle, and 7,190 from the back. The Palm is tighter, with more wooded fairways and nine water hazards; it measures 5,311 yards from the front, 6,461 from the middle, and 6,957 from the back. Both courses have received a four-star ("outstanding") rating from *Golf Digest* magazine. The Magnolia and Palm share two driving ranges and two putting greens.

Oak Trail: This nine-hole, 2,913-yard layout, a walking course tucked into a corner of the Magnolia, was designed for beginners and junior golfers, but it has some tough holes, including two par 5s.

OSPREY RIDGE & EAGLE PINES: These two par-72 courses play from the Bonnet Creek Golf Club. The Tom Fazio–designed Osprey Ridge measures 5,402 yards from the front tees, 6,680 from the middle, and 7,101 from the back. It takes guests into remote areas of WDW property as it winds through wooded landscape near Fort Wilderness. Dramatic contouring puts some tees 20 to 25 feet above the basic grade. In contrast, the Pete Dye–designed

Eagle Pines is a low-profile layout. It plays 4,838 yards from the front tees, 6,309 from the middle, and 6,772 from the pro tees. Many fairways are bordered by scrub and pine needles; water comes into play as well. Osprey Ridge and Eagle Pines share a driving range and a putting green.

LAKE BUENA VISTA COURSE: This Joe Lee design measures 5,194 yards from the front tees, 6,268 from the middle, and 6,819 from the rearmost markers. Among the shortest of the 18-hole, par-72 courses, it has a fair amount of water, and its tree-lined fairways are Disney's narrowest. The course is well suited for beginners but challenges experienced players. A driving range and putting green are available.

Essentials

WHEN TO GO: January through April is peak golfing season. To beat the crowds, play on a Monday or Tuesday, tee off in the late afternoon, and take advantage of low summer rates. From late April through late September, guests pay about $60 at Osprey Ridge and Eagle Pines, and about $60 at Lake Buena Vista, Palm, and Magnolia after 10 A.M. After 3 P.M., the price drops significantly at Osprey Ridge, Eagle Pines, Palm, and Magnolia. Annual golf memberships (available to Florida residents only, for $53) net discounts during this period, too.

RESERVATIONS: Call 407-WDW-GOLF (939-4653) to confirm rates and to secure tee-off times. From January through April, morning and early afternoon tee times should be reserved well in advance; starting times after 3 P.M. are often available at the last minute. Those buying a golf package may reserve tee times up to 90 days prior to their check-in date. Guests with confirmed reservations at a WDW resort or at one of the resorts on Hotel Plaza Boulevard may also reserve 90 days ahead. Others may book tee times 30 days ahead. All reservations must be made with a major credit card. Cancellations must be made at least 48 hours in advance to avoid paying the full fee.

FEES: At the 18-hole courses, greens fees (including a required cart) vary with the course and season. Rates range from about

$45 to $185 for guests at Walt Disney World resorts and the resorts on Hotel Plaza Boulevard, and from about $50 to $190 for day visitors. Twilight rates, available throughout the year, begin in mid-afternoon and run about $53 to $80. Cost for adults to play Oak Trail is $38 for 9 holes; juniors (17 and under) pay $20 for 9 holes. Prices include tax and are likely to change.

INSTRUCTION: At the WDW Golf Studio at the Palm and Magnolia, private lessons cost $63.60 per half hour for adults; $31.80 for juniors. Pros offer 45-minute video sessions; cost is $79.50. Nine-hole playing lessons, in which a pro golfer gives instruction in club selection, strategy, and more, cost $159 for adults and $106 for juniors. Reservations are necessary for lessons; call 407-WDW-GOLF (939-4653). Expect prices to vary.

DRESS: Proper golf attire is required. Shirts must have collars and any shorts must be Bermuda length.

EQUIPMENT RENTAL: Equipment can be rented at all courses; club rentals range from $45 to $55 for men and $45 for women, depending on the season. Photo ID and major credit card (for the $500 refundable deposit) are required for club rentals. Range balls ($6 per basket) are among the items available.

Tournaments

The Funai Classic at the Walt Disney World resort is one of the biggest spectator events on Disney's sports calendar. It features most of the PGA Tour's top players and takes place in October. Guests who plan to golf during their WDW vacation are advised not to visit during tournament week. (You may, however, play with the pros if you are willing to pay for it.)

For additional information about the Funai Classic and other special Walt Disney World golf events, call 407-WDW-GOLF (939-4653). Private tournaments may be arranged by calling the same number. Dates are subject to change.

Tennis, Everyone

No one comes to Walt Disney World strictly for a tennis vacation; it just doesn't exude the country-club ambience of a tennis resort, where everyone is totally immersed in the game. But the facilities and instruction programs here are extensive enough that such holidays are possible. Certainly, playing a couple of sets of tennis on one of the World's 25 resort courts is a good way to unwind after a mad morning in the parks.

With six courts, Disney's Racquet Club at the Contemporary resort is Walt Disney World's major tennis facility for guest use. Located just beyond the hotel's north wing, the club features state-of-the-art hydrogrid clay courts. The Grand Floridian boasts a pair of clay courts. All other Walt Disney World tennis is played on hard courts. Fort Wilderness, Yacht and Beach Club, and BoardWalk have two; Old Key West has three; and the Swan and Dolphin share a four-court facility.

For information about tennis opportunities or to make reservations, call 407-WDW-PLAY (939-7529).

Essentials

WHEN TO GO: Courts are generally open from 7 A.M. to 7 P.M. daily (hours are seasonal, so call ahead for exact times); courts at the Swan and Dolphin are open 24 hours a day; lighted courts are available at each of the above-mentioned resorts. In February, March, April, June, and July the courts endure fairly heavy use, but there is usually a lull between noon and 3 P.M., and again from dinnertime until closing time. January, October, and November are prime months for tennis enthusiasts.

Equipment rental is no longer available at Walt Disney World. Guests must bring their own tennis racquets and balls.

All courts are available on a first-come, first-served basis. Reservations are not accepted. Individual players seeking partners can find them through the player-matching program at Disney's Racquet Club (407-824-3578). During very busy periods, the length of time a single group of players can occupy a court is restricted to two hours on any morning, afternoon, and evening.

LESSONS: The tennis program at the Contemporary resort is open to players of all skill levels. Daily clinics are open to guests 10 years of age and older. Guests under age 14 must be accompanied by an adult. Reservations are required to guarantee play for all programs. Call 407-939-7529 for reservations, more information, and pricing.

TOURNAMENTS: Private tourneys may be arranged by calling 407-827-4433. For information on tournaments at Disney's Wide World of Sports complex, call 407-363-6600.

DRESS: Tennis whites are appropriate, but not required, for play on Disney's courts.

LOCKERS: Lockers are available at the Contemporary and Grand Floridian resorts.

Waters of the World

Boating

Walt Disney World is the home of the country's largest fleet of pleasure boats. Cruising on Bay Lake and the Seven Seas Lagoon can be excellent sport, and a variety of boats are available for rent at WDW resort marinas. Bay Lake excursions originate from the Contemporary, on the lake's western shore; Wilderness Lodge, on the south shore; and Fort Wilderness, which occupies the lake's southeastern shore. The Polynesian and Grand Floridian resorts send boaters out from their marinas on the southern shore of Seven Seas Lagoon. The Caribbean Beach resort leases watercraft for use on its own 45-acre Barefoot Bay. The Yacht and Beach Club, BoardWalk, Swan, and Dolphin share a boating haven in 25-acre Crescent Lake. And marinas at Port Orleans, Old Key West, and the Downtown Disney Marketplace set guests up to cruise the waterways adjoining the 35-acre Lake Buena Vista. Guests at Coronado Springs may rent watercraft for use on the 15-acre Lago Dorado.

To rent, day visitors and resort guests alike must show a resort ID, a driver's license, or a valid passport. Rental of certain craft may carry other special requirements (described below). Note that no privately owned boats are permitted on any of the Walt Disney World waters. Also, all prices and times are subject to change.

CANOEING: A long paddle down the smooth, wooded Fort Wilderness canals is such a tranquil way to pass a misty morning that it's hard to remember that the bustle of the Magic Kingdom is just a short launch ride away. Canoes are available for rent at the Bike Barn at Fort Wilderness (about $7 per half hour, $11 per hour). Most excursions last one to three hours; those with fishing gear often last longer (it's up to the guests in the canoe to decide). Canoes may also be rented at the Caribbean Beach and Port Orleans Riverside marinas. Ocean Kayaks (open-top kayaks) may be rented at La Marina at Coronado Springs and at the marina at Port Orleans Riverside (about $7 per half hour, $11 per hour).

CANOPY BOATS: These 16-foot, V-hulled motorized boats with canopies are a good choice for relaxing cruises. They accommodate up to eight adults, and may be rented for about $27 per half hour at the Downtown Disney Marketplace, Polynesian, Contemporary, Grand Floridian, Wilderness Lodge, Yacht and Beach Club, Old Key West, Port Orleans, Caribbean Beach, and Fort Wilderness marinas.

PARASAILING: Excursions are offered at the Contemporary resort arena. Each seven- to ten-minute flight costs about $75 for one person, $115 for two to ride tandem. Reservations are necessary and may be made up to 90 days ahead; call 407-WDW-PLAY (939-7529).

PEDAL BOATS: These craft rent for about $7 per half hour or $11 per hour at the Caribbean Beach, Port Orleans, Coronado Springs, Old Key West, and Swan and Dolphin marinas. Watercraft are available to all guests at all locations. Hydro Bikes (boats resembling bicycles affixed to pontoons) may be rented at the Swan and Dolphin when it isn't too windy; single-bike units cost about $8 per half hour at each location; doubles, about $16 per half hour at the Swan and Dolphin.

PONTOON BOATS: Motorized, canopied platforms on pontoons are perfect for families, inexperienced sailors, and visitors more interested in serenity than in thrills. Available at most resort marinas, the 20-foot craft hold up to ten adults and cost about $35 per half hour. Guests must be at least 19 years old to rent a pontoon boat.

SAILBOATS: The running room and usually reliable winds of Bay Lake and Seven Seas Lagoon make for good sailing, and the Grand Floridian, Polynesian, Contemporary, and Wilderness Lodge marinas rent a variety of craft so that guests might get a little wind in their sails on the 650-acre expanse. Various types of sailboats are available; models accommodate two to six people and rent for about $25 to $30 per hour. Experience is required for rental of catamarans, available at the Contemporary, Polynesian, and Grand Floridian.

Sailing conditions are usually best in March and April, and before the inevitable late-afternoon thundershowers in the summer—that's when demand is greatest.

SPEEDBOATS: Particularly when the weather is warm, there are always dozens of small boats zipping back and forth across Bay Lake, Seven Seas Lagoon, Lake Buena Vista, Crescent Lake, and Barefoot Bay. These are called Water Mouse boats, and they're just as much fun as they look. The boats, which move as fast as 22 miles per hour, are so small that a rider feels every bit of speed, and they whiz around quickly enough so that a lot of watery terrain can be covered in a half-hour-rental period (for about $22).

Water Mouse boats can be rented at the Grand Floridian, Polynesian, Wilderness Lodge, Contemporary, Yacht and Beach Club, Fort Wilderness, Caribbean Beach, Coronado Springs, and Downtown Disney Marketplace marinas. When the weather is warm, lines form at about 11 A.M. and stay fairly constant until about 4 P.M. Guests must be at least 14 years old and five feet tall to rent Water

Mouse boats. Children under the minimum age and height may ride as passengers but they are not allowed to drive the boat.

WATERSKIING, WAKEBOARDING, AND TUBING: Ski boats with Sammy Duvall instructors and equipment ($125 an hour, for one to five guests) are available at the Contemporary resort marina. Reservations must be made at least 24 hours in advance and may be made up to 90 days ahead; call 407-WDW-PLAY (939-7529).

Fishing

The 70,000 bass with which Bay Lake was stocked in the mid-1960s have grown and multiplied as a result of WDW's restrictive fishing policy. (It's strictly catch-and-release.) No angling is permitted on Bay Lake or the Seven Seas Lagoon, except on the guided fishing expeditions. Largemouth bass weighing two to eight pounds are the most common catch. Excursions depart from the marinas daily (call 407-939-7529 for exact times and prices); five people can be accommodated on a trip. The trip lasts two hours and includes guide, gear, and refreshments (coffee and soft drinks). Guides will pick up guests at the Contemporary, Polynesian, Grand Floridian, Fort Wilderness, and Wilderness Lodge marinas.

Other trips depart from Downtown Disney Marketplace marina at 6 A.M. and 9 A.M. for fishing on Lake Buena Vista and adjoining waterways. Guides will also pick up guests at Old Key West, and Port Orleans Riverside and French Quarter. Two-hour excursions accommodate up to five anglers and include guide, gear, and refreshments.

At Port Orleans Riverside, a two-hour trip tours Sassagoula River and Lake Buena Vista. Daily excursions usually depart at 6 A.M. and 9 A.M. and can accommodate up to five people; includes guide, gear, artificial bait, and soft drinks. Kids under 10 must be accompanied by an adult.

Anglers might also consider two-hour tours that depart from the Yacht and Beach Club at 7 A.M. and 10 A.M. The former is a trip for up to four people, the latter accommodates five. Two-hour trips depart the BoardWalk dock at 7 A.M. and 10 A.M. daily. A guide, gear, and refreshments are included.

Special fishing excursions for kids ages 6 through 12 depart Monday through Friday from the Contemporary, Grand Floridian,

Polynesian, Fort Wilderness, and Wilderness Lodge. Refreshments are provided, as is bait.

Reservations for all fishing excursions must be made at least 24 hours in advance and may be made up to 90 days ahead; call 407-WDW-PLAY (939-7529).

Fishing on your own—again, strictly catch-and-release—is permitted off the dock at the Downtown Disney Marketplace and Board-Walk; in the canals at Fort Wilderness and the stocked fishing hole at Port Orleans Riverside. Fort Wilderness guests may toss in lines from any campground shore. Licenses are not required. Canoes, rods and reels, and cane poles are available for rent at the Fort Wilderness Bike Barn. Bait (in the form of worms) may be purchased. Poles may also be rented at Port Orleans Riverside, BoardWalk, and the Downtown Disney Marketplace.

Swimming

Between Bay Lake and Seven Seas Lagoon, Walt Disney World resort guests have five miles of powdery white-sand beach at their disposal. Although the beaches are strictly for sun-bathing and sandcastle construction, swimmers may splash in one of the many pools that come in every shape and size imaginable. Typhoon Lagoon and Blizzard Beach (see *Everything Else in the World*) only add to the fun.

BEACHES: When Walt Disney World was under construction during the mid-1960s, Bay Lake had an eight-foot layer of muck on its bottom. The lake was drained and cleaned, and below the muck, engineers unearthed the pure, white sand that now edges Walt Disney World resort shorefronts, most notably at the Contemporary, Grand Floridian, Caribbean Beach, and Fort Wilderness. These four sections of beach, plus the ones at the Polynesian, Wilderness Lodge, Yacht and Beach Club, Coronado Springs, and Swan and Dolphin, make up WDW's sandy areas. They aren't walk-forever strands, but they are long enough that most people don't bother to go to the end. Note that all Disney resort beaches are open only to those guests staying at the respective hotels.

POOLS: Walt Disney World resorts have at least one pool apiece. With the exception of the sister resorts (Yacht and Beach Club; Port Orleans French Quarter and Riverside; All-Star Movies, All-Star Music, and All-Star Sports; and Swan and Dolphin), which share some of their recreational facilities, WDW hotel pools are open only to guests staying at those resorts. This policy was initiated to prevent overcrowding. Note that most of the pools are heated in winter.

Featuring one pool apiece are the Animal Kingdom Lodge and Port Orleans French Quarter. The Grand Floridian, Contemporary, Polynesian, Fort Wilderness, Wilderness Lodge, All-Star, and Pop Century resorts have two pools each. BoardWalk features three pools, Coronado Springs and Old Key West have four swimming holes each, Port Orleans Riverside has six, and Caribbean Beach has seven. The Yacht and Beach Club resorts have between them three unguarded pools plus a small water park, called Stormalong Bay, that features slides, jets, and a sand-bottomed wading area. Saratoga Springs Resort & Spa has three pools. The Swan and Dolphin share a lovely, themed grotto pool with a slide, one huge rectangular pool, and a third smaller pool. For descriptions of the themed pools at Walt Disney World resorts, consult the *Transportation & Accommodations* chapter.

There are no diving boards; swimmers in search of a big splash should head for Blizzard Beach or Typhoon Lagoon. Lifeguards are on duty during most daylight hours at the resort's main pools. In addition, each of the resorts on Hotel Plaza Boulevard has its own pool.

Hot Tip!

As signs posted along the beaches indicate, swimming is not permitted in any of Walt Disney World's lakes. It's Disney's way of protecting guests from naturally occurring bacteria common to lakes in the state of Florida. Wading, however, is perfectly safe.

Disney's Wide World of Sports Complex

Variety is the name of the game at Disney's Wide World of Sports complex. The multi-million-dollar complex invites athletes and spectators alike to dive into more than 30 types of sporting experiences. It's a grand slam for die-hard sports fans.

The 200-acre facility hosts amateur and professional events in everything from archery to wrestling. The home of the Amateur Athletic Union (AAU) is also the spring training site for Major League Baseball's Atlanta Braves. The 2003 Super Bowl champion Tampa Bay Bucaneers hold training camp here, too (in late summer).

Designed as a modern vision of old-time Floridian building styles, the architecture harks back to the days when sports facilities were extensions of their neighborhoods; to that end there is even a town commons.

The complex includes a baseball stadium; a field house that accommodates basketball, wrestling, and volleyball; a track-and-field complex; tennis courts; and multipurpose fields fit for football, soccer, and more. Given the possibilities, sports-loving spectators have a world of choices on their hands.

A general-admission ticket costs about $10 for adults and $7.50 for kids ages 3 through 9. Tickets may be purchased at the front gate and allow guests to watch all "nonpremium" events. Note that guests are only admitted on days when events are scheduled. (Though guests may patronize All-Star Cafe any day.)

Tickets to premium events, such as Atlanta Braves spring training games (beginning in late February), may be purchased through TicketMaster (*www.ticketmaster.com*; 407-839-3900) and include general admission.

Premium tickets may also be purchased at the Wide World of Sports complex box office on the day of an event, depending on availability. Prices vary, depending on the event. Note that, in addition to traditional seats, the baseball stadium has lots of lawn seating. (The views of the field are good from all vantage points.)

Essentials

HOW TO GET THERE: WDW resort guests can take a bus to Blizzard Beach and transfer to a bus headed for the complex from 10 A.M. to 6 P.M. From 6 P.M. to 11 P.M., take a bus to Downtown Disney and transfer there. Allow at least an hour for the bus commute (more if you're attending a premium event). If you are driving, take exit 65 off I-4. The complex is between U.S. 192 and Osceola Parkway. Parking is free.

WHERE TO EAT: The big-ticket eatery here is the All-Star Cafe. TVs and a deejay keep you posted with current scores from around the sports world.

There are more than 30 concessions for those seeking a somewhat lighter bite. They offer hot dogs, popcorn, soft drinks, and beer (not to mention peanuts and Cracker Jack), as well as a few more substantial, yet just as portable, snacks.

Touch Base

Get the scoop on all the action at Disney's Wide World of Sports complex by calling 407-939-4263 or visiting the website: *www.disneyworldsports.com*.

More Sporting Fun

BIKING: Pedaling along the rustic pathways and lightly trafficked roads at Fort Wilderness can be a pleasant way to spend a couple of hours. Both areas are spread out, so bicycles are a practical way to get around. Bikes are available for rent at Fort Wilderness, Old Key West, Wilderness Lodge, Port Orleans, Caribbean Beach, BoardWalk, and Coronado Springs. The cost is about $8 an hour or $22 per day; tandem bicycles are offered at some locations. Bikes with training wheels or baby seats are available. Helmets are free.

JOGGING: Except from late fall to early spring, the weather is usually much too steamy in Central Florida for jogging. If you run very early in the morning in warm seasons, the heat is somewhat less daunting. The 1.4-mile promenade around the lake at the Caribbean Beach resort is ideal for jogging, as is the three-quarter-mile promenade that surrounds Crescent Lake, a waterway that's bordered by the Swan and Dolphin, Yacht and Beach Club, and BoardWalk resorts, and the three-quarter-mile path circling Coronado Springs' Lago Dorado. Fort Wilderness and the Wilderness Lodge share a three-quarter-mile path with exercise stations. Old Key West also has scenic routes. Courses range from one mile to about three.

MINIATURE GOLF: The Fantasia Gardens Miniature Golf complex, located near the Swan, Dolphin, and BoardWalk resorts, offers players two 18-hole courses themed to the Disney film *Fantasia.* The Fantasia Fairways course offers a difficult layout sure to tantalize serious golfers. It features traditional golf obstacles, such as sand traps, water hazards, doglegs, and roughs. Don't be fooled by the small size of the course—the challenges are big. (At press time, the record for the par-61 course was 50.)

Fantasia Gardens, on the other hand, is all in fun, with clever things (a dancing hippo, xylophone stairs, brooms dumping buckets of water) at every hole. The degree of difficulty varies from hole to hole, but overall, this is an easy course to conquer. There are several challenges out there, however. Hole 15, for example, is one of the trickier ones. Here golfers aim through four mini-geysers that randomly squirt water into the air.

Disney's Winter Summerland miniature golf course is a mere stone's throw from the Blizzard Beach water park. Designed as a vacation retreat for Santa and his elves, the two 18-hole courses boast a delightfully festive atmosphere, complete with Christmas carol sound tracks. The sandy-surface course is just a bit more of a challenge than its snowy-surface counterpart.

A round on any course costs about $10 for adults, $8 for kids ages 3 through 9. The second round is half price. Typical playing time is about an hour. Hours are generally 10 A.M. to 11 P.M., but vary seasonally. For additional information, call 407-WDW-PLAY (939-7529).

SPAS AND HEALTH CLUBS: While some of the fitness centers within WDW hotels are reserved for guests staying at the resort that houses them, several have open-door policies and are accessible to all WDW resort guests. Health clubs include the Olympiad at the Contemporary, Sturdy Branches at Wilderness Lodge, Zahanati at Animal Kingdom Lodge, La Vida at Coronado Springs, The Fitness Center at Saratoga Springs Resort & Spa, Muscles & Bustles at BoardWalk, and Ship Shape at the Yacht and Beach Club. Rates are $10 per day, $20 per length of stay, and about $40 for a family length of stay (up to five people). The Olympiad health club has Nautilus equipment, cardiovascular machines, and massage. The others have more extensive equipment. Ship Shape has a whirlpool and steam room. Muscles & Bustles has a steam room, tanning bed, and massage services. La Vida has a tanning bed and massage.

Body by Jake at the Dolphin, the fitness center at the Swan, and R.E.S.T. at Old Key West round out the health club options. Body by Jake ($8 per day or $16 for length of stay) is open to guests staying on or off Disney property. The facility at the Swan is free to the hotel's guests. R.E.S.T. is free to all Walt Disney World resort guests.

The spas are located at the Grand Floridian Spa & Health Club, the Saratoga Springs Resort & Spa, and the Wyndham Palace Resort & Spa. The Fitness Center at Saratoga Springs ($15 per day, $35 for a length of stay, $50 for a family of four length of stay) has aerobics, a gymnasium, and a modern facility with the best lineup of Cybex machines on Disney property. The Grand Floridian Spa & Health Club ($12 per day, $30 for three days, and $31.50 for length of stay) has all that plus a luxurious ambience. There are special spa packages available at each of these resorts.

STOCK CAR RACING: The Richard Petty Driving Experience (RPDE) takes motorsports fans out of the grandstands and into a scene that most can only dream about: behind the wheel of a stock car. The RPDE, located at the Walt Disney World Speedway, near the Magic Kingdom guest parking lot, is a training ground for racer wannabes. It offers two different levels of actual driving experience: "Rookie Experience" and "Experience of a Lifetime."

For the less "driven" daredevils, there is the "Riding Experience," which sends guests zooming around the track at blazing speeds while still maintaining their passenger status. No reservations are required for the Riding Experience. Rides begin at 9 A.M. daily. The cost is about $95.

The Rookie Experience includes instruction and eight high-speed (up to 145 miles per hour) laps around the one-mile oval track, as well as a warm-up and a cool-down lap. The three-hour program costs about $370. Reservations are required.

The Experience of a Lifetime is a 30-lap program completed over three sessions. Participants work on building speed and establishing a comfortable driving line. The cost is about $1,300. Reservations are a must.

The RPDE operates daily year-round, with the exception of dates on which actual races are held at the WDW Speedway. Shuttle transportation is provided from the Transportation and Ticket Center (TTC). Call 800-237-3889 for information or to make reservations. To drive, guests must have a valid license and the ability to drive a stick shift. Prices are subject to change.

TRAIL RIDES: Guided horseback rides into pine woods and scrubby palmetto country set off from the front of Fort Wilderness four times daily. This trip is not meant for seasoned gallopers—you can't wander off on your own. The horses have been culled for gentleness, so trips are especially suitable for novices. Cost is about $32 per person for a 45-minute tour. Kids under 9 are not allowed to ride, and there's a weight limit of 250 pounds. (Younger kids can saddle up on ponies at the Fort Wilderness Petting Farm.) Reservations are necessary, and can be made up to 30 days ahead by calling 407-WDW-PLAY (939-7529).

VOLLEYBALL & BASKETBALL: Except for the volleyball court at Typhoon Lagoon, courts are reserved for WDW resort guests. The Grand Floridian, Contemporary, Yacht and Beach Club, Fort Wilderness, Wilderness Lodge, Swan and Dolphin, Coronado Springs, and Old Key West have volleyball courts. Contemporary, Fort Wilderness, and Old Key West have basketball hoops.

Good Meals, Great Times

Although fast food is in great supply, it is hardly the entire Walt Disney World dining story. Epcot adds international flavors to the WDW menu. Tempting options at the other theme parks, BoardWalk, and Downtown Disney—not to mention new dining frontiers in the ever-growing brood of WDW resorts—make deciding where to eat a mouthwatering dilemma. Disney's ongoing effort to expand its culinary horizons has certainly been successful, producing prominent palate pleasers such as California Grill and Artist Point, plus family favorites like Chef Mickey's and Cinderella's Royal Table.

Because there's such a large number and variety of eateries around the World, this chapter presents dining information in two formats. First, we've included an area-by-area rundown—a comprehensive section whose descriptions of food purveyors, including sample menu options, will prove most helpful when you get hungry in a particular part of the World. Second, we've compiled a collection of what we consider to be the best restaurants in a particular category. To select these standouts, we looked at the menu, theme, and overall enjoyability of each restaurant on property.

Finally, in the chapter's last section, we offer a guide to the varied lounges of Walt Disney World, along with a briefing on Disney's priority seating system and dinner show options—and assurance that great times are destined to follow.

The Restaurants of WDW
In the Magic Kingdom

The lion's share of eateries here in Walt Disney World's first theme park are fast-food spots. These establishments' colorful facades and costumed servers are natural extensions of the fantasy surrounding the park's seven distinct "lands." The healthy variety of food available on the fly is a testament to Magic Kingdom visitors' typical preference for a quick bite with no need for firm plans. For those who prefer an all-out meal, the park's small handful of table-service restaurants offer fine mealtime escapes in magical settings that only Disney could create. Visitors interested in character meals have breakfast, lunch, and dinner options here (see page 240 for additional details).

First Things First

The letters at the end of each entry refer to the meals served there: breakfast (B), lunch (L), dinner (D), or snacks (S).
• Eateries in this chapter have been designated inexpensive (under $10), moderate ($11 to $20), expensive ($21 to $45), and very expensive ($46 and up). Prices are based on an adult-sized meal consisting of a beverage, entrée, and either one appetizer, side order, or dessert (not including tax and tip). These classifications are reflected by dollar symbols at the end of each entry (all symbols are defined by the key at the bottom of each page). Note that lunch and breakfast generally cost less.
• All Walt Disney World restaurants and fast-food spots (except some with outside seating or at the Swan and Dolphin resorts) are nonsmoking only. Some restaurants at BoardWalk and Downtown Disney have set aside special sections for smokers.
• Priority seating arrangements for most table-service restaurants should be made in advance by calling 407-WDW-DINE (939-3463).
  We advise guests to call 407-WDW-DINE (939-3463) to confirm all Walt Disney World restaurant information.

Adventureland
Fast Food & Snacks

ALOHA ISLE: This snack stand located near the Swiss Family Treehouse sells pineapple spears and juice, along with other tropical offerings, including pineapple floats and the especially refreshing Dole Whip pineapple soft serve. S $

EL PIRATA Y EL PERICO: The Spanish name of this snack stand, located directly across from the Pirates of the Caribbean attraction, translates to "The Pirate and the Parrot." The offerings here include several traditional Mexican items, such as tacos, taco salads, and nachos, as well as hot dogs with chili and cheese. L S $

SUNSHINE TREE TERRACE: Offerings at this snack spot located near The Enchanted Tiki Room—Under New Management are some of the tastiest in the Magic Kingdom: orange slushes, nonfat frozen yogurt, and a tasty citrus swirl—soft-serve nonfat frozen yogurt swirled with frozen juice concentrate. Cappuccino, espresso, and soft drinks are also available. S $

Fantasyland
Table Service

CINDERELLA'S ROYAL TABLE: Hostesses at this festive establishment wear Renaissance-inspired garb and address guests as "my lady" or "my lord." The hall itself is high-ceilinged and as majestic as the old mead hall it is designed to represent. Its second-story setting offers a pleasantly peaceful view of Fantasyland. Decor tends to royal blues and purples, with tapestry-backed chairs. Cinderella is occasionally on hand to greet children and grown-ups alike in the restaurant's lobby (though such appearances are rare). As guests of the princess, visitors dine on salads and sandwiches on the midday menu. The dinner menu, which changes often, has included prime rib (queen and king cuts, of course), spice-crusted salmon, coconut fried shrimp on chilled noodles, and herbed chicken with sautéed vegetables over polenta.

The Once Upon a Time character breakfast is held every morning. This all-you-can-eat breakfast is about $20 for adults and $10 for children ages 3 through 11. Priority seating is necessary. A 60-day advance booking is required for the character breakfast, along with a deposit (the deposit is refundable with a 24-hour advance cancellation). **B L D** **$$$**

Fast Food & Snacks

ENCHANTED GROVE: A small stand that's the perfect spot to cool off with a lemonade, lemonade slush, or strawberry soft-serve swirl. **S** **$**

MRS. POTTS' CUPBOARD: Ice cream gets top billing at this small spot near The Many Adventures of Winnie the Pooh attraction. There are soft-serve cones in chocolate, vanilla, and swirl; hot fudge, strawberry shortcake, and brownie sundaes; and shakes and floats. **S** **$**

PINOCCHIO VILLAGE HAUS: Located near It's a Small World (some tables offer a peek at the attraction via sizable picture windows), this is another one of those Magic Kingdom restaurants that seem a lot smaller from the outside than they really are, thanks to a labyrinthine arrangement of a half dozen rooms decorated with antique cuckoo clocks, oak peasant chairs, and murals depicting characters from Pinocchio's story—Figaro the Cat, Cleo the Goldfish, Monstro the Whale, and Geppetto, the puppet's creator. The menu offers hot dogs, burgers, turkey sandwiches, and salads. **L D S** **$**

SCUTTLE'S LANDING: Soft drinks and shaved ice are the big draw at this snack spot located near the Dumbo the Flying Elephant attraction. **S** **$**

Frontierland
Fast Food & Snacks

AUNT POLLY'S DOCKSIDE INN: The much-trumpeted sense of getting away from it all that islands always convey can also be found on Frontierland's Tom Sawyer Island. Though only a couple of minutes' ride across the Rivers of America via the Tom Sawyer Island rafts, this landfall manages to seem remote even when there are dozens of youngsters clambering through its caves, over its hills, and

across its rickety barrel bridges. Therein lies the charm of Aunt Polly's. While the adults in a party get some much-needed rest and relaxation sipping lemonade in the shade of the old-fashioned porch and watching the riverboats chugging by, the kids can go exploring. This is also a lovely, removed spot from which to observe the afternoon parade as it makes its way through Frontierland.

It doesn't even matter that Aunt Polly's offers a selection barely wider than the fare that the lady might have served to young Tom Sawyer himself—peanut-butter-and-jelly and ham-and-cheese sandwiches, pickles, apple pie, soft-serve ice cream, root beer floats, cookies, iced tea, lemonade, and soda. **L S** **$**

PECOS BILL CAFE: This is not one of those Magic Kingdom eateries so tucked away that only those who hunt will find it. Sooner or later, almost every guest passing from Fantasyland into Frontierland—ambling along the banks of the river on their way to Splash Mountain—walks by Pecos Bill Cafe. Cheeseburgers, sandwiches, salads, and hot dogs are the staples. The expansive fixin's bar (which includes fresh lettuce and tomato, sautéed mushrooms and onions, and cheese sauce) and ample seating make this spot one of the most popular fast food restaurants in the Magic Kingdom. **L D S** **$**

> ## Hot Tip!
> Most WDW table-service restaurants provide a menu geared to kids, and most fast-food spots offer kid-size value meals. Just ask!

Liberty Square
Table Service

LIBERTY TREE TAVERN: At this pillared and porticoed eatery opposite the riverboat landing, the floors are wide oak planks, the wallpaper looks as if it might have come from Williamsburg, the curtains hang from cloth loops, and the venetian blinds are made of wood. The rooms are chock-full of mementos that might have been found in the homes of Thomas Jefferson, George Washington, and Ben Franklin, and the window glass was made using 18th-century casting methods. Such charming environs make the food served therein seem almost secondary.

The à la carte lunch includes fish, pot roast, turkey, New England clam chowder in a bread bowl, sandwiches, and soups.

Dinner, an all-you-can-eat feast served family-style, is hosted by Disney characters. Menu items have included salad, roast turkey, flank steak, pork chop, macaroni and cheese, mashed potatoes, garden vegetables, and Stouffer's stuffing. The character dinner costs $22 for adults and $10 for children ages 3 through 11. Note that desserts and some beverages cost extra. Priority seating suggested. **L D $ $**

Fast Food & Snacks

COLUMBIA HARBOUR HOUSE: A fast-food fish house with a touch of elegance. Fried fish, fried chicken strips, vegetarian chili or clam chowder in a crusty bread bowl, and assorted sandwiches (including a vegetarian option) and salads grace the menu. (If you order salad, request the dressing on the side or risk it being saturated.) The food is usually quite good, and there are enough antiques and other knickknacks decking the halls to raise this establishment; located near the Liberty Square entrance to Fantasyland, well above the ordinary. Model ships, copper measures, harpoons, nautical instruments, little lace tie-back curtains, and low-beamed ceilings give the restaurant a cozy air. The upstairs dining rooms are particularly enjoyable. **L D S $**

SLEEPY HOLLOW: Ice-cream-cookie sandwiches, warm cobblers prepared with fruit, caramel corn, and other desserts—all made fresh before your eyes—are the sweets for sale at this savory snack stand located in The Hall of Presidents neighborhood, near the Liberty Square bridge. It's pleasant to eat on the secluded brick patio outside. It has a lovely view of Cinderella Castle. **L D S $**

Main Street
Table Service

CRYSTAL PALACE: One of the Magic Kingdom's cherished landmarks, this restaurant takes its architectural cues from a similar structure that once stood in New York, and from San Francisco's Conservatory of Flowers, which still graces that city's Golden Gate Park. The place is huge but not overwhelming because the tables are scattered amid a Victorian-style indoor garden, complete with fresh flowers and hanging greenery. Tables in the front look out on flower beds, while those at the east end have views of a courtyard. The restaurant is located on a pathway at the end of Main Street, U.S.A., heading west toward Adventureland.

Healthier Options

Health-conscious folks need not abandon all restraint for want of suitable sustenance. Most restaurants offer low-fat, low-cholesterol, low-salt, and vegetarian entrées. Even fast-food stands now feature healthier fare such as fresh salads, grilled chicken sandwiches, fresh fruit, turkey burgers, and nonfat frozen yogurt.

Four topiaries—Winnie the Pooh, Tigger, Eeyore, and Piglet—greet guests at the entrance, a sign of the character presence here. None other than Winnie the Pooh himself and his pals from the Hundred Acre wood circulate throughout meals.

Offerings vary according to season and available produce. The all-you-can-eat buffet features a full variety of traditional breakfast items every morning; a salad bar, deli bar, pasta dishes, chicken, and fish for lunch; and spit-roasted beef, chicken, pastas, fish, carved meats, and inventive sides for dinner. The evening salad bar, with its grilled vegetables, peel-and-eat shrimp, cold pasta salads, and variety of greens and grains, is first-rate. Kids particularly like the ice-cream-sundae bar offered at lunch and dinner. Cost for breakfast is $16.99 for adults and $8.99 for children ages 3 through 11; lunch is $17.99 for adults and $9.99 for children; dinner is $21.99 for adults and $9.99 for children. Priority seating suggested. `B L D` `$$-$$$`

THE PLAZA: This airy, many-windowed establishment, around the corner from the Plaza Ice Cream Parlor, is done up in mirrors with sinuous Art Nouveau frames. The menu offers chef's salads, burgers, and hot and cold sandwiches—plus plenty of hard ice cream, milk shakes, floats, and the biggest sundaes in the Magic Kingdom. Café Mocha, which combines chocolate and coffee, is another refreshing specialty of the house. Priority seating suggested. `L D S` `$$`

TONY'S TOWN SQUARE: The decor was inspired by Walt Disney's classic feature *Lady and the Tramp*. The terrazzo-style patio offers a fine view of Town Square. The lunch menu offers Italian specialties, including paninis (sandwiches). Pizzas with selected toppings are good bets. Other staples include Caesar salad, sandwiches, and a variety of pastas.

At dinner select from chicken marsala, grilled pork chop, and spaghetti, along with a variety of daily specials. For dessert, tempting Italian sweets complement a cup of espresso or cappuccino. Priority seating suggested. `L D` `$$$`

Fast Food & Snacks

CASEY'S CORNER: The small round tables at this old-fashioned red-and-white stop on the west side of Main Street (adjacent to Crystal Palace) spill out onto the sidewalk. Except when the weather is hot, this baseball-themed spot is great for ballpark favorites—hot dogs in jumbo sizes, fries, brownies, soft drinks, and coffee. During daytime hours a pianist plinks away on the restaurant's white upright. There's also a back room with bleacher seating. (Seats face a screen showing videos with a baseball theme.) `L D S` `$`

MAIN STREET BAKE SHOP: If the sight of this old-fashioned storefront doesn't lure you in, the heavenly aroma most certainly will. A genteel little tearoom with prim tables and cane chairs, the Main Street Bake Shop is a pleasant place for a light breakfast, midmorning coffee break, or midafternoon rest stop.

Assorted pastries, cakes, and pies are the main temptations. Also offered are fresh cookies: chocolate chunk, oatmeal raisin, sugar, and Nestlé's Original Toll House recipe. Ice-cream-cookie sandwiches are "built to order." **B** **S** **$**

PLAZA ICE CREAM PARLOR: Ice cream lovers from all over the country converge on this corner of the park, which boasts the Magic Kingdom's largest variety of hard ice cream flavors. **S** **$**

Tomorrowland
Fast Food & Snacks

AUNTIE GRAVITY'S GALACTIC GOODIES: This small spot located across from the Tomorrowland Indy Speedway (between Merchant of Venus and Mickey's Star Traders) offers refreshing smoothies, soft-serve ice cream, sundaes, floats, fruit cups, juice, and soft drinks. **S** **$**

COSMIC RAY'S STARLIGHT CAFE: The largest fast-food location in the Magic Kingdom is located directly across from the Tomorrowland Indy Speedway. Three different menus are offered at separate sections along the lengthy counter. *Cosmic Chicken* serves rotisserie chicken and chicken sandwiches; *Blast-off Burgers* has cheeseburgers, vegetarian burgers, and hot dogs; and *Starlight Soup, Salad, Sandwich* offers soups, salads, and cheese steak sandwiches. An Audio-Animatronic lounge lizard known as Sunny Eclipse entertains diners with cheesy songs and (bad) jokes in the main dining area. **L** **D** **S** **$**

LUNCHING PAD AT ROCKETTOWER PLAZA: Located at the base of the Astro Orbiter in the center of Tomorrowland's sprawling concrete plaza, this small dining spot offers sizable smoked turkey legs, character cookies, frozen soda slushies, and soft drinks. **S** **$**

PLAZA PAVILION: Just east of The Plaza restaurant on Main Street, U.S.A., this sleek spot on the edge of Tomorrowland serves deep-dish pizzas, fried chicken strips, Italian specialty sandwiches, and salads. There are some particularly pleasant tables situated toward the water that look past the graceful willow trees nearby, an impressive topiary sea serpent, not to mention Cinderella Castle. **L** **D** **S** **$**

Magic Kingdom Mealtime Tips

- The hours from 11 A.M. to 2 P.M., and again from about 5 P.M. to 7 P.M., are the mealtime rush hours in Magic Kingdom restaurants. Try to eat earlier or later whenever possible.
- When a fast food restaurant has more than one service window, don't just amble into the nearest queue. Instead, inspect them all, because, occasionally, the one farthest from an entrance will be wait-free (or nearly so).
- Table-service restaurants offering full-scale meals are usually less crowded at lunch than they are at dinner.
- To avoid queues, eat lunch or dinner at a restaurant that offers priority seating—Tony's Town Square, Crystal Palace, or The Plaza restaurant on Main Street; Liberty Tree Tavern in Liberty Square; or Cinderella's Royal Table in the castle. Priority seating arrangements may be made in advance by calling 407-WDW-DINE (939-3463). Check for same-day seating at the individual restaurant or City Hall.
- Consider taking the monorail to the Contemporary, Polynesian, or Grand Floridian to have lunch or dinner in a resort restaurant, and then return to the Magic Kingdom later. (Remember to have your hand stamped and keep your ticket for re-entry to the park.)

B breakfast   **L** lunch   **D** dinner   **S** snacks   **$** *under $10*   **$$** *$10–$20*   **$$$** *$21–$45*   **$$$$** *$46 and up*

In Epcot

The various areas that make up Epcot offer a spectrum of eating options that extends from the usual burgers and fries to mouthwatering international specialties. Future World counts a please-all food court among its fast-food spots, plus two table-service restaurants whose menus and atmospheres innovatively reflect the themes of the pavilions they inhabit. World Showcase, on the other hand, is characterized by international flavors. Here, the cuisine of each country is served in settings that strive to transport visitors, if just for the duration of their meal. While the abundance of appealing table-service restaurants makes World Showcase a very popular dining destination, the promenade is also ringed with fast-food spots, most of which feature international fare. Priority seating is an important part of the Epcot dining equation. (To make arrangements, call 407-WDW-DINE.) Character meals are options for breakfast, lunch, and dinner in Future World (for specifics on dining with Disney characters, see page 240).

Future World
Table Service

CORAL REEF (The Living Seas): Decorated in cool greens and blues to complement its surroundings, this restaurant offers diners a panoramic view of the coral reef through large windows. The windows are eight feet high and more than eight inches thick. The dining room has several tiers, so all guests get a decent view. The menu features a bounty of fresh fish and shellfish—including Florida snapper, mahi-mahi, shrimp, and salmon—prepared in a number of delectable ways. The menu may vary seasonally. Priority seating suggested. **L D** **$$$**

GARDEN GRILL (The Land): Sleek wood-trimmed booths illuminated with brass lamps help to make this a festive eatery. The restaurant itself revolves (very slowly), moving past a mural of giant sunflowers and above scenes of the thunderstorm, sandstorm, prairie, and rain forest featured in the Living with the Land boat ride. The scenes were designed with diners in mind, and provide them with a peek into a farmhouse window that's out of viewing range of the waterborne passengers.

Mickey and his friends host two character meals here each day. Lunch and dinner menus feature rotisserie meats, grilled flank steak, and fried catfish. There is a separate menu for children. Cost is $19.99 for adults lunch, $21.99 for dinner. Kids pay $9.99 for lunch and dinner. Beverages and dessert are included. Meals are served family style (communal platters for the table). Priority seating suggested. **L D** **$$-$$$**

Fast Food & Snacks

ELECTRIC UMBRELLA (Innoventions Plaza): This large fast-food establishment is decorated in shades of blue, mauve, and magenta. The fare may not be imaginative, but the restaurant is a good bet when the weather is temperate enough to allow dining at the tables on the terrace outside—or when bound for World Showcase with finicky eaters in tow. Offerings include simple chicken sandwiches, grilled ham-and-cheese sandwiches, grilled vegetable pita sandwiches, hot dogs, burgers, fruit salad, and chef's salad. **L D S** **$**

FOUNTAIN VIEW ESPRESSO AND BAKERY (Innoventions Plaza): Fresh-baked goods and desserts—such as croissants, cheesecake, tiramisu, and more—can be found at this pleasant spot across from the Fountain of Nations. Espresso, cappuccino, wine, and beer are among the assorted beverages available here. **B S** **$**

PURE AND SIMPLE (Wonders of Life): This spot offers a small selection of treats, including menu items such as oat-bran waffles with fruit toppings, frozen yogurt, yogurt shakes, muffins, fruit juices, and more. Vegetable pizzas, soups, Caesar salad with chicken strips, and chicken wrap sandwiches have been among the lunch options. **B L S** **$**

SUNSHINE SEASON FOOD FAIR (The Land): One of the most interesting of the Future World dining options, and a standout in the Walt Disney World fast-food scene, this handful of diverse counter-service stands is on the lower level of the Land pavilion. Each stand in the food court has a farm-style facade done in bright colors, not unlike those that might be found in agricultural exhibit buildings at a midwestern state fair. With umbrella-topped tables beneath colorful hot-air balloons, the effect is quite cheery. Because of the wide variety of foods available here, this is one of the best places in Epcot for a family that can't agree on what to eat—there's bound to be something for everyone.

Soup & Sandwich offers Florida seafood chowder, fruit salad, rotini pasta salad, Caesar salad, and sandwich wraps. The *Ice Cream & Bakery Shop*'s tasty morning offerings include fresh fruit, bagels with cream cheese, jumbo cinnamon rolls, Danish pastries, and muffins. After 11 A.M., cheesecake makes an appearance, along with chocolate cake, strawberry shortcake, rich double-chocolate brownies, and large cinnamon cookies—plus chocolate chip cookies baked on the premises. Ice cream cones and cups, frozen yogurt, and sundaes are also offered. *The Barbecue* stand sells barbecued chicken and ribs smoked on the premises; barbecued pork or chicken breast sandwiches and corn-on-the-cob. The *Pasta and Potato* stand offers Mickey macaroni and cheese; vegetable lasagne; and baked potatoes stuffed with Asian-style chicken and vegetables, cheddar cheese and bacon, and other fillings. **B L D S** **$**

World Showcase
Table Service

AKERSHUS (Norway): The Norwegian castle of Akershus dominates Oslo's harbor, and is the most impressive of all Norway's medieval fortresses. It is actually half fortress and half palace, and many of its grand halls continue to be used for elaborate state banquets. At Epcot's castle-like Akershus, guests are treated to an authentic royal Norwegian cuisine. An all-inclusive price entitles diners to enjoy the appetizer buffet and a choice of entrée. Traditional Norwegian desserts are also available for an extra charge, as are cocktails and Norwegian beer. Hosts and hostesses are on hand to answer any questions about the buffet that guests may have.

The new Princess Storybook breakfast takes place here daily. While guests enjoy the all-you-can eat eat fare (bacon, eggs, breads, and other traditional American breakfast selections are brought to your table), Disney princesses wander about and mingle with guests. Belle, Jasmine, Snow White, Sleeping Beauty, and even Mary Poppins have made appearances. Note that the character appearance schedule varies. Priority seating suggested. **B L D** **$$-$$$**

BIERGARTEN (Germany): Located at the rear of the St. Georgsplatz in the Germany pavilion, this huge tiered restaurant is every bit as jolly as Alfredo's restaurant in the Italy pavilion. This is partly because of the long tables that encourage a certain togetherness among guests—and partly because Beck's beer is served in 33-ounce steins. But equal credit for the gemütlich atmosphere must go to the restaurant's lively entertainment.

At dinner, there may be appearances by traditional Bavarian musicians—each clad in lederhosen or dirndl—who play accordions, cowbells, a musical saw, and a harplike stringed instrument known as the "wooden laughter." The entertaining dinner shows take place at scheduled times in the dining room. Diners are usually invited to join the fun onstage.

The food is hearty and presented as an all-you-can-eat buffet, featuring all sorts of sausages (bratwurst, *Debrizinger, Bauernwurst*), frankfurters, rotisserie chicken, homemade spaetzle, assorted cold dishes, potato salad, cucumber salad, and many more German specialties. Because entertainment is

intermittent, there's plenty of time to enjoy the pleasant setting. Priority seating highly recommended, particularly during peak seasons (book as early as possible). **L D $$–$$$**

BISTRO DE PARIS (France): One flight above Les Chefs de France, this restaurant evokes the charm of early 20th-century Paris. A traditional bistro menu (created by the same trio of French chefs responsible for the fare at Chefs de France) features such robust "preludes" as salmon tartare on black radishes and duck fois gras terrine.

The brief entrée menu includes honey-roasted rack of lamb with grilled vegetables, and a double-cut white veal chop with roasted garlic cloves, potato puree, and spinach. The heartiness of the fare makes it an especially good dining choice in cool weather. Priority seating suggested. **D $$$–$$$$**

LE CELLIER STEAKHOUSE (Canada): Tucked away on the lowest level of the pavilion near Victoria Gardens, this low-ceilinged, lantern-lighted, stone-walled establishment looks a little like the ancient wine cellars for which it is named. It offers a full menu of Canadian foods, with hearty open-face steak sandwiches and steak salads also available for lunch, and roast prime rib and steak added to the offerings at dinner.

Excellent maple-glazed salmon and rosemary garlic seared chicken and pasta round out the selection of entrées. For dessert, try the classic creme brulee or espresso cheesecake. Canada's own Molson and Labatt's beers and Inniskillin wine are served. This tempting menu makes Le Cellier Steakhouse a prime destination. Priority seating suggested. **L D $$**

LES CHEFS DE FRANCE (France): This charming restaurant has a bright, airy feel, with yellow and cream-colored walls drenched in natural light. It boasts a large glass-enclosed "outside" dining area with a conservatory motif.

Behind the restaurant's well-appointed scenes, a team of internationally acclaimed chefs—Paul Bocuse, Roger Vergé, and Gaston Lenôtre—have prepared a tempting nouvelle menu. Bocuse operates a restaurant outside Lyons, France, and Roger Vergé runs one just north of the French Riviera. Together with Gaston Lenôtre (widely recognized as France's premier preparer of pastries and other delicious dessert delicacies), they form a most unusual, and absolutely formidable, gastronomic trio. Their menu features fresh ingredients readily available from Florida purveyors. In addition, the restaurant imports as many key ingredients from France as possible.

As you might expect, the fare here is fiercely French, but the foundation of the menu is nouvelle cuisine, which involves lighter sauces using much less cream and butter than in classic French cooking. Menu items include sautéed chicken breast with wild mushrooms, grilled salmon on polenta, and braised beef in red Burgundy wine beside spinach ravioli.

Special Requests

Full-service eateries can accommodate special dietary needs, providing kosher, low-sodium, lactose-free, and other selections, with 24 hours' notice. Make your request when booking your table by calling 407-WDW-DINE (939-3463).

Soups and appetizers, such as onion soup and escargot, are all-day staples. Apple tart, chocolate crêpes, peach melba, and chocolate mousse cake are dessert specialties of note.

Be aware that this can be one of the most expensive of all World Showcase restaurants. Priority seating suggested (book as early as possible). **L D $$$**

L'ORIGINALE ALFREDO DI ROMA

RISTORANTE (Italy): This restaurant's trompe l'oeil paintings make diners believe they're seeing real scenes, rather than mere murals, and lend character to the decor of this popular establishment. As in the famous Roman restaurant of the same name, the house specialty is fettuccine Alfredo—wide, flat noodles tossed in a sauce made of butter and imported Parmesan cheese. But many other sizes and shapes of pasta are also available. There is also a number of less familiar Italian preparations involving chicken, eggplant, seafood, sausage, and veal.

At lunchtime, it's also possible to order pizza. For dessert, choose from specialties such as ricotta cheesecake, spumoni, tortoni, or gelato. Even if you don't eat here, it's fun to stop and just peer through the glass kitchen windows to watch the cooks cranking out the rigatoni, ziti, linguine, lasagne, fettuccine, and spaghetti (which, the menu reminds guests, were brought from Europe to America by Thomas Jefferson in 1786). Priority seating suggested. **L D $$$**

MARRAKESH (Morocco): The most savory part of the Morocco pavilion features traditional and modern Moroccan cuisine. Waiters are dressed in traditional Moroccan costumes. Menu specialties include roast lamb, chicken brochette, and couscous (steamed semolina served with your choice of lamb, chicken, or vegetables). Sampler platters are also available. The tilework was done by Moroccan craftsmen. Belly dancers and musicians entertain diners at lunch and dinner. Priority seating suggested. **L D $$$**

MITSUKOSHI (Japan): A complex of dining and drinking spots, all run by the Japanese firm for which it is named, occupies the second level of the large structure on the west side of the Japan pavilion. There are two options:

Tempura Kiku occupies a small corner of the Mitsukoshi building that's devoted to the batter-dipped, deep-fried chicken, beef,

seafood, and fresh vegetables that are collectively known as tempura. The individual tidbits are crisp and delicious. Sushi and sashimi round out the offerings. Note that priority seating is suggested. **L D $$$**

Teppanyaki Dining Rooms is composed of five rooms not unlike those popularized by the Benihana chain all around America. Guests sit counter-style around large flat grills while white-hatted chefs chop vegetables, meat, and fish at lightning speed and then stir-fry it all just as quickly. Whether the chopping and cooking accompany a mildly comic routine depends on the chef, but in any case the establishment is quite convivial. The seating arrangements make it natural to strike up a conversation with fellow diners; in fact, it's almost impossible to keep to yourself. Priority seating suggested. **L D $$$**

NINE DRAGONS (China): This stop on Epcot's varied international restaurant tour offers meals prepared in provincial Chinese cooking styles, including Mandarin, Cantonese, Hunan, Szechuan, and Kiangche. Entrées include Hong Kong–style sirloin, Rainbow Kung Pao chicken, and lobster and sea treasure casserole. Appetizers range from Chinese pickled cabbage to pan-fried dumplings and hot-and-sour soup.

A selection of imported Chinese teas, beers, and wines is available. The varied dessert menu features red-bean ice cream, toffee apples, and assorted Chinese pastries. Priority seating suggested. **LD** **$$$**

ROSE & CROWN PUB AND DINING ROOM

(United Kingdom): The fare here tends toward pub grub—that is, fish-and-chips and traditional meat pies. For lunch, however, it's also possible to order Bangers and Mash (sausages with mashed potatoes and Yorkshire pudding), vegetable curry, prime rib, or the Ploughman's Lunch (sliced turkey and ham, English cheeses, and fresh bread). At dinner the standard offerings are supplemented by roast prime rib with horseradish sauce, and fresh salmon. For an appetizer, we recommend the sautéed mushrooms in cream sauce on puff pastry. For dessert there's traditional sherry trifle, a confection of layered whipped cream, custard, strawberries, and sherry-flavored sponge cake; Guinness mousse; and chocolate cake. Bass ale from England, Tennent's lager and McCaffrey's Cream Ale

from Scotland, and Harp lager and Guinness stout, both from Ireland, are on tap. (They're served cold, in the American fashion, not at room temperature, as the British prefer.)

The decor is pretty, mainly polished woods, etched glass, and brass accents. In fine weather it's pleasant to lunch under a canopy on the terrace outside and watch the *FriendShip* water taxis cruising across World Showcase Lagoon; A late dinner on the water has an added perk—a small amount of front-row seating for the nightly fireworks show. Table assignment cannot be requested in advance, but it certainly won't hurt to ask for a table with a view. On the little island just to the east, the wind ruffles the leaves of the Lombardy poplars, a species of tree that is found along roadsides all over Europe.

As for the pub's architecture, it incorporates three distinct styles. The wall facing the World

Showcase Promenade is reminiscent of urban establishments popular in Britain since the 1890s, while that on the south side evokes London's 17th-century Cheshire Cheese pub, with its brick-walled flag-stone terrace, slate roof, and half-timbered exterior. The canal facade, with its stone wall and clay-tile roof, reminds visitors of the charming pubs so common in the English countryside.

The pub section of the Rose & Crown serves such snacks as Stilton cheese and fresh fruit platters, and fish-and-chips—along with all the brews noted above and traditional British mixed drinks, such as shandies (Bass ale and ginger ale), lager with lime juice, black velvets (Guinness stout and champagne), and black and tans (Bass ale and Guinness stout). This drinking and snacking spot is quite popular, so it's often necessary to queue up at the door. But the wait is seldom very long, since few guests choose to linger over their drinks. Note that the pub section also spills out onto the World Showcase promenade—where the first-come, first-served waterside tables make for a nice spot to sip a drink and, possibly, enjoy some fish-and-chips from a nearby stand. Priority seating is not available in the pub areas, but suggested for the adjacent dining room. **LDS** **$$$**

SAN ANGEL INN (Mexico): The food at this establishment located to the rear of the plaza inside the Mexico pyramid (a corporate cousin

of the famous Mexico City restaurant of the same name) may come as a surprise to most visitors. Although the tacos and tortillas and other specialties that usually fall under the broad umbrella of Mexican food are available, the menu also offers a wide variety of more subtly flavored fish, poultry, and meat dishes.

To start, there's *queso fundido* for two (melted cheese and Mexican pork sausage with corn or flour tortillas). As entrées, the menu offers grilled tenderloin of beef served with a chicken enchilada, guacamole, and refried beans; *plato mexicano* (beef taco, quesadilla, and refried beans for lunch; at dinner substitute beef tenderloin or tampiquena for the quesadilla); *ensalada mexicana* (mixed greens with grilled chicken, tomatoes, avocado, turnip, cheese, and cactus strips tossed in a tortilla shell); plus much more that is good and tasty. Mexican desserts are largely unfamiliar to North Americans, with the possible exception of the custard known as flan, but are well worth trying. Dos Equis beer and margaritas make good accompaniments. Priority seating suggested. **L D** **$$$**

Fast Food & Snacks

BOULANGERIE PATISSERIE (France): This bakery and pastry shop in the France pavilion is not hard to find: Just follow the wonderful aroma, then watch the crowds line up to consume the flaky croissants, éclairs, fruit tarts, and chocolate mousse. The treats are served under the management of the stellar trio of chefs who operate the popular Les Chefs de France restaurant not far away: Paul Bocuse, Roger Vergé, and Gaston Lenôtre. Hint for those who hate to wait: This has become a favorite snacking spot among Epcot veterans; your best bet is to stop here as soon as World Showcase opens or half an hour before park closing. **S** **$**

CANTINA DE SAN ANGEL (Mexico): Located along the World Showcase Promenade, just outside the entrance to Mexico's pyramid, this quick-service stand serves beef-filled soft tortillas; *tacos al carbón*, flour tortillas filled with grilled chicken breast strips, onions, and peppers, served with refried beans and salsa; and *churros*, a sort of fried dough rolled in cinnamon and sugar. The Cantina is a nice choice for a tasty rest stop, and even more so for its outdoor lagoonside seating. Beer and margaritas are available. **L D S** **$**

COOL POST (between Germany and China): This is a perfect spot for a refreshing cold drink. Frozen yogurt and ice cream are also served. **S** **$**

KRINGLA BAKERI OG KAFE (Norway): Tucked between the Norway pavilion's wooden church and a cluster of shops, this popular eating spot serves *kringles*, sweet candied pretzels reserved for special occasions in Norway; *vaflers*, heart-shaped waffles topped with powdered sugar and jam; *kransekake*, almond-pastry sticks; and *smørbrøds*, open-face sandwiches of smoked salmon, roast beef, or turkey. Ringnes beer, brewed in Norway, is also available. There is also a pleasant, shaded outdoor eating area. **L D S** **$**

LIBERTY INN (The American Adventure): To many visitors from other countries, American food means burgers, hot dogs, and fries, and these are the staples at the Liberty Inn, located near the entrance to The American Adventure show on the far side of the World Showcase lagoon. Salads, grilled chicken sandwiches, ice cream, apple pastries, and chocolate chip cookies round out the selections. The place is a good choice for children. **L D S** **$**

LOTUS BLOSSOM CAFE (China): Adjacent to Yong Feng Shangdian shopping gallery in the China pavilion, this fast-food counter offers sweet-and-sour pork, egg rolls, and soup. There is a covered outdoor seating area nearby. **L D** **$**

REFRESHMENT PORT (Canada): Another good spot for a quick thirst quencher. Located on the World Showcase promenade, this spot has iced tea and lemonade, plus hot dogs, nachos, fresh fruit, and frozen yogurt. **S** **$**

SOMMERFEST (Germany): Bratwurst sandwiches, soft pretzels, Black Forest cake, apple strudel, Beck's beer, and wine are offered at this outdoor establishment, located toward the rear of the pavilion; seating is nearby. **L D S $**

TANGIERINE CAFE (Morocco): Named for the Moroccan city of Tangier, this casual spot serves lentil salad, hummus, and tabbouleh, as well as rotisserie chicken, beef, and lamb presented as sandwiches (served on Moroccan bread) and combination platters. Specialty coffees and pastries are available. **L D S $**

YAKITORI HOUSE (Japan): Located in the gardens to the left of the plaza, the restaurant occupies a scaled-down version of the 16th-century Katsura Imperial Summer Palace in Kyoto; sliding screens, lanterns, and kimono-clad servers add to the authentic atmosphere.

Among the fare here is *guydon*, a stewlike concoction flavored with soy sauce, spices, and the Japanese rice wine known as sake, served over rice. That staple, along with skewered chicken known as yakitori (it's basted with soy sauce and sesame oil as it broils), teriyaki chicken sandwiches, and Japanese sweets and beverages, typifies the offerings here. The menu has included green tea and red bean ice cream. The nearby garden serves as a peaceful respite for those who wish to take a break from the hustle and bustle of a busy Epcot day. **L D S $**

Epcot Mealtime Tips

- The international restaurants of World Showcase offer some of the best dining on the property. Since many of them are very popular, it's a good idea to arrange advance priority seating for any table-service restaurants by calling 407-WDW-DINE (939-3463) long before arriving. However, it's important to note that some tables may be available for same-day seating. To make arrangements, head to Guest Relations first thing in the morning or to the kiosk located by the Tip Board in Innoventions Plaza. Meals may also be booked at the individual restaurants.

- If you aren't able to secure priority seating for a meal, don't despair. There are many tasty alternatives to a table-service restaurant. Japan has Tempura Kiku, a full-service spot with batter-dipped, deep-fried meats and vegetables (and no priority seating available), and Yakitori House, good for skewered bits of barbecued chicken. Sample Mexican specialties at Cantina de San Angel (whose lagoon-side tables provide a view of the sun setting behind Epcot). Also try the sandwiches at Kringla Bakeri og Kafe, in Norway, or the fish-and-chips in the United Kingdom.

- Cravings for conventional fast foods will be satisfied at the Electric Umbrella, in Innoventions, and at the Liberty Inn, in The American Adventure. A stand near the Rose and Crown Pub offers fish-and-chips. The Sunshine Season Food Fair, in The Land pavilion, offers a bit of everything.

- The most unadventurous eaters can still find something pleasing—even in the more exotic restaurants of World Showcase. If you're undecided, ask at Guest Relations to see a booklet describing the menus. Keep in mind that most restaurants have menus for kids.

- Don't dismiss the idea of an early seating if you can get it: A 5:30 P.M. dinner may not only be welcome, but it may also provide the opportunity to spend the most pleasant and uncrowded evening hours enjoying the Epcot attractions.

- Lunch provides guests with another chance to enjoy the most popular Epcot restaurants. It also has an additional appeal: With priority seating for 1 P.M., it's possible to spend some of the busiest hours in the park consuming a pleasant meal while less fortunate visitors are waiting in some of the longest lines of the day.

In the Disney-MGM Studios

The eateries at the Disney-MGM Studios are a breed apart. Some feature decor that returns guests to a bygone era; others recapture memorable moments from the big or small screen. All reprise a beloved part of Hollywood's star-studded heritage. The Studios has five full-service restaurants, whose atmospheres and menus are so distinct they satisfy altogether different moods and whims. Priority seating is available for these dining rooms; call 407-WDW-DINE (939-3463). Hollywood & Vine offers character meals (see page 240 for specifics). A solid—and fairly diverse—ensemble of fast-food places hits the spot for eaters on the move.

Table Service

50'S PRIME TIME CAFE: The setting is straight out of your favorite sitcoms of the 1950s. Each of the plastic-laminate kitchen tables is set under a pull-down lamp, evoking a suburban kitchenette. Televisions around the room broadcast black-and-white clips from favorite fifties comedies (all related to food). Guests are waited on by "Mom" (and other family members) with considerable enthusiasm—they make recommendations and encourage everyone to keep their elbows off the table and clean their plates (*or no dessert!*). These elements alone make this spot a perennial guest favorite.

Adding to the appeal is the menu, which is packed with "comfort foods." For openers there's a choice of homemade chicken noodle soup or Dad's chili. Specialties of the house include Magnificent Meat Loaf, served with

mashed potatoes and mushroom gravy; fried chicken; and Granny's Pot Roast. There are also Caesar salads, sandwiches, and Aunt Selma's Chicken Salad. Milk shakes, ice cream sodas, and root beer floats are filling accompaniments. And when you've finished everything on your plate, "Mom" will ask if you'd like dessert. Standouts include s'mores, a graham cracker topped with chocolate and toasted marshmallows (you'll feel like you're back at summer camp); sundaes; banana splits; and apple pie à la mode. Kids love this place. A full bar is available. Priority seating suggested. **L D $$-$$$**

HOLLYWOOD & VINE: The distinctive Art Deco facade ushers guests into a contemporary version of a 1950s diner—all stainless steel with pink accents. An elaborate 42-by-8-foot wall mural depicts notable Hollywood landmarks, including the Disney Studios, Columbia Ranch, and Warner Brothers (back when they were the only film studios in the San Fernando Valley). At the center of the mural is the Carthay Circle Theatre, where *Snow White and the Seven Dwarfs* premiered in 1937.

Starlet Minnie Mouse is joined by characters such as Goofy, Pluto, Chip, and Dale, in entertaining guests during breakfast and lunch. (Note that characters are subject to change.) The all-you-can-eat buffet offers a bounty of selections. For breakfast there are eggs, French toast, frittatas, pancakes, Mickey waffles, and more. The lunch buffet features rotisserie turkey, flank steak, seafood, pasta, sautéed vegetables, macaroni and cheese, fried chicken, and hot dogs, plus pastries and a sundae bar. Cost for breakfast is $16.99 for adults and $8.99 for kids ages 3 through 11; lunch is $17.99 for adults and $9.99 for children. The dinner buffet, a non-character affair, costs $19.99 for adults and $9.99 for kids. Priority seating suggested. **B L D $$-$$$**

HOLLYWOOD BROWN DERBY: The home of the famous Cobb salad is alive and well. This re-creation of the former Vine Street mainstay is quite faithful, right down to the caricatures (reproduced from the original Derby collection) that cover the walls. Arch gossip queen rivals Louella Parsons and

B breakfast   **L** lunch   **D** dinner   **S** snacks   **$** *under $10*   **$$** *$10-$20*   **$$$** *$21-$45*   **$$$$** *$46 and up*

twinkle overhead in the "night sky," and real drive-in theater speakers are mounted beside each car. All the tables face a large screen, where a 45-minute compilation of the best (and worst) of science-fiction trailers and cartoons plays in a continuous loop.

The restaurant is also notable for its huge hot and cold sandwiches. Selections include ham sandwiches, barbecue pork sandwiches, barbecue ribs, and flame-broiled hamburgers. There's also a slate of tempting desserts,

including cheesecake, milk shakes, and the Sci-Fi Sundae (a colossal sundae made with vanilla ice cream and many toppings). Priority seating suggested. **L D** **$$–$$$**

Hedda Hopper (portrayed by convincing actresses) may still be spotted dining here, just as they did in the heyday of the real Brown Derby. The restaurant is decorated predominantly in teak and mahogany, and the elegant chandeliers and perimeter lamps (shaped like miniature derbies) are reminiscent of those in the original eatery.

The menu features the famed Cobb salad, created by owner Bob Cobb in the 1930s. It's a mixture of ever-so-finely chopped fresh salad greens, tomato, bacon, turkey, egg, blue cheese, and avocado, served with french dressing. A modern incarnation of the salad is available with shrimp or chicken. The dessert tray is tempting—particularly the grapefruit cake, a Brown Derby institution. The slightly formal atmosphere is not likely to enchant most kids. Priority seating suggested. **L D** **$$$**

MAMA MELROSE'S RISTORANTE ITALIANO: This quirky Italian restaurant (with a California twist) is located in a warehouse that has been converted into a dining room. Appetizer flatbreads are prepared in a wood-burning oven. The menu also features risotto, chicken, pasta, and vegetarian options. More creative dishes include linguini with clams, shrimp, mussels, and calamari in a spicy marinara sauce; veal saltimbocca; and pork and veal paella. Note that the dinner hour ends a bit earlier than usual here. Priority seating suggested. **L D** **$$–$$$**

SCI-FI DINE-IN THEATER: This 250-seat eatery re-creates a 1950s drive-in theater. The tables are actually flashy, 1950s-era cars, complete with fins and whitewalls. Fiber-optic stars

Fast Food & Snacks

ABC COMMISSARY: This restaurant located near the Chinese Theater features savory grilled chicken breast sandwiches, quesadilla club sandwiches, red beans and rice, fresh tomato salad, fruit pies, and milk shakes. The kids' meals are sure to please. As fast-food eateries go, this place is a standout. **L D S** **$**

BACKLOT EXPRESS: This fast-food spot looks like the old crafts shops on a studio backlot. There's a paint shop, stunt hall, sculpture shop, and model shop. The paint shop has paint-speckled floors, chairs, and tables; the prop shop is decked out in car engines, bumpers, and fan belts. There is outdoor seating amid stored streetlights, plants, and trees.

Hot Tip!

Hollywood Brown Derby, Mama Melrose's Ristorante Italiano, and other eateries offer a "dinner and a show" deal. Simply make arrangements upon arrival at the Studios to get special seating (no waiting!) at that evening's performance of Fantasmic! For details, go to Guest Relations.

Menu offerings include burgers, hot dogs, chicken Caesar salad, grilled chicken sandwiches, tuna subs, and chili. For dessert, there's chocolate-chip cheesecake, brownies, and fresh fruit. Beer is available. **L D S $**

MIN AND BILL'S DOCKSIDE DINER: A waterside snack spot offering thick shakes and malts (chocolate and vanilla), as well as chips, cookies, brownies, coffee, soft drinks, and beer. **S $**

STARRING ROLLS BAKERY: Freshly baked rolls, pastries, muffins, croissants, and sugar-free desserts are sold at this sweet-smelling shop. Coffee, tea, and soft drinks are also served, making this a good place for an eat-and-run breakfast. For lunch, ready-made sandwiches with ham and cheese, chicken salad, or tuna salad are available. **B L S $**

STUDIO CATERING CO.: Situated next to the Honey, I Shrunk the Kids Movie Set Adventure, the eatery offers a selection of hearty double-decker sandwiches. The choices include a club sandwich and a turkey and cheddar cheese sandwich served on wheat bread with lettuce and tomato. There is a separate line for cones and sundaes made with chocolate and vanilla soft-serve ice cream. Beer is available at a nearby stand. **S $**

SUNSET RANCH MARKET: Several well-stocked food stands on Sunset Boulevard offer snacking opportunities and quick bites. Blue umbrellas dot the outdoor seating area. *Rosie's All-American Cafe* specializes in burgers, sandwiches, and soups. *Catalina Eddie's* offers plain, pepperoni, and vegetable pizzas, plus salads, brownies, and cookies. Fresh fruit and vegetables, fruit juices, and soft drinks are available at *Anaheim Produce*. The turkey leg cart also offers baked potatoes with toppings, foot-long hot dogs, and soft pretzels. **L D S $**

TOY STORY PIZZA PLANET: This arcade, located near the Muppets attraction, looks as if it were plucked out of the film *Toy Story*. The centerpiece is a Space Crane, complete with aliens and mechanical grabber. Video games line the walls (pay as you play). A perfect spot for children with endless energy and parents who need to rest their feet. The limited menu includes individual pizzas, salads, desserts, and juice. Cappuccino and espresso are also available. **L D S $**

Studios Mealtime Tips

- To avoid traffic jams at fast-food spots, consider eating lunch or dinner at one of the restaurants that offers priority seating—Hollywood Brown Derby, 50's Prime Time Cafe, Sci-Fi Dine-In Theater, Hollywood & Vine (lunch only), or Mama Melrose's Ristorante Italiano. To arrange for priority seating in advance, call 407-WDW-DINE (939-3463). To obtain same-day seating, go to the kiosk at Hollywood Junction (on the corner of Hollywood and Sunset), before 1 P.M. or to the restaurant itself.

- The many indoor and outdoor nooks within the Backlot Express seating area are nicely removed from the beaten path; relative quiet can frequently be enjoyed here even during prime mealtimes.

- Characters appear at the Hollywood & Vine restaurant during breakfast and lunch, so it's one of the best places to meet them at the Disney-MGM Studios.

In Animal Kingdom

Whether you eat like a bird or more like a horse, you'll have no trouble finding something to sink your teeth into at one of Animal Kingdom's many eateries. The emphasis at this theme park is on fast food, with Rainforest Cafe as the only traditional table-service establishment. The menagerie of quick-service options cater to carnivores and herbivores alike, featuring everything from freshly tossed Caesar salad to chicken roasted in a 16-foot "wall of flames." Beer, including Safari Amber specialty brew, and wine are served at most restaurants.

Table Service

RAINFOREST CAFE: Like The Oasis, the region of Animal Kingdom that it borders, this cafe is a lush, soothing tropical jungle. Unlike The Oasis, any quiet moment here is merely a calm before the storm—as brief, dramatic thunderstorms occur throughout the day *inside* the restaurant. Gushing waterfalls, twisting tree trunks, and colorful fish add to the ambience. The environmentally conscious cuisine includes items like Planet Earth Pasta and the Plant Sandwich. (The Calypso Dip—fresh salmon, artichoke hearts, onions, spices, and cheese served with warm pita—is an especially tantalizing appetizer.) There's no net-caught fish on the menu, nor beef from countries that destroy rain forest land to raise cattle.

Note: The restaurant and bar are accessible from inside and outside Animal Kingdom, so admission to the park isn't necessary to enter. It is located to the left side of Animal Kingdom's entrance plaza. Priority seating suggested for breakfast, lunch, and dinner. **B L D S** **$$–$$$**

Fast Food & Snacks

ANANDAPUR ICE CREAM: Cool off with a soft-serve from Asia's local ice cream truck. The refreshing snack is available by the cone, in a soda float, or blended into a flavorful smoothie. **S** **$**

CHAKRANDI CHICKEN SHOP: In Asia, there is a walk-up window dispensing chicken satay dipped in peanut sauce, noodle bowls, corn-on-the-cob, and soft drinks. **S** **$**

CHIP 'N' DALE'S COOKIE CABIN: For a sweet treat, head to Camp Minnie-Mickey for delicious, freshly baked cookies (chocolate chip, macadamia nut, and sugar) and ice-cream sandwiches. **S** **$**

DINO DINER: In DinoLand U.S.A., on the far side of Chester and Hester's DinoRama, is a small wagon that sells pastries and muffins at breakfast and desserts throughout the day. **S** **$**

FLAME TREE BARBECUE: This fast-food establishment serves up a selection of barbecued sandwiches and platters, all wood-roasted. Sample the mild, tomato-based barbecue sauce or the spicy, mustard-based Carolina-style sauce with your smoked beef brisket, St. Louis ribs, and pulled pork. Smoked turkey, a vegetarian wrap, and apple pie round out the options. There's outdoor seating along the river. Located on Discovery Island, near Dino-Land. Open seasonally. **L D S** **$**

HARAMBE FRUIT MARKET: A healthy choice for snacking at Disney's Animal Kingdom is this fruit stand near the entrance to Kilimanjaro Safaris. **S** **$**

KUSAFIRI COFFEE SHOP & BAKERY: The bakery inside Tusker House provides a steady stream of fresh-from-the-oven breakfast treats and assorted desserts, plus cappuccino and espresso. **B S** **$**

MUNCH WAGON: Head to this stand located at Rafiki's Planet Watch for hot dogs and snacks. **L D S** **$**

PIZZAFARI: Individual pizzas are available plain, with pepperoni, and deluxe (with a variety of meats and vegetables). In addition to the

cheese-laden bill of fare, the options here include pasta, a Caesar salad with grilled chicken, and a small vegetable calzone. Brightly colored animal murals decorate this counter-service restaurant, located on Discovery Island, near the bridge to Camp Minnie-Mickey. **L D S $**

RESTAURANTOSAURUS: Located deep in the heart of DinoLand U.S.A., this spot is themed as a campsite for student paleontologists. It's filled with fossils, bones, and such; class notes line the walls. This eatery offers fast food at lunch and dinner: burgers, chicken salad, hot dogs, and salads—plus McDonald's fries, chicken nuggets, and Happy Meals. Breakfast is an all-you-can-eat, character-hosted buffet, called Donald's Prehistoric Breakfastosaurus. It's an entertaining meal, powered by the antics of resident students, who wait tables between classes. Cost is $16.99 for adults; $8.99 for kids ages 3 through 11. Priority seating suggested for the breakfast buffet. Book early. **B L D S $–$$**

TAMU TAMU REFRESHMENTS: Got a hankering for something cool and creamy? Stop by this snack spot in Africa's Harambe (across from Tusker House). Here you can indulge a sweet tooth with soft-serve frozen yogurt and ice-cream cones, floats, and sundaes. There's a small seating nook next door. **S $**

TUSKER HOUSE: Harambe village sets the stage for an exceptional dining adventure at this top-notch fast-food restaurant, themed as a safari orientation center. Seating inside is quite civilized, with cherry-wood-colored tables and carved chair backs; there's also outdoor seating under the thatched roof. The menu—which happens to be one of the best in the park—features rotisserie chicken cooked in a 16-foot "wall of flames." Other highlights include the grilled chicken salad served in a bread bowl, beef stew, roast vegetable sandwiches served with tabbouleh, and grilled chicken with ham and cheese. Fried chicken, and side dishes such as chicken salad, fresh vegetables, and mashed potatoes round out the creative options. **L D S $**

Did You Know?

There are no plastic cup lids, coffee stirrers, or straws used in Disney's Animal Kingdom, since they could be harmful to the animals.

Animal Kingdom Mealtime Tips

- Restaurantosaurus and Rainforest Cafe are the only restaurants to offer full breakfasts; a handful of stands, including Dino Diner, supply light options.

- The only restaurant that offers priority seating for all meals is Rainforest Cafe. To arrange for priority seating in advance, available up to four months ahead for all meals, call 407-WDW-DINE (939-3463). To obtain same-day seating, go straight to the restaurant. We recommend making priority seating arrangements.

- The many seating pavilions along the river near Flame Tree Barbecue provide waterside dining that's nicely removed from the hubbub of Discovery Island; it may be relatively calm here even during prime mealtimes.

- A great place to meet Donald and pals such as Mickey, Pluto, and Goofy is at Restaurantosaurus during the daily character breakfast. (Characters appearing at the breakfast are subject to change—though Donald is always in attendance.) Don't forget to make priority seating arrangements.

B breakfast **L** lunch **D** dinner **S** snacks   **$** *under $10* **$$** *$10–$20* **$$$** *$21–$45* **$$$$** *$46 and up*

In Downtown Disney

The vast region known as Downtown Disney encompasses the Marketplace, Pleasure Island, and the West Side. While an admission fee applies after 7 P.M. for Pleasure Island club-goers, there is no charge simply to dine at any of Pleasure Island's full-service restaurants. (There is never a fee to roam the West Side or Marketplace.) On average, Downtown Disney restaurants operate from 11 A.M. to midnight; most of the snack spots are open from 11 A.M. to 2 A.M. For up-to-the-minute details on hours, call 407-939-4636. It's worth noting that while the restaurants really hop at dinnertime, they are not terribly crowded at lunch (except, possibly, on the weekend).

BONGOS CUBAN CAFE (West Side): This creation of Gloria Estefan and her husband spices up the Downtown Disney dining repertoire with a menu driven by Cuban and Latin American flavors. Its slate of traditional and nouvelle Cuban dishes, such as black bean soup, plantains, steak topped with onions, and flan, tempt taste buds. Indoors, the elaborate mosaic mural and palm-leaf railings set the scene; the patio for outdoor seating wraps around a three-story pineapple. A take-out window provides snacks on the go. Priority seating is not available. **L D S $$–$$$**

CAP'N JACK'S RESTAURANT (Marketplace): This pier house juts right out over Lake Buena Vista, providing water views. The appetizer menu is so full of tasty things—peel-and-eat shrimp, crab cakes, and clam chowder—that it's as good for lunch or dinner as it is for a snack. Entrées extend to king crab legs, lobster, mahimahi, and "landlubber" specials. There is a tempting variety of wines, beers, and other cocktails—and the house's special frozen margaritas are as tasty as they are beautiful. Cap'n Jack's is a terrific place to be, especially in late afternoon, as the sun streams through the blinds and glints on the polished tables and the copper above the bar. **L D S $$**

CHEESECAKE FACTORY EXPRESS (West Side): Located on the top two floors of Disney-Quest, this fast-food restaurant serves much more than the sumptuous sweets it is famous for. The daily offerings are prepared fresh from the four main counters. Highlights include warm spinach and artichoke dip served with chips and salsa, grilled portobello mushroom sandwiches, barbecue chicken pizza, and lasagne in a chicken bolognese sauce. Also available are a selection of hearty soups and salads, tasty sandwiches, and several specialty burgers and hot dogs. Temptations abound at the dessert counter—they come in the form of frozen mud pie, hot fudge brownie sundaes, cookies, cakes, and, of course, cheesecake. Note that DisneyQuest admission is required for access to the Cheesecake Factory Express. **L D S $**

D-ZERTZ (Pleasure Island): Pastries, chocolates, candy, frozen yogurt, and other confections are the desserts available here. Coffee and cappuccino are also served, making it a pleasant spot for a quick snack. **S $**

FULTON'S CRAB HOUSE (Between Pleasure Island and Marketplace): This traditional seafood house, operated by Levy Restaurants, occupies the three-deck riverboat formerly known as the *Empress Lilly*. Permanently docked on the western edge of Lake Buena Vista, it is a tribute to Robert Fulton, who invented the steamboat. The place is so serious about seafood that it has hooked up with fishermen worldwide to ensure that the truckloads of fish and shellfish arriving daily at Fulton's back door are at their freshest.

The menu changes each day to reflect new arrivals, but is always filled with several types of crabs, oysters, and fish, plus lobster, steaks, grilled chicken, grilled vegetables, and combination platters. Signature dishes include cioppino, a savory San Francisco–style seafood stew with a tomato broth base. Accompaniments extend to corn-whipped potatoes and grilled asparagus. Desserts, coffee, and specialty drinks are also served.

GOOD MEALS, GREAT TIMES

Fulton's interior is awash in nautical knick-knacks and nostalgia. Seating on the deck is sometimes available. The adjoining Stone Crab lounge has an excellent raw bar—the perfect place for lunch or a savory snack. Priority seating arrangements suggested for breakfast and dinner at Fulton's. **L D S** **$$$$**

GHIRARDELLI SODA FOUNTAIN AND CHOCOLATE SHOP (Marketplace): San Francisco's famous sweet-maker finally comes east with a soda fountain extraordinaire. Stop in for a chocolaty treat, root beer float, or refreshing malt. Antique chocolate-making equipment demonstrates how the famous Ghirardelli chocolate got its start. There's no better place to please a sweet tooth. **S** **$**

HOUSE OF BLUES (West Side): The night-club that Blues Brother Dan Aykroyd helped launch doubles as a Mississippi Delta–inspired dining spot. House of Blues gives Downtown Disney a culinary boost from the bayou—namely home-style Cajun and Creole cooking. Finally, WDW has a haven for diners desperately seeking their fill of such savory things as jambalaya, étouffée, and homemade bread pudding. A gospel brunch is presented on Sundays. Priority seating is available for groups of 6 to 19 only. **L D S** **$**

MCDONALD'S (Marketplace): The Golden Arches and all of its Mc-specialties (plus pizza) are on hand until the wee hours in this installation of the familiar fast-food establishment, located on the western edge of the Marketplace. **B L D S** **$**

MISSING LINK SAUSAGE CO. (Pleasure Island): Hot dogs, bratwurst, kielbasa, and a variety of savory sausages (including a chicken-apple variety, and both mild and hot Italian links) dominate the menu of this snack spot across from 8TRAX. Submarine sandwiches, burgers, and slushies are also available. **L D S** **$**

PLANET HOLLYWOOD (West Side): This branch of the international restaurant chain is a standout for its spherical silhouette. Built on three levels, this colossal globe is jam-packed with classic movie and television memorabilia.

The creative, wide-ranging menu features first-rate salads, sandwiches, pasta dishes, burgers, appetizer pizzas, fajitas, and dessert specialties. Be sure to consider sampling the blackened shrimp, Far East chicken salad, vegetable burger, or pasta primavera. Cap off the meal with a piece of butter rum cake. Priority seating is suggested. Smoking is permitted in the bar only. **L D S** **$$–$$$**

> ## Hot Tip!
> The lines for Planet Hollywood are usually shortest between 1 P.M. and 5 P.M.

PORTOBELLO YACHT CLUB (Pleasure Island): The inviting, Bermuda-style house combines high gables and beamed ceilings, bright Mediterranean colors and earthy tones. The pleasant establishment is divided into several informal dining rooms, each of which displays an interesting collection of maritime memorabilia.

The bustling open kitchen turns out grilled meat and fish and small gourmet pizzas baked in a wood-burning oven. Try the *quattro formaggi*, a four-cheese pie that's a true taste treat and a great appetizer or snack. Pasta offerings include *spaghettini alla Portobello* (pasta with shrimp, scallops, clams, mussels, crab legs, tomatoes, garlic, olive oil, wine, and herbs) and *penne all'arrabiata* (long pasta

tubes with plum tomatoes, mushrooms, pancetta, garlic, onions, and fresh herbs). Be sure to save room for desserts such as *crema brucciata*, white chocolate custard with a caramelized sugar glaze; or *cioccolato paradiso*, a layer cake with chocolate ganache frosting, chocolate toffee crunch filling, and warm caramel sauce. Portobello also offers a selection of specialty coffees and an impressive wine list. Priority seating suggested. **D** $$$

RAINFOREST CAFE (Downtown Disney Marketplace): There's no mistaking the environmental orientation of this Amazon-emulating eatery near Cap'n Jack's Restaurant. The atmospheric dining environs transport guests to a makeshift rain forest, complete with banyan trees, tropical fish, gushing waterfalls, and a friendly population of hand-raised parrots. A talking tree offers a constant stream of ecological insights, and animal experts are on hand to field questions.

Sophisticated special effects envelop guests in tropical storms, complete with lightning and thunder. Menu items include Planet Earth Pasta, Island Hopper Chicken, and the Plant Sandwich (portobello mushrooms, zucchini, roasted red peppers, and fresh spinach). A merchandise shop stocks logo clothing. Priority seating not available. Note that there is another Rainforest Cafe located at Disney's Animal Kingdom Priority seating is not available at this location. **B L D S** $$–$$$

WOLFGANG PUCK CAFE (West Side): Wolfgang Puck's choice of Walt Disney World for his Florida debut is sure to spur a surge in cravings for his trademark California cuisine.

Among his specialties are gourmet pizzas, Thai chicken satay pastas with fresh vegetables, Chinois Chicken Salad, and rotisserie chicken. The menu is equal parts sophisticated and straightforward—and ever so fresh. There's also an attractive sushi bar. Colorful mosaics decorate his restaurants. Priority seating is not available. **L D S** $$$

WOLFGANG PUCK CAFE—THE DINING ROOM (West Side): The formal upstairs area in the cafe is devoted to the more elaborate of Wolfgang Puck's cuisine. Consider sampling the baby vegetable risotto and grilled chicken with squash ravioli in a sage brown butter sauce. Priority seating is not available. **D** $$$–$$$$

WOLFGANG PUCK EXPRESS (Marketplace and West Side): Renowned chef Wolfgang Puck turns his talents to fast service and signature treats, including gourmet wood-fired pizzas, rotisserie chicken, seasonal soups, focaccia sandwiches, and fresh salads—including his famous Chinois Chicken Salad. **L D S** $

WETZEL'S PRETZELS (Pleasure Island): Whether you prefer pretzels on the salty or sweet side, Wetzel's has something to satisfy. Ambitious snackers enjoy the Mexicali, the Sinful Cinnamon, and the Three Cheese varieties. **S** $

Crossroads of Lake Buena Vista

WDW visitors can get everything from soup to McNuggets at the Crossroads of Lake Buena Vista shopping center, near the resorts on Hotel Plaza Boulevard. Choices include Pebbles (the best bet for adults), Perkins (popular with families), T.G.I. Friday's, Red Lobster, McDonald's, Taco Bell, Jungle Jim's, Pacino's, Chevy's Mexican Restaurant, and Pizzeria Uno.

In the WDW Resorts

Among the more pleasant surprises at Walt Disney World is the delightful theming of the Disney hotels. Each resort sports a fanciful setting quite foreign to Central Florida, reminiscent of such places as the Pacific Northwest; the more regional-minded offer a tasty sampling of the native cuisine to complete the picture. Whereas the deluxe properties provide a variety of dining options, including at least one full-service restaurant, moderate resorts feature a food court plus an informal dining room, and the value-oriented All-Star resorts keep guests' appetites in check with huge food courts.

The possibilities range from dinners served family-style to innovative cuisine, presented in settings worthy of special occasions. Priority seating is an important part of the resorts' full-service dining circuit (call 407-WDW-DINE). Character meals are an option for breakfast, Sunday brunch, and dinner (see page 240).

All-Star Resorts

Each of these resorts features a themed central food court. The *End Zone* food court in Stadium Hall at the All-Star Sports resort, the *Intermission* food court in Melody Hall at the All-Star Music resort, and the *World Premiere* food court in Cinema Hall at the All-Star Movies resort have similar food stands. The selections include pasta, pizza, chicken, ribs, burgers, hot dogs, sandwiches, salads, frozen yogurt, and a wide variety of breakfast and baked goods. **B L D S $**

Animal Kingdom Lodge

BOMA—FLAVORS OF AFRICA: Big and bustling, this family restaurant, designed to resemble an African marketplace, features

buffet fare from more than 50 African countries. Priority seating suggested. **B D $$–$$$**

JIKO—THE COOKING PLACE: Food with an international flair fills the menu at this sophisticated spot. Priority seating suggested. **D $$–$$$**

THE MARA: An enormous fast-food restaurant located near the pool. **B L D S $–$$**

BoardWalk

BIG RIVER GRILLE & BREWING WORKS: Guests observe (and later sample) as the brew master creates three flagship ales and two seasonal brews at this working brew pub. The menu features a selection of sandwiches and salads, plus variations on pub favorites, such as veal meat loaf with Tilt Pale Ale sauce and lobster pot pie. **L D S $$**

BOARDWALK BAKERY: The aromas wafting from Spoodles' next-door neighbor on the boardwalk reveal the fresh-baked goods therein. Display windows allow guests to watch bakers at work. **B S $**

ESPN CLUB: A sports bar/family restaurant one-two punch, ESPN Club surrounds guests with no fewer than 80 TV monitors, so no one misses a play. The standard fare includes burgers, sandwiches, and a variety of salads and entrées. **L D S $$**

FLYING FISH CAFE: This upbeat eatery delivers creative seasonal menus with an emphasis on seafood and healthy options. As

GOOD MEALS, GREAT TIMES

an example of the entrées created in the open "on-stage" kitchen, consider the potato-wrapped yellowtail snapper. While seafood is the specialty, steaks are also served. Save room for a nice, homemade dessert. Priority seating suggested. Seating is available at the chef's counter. `D` `$$$`

SEASHORE SWEETS': Located next to the Flying Fish Cafe, this old-fashioned spot sates sweet tooths with candies, saltwater taffy, and ice cream and frozen yogurt. Specialty coffees are also offered. `S` `$`

SPOODLES: This family restaurant with butcher-block tables and Mediterranean tastes is between Seashore Sweets' and the BoardWalk Bakery. Dinner menus highlight specialties from Greece, Spain, Northern Africa, and Italy, and encourage diners to share dishes and try new foods. Offerings range from pizza to braised lamb shank with a creamy herb polenta. The breakfast menu features eggs, meats, fish, cereal, and French toast. A take-out window allows passersby to pick up pizza by the slice. Priority seating suggested. `B` `D` `$$-$$$`

Caribbean Beach

OLD PORT ROYALE: The food court in Old Port Royale features a large dining area and the following fast-food eateries. *Cinnamon Bay Bakery* serves croissants, freshly baked rolls, pastries, ice cream, and other high-calorie treats. Italian specialties are the order at the *Kingston Pasta Shop*. Soups, salads, and hot and cold sandwiches make up the selections at *Montego's Deli*. Burgers and grilled chicken sandwiches are among the offerings at *Port Royale Hamburger Shop*. And pizza is available by the slice or the pie at *Royale Pizza Shop*. `B` `L` `D` `S` `$`

SHUTTERS AT OLD PORT ROYALE: Prime rib, lamb chops, and pork loin are among the items on the menu at this cozy restaurant within Old Port Royale. Tropical drinks, beer, wine, and cocktails are also served. Priority seating suggested. `D` `S` `$$-$$$`

Contemporary

CALIFORNIA GRILL: Perched on the hotel's 15th floor, with terrific views of sunsets and Magic Kingdom fireworks, this acclaimed restaurant offers the best in West Coast cuisine in a stylish, relaxing atmosphere. (It has been named "restaurant of choice" by *Orlando Magazine*.) The ever-changing menu is defined by sophisticated use of fresh produce. Wood-fired California pizzas, alderwood-smoked salmon, sushi, spit-roasted chicken, and jumbo soufflés are made to order in an open kitchen. Grilled pork tenderloin with polenta and balsamic-vinegar-smothered cremini mushrooms suggest the chef's culinary prowess. There's even a vegetarian zone on the menu. The extensive wine list is updated daily. Priority seating suggested. `D` `$$$`

CHEF MICKEY'S: Chef Mickey and his pals host this buffet-style feast, with dramatic views of the monorail passing above. Colorful life-size illustrations of Disney characters decorate the room. The changing menu takes advantage of seasonal offerings; a sundae bar provides a sweet finish. This is a popular eatery with a loyal following. Be prepared to drop your fork and swing your napkin on a moment's notice. Priority seating suggested. `B` `D` `$$-$$$`

CONCOURSE STEAKHOUSE: This spot offers omelettes, pancakes, and fresh fruit for breakfast. At lunch there are salads, soups, burgers, pizzas, and sandwiches to choose from. Dinner adds steaks, seafood, and oak-roasted prime rib to the menu. The wine list is updated daily. Priority seating suggested. **B L D** **$$$**

FOOD AND FUN CENTER: On the first floor by the arcade, this no-frills snack bar serves light fare around the clock (though there is a bigger selection of food by day). **B L D S** **$**

Coronado Springs

MAYA GRILL: The only full-service restaurant at this resort, it features steak and seafood with a Latin American flair. Many items are cooked over an open-pit wood-fired grill. Breakfast is presented as an all-you-can-eat buffet. Priority seating suggested. **B D** **$$$**

PEPPER MARKET: This colorful food court, modeled after an open-air market, has a large seating area and lots of stands where vendors sell pizza, sandwiches, salads, burgers, stir-fry, Mexican specialties, baked goods, margaritas, and more. Note that a 10 percent gratuity is automatically added to the bill whether you eat in the dining area or not. **B L D S** **$–$$**

Disney's Old Key West

GOOD'S FOOD TO GO: Hamburgers, cheeseburgers, grilled chicken sandwiches, salads, ice cream, and frozen yogurt are among the offerings. **B L D S** **$**

OLIVIA'S CAFE: An assortment of Key West favorites, including tasty shrimp dishes and conch fritters, are featured alongside contemporary southern fare. The menu changes frequently. **L D** **$$**

Fort Wilderness

Most people cook their own meals here; ample supplies are available at both the Meadow Trading Post and the Settlement Trading Post (open from 8 A.M. to 10 P.M. in winter, to 11 P.M. in summer).

TRAIL'S END BUFFET: It's a little off the beaten path for anyone but Fort Wilderness guests, but for many it's well worth the trip. The informal log-walled restaurant offers an inexpensive, all-you-can-eat breakfast (one of the biggest bargains on DisneyWorld property), including cheese grits, biscuits, gravy, and a tasty "breakfast pizza" that vaguely resembles an omelette. Hearty lunches and dinners feature barbecued chicken, fish, chicken pot pie, and spareribs. There are sandwiches and a taco bar at lunch. Pizza is served every night from 9:30 P.M. until 11 P.M. (until midnight on weekends). Beer and wine are served by the glass or by the pitcher. **B L D S** **$–$$**

Grand Floridian

CÍTRICOS: The most recent addition to the Grand Floridian's impressive restaurant lineup specializes in market-fresh Southern French cooking. The fare varies seasonally but may include items such as sautéed tiger shrimp with ziti, artichokes, bell peppers, and roasted garlic in a spicy wine sauce; or rack of lamb.

The menu suggests a wine from the extensive international list for each appetizer, entrée, and dessert; for $25 the waiter will bring one for each of three courses. The stunning view of the Seven Seas Lagoon is a year-round staple. A private dining room is available for parties of up to 14 people. Priority seating suggested. Closed Monday and Tuesday. **D** **$$$–$$$$**

GASPARILLA GRILL & GAMES: Grilled chicken, burgers, pizza, hot dogs, and soft-serve ice cream are the mainstays at this 24-hour take-out restaurant near the marina. There is indoor and outdoor seating. Continental breakfast is also available. **B L D S** **$**

GRAND FLORIDIAN CAFE: Traditional American cooking is the specialty at this picturesque spot. Although the menu varies, selections have included fried chicken and Atlantic swordfish. There are also salads and an assortment of more traditional entrées. Priority seating available. **D** **$$$**

NARCOOSSEE'S: The partially open kitchen is the focal point at this casual, airy octagonal dining spot on the shores of the Grand Floridian beach. Specialties of the house, which vary seasonally, may include Maine lobster, grilled lamb chops, or pepper-seared jumbo scallops. House staples include charbroiled meats, Florida seafood, and vegetarian options. It's also possible to enjoy a cocktail on the veranda overlooking the Seven Seas Lagoon. Priority seating suggested. **D** **$$$**

B breakfast   **L** lunch   **D** dinner   **S** snacks   **$** under $10   **$$** $10–$20   **$$$** $21–$45   **$$$$** $46 and up

1900 PARK FARE: A sophisticated buffet menu and subtle decor make this the most elegant character restaurant on property. Big Bertha, a band organ built in Paris nearly a century ago, sits 15 feet above the floor in a proscenium. Mary Poppins and friends (characters vary) mingle with guests during the bountiful daily breakfast. Cinderella and her storybook friends visit the dining room during the dinner hours. Keep in mind that the lineup of characters does change from time to time. Dinner features seafood, salads, pastas, vegetables, breads, and prime rib. The offerings change weekly. Priority seating suggested. **B D $$$**

VICTORIA & ALBERT'S: The intimate dining room seats only 60, and elegant touches include Royal Doulton china, Sambonet silver, and Schott-Zweisel crystal. The menu is customized daily. Each night there are fish, fowl, red meat, veal, and lamb selections, which depend on the best ingredients in the market and are described in detail by your waiter. The chef may even make a personal appearance to say hello or to accommodate special requests from patrons, or guests may choose to dine at the chef's table in the kitchen (for an additional charge).

There are also choices of two soups, two salads, and desserts, including specialty soufflés of fresh berries, chocolate, or Grand Marnier. There is an extensive wine list, and wine pairings are available (for an additional $45).

Once guests have made their selections, they are presented with a personalized menu as a souvenir of the event. A harpist provides background music. At the completion of the meal, women receive a long-stemmed rose. Jackets are required. One oddity of note: Every host and hostess at the restaurant is named Victoria or Albert (or at least claims to be). Priority seating is necessary. **D $$$$**

Polynesian

CAPTAIN COOK'S SNACK COMPANY: A good spot for continental breakfast, hamburgers, hot dogs, fruit salad, sandwiches, and snacks; cans of beer and small bottles of wine are also available. Open 24 hours a day. **B L D S $**

KONA CAFE: Located on the second floor of the Great Ceremonial House, just around the corner from 'Ohana, this casual restaurant features a South Seas decor and an exotic menu. Lunch and dinner menus has Asian-influenced entrées. Possibilities include calamari in a sweet chili-mint sauce; char-grilled ahi tuna with pan-fried noodles and bok choy; and char-crusted strip sirloin in a teriyaki marinade. A variety of desserts are among the offerings. Adjoining the cafe is a coffee counter that's perfect for a quick bite en route to the monorail. The coffee is quite good. Priority seating is available at the restaurant. **B L D S $$–$$$**

'OHANA: On the second floor of the resort's Great Ceremonial House, this restaurant features a dramatic, 16-foot-long open fire pit. Dinner choices in the all-you-can-eat, family-style feast include shrimp, poultry, pork, and beef, all roasted on skewers up to three feet long. Meats are marinated in original combinations of soy, ginger, lemongrass, or garlic, and are served family-style with an assortment of vegetables, salads, and homemade bread.

The meal ends with fresh pineapple with caramel dipping sauce, or additional dessert offerings (for an extra charge) such as banana tarts. Polynesian singers entertain at dinner, while periodic hula hoop and coconut-rolling contests amuse young children.

Par for the Course

The pleasant **Sand Trap Bar & Grill** in the Bonnet Creek Golf Club is a convenient dining option for golfers playing the adjacent Eagle Pines and Osprey Ridge courses. It's also close to the Magic Kingdom resorts. In addition to the traditional breakfast items, the Sand Trap serves a variety of appetizers, burgers, soups, and sandwiches. There is a full bar; ice cream and milk shakes are also available. **B L D S** $$

There's no menu from which to order. Waiters simply deliver course after course. By all means sample everything that comes your way.

The dining room itself is large and open and offers fine views across the Seven Seas Lagoon all the way to Cinderella Castle in the Magic Kingdom. Mickey and his friends host a character breakfast each morning. Breakfast fare is basic and presented "family style." Priority seating suggested. **B D** $$$$

Pop Century

Guests of the Pop Century resort dine in the food court in Classic Hall. The selection includes pasta, pizza, chicken, burgers, hot dogs, sandwiches, salads, breakfast items, and baked goods. **B L D S** $

Port Orleans French Quarter

SASSAGOULA FLOATWORKS & FOOD FACTORY: The stands at this festive food court feature pizza, pasta, gumbo, burgers, sandwiches, soups, salads, spit-roasted chicken, barbecued ribs, ice cream, and a full selection of fresh bakery products, including tempting beignets. **B L D S** $

Port Orleans Riverside

BOATWRIGHT'S DINING HALL: Be sure to notice the boat that's being built in this table-service eatery. Specialties include Southern dishes as well as American home-style favorites. Priority seating suggested. **B D** $$–$$$

RIVERSIDE MILL: This high-ceilinged food court styled in the image of a working cotton mill offers half a dozen food counters and a sprawling seating area. Collectively, the stands offer pizza; pasta; calzone; fried, grilled, and spit-roasted chicken; burgers; barbecued ribs; salads; sandwiches; and fresh baked goods.

For guests on the go, the food court's deli does double duty as a convenience store, stocking sandwiches, soft drinks, beer, wine, snack items, and prepared salads. In the past, it's been possible to have pizza delivered to guestrooms. Ask a food court attendant if this service is offered during your stay. **B L D S** $

Swan & Dolphin

CABANA BAR & GRILL: Burgers, grilled chicken sandwiches, fruit, and yogurt are offered at this full-service poolside eatery. **L S** $

CORAL CAFE: Buffets are offered for breakfast and dinner in this bright and casual restaurant. An à la carte menu is also available, offering turkey burgers, chicken, sandwiches, pasta, and cheese steaks. Located at the Dolphin. **B L D S** $$

DOLPHIN FOUNTAIN: Homemade ice cream is the palate-pleasing highlight here. Flavors include dark chocolate, cappuccino, and mint chocolate chip. Oreo and Heath Bar mixes are available in waffle cones, cups, or as part of super sundaes. Burgers, shakes, and malts are also available. The old-time 1950s atmosphere is enhanced by an energetic staff that breaks into song and dance several times a day. **L D S** $-$$

GARDEN GROVE CAFE: Situated in a five-story greenhouse, this Swan dining spot offers a full breakfast menu and fresh fish and shellfish at lunch. At dinner, the restaurant is transformed into Gulliver's Grill, where large servings are presented before you, and a magician is on hand to entertain.

Desserts are baked fresh daily in an open pastry kitchen. As you approach the restaurant, take a look through the glass windows to see the chefs at work. Character breakfasts and dinners are held here on certain days. Priority seating suggested for dinner. **B L D S** $$$

PALIO: This Italian bistro gets high marks for its bruschetta, focaccia, pasta, and pizza. Other specialties include veal and fish dishes. A strolling musician adds to the ambience. Priority seating suggested. Located at the Swan. **D** $$$

SHULA'S STEAK HOUSE: Like the original Shula's in Miami, this Dolphin dining spot specializes in generous portions of certified Angus beef, in addition to chicken and fresh fish dishes. The eatery pays tribute to the 1972 Miami Dolphins—the year legendary Coach Don Shula led his team to a perfect NFL season. Photos and souvenirs abound, and the menu comes on an autographed football (yours to keep for about $250). Priority seating recommended for dinner. There is no children's menu. **D** $$$-$$$$

SPLASH GRILL: Burgers and other grilled fare join ice cream and frozen yogurt on the menu at this Swan poolside spot. Beer and frozen drinks are served. Prepackaged snacks are also on hand. **L S** $

TUBBI'S: Checkerboard decor and a jukebox raise this cafeteria a bit above the norm. The food, including meatball subs, burgers, sandwiches, and pizza, is usually fresh, and the lines are seldom long. The adjoining convenience store (which is, conveniently, open 24 hours) offers snacks and sundries. **B L D S** $

Wilderness Lodge

ARTIST POINT: Housed in a cavernous dining room decorated with artwork representing painters who first chronicled the Northwest landscape, this fine dining spot offers a creative menu that incorporates wild game (ostrich, buffalo, etc.), in addition to more traditional items such as steak, as well as salmon and other Pacific seafood. One specialty of the house, the tomato salad, is a perennial favorite (it's available both as an appetizer or an entrée). The solid wine list spotlights wines from the Pacific Northwest. Priority seating suggested. **D** $$$

ROARING FORK SNACKS: Salads, burgers, fries, sandwiches, yogurt, chili, and snacks are available at this stone-walled nook near the arcade. **B L D S** $

WHISPERING CANYON CAFE: This family-friendly restaurant is open for all-day dining. Hearty all-you-can-eat fare includes smoked barbecued meats with a variety of sides and salads, plus homemade desserts (for an extra charge). Assorted sandwiches and entrées are available à la carte at lunch and dinner. Priority seating suggested. **B L D** $$$

Yacht & Beach Club

BEACHES & CREAM SODA SHOP: This restaurant lies between the Yacht and Beach Club. It features oversize sundaes, cones, floats, shakes, and sodas, as well as the Fenway Park Burger—which may be ordered as a single, double, triple, or home run. Breakfast items are available as well. **B L D S** $-$$

CAPE MAY CAFE: A wonderful all-you-can-eat New England clambake is held each evening at the Beach Club. A cooking pit used for steaming is in full view of diners, and favorite menu items include clams, mussels, chicken, shrimp, red-skin potatoes, and chowder. There is a character breakfast buffet each morning. Priority seating suggested. This is one of the better WDW values. **B D** $$-$$$

HURRICANE HANNA'S GRILL: Located in the Stormalong Bay area. Hot dogs, burgers, sandwiches, and ice cream are on the menu. There is also a full bar. **L S** $

YACHT CLUB GALLEY: Vivid ceramic-tile tabletops emphasize the nautical theme at the Yacht Club. Breakfast features a buffet and a full menu; lunch and dinner are à la carte only. Priority seating suggested. **L S** $

YACHTSMAN STEAKHOUSE: As its name implies, beef is the house specialty. Guests may watch the butcher choose cuts of meat in the glassed-in shop and observe as meals are prepared in the display kitchen. Seafood and chicken are also available. Located at the Yacht Club. Priority seating suggested. **D** $$$

WALT DISNEY WORLD

Name/Location Page Number	Meals Served	Style*	Price**	Characters	Theme
Cinderella's Royal Table Magic Kingdom (page 214)	Breakfast	Family-style	B: $20/10	Cinderella and friends like Snow White and Belle	Medieval banquet
Liberty Tree Tavern Magic Kingdom (page 216)	Dinner	Family-style	D: $22/10	Minnie, Goofy, Pluto, Chip, and Dale	Traditional Thanksgiving dinner
Crystal Palace Magic Kingdom (page 216)	Breakfast Lunch Dinner	Buffet	B: $17/9 L: $18/10 D: $22/10	Pooh, Eeyore, Tigger, and Piglet	Sunlit conservatory
Garden Grill Epcot (page 219)	Lunch Dinner	Family-style	L: $20/10 D: $22/10	Mickey, Pluto, Chip, and Dale	Home-style country cooking
Hollywood & Vine Disney-MGM Studios (page 226)	Breakfast Lunch	Buffet	B: $17/10 L: $18/9	Minnie, Pluto, Goofy, Chip, and Dale	Hollywood heyday
Restaurantosaurus Disney's Animal Kingdom (page 230)	Breakfast	Buffet	B: $17/9	Donald, Pluto, and Goofy	Paleontologist hangout
Chef Mickey's Contemporary Resort (page 235)	Breakfast Dinner	Buffet	B: $16/9 D: $22/10	Mickey, Minnie, Goofy, Donald, Chip, and Dale	Party central!
1900 Park Fare Grand Floridian Resort (page 237)	Breakfast Dinner	Buffet	B: $17/10 D: $24/11	B: Stars like Mary Poppins D: Cinderella and friends	Turn-of-the-century circus
'Ohana Polynesian Resort (page 237)	Breakfast	Family-style	B: $17/9	Mickey, Goofy, Chip, and Dale	Tropical hut
Akershus Norway Pavilion, Epcot (page 220)	Breakfast	Buffet	B: $20/10	Belle, Jasmine, Snow White, Sleeping Beauty, Mary Poppins	14th-century Norwegian castle
Cape May Cafe Yacht and Beach Club Resorts (page 239)	Breakfast	Buffet	B: $17/9	Goofy, Minnie, Chip, and Dale	Seaside picnic

* Family-style and buffet meals are all-you-can-eat dining experiences. Family-style features a set menu and table service; buffet-style meals usually present more dining options and are self-serve.
** Adult prices are followed by children's prices (diners ages 3 through 11)

CHARACTER DINING

Featured Items	For Dessert	Tip	Wins the Award for . . .
French toast, eggs, bacon, fruit	Danish	Book the first seating and request a table by the window for a prime view	**Best Setting** (in Cinderella Castle)
Turkey, flank steak, ham, stuffing, mashed potatoes, vegetables, Stouffer's mac and cheese	Not included with the meal, but available for an additional charge: fruit pie.	Though the fare, which is served family style, isn't exactly gourmet, it tends to please picky, young eaters.	**Heartiest Fare** (Most guests feel stuffed after dinner—much like they do on Thanksgiving.)
B: French toast, eggs, cereal, frittata, fruit L/D: Shrimp, carved meat, pasta, veggies, pizza, salad	B: Sticky buns D: Cakes, pies, make-your-own-sundaes, cookies	Don't be put off by this restaurant's size—the characters make the rounds surprisingly quickly	**Best Theme Park Buffet** (Lovely setting, convenient location, and an appetizing menu.)
B: Eggs, potatoes, sausage L/D: Catfish, beef, chicken, veggies, potatoes, stuffing, (mac and cheese for kids)	B: Bakery basket L/D: Strawberry shortcake or fruit cobbler à la mode	Expect to pay an additional $3 per table for salad at lunchtime	**Best for Vegetarians** (Ask for the vegetarian meal—it's a tasty ravioli primavera.)
B: Chocolate French toast, pancakes, eggs, fruit L: Carved meats, seafood, pasta, hot dogs, salads	B: Pastries, muffins L: Make-your-own-sundaes, pies, cakes	Ask to sit near the center of the restaurant for the best view of the characters' performances	**Most Elaborate Costumes** (Features Starlet Minnie and Gangster Goofy.)
Pancakes, French toast, eggs, breakfast burritos, frittata, sausage, grits, cereal, fresh fruit	Danish, muffins	Beware of prankster waiters!	**Best Place to Find Donald Duck** (As the host, he makes the rounds all morning long.)
B: Eggs, frittata, pancakes, Mickey waffles, fruit, cereal D: Carved meats, seafood, pasta, veggies, pizza, salads	Make-your-own cupcakes and sundaes, cheesecake, pies, cookies	The party break happens every 45 minutes. Be sure to stick around for at least one celebration.	**Best All-Around Character Meal** (It has a fun and festive setting and a kid-pleasing menu.)
B: Pancakes, eggs, waffles D: Carved meats, cheese ravioli, lo mein, brie and crackers	B: Sticky buns, muffins, Danish D: Key lime pie, cheesecake, bread pudding	Breakfast here is a nice way to start a Magic Kingdom day. The park is just one monorail stop away.	**Fanciest Foods** (The quality is superior to the other buffets, but there's still plenty to please the kids.)
Mickey waffles, eggs, biscuits, fruit, bacon	Sweet pineapple bread	Don't forget your autograph book and camera. The characters spend a good amount of quality time at each table.	**Speediest Service** (This restaurant is rarely packed, which makes for faster service.)
B: Scrambled eggs, potato casseroles, French toast sticks, bacon, sausage, fruit	Danish, pastries	This is the only place to have breakfast at Epcot's World Showcase. (And it's the only table service breakfast option in the whole park.)	**It's not Cinderella's Castle, but it's still pretty cool** (It's much easier to score priority seating here, too.)
Eggs, French toast sticks, pancakes, sausage, fruit, cereal, grits	Cheese crepes	For guests staying in the Epcot area, Cape May is one of the best breakfast options.	**Best Chance of Getting a Table Without Priority Seating** (But make the arrangements, anyway!)

All characters, menu items, and prices are subject to change. Prices are rounded to the nearest dollar.
Call 407-WDW-DINE for current details or to make priority seating arrangements.

RESTAURANT ROUNDUP

Dining Disney-style is one of the most enjoyable aspects of the vacation for many visitors. But with so many different restaurants to choose from, it can be difficult to select the spots that will best suit your family. Regulars to WDW are quick to recommend their favorites to newcomers. We, of course, are no exception to the rule. What follows is a rundown of the restaurants that we always try to include in our trips to the World and wholeheartedly recommend to those who are planning a visit. To pick these Birnbaum's Bests, we considered such factors as food quality, restaurant atmosphere, location, and overall value.

GOOD MEALS, GREAT TIMES

TOP WDW RESTAURANTS FOR FAMILIES WITH KIDS

TABLE SERVICE

Biergarten . . . . Epcot (p. 220)
Boma—Flavors of Africa . . . . Animal Kingdom Lodge (p. 234)
Cape May Cafe . . . . Beach Club resort (p. 239)
Chef Mickey's . . . . Contemporary resort (p. 235)
Cinderella's Royal Table . . . . Magic Kingdom (p. 214)
Crystal Palace . . . . Magic Kingdom (p. 216)
50's Prime Time Cafe . . . . Disney-MGM Studios (p. 226)
Garden Grill . . . . Epcot (p. 219)
Rainforest Cafe . . . . .Animal Kingdom and Downtown Disney (pp. 229, 233)
Sci-Fi Dine-In Theater . . . . Disney-MGM Studios (p. 227)

FAST FOOD

ABC Commissary . . . . Disney-MGM Studios (p. 227)
Columbia Harbour House . . . . Magic Kingdom (p. 216)
Liberty Inn . . . . Epcot (p. 224)
Pecos Bill Cafe . . . . Magic Kingdom (p. 215)
Pinocchio Village Haus . . . . Magic Kingdom (p. 215)
Sunset Ranch Market . . . . Disney-MGM Studios (p. 228)
Sunshine Season Food Fair . . . . Epcot (p. 220)
Tusker House . . . . Animal Kingdom (p. 230)

BEST KID'S MEAL PRESENTATION

Old Port Royale . . . . Caribbean Beach resort (p. 235);
The meal comes in a sand bucket with a shovel.

RUNNER-UP

Sci-Fi Dine-In Theater . . . . Disney-MGM Studios (p. 227);
Dessert is served on a glow-in-the-dark Frisbee.

BEST PLACE TO CELEBRATE A CHILD'S BIRTHDAY

Chef Mickey's . . . . Contemporary resort (p. 235)

RUNNER-UP

Mickey's Backyard Barbecue . . . . Fort Wilderness (p. 248)

BEST FIREWORKS VIEW

California Grill . . . . Contemporary resort (p. 235)

BEST VEGETARIAN MEALS

Artist Point
Wilderness Lodge (p. 239)

BEST SPLURGE FOR GROWN-UPS

California Grill . . . . Contemporary resort (p. 235)

RUNNERS-UP

Artist Point . . . . Wilderness Lodge resort (p. 239)
Jiko—The Cooking Place . . . . Animal Kingdom Lodge resort (p. 234)
Les Chefs de France . . . . Epcot (p. 221)
Stone Crab Lounge (inside Fulton's) . . . . Downtown Disney (p. 231)
Victoria & Albert's . . . . Grand Floridian resort (p. 237)
Wolfgang Puck Cafe . . . . Downtown Disney (p. 233)

BEST DINNER SHOW

Hoop-Dee-Doo Musical Revue: This crowd-pleasing saloon hall show has been going like gangbusters since 1974. Kids enjoy the silly humor, while adults eat up the bottomless buckets of ribs, fried chicken, and other down-home dishes. Presented at Fort Wilderness (p. 248).

RUNNER-UP

Mickey's Backyard Barbecue: If it were offered year-round, this would be our number-one choice. It's more of a big, informal party than a show, complete with a kickin' country band, games for the kids, and line dancing with Disney characters. The self-serve, all-you-can-eat barbecue fare is varied and plentiful. Presented at Fort Wilderness (p. 248).

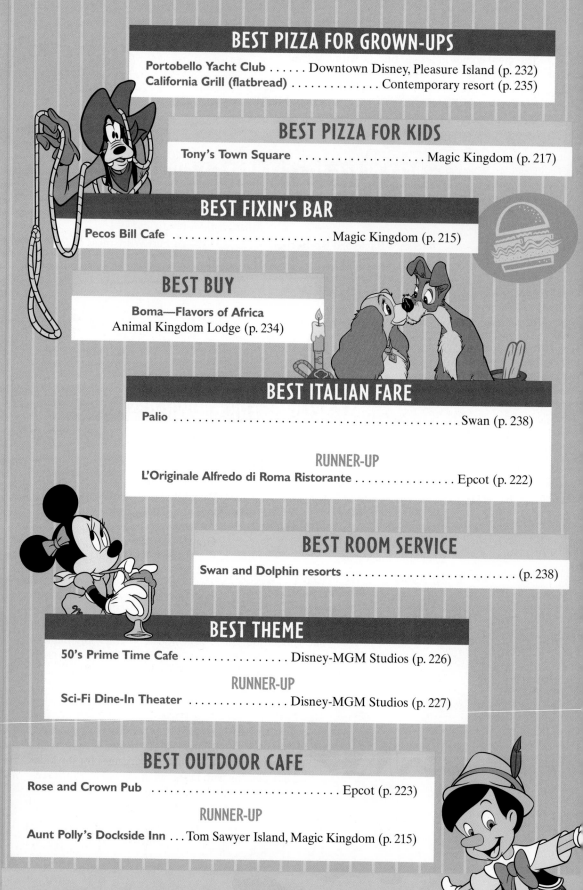

BEST PIZZA FOR GROWN-UPS

Portobello Yacht Club . . . . . . Downtown Disney, Pleasure Island (p. 232)
California Grill (flatbread) . . . . Contemporary resort (p. 235)

BEST PIZZA FOR KIDS

Tony's Town Square . . . . Magic Kingdom (p. 217)

BEST FIXIN'S BAR

Pecos Bill Cafe . . . . Magic Kingdom (p. 215)

BEST BUY

Boma—Flavors of Africa
Animal Kingdom Lodge (p. 234)

BEST ITALIAN FARE

Palio . . . . Swan (p. 238)

RUNNER-UP

L'Originale Alfredo di Roma Ristorante . . . . Epcot (p. 222)

BEST ROOM SERVICE

Swan and Dolphin resorts . . . . (p. 238)

BEST THEME

50's Prime Time Cafe . . . . Disney-MGM Studios (p. 226)

RUNNER-UP

Sci-Fi Dine-In Theater . . . . Disney-MGM Studios (p. 227)

BEST OUTDOOR CAFE

Rose and Crown Pub . . . . Epcot (p. 223)

RUNNER-UP

Aunt Polly's Dockside Inn . . . Tom Sawyer Island, Magic Kingdom (p. 215)

BEST SEAFOOD

Fulton's Crab House . . . . Downtown Disney (p. 231)

RUNNERS-UP

Flying Fish Cafe . . . . BoardWalk resort (p. 234)
Coral Reef . . . . Epcot (p. 219)

BEST CRAB CAKES

Stone Crab Lounge . . . . Fulton's Crab House,
Downtown Disney Marketplace (p. 232)

BEST BLOODY MARY

Stone Crab Lounge . . . . Fulton's Crab House,
Downtown Disney Marketplace (p. 232)

BEST BUFFALO WINGS

ESPN Club
BoardWalk resort (p. 234)

BEST ICE CREAM

The Plaza . . . . Magic Kingdom (p. 217)
Ghirardelli Soda Fountain and
Chocolate Shop . . . . Downtown Disney Marketplace (p. 232)

BEST STEAK

Shula's Steak House . . . . Dolphin resort (p. 239)

RUNNERS-UP

Concourse Steakhouse . . . . .Contemporary (p. 236)
Yachtsman Steakhouse . . . . .Yacht Club resort (p. 239)

BEST SUSHI

Wolfgang Puck Cafe . . . . . . Downtown Disney West Side (p. 233)

RUNNER-UP

Matsu No Ma Lounge . . . . Epcot (p. 250)

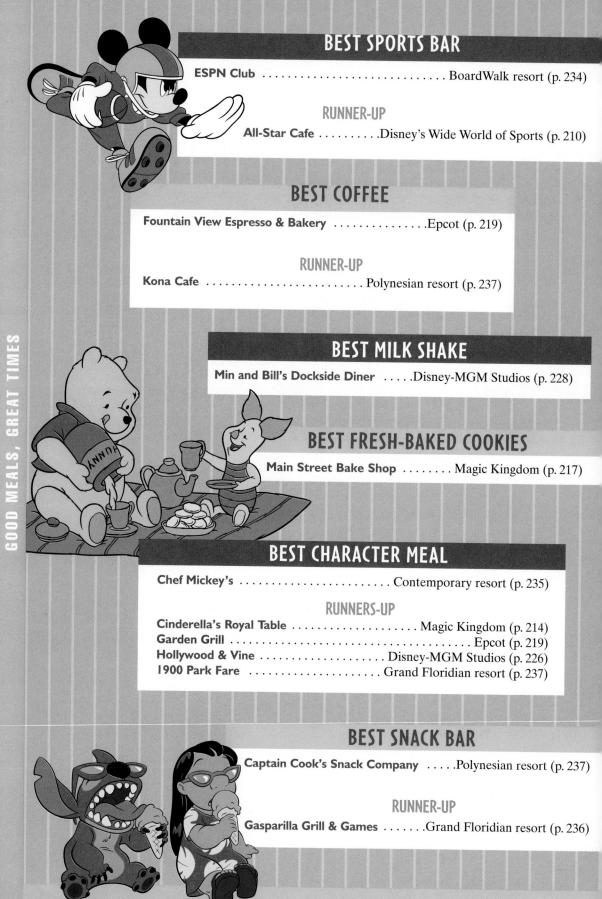

GOOD MEALS, GREAT TIMES

Priority Seating Explained

Priority seating has replaced reservations at most of WDW's full-service restaurants. Disney started the policy to provide the assurance of a reservation without delays caused by no-shows and late-comers. Ideally, the system ensures that guests are not left waiting if a table is available. Here's how it works: You call ahead to request a priority seating time; you arrive five minutes before the assigned time and check in at the podium; you receive the next available table that can accommodate your party. The system works like reservations, so you will always be seated before any walk-ins.

We recommend making advance arrangements. Priority seating times can generally be secured up to four months ahead by calling 407-WDW-DINE (939-3463). Hours are Sunday through Saturday from 7 A.M. to 11 P.M. The number of tables available in advance varies. If you are unable to book ahead of time, try to make same-day arrangements.

Hot Tip!

At most WDW restaurants, priority seating arrangements are scheduled in five- or ten-minute intervals. If they don't have a 6 P.M. availability, ask about a 6:05 P.M.

Most WDW resorts have at least one phone in the main lobby that provides direct contact with the "Dine Line." Simply touch 55—the call is free. From other locations, dial 407-WDW-DINE. Once at the theme parks, priority seating arrangements can be made at the restaurant itself; at City Hall in the Magic Kingdom; in Epcot at Guest Relations in Innoventions Plaza; by Hollywood Junction in the Disney-MGM Studios; and at Guest Relations in Animal Kingdom. Bookings can also be made at Guest Services in Downtown Disney Marketplace and at the West Side.

While the priority seating system is often successful, there are times when the wait for a table can be unexpectedly long. This is most likely to occur during peak mealtimes at restaurants that offer buffets or family-style meals, where patrons will often opt for seconds (or thirds). For this reason, be sure to check in at the restaurant particularly early for all character-hosted meals.

Priority seating is the prevalent policy at Walt Disney World restaurants, but there are some exceptions where tables may be booked solely via traditional reservations. Most notably, reservations are necessary for all dinner shows—the Hoop-Dee-Doo Musical Revue, Mickey's Backyard Barbecue, and the Polynesian Luau; they can be made by calling 407-WDW-DINE (939-3463). With the exception of Mickey's Backyard Barbecue, dinner show reservations can be booked up to two years in advance; the Barbecue accepts reservations one year ahead. If you can't get a table for an early performance, consider a later one (they are usually less heavily booked).

Keep in mind that a priority seating assignment is not a traditional reservation. Don't be surprised if you have to wait a bit when you arrive at your assigned time. Your party will be given the first table that opens up.

Note: Because the dining scene at Walt Disney World is ever-evolving and procedures have changed more than a few times over the years, we advise calling 407-WDW-DINE (939-3463) to confirm current priority seating policies.

Advance Planning

While some WDW restaurants always seem to have an available table (like the Marrakesh in Epcot's World Showcase), others are booked far in advance. The restaurants for which careful planning is essential include Cinderella's Royal Table in the Magic Kingdom (call 60 days ahead and keep your fingers crossed!); Les Chefs de France in Epcot; Donald's Prehistoric Breakfastosaurus in Animal Kingdom; and California Grill in the Contemporary resort.

Dinner Shows

The fact that Disney is expert in family entertainment is nowhere more readily apparent than amid the whooping and hollering troupe of singers and dancers who race toward the stage at Fort Wilderness resort's Pioneer Hall. As guests plow through ribs, fried chicken, and strawberry shortcake, these enthusiastic performers sing, dance, and joke up a storm.

The gags are groaners, but the audience eats 'em up. It's all in the course of an evening at the ***Hoop-Dee-Doo Musical Revue***, presented nightly at 5 P.M., 7:15 P.M., and 9:30 P.M. Cost is $49.01 per adult and $24.81 for children (ages 3 through 11).

> ## Hot Tip!
> The Hoop-Dee-Doo Musical Revue is a tremendously popular show. Make your reservations as far in advance as possible.

Note that the dining room in Pioneer Hall is exceptionally chilly year-round. Be sure to bring a sweater to combat the intense air-conditioning.

Also presented at Fort Wilderness is ***Mickey's Backyard Barbecue***. A country band gets guests out on the floor to kick up their heels (the line-dance lessons help, too), and Disney characters join in the fun.

Dinner consists of plenty of picnic favorites: barbecued ribs and chicken, corn on the cob, and baked beans. The seasonal dinner show costs $38 per adult and $25 for children. Tickets are required, so remember to book ahead.

Disney's new-and-improved Polynesian Luau show is called ***The Spirit of Aloha***. Set in the beachfront backyard of a Hawaiian house (at the Polynesian resort), the show invites guests to participate in a musical celebration.

The luau experience combines traditional music as well as more contemporary ditties from the animated Disney film *Lilo and Stitch*. The performers' dancing is some of the most authentic this side of Hawaii. *The Spirit of Aloha* is presented in an open-air dining theater in Luau Cove, adjacent to the Seven Seas Lagoon.

The all-you-can-eat feast is influenced by the flavors of Polynesia and includes draft beer, wine, soft drinks, and dessert. Menu items include roasted chicken (made with a new recipe), wild rice, and vegetables. The kids' menu features peanut butter and jelly sandwiches, mac and cheese, chicken nuggets, and hot dogs. Cost is $49.01 for adults and $24.81 for kids.

Plan to arrive at least fifteen minutes before showtime, and allow extra time for transportation and parking. (Note that prices include tax and gratuity and are subject to change.) The show may be canceled due to inclement weather.

Reservations: Arrangements for dinner shows mays be made up to two years in advance (except for the Backyard Barbecue, which accepts reservations up to one year ahead) by calling 407-WDW-DINE (939-3463). Groups of eight or more should call 407-939-7707.

Note that a credit card number is required for all dinner show reservations. *Also, it's very important to remember that cancellations for any dinner shows must be made at least 48 hours prior to showtime to avoid paying full price.*

GOOD MEALS, GREAT TIMES

Lounges of WDW

No one ever said the Magic Kingdom's no-liquor policy means that everyone in the World is a teetotaler. Actually, some of WDW's tastiest offerings are liquid (and decidedly spirited), and some of its most entertaining places are its bars and lounges.

Hours vary depending on the locale, but generally watering holes at Epcot, Disney-MGM Studios, and Animal Kingdom shut their doors at park closing. Pool bars at the resorts generally keep daytime pool hours. Last call at lounges in the resorts is anywhere from 10 P.M. to midnight. Downtown Disney Marketplace spots stay open until the shops close, usually 11 P.M. Pleasure Island and the West Side keep things going until about 2 A.M.

All-Star Movies, All-Star Music & All-Star Sports

Silver Screen Spirits at All-Star Movies, **Singing Spirits** at All-Star Music, and **Team Spirits** at All-Star Sports serve beer, wine, and specialty drinks by the pool.

Animal Kingdom

DAWA BAR: Enjoy Safari Amber beer and African music under the thatched roof.

RAINFOREST CAFE: The diminutive Magic Mushroom bar serves, among other things, fruit blends and specialty drinks.

Animal Kingdom Lodge

CAPETOWN LOUNGE AND WINE BAR: Sip African wines at this tiny spot near Jiko—the Cooking Place.

UZIMA SPRINGS: Poolside bar serving cocktails and snacks during pool hours.

VICTORIA FALLS: Mezzanine-level lounge offering coffee, tea, wine, and other spirits.

BoardWalk

ATLANTIC DANCE: This dance hall showcases hors d'oeuvres, desserts, a full bar, 25 specialty drinks, and premium cigars.

BELLE VUE ROOM: Snacks and a full bar accompany old-time tunes from antique radios in this lobby cocktail lounge.

BIG RIVER GRILLE & BREWING WORKS: A working brewpub where patrons may order appetizers at the bar and sample the brew master's flagship ales and specialty beers.

ESPN CLUB: The ultimate sports bar provides live radio and television broadcasts along with a menu of ballpark favorites.

JELLYROLLS: Dueling pianos and lively sing-alongs are the draw at this unique club, serving beer and other drinks.

LEAPING HORSE LIBATIONS: The pool bar offers cocktails, tuna sandwiches, fruit salad, and garden salads in a carnival setting.

Bonnet Creek Golf Club

SAND TRAP BAR & GRILL: Appetizers and sandwiches supplement the libations here.

Caribbean Beach

BANANA CABANA: Refreshing drinks and snack items are served at this poolside bar.

CAPTAIN'S TAVERN: Tropical drinks, beer, wine, and cocktails are served at this restaurant lounge in Old Port Royale. Items from the restaurant are available during dinner hours.

Contemporary

CALIFORNIA GRILL LOUNGE: Prime 15th-story digs eye level to the Magic Kingdom fireworks. A selection of California wine, all manner of other drinks, and items from the restaurant menu are offered in this tiny space within the California Grill restaurant.

OUTER RIM: This lounge overlooking Bay Lake serves cocktails, appetizers, and desserts.

SAND BAR: A full bar is offered poolside, weather permitting. Fast food is available at the adjacent counter area.

Coronado Springs

FRANCISCO'S: Located in the main building, this lounge serves specialty drinks, beer, wine, and light Mexican snacks.

SIESTA'S: Swimmers can take time out for burgers, sandwiches, tacos, and cocktails at this spot near the pool in the Dig Site area.

Disney-MGM Studios

TUNE-IN LOUNGE: A sitcom living room setting, with comfy couches and chairs, characterizes this lounge next to the 50's Prime Time Cafe. Waiters play the roles of sitcom "Dads," and old TV sets play scenes from beloved sitcoms (all of which feature food). Appetizers, mixed drinks, beer, and wine are served.

Disney's Old Key West

GURGLING SUITCASE: This pocket-size lounge on the Turtle Krawl boardwalk serves an assortment of Key West specialties along with traditional cocktails, beer, and wine.

TURTLE SHACK: Refreshments at this poolside spot include cocktails and fast-food items.

Downtown Disney

All clubs have bars serving specialty drinks, beer, wine, and cocktails. The excellent *Stone Crab* lounge inside *Fulton's Crab House* (located between Pleasure Island and the Marketplace) and *Bongos Cuban Cafe* (West Side) are notable for exotic cocktails and scenic outdoor seating. Pleasure Island's *Portobello Yacht Club* also has a pleasant lounge. The *Rainforest Cafe* (Marketplace) is the site of the Magic Mushroom bar.

CAP'N JACK'S RESTAURANT (Marketplace): Agleam with copper and right on the water, this bar's specialty is its delicious strawberry margaritas. The nibbles of garlic oysters, clam chowder, and shrimp on the appetizer menu are great for a snack or a meal.

> ## Hot Tip!
> For a late-night cocktail, head to Downtown Disney. The resort lounges tend to have last call before midnight.

Epcot

All restaurants, including some fast-food spots, serve alcoholic beverages. Some have a small lounge at which patrons may wait for tables. A few other Epcot locales actually specialize in liquid refreshments:

MATSU NO MA: In addition to exotic sake-based specialty drinks, this Japan pavilion establishment offers a fine panoramic view over the whole of Epcot—including the World Showcase Lagoon, with Spaceship Earth as a backdrop—one of the best vistas of the property available. Japanese beer, green tea, and sushi are also served.

ROSE & CROWN PUB: This watering hole—a veritable symphony of polished woods, brass, and etched glass—adjoins the Rose & Crown Dining Room in the United Kingdom pavilion. British, Scottish, and Irish beers are available, along with a score of specialty drinks and appetizing snacks imported from the other side of the Atlantic. On special occasions, there may be live (and lively) piano music.

SOMMERFEST: Just outside the Biergarten restaurant in Germany, there's a small shaded terrace where soft pretzels, bratwurst, Black Forest cake, Beck's beer, and German wine are available.

Fort Wilderness

CROCKETT'S TAVERN: Cocktails, beer, wine, appetizers, and light sandwiches are served in a rustic setting.

Grand Floridian

GARDEN VIEW: A lovely view of the pool and garden area makes this lounge a pleasant place to meet for a drink or dessert. Traditional afternoon tea is also served each day. Priority seating is suggested for tea.

MIZNER'S: Named after the eccentric architect who defined much of the flavor of southeastern Florida's Gold Coast, this handsome retreat is on the second floor of the main building. Ports, brandies, and appetizers are featured.

NARCOOSSEE'S: This lagoonside bar-within-a-restaurant offers many international wines.

POOL BAR: This bar stands by with beer, frozen drinks, and fast-food items.

Polynesian

BAREFOOT BAR: This oasis next to the swimming pool lagoon serves beer, frozen tropical drinks, and fast food. Seasonal.

TAMBU: Adjoining 'Ohana restaurant, this small bar offers Polynesian-style appetizers and specialty drinks in a tropical setting.

Pop Century

POOL BARS: In both the Legendary Years and Classic Years areas, watering holes near the main pools serve beer, wine, and cocktails.

Port Orleans French Quarter

MARDI GROGS: Beer, specialty drinks, popcorn, hot dogs, and hot pretzels are among the offerings at this poolside spot.

Port Orleans Riverside

MUDDY RIVERS: The poolside bar serves beer, specialty concoctions, and fast-food items.

RIVER ROOST: Situated in a room designed as a cotton exchange, this lounge features specialty drinks, as well as light hors d'oeuvres.

Swan & Dolphin

CABANA BAR & GRILL: Beer, frozen drinks, and fast-food selections are the main offerings at this Dolphin poolside spot.

COPA BANANA: The tabletops in this Dolphin bar resemble oversize slices of fruit, and giant pineapples and palm trees offer a fitting backdrop for tempting tropical libations, as well as more traditional cocktails.

KIMONOS: This Swan spot, attractively decorated in Japanese style, has a full bar, as well as sushi and other tasty treats.

LOBBY COURT: The winding corridors of the Swan lobby have comfortable couches and chairs, punctuated by pianos where able musicians often perform. A special menu with international wines, ports, cognacs, and cigars is offered seasonally.

SHULA'S STEAK HOUSE LOUNGE: This cozy cigar bar adjoining Shula's Steak House features rich wood tones and leather chairs— the perfect place to sip a cocktail and puff a stogie while playing armchair quarterback.

SPLASH GRILL: Beer, frozen drinks, and fast food are served at this Swan poolside cafe.

Wilderness Lodge

TERRITORY: Located between Artist Point and Whispering Canyon Cafe, this homage to the Old West is a nice spot for a light lunch or predinner treat. Appetizers, microbrewed beer, wine, and specialty drinks are served.

TROUT PASS: This poolside bar serves beer, frozen drinks, and snacks.

Yacht & Beach Club

ALE AND COMPASS: The cozy lobby watering hole proffers a specialty drink menu complete with coffee and ale.

CREW'S CUP: Styled after a traditional New England waterfront pub, this lounge has a seafaring feel to it. It's next door to the Yachtsman Steakhouse, has almost 40 beers, and is a choice spot for a drink before dinner. There is a tempting appetizer menu, too.

HURRICANE HANNA'S GRILL: This poolside spot, located near Stormalong Bay between the Yacht Club and Beach Club, offers specialty beverages, frozen drinks, and beer as well as a selection of fast-food items.

MARTHA'S VINEYARD: While a full bar is available, wines from a Martha's Vineyard winery (and other areas) are this spot's specialty. Hors d'oeuvres and snacks are served.

RIP TIDE: This lobby bar features California wines, wine coolers, and frosty drinks that are consistent with the hotel's beachside theme.

INDEX

10% OFF ADMISSION
for up to 4 Guests

Subject to terms and conditions on reverse side

10% OFF
Food and Beverage

**Between
11 A.M. and 4 P.M.**

(Excludes taxes, gratuities,
and alcoholic beverages)

at DOWNTOWN DISNEY® West Side

Subject to terms and conditions on reverse side

**DISNEY'S
VERO BEACH
RESORT**

Up to 20% off
Accommodations

- Receive 10% off when arriving 2/5/04–2/12/04 and 2/16/04–3/27/04.
- Receive 20% off when arriving 1/1/04–2/4/04,
  4/18/04–5/27/04, 5/31/04–7/1/04, 7/5/04–9/2/04,
  9/6/04–11/23/04, and 11/28/04–12/19/04.

For reservations, call 407-939-7450 and ask for the Birnbaum offer.

Subject to terms and conditions on reverse side

**Disney
Information
Center**

Disney
Souvenir

Present this coupon at the Disney Information Center in Ocala,
Florida, and receive one Disney souvenir as selected by the Disney
Information Center Cast Members. Stop in and receive assistance
with purchasing *Walt Disney World*® theme park tickets, making
room reservations, and dining priority seating.

Exit 350 on I-75 in Ocala, Florida

Subject to terms and conditions on reverse side

15% off Epcot
Dive Quest
admission

Epcot Dive Quest is a scuba-diving adventure open to
all certified scuba divers ages 10 and up.

Call (407) 939-8687 for reservations.

Subject to terms and conditions on reverse side

15% OFF
Disney's Dolphins
in Depth admission
for up to 4 guests

Disney's Dolphins in Depth is an educational dolphin
interaction program open to all guests ages 13 and up.

Call (407) 939-8687 for reservations.

Subject to terms and conditions on reverse side

**DISNEY'S
HILTON HEAD ISLAND
RESORT**

Up to 20% off
Accommodations

- Receive 10% off when arriving 5/6/04–5/27/04
  and 5/31/04–6/2/04.
- Receive 20% off when arriving 1/1/04–2/12/04,
  2/16/04–4/7/04, 4/25/04–5/5/04, 8/29/04–9/2/04,
  9/6/04–11/23/04, and 11/28/04–12/31/04.

For reservations, call 407-359-8000 and ask for the Birnbaum offer.

Subject to terms and conditions on reverse side

10% OFF
admission for up to 4 guests

at *Disney's Fantasia Gardens* or
Disney's Winter Summerland Miniature
Golf Course.

Subject to terms and conditions on reverse side

10% OFF*
Food and
Non-alcoholic
Beverage

*10/31/03–12/31/04

at Disney's Wide World of Sports® Complex

Subject to terms and conditions on reverse side

10% OFF ADMISSION
for up to
4 guests

at DOWNTOWN DISNEY® Pleasure Island

Subject to terms and conditions on reverse side